Transforming Financial Institutions

Transforming Financial Institutions

Value Creation through Technology Innovation and Operational Change

JOERG RUETSCHI

WILEY

Library of Congress Cataloging-in-Publication Data

Names: Ruetschi, Joerg, author.
Title: Transforming financial institutions : value creation through technology innovation
    and operational change / Joerg Ruetschi.
Description: First edition. | Hoboken, NJ : Wiley, 2022. | Series: Wiley
    finance series | Includes bibliographical references and index.
Identifiers: LCCN 2021043867 (print) | LCCN 2021043868 (ebook) | ISBN
    9781119858836 (paperback) | ISBN 9781119858843 (adobe pdf) | ISBN
    9781119858850 (epub)
Subjects: LCSH: Decision making. | Strategic planning. | Problem solving. |
    Financial institutions—Management. | Information
    technology—Management.
Classification: LCC HD30.23 .R84 2022 (print) | LCC HD30.23 (ebook) | DDC
    658.4/03—dc23
LC record available at https://lccn.loc.gov/2021043867
LC ebook record available at https://lccn.loc.gov/2021043868

Cover Design: Wiley
Cover Image: © oxygen/Getty Images

To Parissa and Leila, the true loves of my life.

Contents

About the Author   xi

Introduction   1

PART ONE

Managerial Fundamentals

CHAPTER 1
Strategic Decision Making   7

1.1 Strategic analysis	7
1.1.1 Hypothesis-driven problem solving	8
1.1.2 System theory	12
1.1.3 Coherence	13
1.2 Strategic planning	17
1.2.1 Roadmap	17
1.2.2 Impact assessment	17
1.2.3 Strategic options and portfolio choices	20
1.2.4 Action and response plan	21
1.3 Operational excellence	23
1.3.1 Operating model	23
1.3.2 Balance scorecard	24
1.3.3 Best practice and benchmarking	26
1.4 Business performance improvement	26
1.4.1 Portfolio optimisation	27
1.4.2 Divestments and disposals	28
1.4.3 Front-to-back optimisation	28
1.4.4 Cost reduction	29
1.4.5 Technology replatforming	31
1.5 Merger and acquisition	32

CHAPTER 2
Financial Decision Making   35

2.1 Financial analysis	35
2.1.1 Financial statements	35

2.1.2	*Financial ratios*	44
2.1.3	*Leverage analysis*	46
2.2	Financial valuation	47
2.2.1	*Valuation methods and principles*	48
2.2.2	*Valuation models and techniques*	53
2.3	Financial modelling	61
2.3.1	*Risk and return*	61
2.3.2	*Asset pricing*	68
2.3.3	*Contingent claims*	74
2.4	Financial stress	86
2.4.1	*The cycle of financial stress*	86
2.4.2	*Liquidity risk*	88
2.4.3	*Market dislocations*	90
2.4.4	*Systemic crises*	96

CHAPTER 3
Asset-liability Management   **101**

3.1	Risk transfer	101
3.1.1	*Principles of risk-taking*	101
3.1.2	*The pricing taxonomy of risk*	102
3.2	Financial engineering	116
3.2.1	*Cash instruments*	117
3.2.2	*Forwards and futures*	120
3.2.3	*Swaps*	124
3.2.4	*Options*	132
3.2.5	*Securitisation*	138
3.3	Risk management	141
3.3.1	*Enterprise-wide risk management*	142
3.3.2	*Value-at-risk*	143
3.4	Capital management	145
3.4.1	*Capital adequacy*	145
3.4.2	*Capital structure*	145
3.4.3	*Funding mix*	147
3.4.4	*Capital allocation mechanism*	148
3.5	The Basel framework	149
3.5.1	*Historical context and development*	149
3.5.2	*Methodological framework*	150
3.5.3	*Regulatory capital*	151
3.5.4	*Risk-weighted assets*	154
3.5.5	*Liquidity requirements*	161
3.5.6	*Additional regulatory considerations of the G20 reform*	163

CHAPTER 4
Technology Management and Innovation 165

4.1 Financial technology management 166
    4.1.1 Traditional role and innovation 166
    4.1.2 Targeted replatforming 167
4.2 Emerging technologies 168
    4.2.1 Software and infrastructure 169
    4.2.2 Artificial intelligence 173
    4.2.3 Distributed ledger technology 177
4.3 The transformational impact of financial technology 182
    4.3.1 Operational efficiency 182
    4.3.2 Augmented decision making 189
    4.3.3 Digital financial innovation 193

PART TWO
Repositioning Financial Institutions

CHAPTER 5
Turnaround and Transformation 203

5.1 Reorganisation and wind-down 204
    5.1.1 Legal principles 205
    5.1.2 Reorganisation and wind-down of financial institutions 212
5.2 Turnaround process 217
    5.2.1 Crisis management 217
    5.2.2 Turnaround plan 220
    5.2.3 Financial restructuring 223
    5.2.4 Operational restructuring 228

CHAPTER 6
Value Creation and Growth 231

6.1 Intrinsic value 231
    6.1.1 Growth initiatives 232
    6.1.2 High-impact situations and the M&A transaction life cycle 233
    6.1.3 Value creation plan 241
6.2 Value optimisation 244
    6.2.1 Commercial optimisation 244
    6.2.2 Operational optimisation 246
    6.2.3 Financial optimisation 247
6.3 Value realisation 248
    6.3.1 Governance and central programme management 248
    6.3.2 Operational blueprint 250
    6.3.3 Targeted implementation 254

PART THREE
Conclusion

CHAPTER 7
Rebuilding the Global Banking Industry   **259**
    7.1   The industry's change and growth agenda   259
    7.2   The transformational impact of technology   261
    7.3   Specialisation and inclusive risk transfer   262

Afterword and Acknowledgment   **265**

Bibliography   **269**

Index   **275**

About the Author

Dr Joerg Ruetschi specialises in turnaround and value creation at the intersection of finance and technology. He has been working with financial institutions, technology companies, and private equity as well as venture capital firms on special and entrepreneurial situations for almost 20 years. Joerg's core professional interests have been in building, growing, and transforming businesses through delivering comprehensive end-to-end solutions from strategy through execution.

Originally trained in investments and quantitative analysis, Joerg gained early experience in risk management and capital markets during his academic studies, which led to a PhD in Finance in 2005. He spent 10 years in investment banking at Goldman Sachs and alternative investments at StepStone Global with focus on asset-liability management and asset restructuring. He joined Booz & Company (now Strategy& as part of the PwC network) in 2013 to lead the advisory proposition for bank restructuring and the broader transformation agenda of financial institutions. After the merger of Booz & Company with PwC, Joerg operated on its Deal Advisory platform with focus on operational restructuring and merger and acquisition (M&A) in financial services. He set up his own independent platform, Evolve Enterprise Solutions (EES), in 2019 to fully focus on emerging technologies and specialty finance, driving the broader change and growth agenda of financial institutions.

As an operating executive and advisor, Joerg worked across the life cycle in turnaround and transformational M&A. This included strategy development, operational execution, and technology solutions. In this capacity, he led the commercialisation, reorganisation, and integration of emerging financial technologies, assuming executive roles in artificial intelligence and enterprise software businesses. He led a series of engagements for the restructuring of the international wholesale businesses of global European banks; advised regional, systemic banks across Europe, the Middle East, and Africa on nonperforming assets, business performance improvement, and technology solutions; and assisted neo-banks in the operational build-up of their consumer and commercial finance businesses. He further brings extensive experience in alternative investments through which he also worked in the international specialty and reinsurance markets.

Joerg has a dedicated technical background in value creation, restructuring, and finance which includes in addition to his PhD, the Certified Turnaround Professional (CTP), Chartered Financial Analyst (CFA), and Financial Risk Manager (FRM) designations. His long-term academic and research interests have been risk transfer and financial engineering, financial stress, and restructuring as well as entrepreneurship and technology innovation. During his professional career, he has been specialising in the combination of strategic and financial decision making as well as the transformational impact of technology. He developed a comprehensive transformation and value creation methodology to build and transform financial institutions that is further discussed in this book.

BACKGROUND TO EES

Evolve Enterprise Solutions is an independent platform for entrepreneurial and special situations. The firm drives the change and growth agenda in financial services with core focus on emerging technologies and specialty finance and their integration into the ecosystem of incumbent financial institutions.

EES Value Advisory offers executive and managerial services across the incubation, scale-up, transformation, and turnaround of businesses as well as creating and defending value in principal investments (M&A). It further leads advisory mandates across strategy development, validation, and roadmaps (e.g. turnaround and value creation plans), investor and due diligence support with commercial and operational focus, and the planning and execution of business transformation initiatives, restructurings, divestments, greenfield build-ups, and buy-to-build strategies.

Through EES Capital Advisory, the firm keeps a strong focus on building equity participation in the companies it works with.

Further information can be found at www.eesadvisory.com.

Introduction

This book is a reflection of my own journey in finance through my experience in financial technology, advisory, investment banking, and alternative investments over the last 20 years. After having the opportunity to be trained in investment management at an early stage, I developed during my studies a deep interest in risk transfer and financial innovation with a fascination for financial history and dynamic system theory. Impressed by the publications of Charles Kindleberger and Edward Chancellor, I lived through my first financial crises as a student with the downfall of the hedge fund Long-term Capital Management in 1998.[1] These interests fundamentally shaped my academic studies that eventually led to a PhD. Ten years followed as a derivatives specialist in investment banking and alternative investments before moving into advisory to focus on bank restructuring and the broader transformation agenda of financial institutions. Over the last years, I have dedicated my focus on emerging technologies, specialty finance, and their transformational impact on financial institutions. My core interests, as we are going to explore further in this book, remain on how financial institutions can be transformed with regard to value creation for shareholders but also with regard to system reliance as well as financial effectiveness and inclusion.

With the Global Financial Crisis (GFC) of 2007–2009, a boom of 30 years of deregulation and growth that started with the Big Bang in 1987 came to an abrupt end. With it, the fundamental beliefs in modern risk transfer mechanisms and financial engineering were shaken. In response, the G20 regulatory reform addressed several of the issues through new capital requirements, leverage constraints, and regulatory scrutiny. These incoming regulations have challenged the established commercial models with their profitability thresholds, leading to the immanent result that large complex financial institutions operate way below their cost of capital. At the same time, emerging technologies have fundamentally transformed operating platforms and the decision-making frameworks. The incoming technology agenda has the potential to reinnovate the industry and put it back on a growth path. However, this requires substantial investments and the break-up of the industry's existing organisational structures. Accordingly, this book

---

[1] Further information can be found in Charles Kindleberger's "*Manias, Panics, and Crashes. A History of Financial Crisis*" from 1992; Edward Chancellor's "*Devil take the hind most. A history of financial speculation*" from 1988 and Roger Lowenstein's, "*When Genius Failed: The Rise and Fall of Long-Term Capital Management*" from 2014.

introduces a business and management methodology that is shaped by the analysis of a number of core hypotheses:

- **Hypothesis 1:** Post GFC and the G20 regulatory reform, size, and operational complexity have become core value drivers for financial institutions. Both impact and endanger the creation and delivery of shareholder value.
- **Hypothesis 2:** Emerging technologies facilitate new business and target operating models (TOM). Technology-enabled service components allow financial institutions to differentiate and gain a competitive market positioning. Efficient system and infrastructure platforms build the core of the delivery of targeted client services. The latter is play between technology providers and incumbent financial institutions. Inherent to these developments is an open question around the regulatory treatment of those components, that is, the client-facing services and systems as well as infrastructure platforms are fully regulated whereas the backup infrastructure may operate outside of today's regulatory regimes.
- **Hypothesis 3:** There is inherent value in specialised finance and risk transfer capabilities such as dedicated lending, trading, and related risk transfer mechanisms across specific client segments and product portfolios. Specialty finance businesses operate at a much lower cost-income ratio and higher return-on-equity targets than large-scale, aggregated financial businesses.
- **Hypothesis 4:** Strategic coherence becomes a major driver in structuring financial institutions with profitability as core focus.
- **Hypothesis 5:** Open architecture models allow incumbent financial institutions to specialise on their core competence and to integrate best-in-class services with the objective to provide customer a coherent experience through core platform offerings.
- **Hypothesis 6:** Balance sheets of financial institution need to be managed under fair value considerations and marked-to-market on a consistent basis. Direct lending and investment facilities through stable pools of capital can further facilitate the structured loss of funding facilities under such a regime.

In validating these hypotheses, this book develops a methodology to transform financial institutions and create value through risk transfer businesses. Business transformation is usually applied to specific situations. It describes the outright turnaround and restructuring of a business following a crisis or change agenda with emphasis on operational efficiency, often under financial stress. Value creation, on the other hand, refers to an agenda of strategic growth initiatives. These initiatives are either driven by expansion through organic and acquisition-based growth or operational efficiency through business improvement and capital optimisation. Value creation therefore often implies the acquisition of a business, followed by a series of initiatives to build and reposition it. The term is applied narrowly in an investor context with financial sponsors such as private equity and hedge funds taking an important role as financial or even strategic buyers through principal investments. This book uses value creation in the broader context of a management and entrepreneurial philosophy. Exhibit I illustrates this framework graphically.

The introduced methodology follows a strategy through execution mindset, applying commercial evaluation through operational execution in repositioning banking and financial services business. In its core, it is about how to transform a financial services business front to back by combining commercial and operational change with disciplined balance-sheet management and cutting edge technology. Before these fundamental drivers can be assessed in a comprehensive value creation framework, a common understanding of strategy, financial decision making, asset-liability management and, most important, financial technology has to be established. The book is organised in two parts. Part One covers the managerial fundamentals and building blocks of the end-to-end business transformation and value creation framework that is discussed holistically in the second part. Exhibit I provides an overview of the content modules on which the management framework is built.

The book's focus is on presenting an experience-based methodology for practitioners with no further aspiration for an academic contribution on the topic. I have borrowed heavily from existing concepts in professional and academic literature and refer back to these as "Resources and Further Reading" at the end of each chapter. Readers will further find in the chapter "Afterword and Acknowledgment" references to many of the individuals, that is, colleagues, mentors, and friends, who were part of

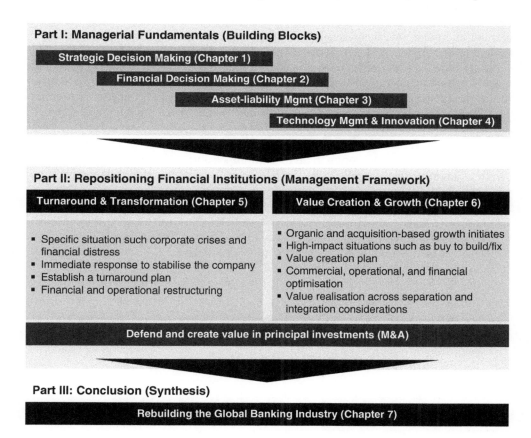

Part I: Managerial Fundamentals (Building Blocks)

Strategic Decision Making (Chapter 1)

Financial Decision Making (Chapter 2)

Asset-liability Mgmt (Chapter 3)

Technology Mgmt & Innovation (Chapter 4)

Part II: Repositioning Financial Institutions (Management Framework)

Turnaround & Transformation (Chapter 5)

Value Creation & Growth (Chapter 6)

- Specific situation such corporate crises and financial distress
- Immediate response to stabilise the company
- Establish a turnaround plan
- Financial and operational restructuring

- Organic and acquisition-based growth initiates
- High-impact situations such as buy to build/fix
- Value creation plan
- Commercial, operational, and financial optimisation
- Value realisation across separation and integration considerations

Defend and create value in principal investments (M&A)

Part III: Conclusion (Synthesis)

Rebuilding the Global Banking Industry (Chapter 7)

Exhibit I   Content modules of the book's business transformation and value creation framework

this journey and experience. My professional and research interests across the different stages of my career has been centred on solving complex financial, commercial, and operational problems, and in particular how technology has impacted decision making and operational delivery. This experience provides a base to express a personal view on what works and what does not in accordance with my own professional development path. I wanted to be as illustrative as possible by adding tangible examples as well as reported and unreported stories to the book's narrative. I aimed to reference existing literature at a minimum under the dedicated section at the end of each chapter but sometimes also consulted public resources to validate my own understanding without further quoting them (in addition to the references in the already quoted literature). Last but not least, the entire book (in particular in Chapters 2 and 3) applies pragmatically a quantitative terminology and uses for instance discrete and continuous compounding alternatively in the introduction of different models. The target audience is decision makers and business leaders while appreciating that the industry's language remains a mathematical one.

The title of the book implies the coverage of a broad spectrum of financial institutions across banking, capital markets, insurance, asset management, technology, and infrastructure. My core focus over the years though has been on international commercial and wholesale businesses in banking and asset management with risk transfer as the key engine of the underlying business model. My own transformation and value creation experience has been in particular centred in the repositioning of capital market, corporate, and investment banking businesses of global European T1 banks; the restructuring of nonperforming assets of Southern European regional [systemic] T2,3 banks; and the build-up of specialty finance[2] platforms and financial technology businesses. This book is very much a reflection of these experiences and therefore focuses its coverage mainly on corporate and institutional as well as specialised, commercial lending businesses, often in an international setting. The term "financial institution" therefore always implies a banking perspective which includes deposit taking, payment, lending and borrowing, underwriting and placement of securities, brokerage, trading, clearing as well as institutional asset management. Furthermore, the book covers private placement and alternative risk transfer mechanisms with the objective to take risks from bank balance sheets and replace them with stable pools of capital which includes direct lending and investment facilities. The text further refers to those vehicles as asset-management solutions.

---

[2]A series of challenger banks have been built across Europe that focus on specific niche segments across consumer and commercial finance.

One

Managerial Fundamentals

The first part introduces the fundamentals concepts and managerial fundamentals that drive decision making and operational excellence in financial services. These building blocks cover strategic and financial decision making, asset-liability management as well as technology management and innovation. The first two chapters frame the decision-making methodology for financial institutions and the later chapters discuss with balance-sheet strength and technology management two key capabilities of a successful financial-institution model.

CHAPTER 1

Strategic Decision Making

$\mathbf{S}$ trategy is a very broadly used term applied in military, political, and business situations. Lawrence Freedman illustrates in his book *Strategy—A History* the origin of strategy though mythical figures, politicians, and business leaders. They all have in common to take decisions under uncertainty and confusion of the human affair. Strategic decision making aims to clarify these moments of uncertainty with an applied set of problem-solving principles. It is therefore a problem-solving methodology that is applied to complex, unstructured, and multidimensional issues, driven by the uncertainty of human behaviour and decision making. Max McKeown specifies in *The Strategy Book* that strategy is about shaping the future by which people attain desirable ends with available means. Authors such as Igor Ansoff, Henry Mintzberg, and Michael Porter established during the last 50–60 years a corporate discipline that aims to combine a rigorous planning approach with adaptability to the circumstances given the uncertainty of the situation.

Corporate and business strategy follows a vision for a business in accordance with an executable mission of a specific commercial and operational plan. This involves determining and implementing long-term goals and objectives, with the considerations of a financial institution's market positioning and available capabilities. These considerations include competitive analysis, macroeconomic and industry conditions, regulatory constraints, and other dimensions of the internal organisation and external environment. The following chapter introduces a series of core strategic principles and applies them to financial, commercial, and operational problem solving in financial institutions. It covers tools of strategic analysis such as hypothesis-driven problem solving, system theory and coherence, as well as strategic planning such as roadmaps; heat maps; strengths, weaknesses, opportunities, and threats (SWOT); and scenario analysis. It further discusses the operational efficiency and the design of target operating models (TOM), performance improvement, and merger & acquisition (M&A) as fundamental tools of the strategic decision-making process. The ability of an institution to convert strategy into a success business is directly related to the continuous testing of the logic and the assumptions when making structured decisions about how to win in a competitive marketplace.

1.1 STRATEGIC ANALYSIS

Strategic decision making develops a systematic approach and defines a methodology to analyse business situations and solve entrepreneurial issues that are by nature complex and unstructured. It solves the key question on how to get a competitive advantage over the opponent in resolving the issues. The complex nature and dynamic relationship of the underlying drivers require a systematic problem-solving mindset. In business and finance, this problem-solving mindset establishes a clear understanding of the dynamics of the market positioning of a business with its revenue stream and the effectiveness of the operating platform with its cost structure. System theory is used to further assess the dynamics within the assumptions and limitations of theoretical models. At the same time, every strategy has to be coherent with an organisation's market positioning, capability set, and product and services fit while following a best-in-class benchmark. The following section introduces those three tools of strategic analysis.

1.1.1   Hypothesis-driven problem solving

Strategic analysis is by nature solution oriented and hypothesis driven while being fact-based at the same time. The process of coming up with a good strategy has the same logical structure as the problem of coming up with a good scientific hypothesis, as strategy deals with the edge between the known and the unknown. It is an educated guess about what will work in a specific situation. As a decision process, it applies a structured framework to generate fact-based hypotheses followed by data and information gathering with the objective to prove or disprove the hypotheses.

This decision and problem-solving process is therefore often referred to as a hypothesis-driven approach. The hypothesis-driven approach is a cornerstone in strategic analysis. It starts with understanding the situation, framing the problem, analysing through gathering information as well as data, and finally concluding the analysis by guiding policies and coherent action plans. In its analytical approach, it simplifies the often overwhelming complexity and reality by identifying certain aspects of the situation as critical.

This hypothesis-driven analysis is driven by three core principles that can be summarised as follows:

1. Simplify and reduce complexity by stating early an initial hypothesis which leads to a result-driven analysis.
2. Specify and focus through identifying key drivers in a designated analytical framework that is mutually exclusive collectively exhaustive (MECE).
3. Quantify and validate through available information and related data.

As Exhibit 1.1. illustrates, every strategic issue, as any complex und unstructured problem-solving challenge, starts with developing and testing a bunch of hypotheses that sets out the path how a situation can be resolved. This path knows five major steps.

The principles of the hypothesis-driven approach provide a central decision platform, based on which efficient problem-solving process can be applied. The process is defined through a structured framework that is centred on the initial hypothesis. It begins with framing the problem through understanding the situation and defining the boundaries of the analysis. It early comes up with an initial hypothesis and further breaks down the issue in its core components. By gathering information and data and through analysing them, it is continuously refined until a synthesis and conclusion can be reached. There are five steps that further define this methodology.

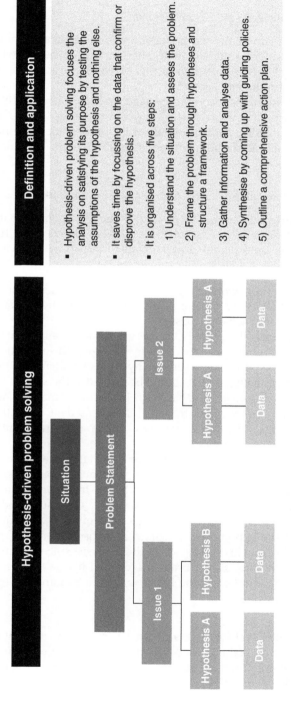

Hypothesis-driven problem solving

Definition and application

- Hypothesis-driven problem solving focuses the analysis on satisfying its purpose by testing the assumptions of the hypothesis and nothing else.

- It saves time by focussing on the data that confirm or disprove the hypothesis.

- It is organised across five steps:

  1) Understand the situation and assess the problem.

  2) Frame the problem through hypotheses and structure a framework.

  3) Gather information and analyse data.

  4) Synthesise by coming up with guiding policies.

  5) Outline a comprehensive action plan.

Situation

Problem Statement

Issue 2

Hypothesis A

Hypothesis A

Data

Data

Issue 1

Hypothesis A

Hypothesis B

Data

Data

Exhibit 1.1 Hypothesis-driven problem solving[1]

[1]Exhibit 1.1 follows a standard presentation used in strategy consulting and is more formally described in publications such as Rasiel, Ethan M. and Paul N. Friga (2010).

Baseline, structure, and hypotheses

Step 1: Understand the situation and assess the problem

The objective here is to fundamentally comprehend the situation of a business by look-ing into initially available information and data. The step is known as baselining as it organises available data in a format that then further drives the structure of the analyt-ical framework and the solution path around it.

In a restructuring situation, the incoming management team assesses the situation with readily available information while starting to work on a more detailed baselining. The baselining provides a detailed description of the business model, outlines the tar-get operating model with its value chain, and provides a functional breakdown of the operational cost base.

Step 2: Frame the problem through hypotheses and structure a framework

In a first diagnosis, a clearly defined framework allows the management team to come up with an initial hypothesis on how to resolve the problem directionally. It is shaped across the core elements of the situation and its related issues. The following key ele-ments are to be considered:

- Set up the analytical framework through defining the issues in a structured approach with its key drivers and major factors: It is followed by an issue tree that sets out a logical order for each of the issues.
- State an initial hypothesis that speeds up the quest for a solution and sketches out a roadmap for the analysis: It will guide the work throughout the entire problem-solving process. Forming an initial hypothesis will make the decision making more efficient and effective. It should be formed at the start of the process as it allows one to reach conclusions based on limited information. As different hypotheses are proven or rejected through gathering data and information, validate them accordingly. The initial hypothesis remains central in outlining the framework of the analytical process.
- Develop issue trees to bridge the gap between the analytical framework and hypotheses: An issue tree structures the issues that must be addressed to prove or disprove a hypothesis. Every issue generated by the framework can be further broken down to subissues. By creating an issue tree, the issues and subissues are laid out in visual progression. This allows determining what questions to ask in order to form the hypothesis and serves as a roadmap for the analysis. It also allows eliminating quickly dead ends of the analysis, since the answer to an issue immediately eliminates all the branches falsified by the answer. To reduce complexity, simplify by numbering the issues and state hypothesis in the MECE approach along an issue tree.

Mutually exclusive collectively exhaustive (MECE) refers to the concept of sep-arating the problem into distinct, nonoverlapping issues while making sure that issues relevant to the situation and problem have not been overlooked. All possible options are to be considered or rejected in the problem-solving process.

In our restructuring case, a global T1 bank experienced a capital shortfall and had to sell a series of asset portfolios and businesses in a fire sale. A new management was appointed to execute a broader turnaround of the global markets business where the issues were located. During the baselining, an initial hypothesis was established that post sale the operational capabilities and their cost base were outsized with regard to the remaining portfolio of assets and businesses. The management team developed a functional breakdown of the cost base and identified the major cost driver for each function. Based on this analysis, a group of hypotheses was built to take costs out rapidly and stabilise the operations as base to further reposition the business.

Analysis, refinement, and elimination

Step 3: Gather information and analyse data

After setting up the framework and defining the set of applicable hypotheses, the next step is to design the analyses that must be pursued to prove and/or reject the hypotheses. It is followed by gathering the data and information needed for the analysis. Those steps include:

- Gather information and data to identify and verify the different issues specified by each hypothesis.
- Analyse and diagnose through, continuously refining the hypotheses along the issue tree.
- Isolate the core issues by a process of segmentation and elimination.

In our case study, the management team gathered detailed financial data across the different initiatives and conducted interviews with respective stakeholders. Through the received data streams and information, it validated and eliminated several of the cost reduction hypotheses. The hypotheses that got confirmed were further refined until the management team was in a position to agree on the cost targets with the different business leaders. The aggregated quantum was then presented and approved by the board of directors and subsequently communicated to the market.

Conclusion and action plan

Step 4: Synthesise by coming up with guiding policies

In a first conclusion, the key findings are summarised and synthesised to an overall conclusion. Additional factors may further be considered when they impact the outcome. This leads to the evaluation of which strategic options might be applicable while keeping the big picture.

Step 5: Outline a comprehensive action plan

In the final step, the management's action plan is outlined. This often implies several strategic options with different choices. Tangible recommendations need to be articulated as a conclusion before the implementation process can be started. Action steps are to be coordinated with one another to work together in accomplishing the guiding policy. What is important to realise is that good strategy and good organisation lie in specialising on the right activities and imposing only the essential amount of coordination.

1.1.2 System theory

Systems theory is a multi- and interdisciplinary approach that integrates different theories with their individual premises and dynamic behaviours in a comprehensive setting. A problem-solving methodology follows specific theoretical assumptions that define a system with its boundaries, surrounded and influenced by its environmental factors. A system is a group of things that are interconnected and demonstrate their own behaviour patterns over time. This may be a natural system that exists in reality. It may be replicated through a logical system and theoretical model as an approximation of its reality. The combination of several systems represents an overarching system. Changing one part of the system may affect other parts and with it the whole system with predictable and unpredictable behavioural patterns. Some systems are self-adapting. Others need to adapt and their growth depends on how well they can adjust to the environment.

The goal of system theory is to discover dynamics, conditions, and constraints across systems that can be generalised to overarching principles. Whilst we aim to avoid the deep coverage of theoretical concepts such as dynamic system theory and cybernetics, it needs to be emphasised that interdisciplinary thinking is a crucial element of any strategy toolkit. The modern financial system is global in scale and intertwined. As a result, it has become immensely complex. Often several theories (i.e. systems) need to be applied as a fair proxy of reality. Different systems may model different dynamics and outcomes. The interdependence between the models is crucial and encourages us to use different disciplines to analyse a situation. Financial analysis, valuation, and modelling are by definition quantitative driven and highly dependent on specific premises as will be further covered in Chapter 2. This leads to a simplification of the real world dynamics, and as we will further learn similar behaviour patterns and decision making that consequently may destabilise the entire system.

System theory can crucially support strategic analysis by outlining the dynamics and impact factors on aggregated levels. It allows one to think through problems from different standpoints and interdependencies. Dynamic system theory in particular describes the long-term qualitative behaviour of complex system dynamics by using mathematics in the area of differential equations. Its focus is not on finding precise solutions through formal equations but by describing the dynamics of a system depending on its initial conditions. The study of chaotic systems is attributed to dynamic system theory. It has found its application in advanced financial modelling.

Exhibit 1.2 illustrates a simplified decision model based on system theory. Similar to more advanced applications such as the St. Galler Management Model, it uses an institution's ecosystem as the overarching system at the highest level and then applies subsystems to describe the organisational-level implications. Systems are interrelated and driven by feedback loops between output and input. Data, market intelligence, people, and resources are input factors. Products and services as well as processes and

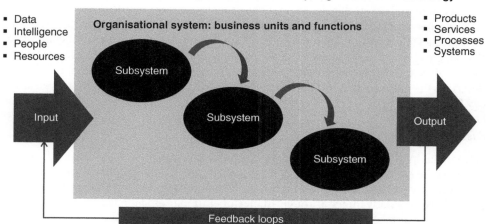

Exhibit 1.2   System theory and its application for strategic analysis

systems are output factors. The interdependencies drive the subsystem while organisational and ecosystem levels provide the constraints and requirements that need to be fulfilled.

When analysing broader trends in financial systems, macro-history that looks at events in financial history and approximates long-term trends with respective implications for decision making should be applied in combination with dynamic system theory. Chapter 2 will apply in its analysis of financial stress and banking crises a respective methodology that is based on the combination of quantitative analytics, dynamic system thinking, and macro-history.

1.1.3   Coherence

The term "coherence" refers to the degree of alignment among an institution's strategy, its capabilities set as well as the options and portfolio choices it encounters. It is a reflection of its successful commercial positioning. In its analysis, this methodology covers a range of fundamental questions on the effectiveness of the market position, the strategic fit of its business as well as portfolio and services, and the gap between available and required capabilities. It further assesses how capabilities can be built successfully either organically or through acquisitions. On the other hand, it provides a framework on how incoherent capabilities are to be disposed or divested. Every roadmap needs to be assessed with regard to its strategic coherence. This is equally applicable to turnaround and transformation as well as value creation plans.

Following the methodology, originally developed by Booz & Company (now Strategy& as part of the PwC network), a strategy is coherent across three core elements: the market position of a business, its capabilities set, and its services and product fit. To have a successful execution of the strategy, those three elements are to be in full alignment. Every strategic decision needs to be targeted towards coherence and needs to be consistent with its strategic identity. Crises that lead to restructuring and turnaround, underperformance that requires business transformation, and/or an acquisition that demands a value creation are to be assessed against these three elements of coherence. If strategic coherence is not ensured, the strategy may fail, which applies in particular for complex and diverse businesses such as banking and financial services. Exhibit 1.3 describes the different factors of coherence that is also known as capability-driven strategy (CDS).

Sustainable competitive advantage

A financial institution needs to have a sustainable advantage to competitive advantage which is the overarching objective of a coherent strategy. There are three main sources of competitive advantages. The first one is economic success factors such as absolute and relative cost advantage through higher operational efficiencies as well as differentiation advantages through risk-based credit underwriting and technology-enabled distribution channels. The second one is organisational factors which relate to specific institutional and management capabilities. The third and last one comes from political and legal factors through high market entry costs and market protection such as high regulation.

Market positioning

The market positioning defines the way a business creates and realises value for its stakeholders and differentiates itself from competitors. Although the positioning needs to be nimble and adaptable for growth opportunities, it needs to be ultimately focused and tangible for decision making. It is a distinctive feature that is core to the strategic identity. At the core is an institution's value proposition. Financial institutions usually have multiple and often diverse businesses. Diversification benefits with regard to managing the economic cycle and the different risk factors as well as complex client requirements, franchise relationships, and distribution opportunities are often quoted as rationale. In the late 1990s and early 2000s, universal financial conglomerates were created that consisted of banking, insurance, and investment management businesses. The management complexity was dramatic and most of them spectacularly failed when the technology, media, and telecommunication bubble burst. Goldman Sachs, on the other hand, is known for its unique market positioning, business profile, and talent culture. Until very recently, the firm had remained loyal to its core strategic identity as an investment bank with risk-taking and advisory businesses at the core of its franchise. In looking for additional growth areas, Goldman Sachs has more recently ventured out to consumer finance although it had been struggling previously with its ultra-high net worth wealth management business. Applying the coherence methodology to this strategy move, it remains an open question whether this strategic change will be a successful one.

Capabilities set

A capabilities set is a combination of several mutually reinforcing activities that, together, constitute the market position of a business. On an individual level, a capability is the ability to reliably and consistently deliver a distinctive outcome

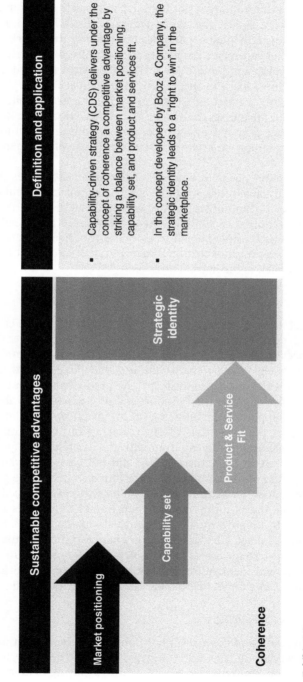

Exhibit 1.3 Capability-driven strategy (CDS)

for the business. This is ensured through the right combination of processes, tools, knowledge, skills, and organisation. Each of the capabilities has to be distinctive on its own and represents an extraordinary if not unique competence that is differentiating. When deployed effectively as set, the combined capabilities lead to a competitive advantage. It is not about individual capabilities but the way they work together. For financial institutions, this can mean the ability to centralise data analytics to assess and manage risk, to develop and bundle products and services in a unique way, or to effectively manage relationships with specific client segments. The capabilities deliver value as a combined entity. In case of Goldman Sachs, the firm's ability to manage data across products and businesses, and steer its balance sheet to transparent daily mark-to-market valuation, gave it a massive competitive advantage in managing the risks of the accelerating subprime crisis before the collapse of Lehman Brothers in autumn 2008.

Every strategic decision needs to consider if the organisation has the ability to deliver and the required capabilities set to do so. If a financial institution does not have them now, can they be built organically or acquired externally? To do so, the gap between available and required capabilities has to be assessed and clearly described. Then specific actions can be implemented to close the gap. Every strategic roadmap, if it is a turnaround plan or a value creation blueprint, needs to reflect this and, most important, always link back to the market position.

Product and service fit

Finally, every product and service offering has to be supported by the capabilities set and fully aligned with the market position. Products and services deliver revenues and add the financial aspect to every strategic decision. If they are not in alignment, then the overall impact of the strategic move remains questionable. Furthermore, if the product and services fit is not ensured, the exit of the respective product portfolios is to be considered. Often during periods of growth, the product and service portfolios are extended to nonaligned and/or not supported capabilities. UBS, for instance, added late in the cycle, leading up to the Global Financial Crisis (GFC), a series of fixed-income and credit businesses in a desperate attempt to catch up with the established American investment banks. When the credit cycle turned, UBS did not have the risk-management capabilities to manage the position and client exposure effectively. The group with its differentiating and sustainable wealth management business experienced losses in the area of US$40–50 billion. It was at the edge of collapse and had to be rescued in a combined operation by the Swiss government and the Swiss national bank. Following the stabilisation of its balance sheet, UBS, as many other banks in similar situations, moved all its incoherent or nonstrategic assets and businesses to a noncore unit and wound them down in a disciplined manner. Financial institutions complete pricing analyses in relation to the addressable target market and customer segmentation.

Strategy identity with winning ambitions

The thorough understanding of the market positioning and the institution's capability set and product and services fit lead to the strategic identity. The strategic identity sets the winning ambitions and initiatives in the competitive playing field for success. The winning ambitions are shaped by an institution's vision and purpose that gets captured by the mission statement. It must be coherent across the firm's market positioning, capability set, and product and service fit. It eventually describes the way an institution intends to gain a competitive advantage through its value proposition and growth initiatives in the marketplace.

1.2 STRATEGIC PLANNING

Strategic planning follows a structured process that combines several layers of analysis to a roadmap. The roadmap evaluates a situation and concludes on a strategic direction. It starts with an impact assessment that outlines the available options and portfolio choices to be aligned with the requirements of the commercial and operating model. Finally, a coherent action plan is to be established.

1.2.1 Roadmap

A strategic roadmap summarises the cornerstones of a strategic plan. It is designed to help the management team to make its strategic choices. The roadmap starts with an evaluation of the situation, followed by impact assessment that leads to a response plan. The situational evaluation is shaped by the set of hypotheses that have been built in to understand the situation. The action plan outlines the strategic direction with its different options, defines the specific problem-solving process for a situation, and comes up with an action plan that further moves the analysis towards implementation. A turnaround and value creation plans that we are going to introduce in Chapters 5 and 6 are to be understood as such strategic roadmaps. For the time being, it remains crucial to be familiar with the term and understand its role. Conceptually, the hypothesis-driven approach as an efficient problem-solving process leads and shapes the strategic roadmap. It moves the focus from identification and evaluation to action and implementation.

1.2.2 Impact assessment

Every new situation such as a crisis, a major transformative event (e.g. new capital requirements), or the circumstances of an underperforming business require the detailed evaluation and impact assessment. Strategy offers a series of tools that facilitate this initial analysis. The following paragraphs are focussing on heat maps, SWOT, and scenario analysis as proposed tools. In its approach, all those tools are usually expert driven and supported by quantitative analysis. It allows illustration of the situation with its core drivers while getting senior decision makers and stakeholders aligned to the problem-solving process.

Heat map analysis

A heat map visualises and graphically illustrates an initial evaluation and impact assessment with its core issues against several dimensions. The individual outcomes are contained in a matrix, often as an expression of an institution's organisational structure and its operating model's functional structure. The important role of the target operating model will further be discussed in a subsequent section. As illustrated in Exhibit 1.4, the outcomes of a heat-map analysis are represented in accordance with a

Functions

Dimensions	Front office	Mid office	Back office
Governance	High	Low	Medium
Organisational design	Low	Medium	Low
Regulatory requirements	High	High	Low
Capital considerations	High	High	Medium
Brand and marketing	Low	Medium	Medium
Operational implications	Low	High	High
Technology	Medium	Low	Low

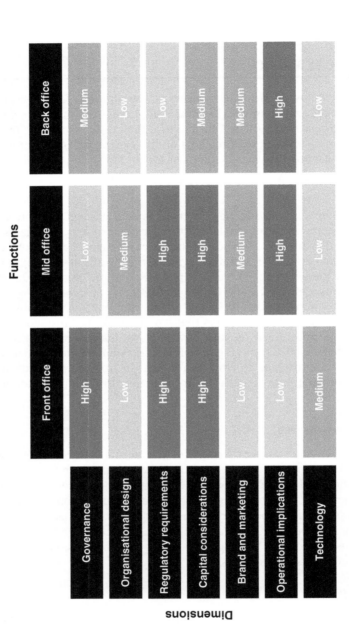

Exhibit 1.4 Heat map with high, medium, and low impact

colour scheme, for example, red for high impact, amber for medium impact, and green for low impact.

Heat maps can be applied to a variety of situations such as specific events in case of a crisis or a strategic shift. The heat map allows quick assessment of the situation and provides initial guidance and direction for how the situation can be approached and the issues resolved. It is a powerful tool for internal coordination and alignment across decision makers.

SWOT analysis

The SWOT analysis further provides helpful information for matching resources to an institution's capabilities and market positioning. It is one of the most commonly used approaches in strategic planning. It covers strengths (S) and weaknesses (W) from an internal view, and opportunities (O) and threats (T) from an external perspective. The analysis outlines advantages and disadvantages and identifies the environment's favourable and unfavourable factors in achieving the objectives of a strategic decision. It naturally illustrates the competitive advantage or disadvantage of an institution in a specific situation which can impact the decision dramatically.

Prior to performing a SWOT analysis, it is important to first develop the proper context by working through the process of a market assessment and identify the competitive advantage an institution. The assessment must follow the framework and requirements of strategic coherence. It is always applied within the context of a defined market that sets the barriers to implement a particular strategy at the organisational or product level. Through the combination of different scenarios, the SWOT analysis helps in developing strategic options and priorities. The combination of strengths and opportunities indicates the right or a strong strategic fit. The combination of weaknesses and opportunities allows to overcome gaps. The combination of strengths and threats leads to the reduction of organisational vulnerabilities. Finally, the combination of weaknesses and threats preempt threats that may attack vulnerable areas. Exhibit 1.5 illustrates the core components of a SWOT analysis with its applications.

Scenario analysis

A scenario analysis further evolves the initial assessment by analysing possible future outcomes by stressing specific factors for the evaluation. It assumes specific scenarios

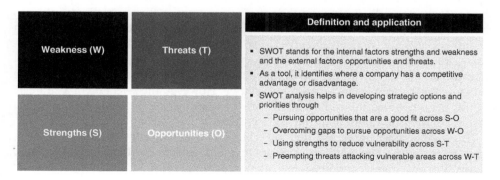

Exhibit 1.5 SWOT analysis

for the factors and assesses the possible outcomes under these developments. Each scenario normally combines optimistic (best case), standard (base case), and pessimistic or less probable (worst case) developments. The scenarios are built with the objective to assess the implications for decision making. The four combinations outlined under the SWOT analysis can be the starting point for an extended scenario analysis framework.

The scenarios can be qualitative or quantitative. Qualitative scenario analysis applies graphic factors to illustrate the dynamics and interdependencies by using instruments from system theory. Quantitative scenario analysis often uses a binominal or trinomial tree by applying specific probability distributions. As we are going to discuss further in Chapter 2, a probability distribution is a mathematical description of the probabilities of events of a sample space. The sample space describes the set of all possible outcomes of a random phenomenon being observed. There are discrete and continuous probability distribution with different specifications such as normal or t-shaped distributions. Monte Carlo simulation uses stochastic processes in forecasting the different outcomes. It develops a better view regarding the risk and uncertainty of an outcome and is often applied in financial analysis and valuation. Chapter 2 covers in detail the fundamentals of a scenario-based approach in the context of a financial decision-making process.

Game theory allows the simulation of the strategic interaction among rational decision makers. It can apply to a variety of situations in strategic decision making. In its simplest form, it applies zero-sum games, in which each participant's gains or losses are exactly balanced by those of the other participants. More advanced forms change assumptions and introduce behavioural relations to simulate the outcomes of the interactions. As we explore further, in financial decision making the behavioural element is usually approximated by utility functions that can be described by mathematical models. Through the application of deep-learning machine learning models, game theory can use today large amounts of data and apply advanced simulation for complex decision making. Chapter 4 will cover these developments further under the section on artificial intelligence and augmented decision making.

1.2.3   Strategic options and portfolio choices

The establishment of strategic options follows the impact assessment. This allows the structured evaluation of the relative merits and feasibility of different ways forward expressed by the available options. A strategic option is nothing else than an available choice. There naturally is always a chance of an inherent challenge or disadvantage to choice made. Options are therefore often aggregated and become portfolio choices in accordance with the strategic direction of an institution. Probability theory offers several quantitative techniques to quantify the options and their aggregation. Contingent claim models that are introduced in Chapter 2 apply binominal trees in a discrete setting and closed-end formulas in a continuous setting. However, the selection of a strategic options often remains subjective and is likely to be influenced by the specific political interests or cultural values of the decision makers.

It remains most important that any choice is coherent with the firm's strategy, market positioning, capability set, and product and services portfolio. The introduced methodology of strategic coherence articulates a paradigm against which all choices and decisions are evaluated. In turnaround and transformational situations, the rationalisation of business portfolios is often required in accordance with the strategic direction chosen. Up to the GFC, many global European banks had pursued lofty ambitions, trying to build themselves into global powerhouses in some cases by expanding into businesses where they had little expertise such as investment banking. They suffered accordingly in the period following the crisis, incurring losses and, in some cases, had to accept government bailouts. However, a group of them radically restructured their business portfolio and significantly scaled back on major business lines and geographies. UBS, for instance, scaled back their investment bank to provide services to their core wealth management business. Royal Bank of Scotland (RBS) reduced their corporate and institutional bank substantially (now known under the Nat West Markets brand) to the requirements of their UK-domestic corporate and institutional client base. Other banks made none or only incremental changes to their strategy and had to go through an accelerated restructuring at a much later stage in the cycle. In value creation situations such as buy-to-build or buy-to-fix acquisitions, the same principle applies. Each value creation initiative must be coherent to the build-up and/or repositioning strategy, the market opportunities, and the capability set. As part of the broader transformation cycle of the industry, a group of specialty finance providers popped up after the GFC. They challenged the existing market structure by either focussing on underserved client and product segments or providing technology-enhanced services in a very effective manner. The profitability of these challenger banks has been much higher with a return on equity (ROE) of more than 30% and cost-income ratios below 40%. Targets that could have never been fulfilled as part of a large and complex organisation.

1.2.4 Action and response plan

An action and response plan is the part of the strategic roadmap that describes the set of actions to get the solutions to the respective situation implemented. It is often used for illustration and approvals in discussions with senior management with regard to next steps. It provides a detailed documentation that consists of an executive summary, a section on the evaluation and impact assessment, consisting of a combination of a heat map, scenario, and SWOT analysis, as well as a Gantt chart. The Gantt chart proposes a response schedule with its timeline, activities, and key milestones. This plan usually outlines the going-forward direction though a comprehensive business plan which then further describes the overall commercial considerations. It includes financial information, operational requirements, and specific implementation initiatives for the execution. Good examples of such action and response plans are separation and integration plans that are further covered in Chapter 6 under value creation and growth.

A Gantt chart is a bar chart, named after its inventor Henry Gantt, that uses a bar for each activity in accordance with its timeline while showing the dependency between activities and response status. Each activity is represented by a bar. The position and length of the bar reflect the start date, duration, and end date of the activity. Tasks and specific subtasks are created, and interdependencies and overlaps are visualised. Each activity is a response to mitigate or influence the outcome described by the evaluation and impact assessment. It illustrates the response schedule graphically and often describes milestones with specific marks to complete it. Exhibit 1.6 illustrates a Gantt

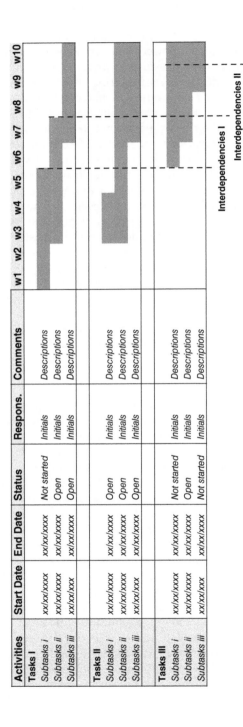

Exhibit 1.6 Gantt chart and performance tracking template

chart with its visible features. There are several software solutions available that allow a flexible integration in an institution's programme management.

A quantitative performance tracker accompanies the plan with the aim to track progress and associated costs. The tracker applies a selected set of key performance indicators (KPIs) that allows the management team to measure progress towards plan and highlights areas that need attention. The right set of indicators needs to be selected as a representation of the respective situation and desired outcomes. Important is to identify and select the critical few management metrics. KPIs can be grouped in a financial, commercial, and operational perspective. Its role will further be discussed in Chapter 6 when the different components of a value creation plan are going to be established.

1.3 OPERATIONAL EXCELLENCE

With strategic coherence, a methodology and group of core principles were introduced. A business must establish itself with a clear identity in the marketplace and create a set of differentiating capabilities to which all product and services have to fit. The operating model brings this all together with focus on operational excellence and efficiency. It outlines the governance structure of a business across locations and the different operational functions such as front office, operations, technology, and support functions, that is, finance, risk, human resources, and legal. It defines processes and systems as well as the services provided by each function across the value chain. It sets the people agenda by articulating skills and motivations of its people across each function and defines performance management and incentivisation as well as organisational development.

1.3.1 Operating model

The operating model facilitates the realisation of an organisation's strategic ambitions as an expression of its strategic identity in coherence and alignment with its market position, capability set, and product and services fit. It links back to vision, culture, and specific management processes and is organised in accordance with the paradigm of operational efficiency in transparent alignment with its KPIs. It most importantly clarifies if resources and costs are correctly allocated and its cost base and drivers in line with benchmarking peers and best practice. The information flow must be guaranteed and controlled back-to-front.

The operating model can be distinguished in an as-is and target operating model (TOM). The as-is operating model is a description of today's processes, systems, and services. It delivers a functional front-to-back view of today's cost base which is the starting point for the performance analysis. The TOM on the other hand implies a target state that is to be attained on a going-forward basis. For any turnaround and value creation plan, the TOM is fundamental to any business performance improvement initiative such as cost reduction, restructuring, or commercial as well as operational transformation. They all start with the design of the targeted state of the operation and its functions that are defined by the TOM. There are several design principles that have to be incorporated.

The TOM outlines where operations and people are going to be located. It defines the organisational structure with its major business units, sets roles and responsibilities, and allocates resources respectively. Tasks are defined and divided, and authorities are distributed to ensure efficient delivery. It is an expression of an institution's day-to-day activities, organised front to back across functions, representing the value chain of a business. It starts with the front office which includes all revenue-based activities such as product and sales-related ones. It defines the market position and how the organisation faces off to customers and competitors. It is followed by operations and technology and outlines the services that are provided. It can be divided in middle office which includes product control and compliance functions as well as client services support. There also is a classic back-office which settles products and issues documentation and drives standardised operational services. The shared or support functions support the different business units, operations, and technology across the organisation. These are finance, risk, human resources, legal, and compliance. Technology can also be organised as a shared function, delivering services across business units. Given the specific requirements of individual business units, they usually remain close to operations or a hybrid model of group and business unit technology services is established. Within the risk function sits the second line of defence while the first line remains a responsibility of the front office, and auditing as the third line is part of the finance function.

The TOM design should be inspired by the quality and range of possibility that are open for the business. It is usually defined along six key dimensions or building blocks such as organisational structure, governance, authority matrix, decision rights, processes, policies, and procedures as well as staffing requirements. This incorporates which customers and markets to serve and the range and type of products and services to offer. In accordance with its coherent strategy, it is a well-defined system for planning, setting goals, delegating authority, budgeting, and measuring performance. The hierarchical structure is shaped by spans of control. Decision rights are at the same time a critical determinant of organisational performance. They describe the decision-making authority and accountability across the organisation. Efficient decision making is ensured through a good balance between centralisation and decentralisation in the way the decision making is structured. Exhibit 1.7 describes the front-to-back TOM of an international banking business together with the six key dimensions of an operating model design.

1.3.2 Balance scorecard

Business performance is captured by the balanced scorecard (BSC) as a standardised tool of management reporting, originally developed by Robert Kaplan and David Norton in the 1990s. It is used by executives to measure business performance through both financial and nonfinancial data as well as to keep track and monitor ongoing initiatives. The BSC combines financial and operational considerations through tangible KPIs and incorporates additional perspectives such as competition, customer, internal processes, and learning and growth. It is based on an institution's strategic agenda and monitors performance against its set objectives. Chapter 2 on financial decision making outlines KPIs with its different dimensions in more detail.

Functions

Front office	Mid office	Back office
Client & markets	Compliance & Surveillance	Processing
Sales & business development	Product control	Settlement
Onboarding and know your customer	Data quality and control	Transaction management
Product development	Financial reporting and valuation	Data management
Accounts & deposits	PnL attribution and substantiation	
Credit underwriting	Reconciliation	
Trading		
Advisory		

Services

Six key dimensions of operating model design

Organisational structure	Governance	Authority matrix
Decision rights	Processes, policies, and procedures	Staffing requirements

Exhibit 1.7 Front-to-back TOM of an international banking business

25

1.3.3 Best practice and benchmarking

Best practice defines a management method of market and peer comparison that focuses on achieving results superior to those achieved by other market participants. It is used as a benchmark and reference point in implementing strategic initiatives on operational effectiveness that applies cost benchmarks across the operating model. The challenge is to make the benchmarks comparable in accordance with a standardised framework. Most methods use surveys and quantitative techniques to build a data and market insight database that aggregates best-practice principles and sets of data point to the management information system (MIS). These data points represent an effective way to identify opportunities for performance improvement.

Several consulting firms have established independent platforms that provide independent, impartial, and anonymous benchmarks of competitors' businesses, operations, and technology performance. The Boston Consulting Group (BCG), for instance, offers through its subsidiary Expand benchmark services to financial institutions with the objective to validate in particular operational strategies in a peer comparison. Other consulting firms such as Oliver Wyman, McKinsey & Company, and Coalition offer similar services where independence and anonymous information gathering is core to the offering. McKinsey got in the news after closing its Corporate & Investment Banking (CIB) Insight service unit in early 2021 after it became apparent that its research team inappropriately took information from its former employer, Coalition.

1.4 BUSINESS PERFORMANCE IMPROVEMENT

The term business performance improvement is used in a broad format but often links back-to-back cost reduction with other efficiency considerations. However, it is a decision-making methodology and principle that is in particular relevant for stabilising businesses and repositioning them for growth. As a methodology, it replaces uncertainty and provides an execution plan with a number of available tools. It incorporates portfolio optimisation, business simplification, disposal and divestments, business simplification, cost reduction, and technology replatforming that are all covered in the following sections. It is all about operational change in accordance with the defined TOM design and starts with the definition of an agreed set of KPIs on which the organisational achievements and initiatives can be measured.

Operational change begins with an evaluation if the TOM is aligned with the strategic identity across market positioning, differentiating capability set, as well as product and services fit. Everything is assessed from a perspective of coherence and measured against a group of defined KPIs. The operational cost base is often the starting point but the KPIs are more broadly aligned. There may be an enormous franchise value in specific business segments with their services although they operate below the profitability targets. Corporate and institutional banking, for instance, depend heavily on auxiliary services such as foreign exchange trading or sophisticated cash management. The TOM further sets out the design for the location of operations and people. It is to be organised across principles of operational effectiveness with its KPIs fully aligned. KPIs translate strategic coherence in tangible outcomes. KPIs that are applied for financial institutions are covered in more detail in Chapter 3 on financial decision making. A balance scorecard may further enforce financial and operational discipline by continuously monitoring a group of KPI dimensions.

1.4.1 Portfolio optimisation

As outlined previously, incoherent capabilities and businesses in institutions are to be disposed and investments in them scaled back. The same logic applies to portfolios of products and clients. More diverse product and client portfolios lead to operational complexity with high costs and inefficiencies. Often portfolio complexity is a result of aggressive growth. The 30 years of dramatic growth that the financial industry had gone through up to the GFC led not only to incoherent business but also to outsized product and client portfolios.

Business portfolios

Business portfolios are rationalised under the principle of coherence, crucially clarifying whether the business has a competitive advantage and operates above a profitability threshold or has a specific franchise value overall within a group structure. Incoherent and misaligned businesses should be disposed and their investments scaled back dramatically. With the incoming regulatory agenda post GFC, there had been a huge focus on streamlining balance sheets and mitigating higher risk-weighted assets implications at financial institutions. Often previously profitable businesses were heavily impacted by higher capital requirements. Correlation risk of high-rated senior credit tranches made the business unattractive and many trading desk and asset portfolios were liquidated as part of noncore legacy units. Chapter 2 introduces the economic value added (EVA) methodology that applies an excess economic spread in making those decisions and facilitates capital allocation respectively. A pure financial view often has to be balanced by the franchise value which is harder to measure quantitatively given the impact on customer relationships.

Product and client tails

Many financial institutions accumulated over the 30-year growth period dramatically outsized product and client portfolios. Often 90% of the revenues are eventually produced by 10% of the products and clients. In investment banking in particular, specific clients traded tailored products on a very infrequent basis. Those tailored products were often exotic in nature and required specific structuring and technology capabilities. Client segmentation provides a transparent picture of the net-profit contribution of each client, organised across segments. It illustrates comparative advantages and identifies inefficiencies. It further allows a focussed distribution model as well as risk-based and funding-based pricing model.

Product portfolio can be standardised across defined transparency requirements that are linked back to the KPIs. Exotic derivatives products were a strong profit driver for trading and sales units of international banks. The incoming regulatory agenda introduced very punitive capital and transparency requirements to address the systemic risk of those businesses post-crisis. Deutsche Bank and many other European banks shifted strategy quickly and moved back to highly standardised instruments with large trading volumes. The exotic businesses that often just had been built prior to the GFC were disposed. As a result, the profit and profitability levels of those business units plunged and triggered a series of restructuring activities.

1.4.2 Divestments and disposals

A divestment, divestiture, or disposal is the sale of an existing asset or business by a financial institution. From a strategic perspective, a divestments allow to refocus the business portfolio with its capabilities and product and service mix on its market positioning. Post GFC, most international banks rationalised their asset and business portfolios by establishing noncore units for nonstrategic assets and businesses. This applied equally to distressed and nonperforming assets as well as businesses that were no longer coherent with the rescaled strategic objectives. A big driver of this development was the incoming regulations. They either constrained balance-sheet leverage or led to higher capital requirements which substantially impacted profitability as we covered in the previous section on portfolio optimisation.

1.4.3 Front-to-back optimisation

After applying the principles of coherence within a portfolio rationalisation framework, front-to-back optimisation applies business simplification and automation by streamlining the TOM with regard to people, processes, and systems. It often applies automation and straight-through-processing as core principle. Businesses with diverse product and service features lead to high organisation and operational complexity that require manual intervention with a lot of personnel. The respective full-time equivalent (FTE) requirements to provide those manual interventions can be extensive and expensive. In addition, there are often specific technology requirements that are outside standardised software solutions.

In financial institutions, structured derivatives businesses had gone through a dramatic growth period fuelled by financial innovation, laxer regulations, and a broader acceptance of more complex financial instruments. Tailored products grew across asset classes with different operational and technology requirements. The combination of a more difficult market and a more scrutinised regulatory environment made the complexity of those businesses transparent. The tailored and bespoke nature of these derivatives required a lot of manual work or specific applications on technology platforms which elevated the cost dramatically. This was very different from standardised flow products which could be fully automated and processed by standard software packages. By separating the processing of highly bespoke products and standardised flow products, operational efficiency could be increased dramatically. Standardised products were fully automated through off-the-shelf software solutions while eliminating breaks and errors caused by processing nonflow products in the same fashion. Dedicated and specialised teams with deep product expertise processed the bespoke products in accordance with its specific requirements. The operational costs of those teams became fully transparent which allowed management to incorporate a more comprehensive analysis of their profitability. More advanced and structured derivatives products are usually traded on an infrequent basis by a specific set of clients. In addition to the higher capital requirements, management needs to assess each of these transactions to get full transparency on the cost of the transaction and its fit for the business holistically. Front-to-back optimisation is closely related to cost reduction and technology replatforming.

1.4.4 Cost reduction

Successful cost reduction is based on a comprehensive understanding of the operational cost base which is a derivative of the as-is operating model. The process of establishing this understanding is called baselining. The baselining starts with the development of a functional cost model that tracks costs front to back across functions with their respective services and activities for each function. Based on financial and management reporting, the baselining is derived by mapping the different cost components to each function which provides a comprehensive front-to-back view. For financial institutions, it is to be mentioned that the fixed costs consisting, for instance, of salaries are usually a major contribution factor for the production cost and cost of goods sold (COGS). In addition, capital costs are to be considered when respective decisions have been made. The product and sales costs will be allocated to the front office, reporting and valuation costs to the mid office, the finance costs to the share or support function, and so on and so forth. Through the cost mapping, the cost driver for each function can be identified which further requires a top-down view of the financial institution's strategy across market positioning, capabilities set, and product portfolio. Exhibit 1.8 describes a typical baselining and cost mapping for an international wholesale banking business. It further outlines some common cost reduction hypotheses for these types of businesses.

A comprehensive baselining allows the development of initial cost reduction hypotheses that are usually organised by function. The initial hypotheses are developed from experience and peer-to-peer comparison by applying benchmarking and best-practices. External advisors have established large pools of comparable data that allows to identify outsized cost components and articulate hypotheses around it. For illustration, a cash equity business with US$1 billion in revenues employs 260 full-time equivalents (FTEs) whereas the average peer group only needs 200 FTEs. An initial cost reduction hypothesis for this business of 60 FTEs can be established with an average cost per FTE across grades of US$220,000 which leads to a total cost saving of US$13.2 million. All initial cost reduction hypotheses are to be presented to the management team in a workshop and then further categorised and ranked according with the experienced-based consensus on the opportunities. Activity-based costing has been in particular applied to allocate overhead costs for shared and support function. It allows to extend traditional cost systems by linking resource expenses to the respective functions.

As a result of the increased regulatory requirements, overhead costs in compliance and regulatory functions exploded and became a major contribution factor for segment and product profitability as they were allocated to different business units in accordance

Common cost reduction hypotheses

1 Front-office effectiveness
- Optimising client and product portfolios
- Optimising coverage model
- Increasing digital penetration

2 Trade-flow optimisation
- Right-sizing front-office headcount
- Optimising life cycle management
- Improving booking discipline

3 Operational effectiveness
- Optimising management layers
- Rationalising support activities
- Automate manual processes

Baselining

Sales	Trade execution	Mid office	Back office
20% Costs/25% FTE	30% Costs/25% FTE	10% Costs/15% FTE	5% Costs/10% FTE
Sales	Trading	Product control	Cash settlement
Structuring	Prime services	Trade control	Confirmations
Compliance	Modelling	Reconciliation	Settlement
Client services	Risk management	Reporting	Asset servicing
Sales support		Client valuation	Collateral mgmt
			New issue support
			Risk & control

Technology

45% Costs/25% FTE

- Integrated software solutions
- Product-specific applications
- Technology management

Exhibit 1.8 Baselining and cost mapping

with an allocation formula. The initial hypotheses then further have to be validated and refined by interviews with the business leaders. Many hypotheses are getting eliminated during this process. The selected and refined hypotheses can then be quantified as opportunities and then aggregated to overall cost reduction target. Often, it is the other way around and the management team articulates an initial cost target and the needs to outline the specific opportunities. In the second restructuring wave after the GFC, many global banks communicated specific cost targets as part of investor presentations. Through lean management, a systematic method for continuously eliminating overhead and non-value-added steps across financial institutions' value chain and business processes, strategic cost reduction targets can be reached over time. It is a commitment to efficiency and performance improvement on an ongoing basis.

1.4.5   Technology replatforming

Historically, technology was developed in-house tailored to the different commercial requirements of individual financial institutions. The core systems were often designed in the 1970s and 1980s, and the operational complexity increased dramatically as result of dramatic growth in client and product portfolios during the 1990s and 2000s. Different systems with individual databases were integrated through aggregators which increased their operational costs dramatically and often required manual work in processing the system adjustments. After asset and businesses were rationalised, many financial institutions were left with outsized and heterogeneous technology platform that were no longer in line with the product and client requirements.

As part of their business performance improvement initiatives, many financial institutions started to reorganise their technology platform through targeted replatforming initiatives. Off-the-shelf software solutions were replacing internally developed banking applications which often required the rationalisation and simplification of product portfolios beforehand. Providers such as Temenos, Avaloq, FIS, and Murex provided standardised software across core systems and specific product solutions. Cloud computing allowed new forms to centrally store crucial data which can resolve data fragmentation as one of the industry's core issue. Goldman Sachs previously created Securities DataBase (SecDB) in the early 1990s with the objective to have one data reference pool across products and asset classes for its securities business. It allowed the firm's pricing and risk management engines to access one unified data pool across the organisation which was efficient and transparent. SecDB was later credited to have been a crucial factor in Goldman Sachs' superior approach in managing the subprime crises in the United States. J.P. Morgan created at a later stage something similar called Athena for their integrated CIB unit.

Technology innovation and open architecture will accelerate the consolidation of the banking industry as digital distribution channels increase the scalability of services. Open architecture solutions such as application programming interface will allow the banks to become global digital banking platforms, partnered with best-in-class service providers, who will utilise their core infrastructure and customer base. This may lead to a competitive selection process as only a small group of global digital banking platforms is needed in this new world, connecting clients to the best-in-class service universe. Differentiation will happen on a regional or even a local level and in service areas where specific skill sets are required. Participants must assess their competitive advantage and decide which role they want to play. Chapter 4 covers technology management and innovation in further detail.

1.5 MERGER AND ACQUISITION

Merger and acquisition (M&A) is an efficient tool to consolidate a market positioning and acquire a specific capability set and asset portfolio in building a business and an operating platform. Every M&A transaction must have a clear rationale that follows a clearly articulated hypothesis and is coherent with an institution's strategy, that is, market position, capabilities set, and product and service fit. Such transactions may follow a horizontal or vertical logic with focus on the same product and service areas or different stages of the value chain. M&A follows a life cycle across deal strategy, due diligence, and execution as well as the post-deal implementation which either is an integration and/or separation. Chapter 7 will cover this life cycle from a value creation perspective and outline the different steps within each stage. Chapter 2 covers different valuation methods that are a crucial part of the M&A process. M&A must be coherent with the existing businesses strategic direction and capability set, else there is an inherent risk that it distracts and concludes in additional cost layers driven by the increased regulatory complexity. M&A in banking and financial services has heavily been driven by regulations.

In the late 1980s and the 1990s, a series of mega mergers happened between financial institutions. JPMorgan Chase, in its current structure, is the result of the combination of several companies that started 1996. It includes Chase Manhattan Bank, J.P. Morgan & Co., Bank One, Bear Stearns, and Washington Mutual. UBS as we know it today was formed by the merger of Schweizerische Bankgesellschaft with Swiss Bank Corporation in autumn 1998. Citigroup is another company that followed an aggressive M&A strategy during 1990s. The US Congress further passed the Gramm-Leach-Bliley act in the late 1990s. It repealed parts of the Glass-Steagall Act of 1933 which aimed to prevent a broader bank crisis during the Great Depression. It separated conventional areas of banking from the risky areas of securities trading and investment banking. The passing of the Gramm-Leach-Bliley led to a big boom in banking mergers as traditional banking giants started to scale their traditional operations by acquisition of smaller players while accessing cheap capital that could put to work in the brokerage and advisory businesses. In the early 2000s, there were over 1000 banking deals in the United States alone in which Wachovia bought Commerce National, Wells Fargo bought H.D. Vest, and Bancorp bought Commercial Bank of New York. This consolidation was further accelerated during and after the GFC where several distressed banks such as Wachovia were acquired by Wells Fargo or Bank of America bought Merrill Lynch in 2008 after the collapse of Lehman Brothers. Those M&A activities slowed down dramatically when the G20 regulatory reform was implemented, and banks faced a new regulatory landscape with increased complexity.

Successful large-scale M&A in banking and financial services has always been challenging given the complexity and multigeography of the businesses. Often an integration must be combined with a business transformation which includes performance improvement and operational change. Citigroup was formed by the merger of Citicorp and the financial conglomerate Travelers Group in 1998. It subsequently spun off its insurance businesses which included property and casualty as well as life insurance and annuities. ABN AMRO Bank N.V. was established in its current form in 2009, following the acquisition and break-up of the original ABN AMRO by a banking consortium consisting of RBS Group, Santander Group, and Fortis. This consortium, known as RFS Holdings B.V., acquired the bank in October 2007 and divided it into three parts. Each part was owned by one of the members of the consortium. RBS and Fortis soon ran into serious trouble as soon as the GFC started shortly after. The large debt created to fund the takeover had depleted the two financial institutions' reserves. The Dutch and UK government stepped in and bailed out Fortis, before splitting ABN AMRO's Dutch assets from those owned by RBS. The operations owned by Santander, notably those in Italy and Brazil, were merged with the rest of the group or divested.

The modern Santander Group was created through a series of global mergers, initially with Cantral Hispano in the early 1990s, followed by acquisitions in Latin America and the United Kingdom. Its management team was very strong in efficiently integrating the acquired businesses, combined with substantial performance improvement through cost reduction and digitisation. Every acquisition of Santander had been coherent with its positioning, capability set, and product portfolio as a leading retail bank across jurisdictions. This was very different from Deutsche Bank who established its global presence in investment banking through a series of acquisitions such as Morgan, Grenfell & Co., and Bankers Trust, which completely changed its traditional model as a domestic German banking giant. Similar to Credit Suisse, who acquired First Boston and struggled to integrate it in the broader group structure, Deutsche Bank had to substantially downsize its investment banking operations post GFC and return to its core commercial model as a domestic bank for German retail and corporate customers. Credit Suisse also returned to its domestic focus and original role as international wealth manager. RBS by itself had to accept government capital post crisis and scale down its global aspirations after a series of wrong investments, mainly related with the aggressive build-up of its trading and investment banking businesses. Those large global European banks together with UBS and Barclays drove the restructuring and transformation activities post the GFC with core focus on new organisational structures and performance improvement.

RESOURCES AND FURTHER READING

Ansoff, Igor H. (1988b). *Corporate Strategy*; Business Library.

Besanko, David et al. (2000). *Economics of Strategy*; Wiley.

Couto, Vinay, John Plansky, and Deniz Caglar (2016). *Fit for Growth: A Guide to Strategic Cost Cutting, Restructuring and Renewal*; Wiley.

Evans, Vaughan (2013). *Key Strategy Tools*; FT Publishing

Freedman, Lawrence (2013). *Strategy—A History*; Oxford University Press.

Gemes, Alan and Joerg Ruetschi (2016). "Banking's Biggest Hurdle: Its Own Strategy—Why coherent institutions were the first to rebound after the financial crisis"; *strategy+business*

Kaplan, Robert S. and David P. Norton (1996). *The Balanced Scorecard: Translating Strategy into Action*; President and Fellows of Harvard College.

Kiechel, Walter III (2010). *The Lords of Strategy*; Harvard Business Press.

Leinwand, Paul and Cesare Mainardi (2010). *The Essential Advantage: How to Win with a Capabilities-Driven Strategy*; Harvard Business Review Press.

Leinwand, Paul and Cesare Mainardi (2016). *Strategy That Works*; Harvard Business Review Press.

Mckeown, Max (2019). *The Strategy Book*; Pearson.

Meadows, Donella (2008). *Thinking in Systems: A Primer*; Chelsea Green Publishing.

Mintzberg, Henry (1993). *Rise and Fall of Strategic Planning*; Pearson Education Limited.

Porter, Michael E. (1980). *Competitive Strategy: Techniques for Analyzing Industries and Competitors*; Free Press.

Rasiel, Ethan M. and Paul N. Friga (2010). *The McKinsey Mind*; McGraw Hill.

Rumelt, Richard (2011). *Good Strategy, Bad Strategy*; Profile Books.

Rutherford, Albert (2018). *The Systems Thinker*; Kindle Direct Publishing.

CHAPTER 2

Financial Decision Making

After discussing the fundamentals of strategic decision making, the objective of this chapter is to establish a financial decision framework that can be incorporated in a comprehensive business transformation and value creation methodology. The chapter covers financial decision making across the four fundamental areas of financial analysis, valuation, modelling, and stress. These areas define the quantitative step stones to measure and capture value and transformational impact of different commercial and operational initiatives on a business. Financial analysis covers the information provision with regard to the applicable key performance indicators (KPIs). Financial valuation discusses the methodology to translate the KPIs into business valuation. Financial modelling outlines the mathematical fundamentals of a risk-based decision process applied in particular to financial institutions. This decision process is further outlined in Chapter 3 under asset-liability management. The last section on financial stress establishes a framework to assess market dislocations and banking crises that allow one to generalise the decision framework and brings it more closely to economic realities.

2.1 FINANCIAL ANALYSIS

The first step stone in financial decision making is established through three core components of traditional financial analysis, namely the financial statements, ratios, and leverage. Financial analysis applies a static accounting methodology to provide the information base and identify the KPIs for dynamic risk-based methods that are covered in the second part of this chapter.

2.1.1 Financial statements

The financial statements provide the information base for all financial decisions. It is the starting point for financial analysis that also is often referred to fundamental analysis. They report the results of a business's past performance and its current financial position. While the interests of financial stakeholders may relate to the future financial performance and health of a business, financial statements summarise all the core information that are required for the financing, operating, and investment decisions in accordance with a firm's commercial positioning. This section focuses on the evaluation and interpretation of financial statements for decision making in financial institutions. It provides an overview in accordance with International Financial Reporting Standards (IFRS)[1], following the objective to extract for information from a value creation and transformation perspective.

International Accounting Standard (IAS) 1 on presentation of financial statements sets out the guidelines and minimum requirements for the presentation of financial statements. It defines their purpose in information provision on the financial position, financial performance, and cash flows of an entity and categorises the information provided into assets, liabilities, income and expenses, contributions by and distribution to owners, and cash flows. It follows the principle of consistency and materiality from one period to the next with the objective to provide transparency and comparison. A complete set of financial statements consists of five main components:

- a statement of profit and loss (PnL) and other comprehensive income (OCI) for the period (income statement)
- a statement of financial position at the end of the period (balance sheet)
- a statement of changes in equity for the period
- a statement of cash flow for the period (cash flow statement)
- a comprehensive set of explanatory notes

We are following a focused approach with the objective to establish the fundamentals for financial institution. The core focus is on the respective KPI inputs such as profits, several applicable balance-sheet items such as equity or working capital, and eventually free cash flow. All these items provide the base for business valuation and economic risk assessment.

Income statement

The income statement measures a company profit or loss over a specific period of time. A business is required to record and report for tax purposes at a minimum and for its shareholders/owners in particular when it operates in the public space. IFRS defines a statement of profit and loss and other comprehensive income. Exhibit 2.1 describes its categories.

Revenue is the sales or gross income a company has made during a specific operating period. It is recognised when realised and earned which is when products and services have been delivered. For a financial institution and bank, it consists of interest income, fees, and commission income as well as trading income and is usually presented net of all directly allocated expenses.

Cost of sales is the costs directly associated to the revenues and attributable to the production of the products and services of a company. For financial institutions, cost of sales mainly consists of personnel expenses. The net value of revenue is often determined after the cost of sales (i.e. personnel expenses for a bank) is removed and then presented in the form of gross profit as a totalling item equal to revenue less the cost

---

[1] It has to be kept in mind though that IFRS finds its particular application in the European Union while the United States follows US Generally Accepted Accounting Principles.

in millions	20xx
Net interest income	'000
Net fee and commission income	'000
Net trading income	'000
Net income from other financial instruments	'000
Other revenue	'000
Net loss arising from de-recognition of financial assets	'000
Revenues	**'000**
Personnel expenses	'000
Other operating expenses	'000
Impairment losses of financial instruments	'000
Depreciation and amortisation	'000
Expenses	**'000**
Other net income	'000
Profit before tax	**'000**
Income tax expense	'000
Profit for the period	**'000**
Items that will not be reclassified to profit or loss	'000
Items that are or may be reclassified subsequently to profit or loss	'000
Other comprehensive income	**'000**
Total comprehensive income	**'000**

Exhibit 2.1 Illustrative financial institution's statement of PnL and OCI in accordance with the requirements of IAS 1 and IFRS 9

of sales. Distribution costs and administrative expenses represent operating expenses. Operating expenses are indirect costs related to generating the company's revenue and supporting its operations. They are incurred as a result of performing its normal business operations.

Income that is recorded on the income statement and taxable but not core to the business is classified as other income. This may include the distribution of investment, insurance, and pension products as well as a range of nonbanking activities. Often other income is not considered as revenue. In addition, there may be other expenses, gains, and losses that need to be considered so it is usually represented as other net income in a separate line.

All combined, this leads to the profit before tax which is also equal to earnings before taxes (EBT). Deducting income tax expense leads to profit for the period as core measure for the KPI return on tangible equity or ROTE. IFRS further requires the detailed presentation and disclosure of other comprehensive income which is a very important role for financial institutions with regard to fair value considerations, change in asset values, and hedging for managing their balance sheets. IFRS 7 and 9 on financial instruments provide detailed guidance on disclosure and presentation in particular with regard to the profit and loss impact. The accounting and regulatory principles of financial instruments will be covered separately in preparation for

Chapter 4 on asset-liability management. Total comprehensive income then represents the combination of profit for the period and other comprehensive income, net of tax.

For the valuation of a business and hence value creation, earnings before interest, taxes, depreciation, and amortisation (EBITDA) is a core and very important input factor as cash flow proxy. Depreciation is an accounting requirement for aging and depletion of fixed assets over a period of time and is covered explicitly by IFRS under IAS 16 property, plant, and equipment. Amortisation is the accounting for the cost base reduction of intangible assets such as intellectually property (patents and copyrights) and trademarks over their useful life. IFRS covers the respective requirements under IAS 38.

Balance sheet

The balance sheet measures an institution's financial position at a specific point in time. With assets, liabilities, and shareholder equity, it is broken up in three major categories. The total value of assets is equal to the sum of the liabilities and shareholders' equity. Assets are resources held to produce some economic benefit. They are distinguished between current assets with an economic benefit expected within one year and noncurrent assets with an expected benefit of more than one year. The same applies for current liabilities and noncurrent liabilities.

Current assets include cash and cash equivalents, assets that are readily convertible into cash such as money market instruments, short-term government bonds, and other marketable securities. As Exhibit 2.2 outlines, IAS 1 also includes financial assets at fair value through profit and loss, other financial assets at amortised costs, derivative financial instruments, and assets classified as held for sale. Banking specific, these are often pledged and nonpledged trading assets for collateral management, derivatives assets held for risk management, and investment securities. Inventories, which usually refer to raw materials and goods, have little or no importance for financial instruments. However, the term is used for securities that are hold for a short period of time with the purpose of market-making, facilitating client activities, and financing securities.

Noncurrent assets include all financial assets such as loans, held-to-maturity investments, and derivative position for more than a year and all fixed assets such as physical properties and equipment that belong to financial institutions. They also include intangible assets such as goodwill, brand recognition, and intellectual property, covered under IAS 38. Financial institutions can also build capital expenditure (often referred to as CAPEX) when they build, maintain, and improve specific technology capabilities. An item is considered a CAPEX when the asset is newly acquired or when cash is used towards extending the useful life of an existing asset. It can be important measure to build capital in particular for neo-banks, although it will be heavily scrutinised. In contrast to operating expenses, CAPEX is a cost that cannot be deducted in the year in which it is paid or incurred and must be capitalised. The general rule is that if the acquired property's useful life is longer than the taxable year, then the cost must be capitalised and activated on the balance sheet. CAPEX is then amortised or depreciated over the life of the asset.

Deferred taxes result from timing differences between net income recorded for accounting purposes in accordance with the respective principles (IFRS in our

in millions	20xx
ASSETS	
Cash and cash equivalents	'000
Nonpledged trading assets	'000
Pledged trading assets	'000
Derivative assets held for risk management	'000
Loans and advances to banks	'000
Loans and advances to customers	'000
Investment securities	'000
Current tax assets	'000
Property and equipment	'000
Intangible assets	'000
Deferred tax assets	'000
Other assets	'000
Total assets	**'000**
LIABILITIES	
Trading liabilities	'000
Derivative assets held for risk management	'000
Deposits from banks	'000
Deposits from customers	'000
Debt securities issued	'000
Subordinated liabilities	'000
Provisions	'000
Deferred tax liabilities	'000
Other liabilities	'000
Total liabilities	**'000**
EQUITY	
Share capital and share premium	'000
Preference shares	'000
Reserves	'000
Retained earnings	'000
Total equity attributable to owners of the Bank	**'000**
Noncontrolling interests	'000
Total equity	'000
TOTAL LIABILITIES AND EQUITY	**'000**

Exhibit 2.2   Illustrative financial institution's balance sheet in accordance with IAS 1

analysis) and the net income recorded for tax purposes. They can act as an asset in case of a loss and a liability in case of a profit. Liabilities include deposits from banks and customers as well as other amounts due to financial institutions, payables from securities financing transaction, trading liabilities, as well as derivative liabilities held for risk management. It further includes trading liabilities, derivatives liabilities held for risk management, provisions as well as debt securities issued, and subordinated liabilities. Shareholders' equity consists of common, preferred, or treasury shares as well as retained earnings, reserves, and other comprehensive income or loss. Equity capital together with different classes of debt will be covered separately in Chapter 3 under capital structure. Those elements remain core in defining the KPIs from a value creation perspective.

A statement of changes in equity explains the changes in a financial institution's share capital, accumulated reserves, and retained earnings over the reporting period. It breaks down changes in shareholders' interest in the organization and in the application of retained profit or surplus from one accounting period to the next. In accordance with IAS 1, the statement of changes in equity consists of total comprehensive income and transactions with owners of the financial institution. Exhibit 2.3 outlines its line

in millions	20xx
TOTAL EQUITY—Balance at the beginning of the period	**'000**
TOTAL COMPREHENSIVE INCOME	**'000**
Profit for the period	**'000**
Other comprehensive income	**'000**
Remeasurements of defined benefit liability and asset	'000
Fair value reserve (available-for-sale financial assets):	'000
Available-for-sale financial assets—net change in fair value	
Available-for-sale financial assets—reclassified to profit or loss	
Translation reserve:	'000
Foreign operations—foreign translation differences	
Net loss on hedge of net investment in foreign operations	
Hedging reserve:	'000
Cash-flow hedges—effective portion of changes in fair value	
Cash-flow hedges—reclassified to profit or loss	
Tax on other comprehensive income	'000
Transactions with owners of the bank	
Equity-settled and share-based payment	'000
Dividends to equity holders	'000
Share options exercised	'000
Total contributions and distributions	**'000**
TOTAL EQUITY—Balance at the end of the period	**'000**

Exhibit 2.3   Financial institution's consolidated statement of changes in equity in accordance with IAS 1 and IFRS 9

items such as profits or losses from operations, revaluation reserve, items charged or credited to accumulated other comprehensive income and dividends paid, and issue or redemption of shares. It also includes the noncontrolling interest attributable to other individuals and organisations.

Cash flow statement

Cash flow forms one of the most important parts of business operations and accounts for the total amount of tangible liquidity that is being transferred into and out of a business. It allows the management team to evaluate the cash generation and maintenance for operational efficiency and other requirements while supporting them in key investing and financing decisions. The cash flow statement is a standard reporting tool and integral part of a primary financial statements as required and further specified under IAS 7. Cash flows are classified and presented into operating activities, investing activities, and financing activities. The latter two categories are generally presented on a gross basis. From a value creation perspective, the free cash flow, defined as operating minus the investing cash flow, is an important KPI and input factor for financial valuation. EBITDA is a common proxy for free cash flow as it can evaluate a company's profitability based on net working capital. Its application will be further discussed in the next section on valuation. Exhibit 2.4 illustrates a financial institution's consolidated statement of cash flow in accordance with IAS 7

Operating cash flows

The cash flow from operating activities (short operating cash flows) constitutes the cash-generating abilities of a business's core activities and refers to the cash amount generated from revenues. There is the direct or indirect calculation method. The direct method aggregates each major class of gross cash receipts and gross cash payments which is encouraged by IAS 7. The indirect method, on which we focus here as it exhibits the relationships between the items for decision making, includes the profit for the period (or net income) from the income statement, the noncash adjustments to net income, and changes in working capital.

The indirect calculation, applied to a banking business, starts with the profit for the period. It then adds all noncash items of the income statement such as depreciation and amortisation, net impairments, as well as gains and losses at fair value through profit and loss (FVTPL) on loans, advances, investment and issued debt securities, and the net loss arising from derecognition of financial assets measured at amortised cost. Net interest income, dividends, and tax expenses (including the ones from other income and other comprehensive income) are deducted and replaced by the interest, dividends, and taxes actually received and paid during the reporting period. Note that interest and dividends received and paid may be classified as operating, investing, or financing cash flows under IAS 7. For an operating banking business, however, they should be part of the operating cash flow. Cash flows arising from taxes on income, on the other hand, are normally classified as operating, unless they can be specifically identified with financing or investing activities.

in millions	20xx
CASH FLOWS FROM OPERATING ACTIVITIES	
Profit or loss for the period	'000
Adjustments for:[2]	
Depreciation and amortisation	'000
Net impairment loss on investment securities	'000
Net impairment loss on loans and advances	'000
Net interest income	'000
Net gain on investment securities	'000
Net gain on loans and advances at fair value through PnL	'000
Net loss on debt securities issued at fair value through PnL	'000
Net loss on sale of available-for-sale investment securities at fair value through OCI	'000
Net loss arising from derecognition of financial assets measured at amortised cost	'000
Dividends on available for-sale equity securities at fair value through OCI	'000
Equity-settled share-based payment transactions	'000
Tax expense	'000
Changes in:	
Trading assets	'000
Derivative assets held for risk management	
Loans and advances to banks	'000
Loans and advances to customers	'000
Other assets	'000
Trading liabilities	'000
Derivative liabilities held for risk management	'000
Deposits from banks	'000
Deposits from customers	'000
Other liabilities and provisions	'000
Interest received	'000
Dividends received	'000
Interest paid	'000
Income taxes paid	'000
Net cash provided/used in operating activities	**'000**

Exhibit 2.4 Illustrative financial institution's cash flow statement in accordance with IAS 7

---

[2]Adjustments to reconcile profit to net cash by operating activities.

CASH FLOWS FROM INVESTING ACTIVITIES	
Acquisition of investment securities	'000
Proceeds from sale of investment securities	
Acquisition of property and equipment	'000
Proceeds from the sale of property and equipment	'000
Acquisition of intangible assets	'000
Net cash provided/used in investing activities	**'000**

CASH FLOWS FROM FINANCING ACTIVITIES	
Proceeds from issue of debt securities	'000
Repayment of debt securities	
Repayment of debt securities	'000
Proceeds from issue of subordinated liabilities	'000
Proceeds from exercise of share options	'000
Dividends paid	'000
Net cash provided/used in financing activities	**'000**

NET DECREASE IN CASH AND CASH EQUIVALENTS	
Cash and cash equivalents at the beginning of the year	'000
Effect of exchange rate fluctuations	'000
Cash and cash equivalents at the end of the year	'000

Exhibit 2.4   (*Continued*)

Changes in working capital which cover all of a business's short-term expenses such as trading, assets, derivative assets held for risk management, loans and advances to customers and financial institutions, and other assets as well as trading liabilities, derivative liabilities held for risk management, deposits from customers and financial institutions, as well as other liabilities and provision are further considered. The profit for the period, the noncash items of the income statement, and the changes in working capital lead to the net cash used in operating activities.

Investing cash flows

To attain a measure of free cash flow from the operating cash flow, the effect of investment activities has to be incorporated. Investing activities are defined as the acquisition and disposal of long-term assets and other investments that are not considered to be cash equivalents. The cash flows from investing activities therefore include the acquisition of investment securities, proceeds from sale of investment securities, acquisition of property and equipment, proceeds from the sale of property and equipment, and acquisition of intangible assets.

Financing cash flows

Financing activities are activities that alter the equity capital and borrowing structure of the entity. The net cash from financing activities include proceeds from issue of debt securities, repayment of debt securities, proceeds from issue of subordinated liabilities, proceeds from exercise of share options, and dividends paid.

Net decrease in cash and cash equivalent then consists of all the cash flow components. The cash flow of financial institutions can be very volatile as the nature of the business changes financing and investing conditions that are further impacted by regulatory requirements. Financial institutions heavily invest in intangible assets such human capital and their brand name. Investments in future growth are therefore often categorised as personnel and operating expenses in the income statement that cannot be activated on balance sheets. Historically, CAPEX such as physical properties and equipment has been low. However, given the huge focus on technology replatforming, the CAPEX element may be changing when specific technology is built in-house and activated on the balance sheet. Large parts of banks' balance sheets are nevertheless categorised as working capital, defined as the difference between current assets and current liabilities. These financial assets and liabilities may further fluctuate substantially with interest rates and other macroeconomic conditions. All these factors add volatility to the cash flow statements and challenges in particular the estimation of free cash flows as a KPI and value creation driver.

2.1.2 Financial ratios

Fundamental analysis uses financial ratios to enhance the understanding and interpretation of a business. The ratios illustrate the relationship between financial performance measures. They are determined by dividing one metric by another metric. Financial statements provide the accounting information to calculate a series of KPIs that we are going to introduce in this section. In addition, there is a series of trading multiples that references accounting to market information such as the stock price of a publicly listed company. These metrics are crucial for financial valuation in particular with regard to precedent transaction analysis that allows the historical comparison of a valuation outcome within a peer group or in a historical comparison. We cover those elements in the next section on financial valuation.

There are three major financial ratios that are in particular relevant to measure financial institutions' performance and profitability. These are return on invested capital (ROIC), return on assets (ROA), and return on equity (ROE). All of them are based on earnings, profit, or income, defined as the net benefits of an institution's operations on which corporate tax is due. These terms are used alternatively, depending on their context and the applied accounting standards. Several more specific terms are used for the analysis of specific aspects of an institutions' operations such as earnings before interest and taxes (EBIT) and EBITDA. EBIT represents operating income and summarises the profitability of a business's operations, excluding nonrecurring and restructuring-related income and expense. EBITDA is often use as proxy for cash flow. As the ratios' numerators reflect a specific time period, the denominator should reflect the average assets for that same time period. Where the business does not experience seasonality, an average of the beginning and ending assets for the period can be used.

ROIC measures the return generated by all capital provided to a company. ROIC focuses on operating income, using EBIT as a preinterest earning metric in the numerator and the average of equity and debt in the denominator. It is formally defined as

$$ROIC = \frac{EBIT}{Average\ (equity + net\ debt)}.$$

ROA provides a reference of the asset efficiency of a business by measuring the return generated by a company's asset base. ROA incorporates the profit for the period (or net income), formally expressed as

$$ROA = \frac{Profit}{Average\ (total\ assets)}.$$

ROIC and ROA are equal if an institution's investment in its assets is not financed by debt but equity only.

ROE measures the return generated on the equity provided by shareholders. Given the equity-based business model, ROE is the core performance and profitability measure for financial institutions. The ratio also uses profit as an earning metric, net of interest expense, in the numerator and average shareholders' equity in the denominator. It can formally be expressed as

$$ROE = \frac{Profit}{Average\ (shareholder's\ equity)}.$$

The DuPont equation further decomposes the ROE metrics into three subcomponents:

$$ROE = net\ profit\ margin \times total\ asset\ turnover\ ratio \times financial\ leverage,$$

which can formally be expressed as

$$ROE = \left(\frac{profit}{revenues}\right)\left(\frac{revenues}{asset}\right)\left(\frac{asset}{equity}\right).$$

The last two terms of the DuPont equation refer to asset efficiency. Asset turnovers describes an institution's effectiveness to turn its assets into revenues. Financial leverage illustrates how the use of lower-cost debt and preferred stock increases the return of common shareholders which is discussed in more detail in the following section.

Earnings per share (EPS) are a common performance and reporting measure for financial institutions that is often used in financial reporting. It is calculated by dividing net income applicable to common shares or shareholders, that is, net income minus dividends on preferred shares, by the average number of common shares outstanding during the period. If an institution has outstanding securities that holders can convert into or exchange for common shares such as employee stock options or convertible debt, it will calculate a fully diluted EPS amount. The popularity of EPS originates from the ease with which earnings can be related to an institution's market price per share which is known as the price–earnings (PE) ratio. The importance of the PE ratio is further covered under the dividend discount model (DDM) in the valuation section of this chapter.

2.1.3 Leverage analysis

The application of leverage is a crucial element in analysing the businesses of financial institutions. The term leverage comes from gearing and is usually applied to debt financing with the objective to enhance ROE. Financial institutions may be seen as leveraged organisations as they use their equity for lending and managing risk. Leverage increases risk exponentially though and can be backfiring in a time of financial dislocation and crisis. In comparison to corporates, financial institutions have a large fixed cost base, defined by their staff costs. Besides the technology platforms, there is no tangible production facilities or real inventories other than assets that are used for business (e.g. trading). Operational leverage is another dimension that needs to be considered in the analysis of financial institutions. Accordingly, this section uses the term of leverage broadly for assessing the risk of a business when returns are enhanced, either financially through borrowing and financial engineering[3] or operationally through gearing revenues contribution to the cost structure.

Financial leverage

Financial leverage (FL) is the means to increase shareholder value through leverage, formally defined as

$$FL = \frac{Total\ Debt}{Shareholder\ Equity},$$

which can further be expressed as a degree of financial leverage (DFL) equal to

$$DFL = \frac{EBIT}{EBIT - Total\ Interest\ Expense}.$$

The DuPont formula that decomposes the different drivers of ROE across its three components incorporates financial leverage through the equity multiplier. It can be calculated by dividing a financial institution's total assets by its total equity. The expected ROE increases with the leverage factor, defined as

$$E[ROE] = E[ROA] + FL \times (R[ROA] - R[ROD]),$$

$$for\ which\ ROD = Return\ on\ Debt.$$

At the same time, the expected return volatility increases by $(1 = FL)^2$ and therefore shows the exponentially increased risk of financial leverage. This is called the leverage effect.

Operating leverage

Operating leverage (OL) is a metric that measures the degree to which a business can increase operating income by increasing revenue. It refers to the proportion of fixed costs versus variable costs in a company's cost structure and the relative impact on profit

---

[3]Leverage strategies through financial engineering are defined by the applications of financial instruments. It will be covered separately in a dedicated section of Chapter 3 on asset-liability management.

given a change in sales. A business that generates revenues with a high gross margin and low variable costs has high operating leverage. Businesses with high operating leverage must cover a larger amount of fixed costs with revenues. However, they also earn more profit from incremental sales as the fixed costs are being spread over more product units. On the other hand, they will suffer more from a drop in sales volume because each lost unit will reduce profit by a relatively large amount. Low-operating-leverage businesses may have high costs that vary directly with their revenues but have lower fixed costs.

Formally, OL is defined as

$$OL = \frac{Revenues - variable\ costs}{Revenues - variable\ cost - fixed\ costs} = \frac{Revenues}{Operating\ income},$$

and the degree of operating leverage (DOL) can further be expressed as

$$DOL = \frac{Contribution\ margin}{Profit},$$

for which contribution margin = price – variable cost per unit.

DOL reveals how well a financial institution is using its fixed-cost structure to generate profits. The higher the degree of operating leverage, the greater the potential risk of a business. A revenue increase of x% should result in an increase in operating income of %revenue increase by the respective DOL. It can also be calculated by dividing the percentage change of an institution's earnings per share by its percentage change in its earnings before interest and taxes over a period. A higher DOL shows a higher level of volatility in EPS. We need to keep in mind though that financial institutions usually have large fixed costs, defined by salaries and other compensation elements as well as operational costs that are shaped by its technology stack.

Combined leverage measure

On an aggregated level a financial institution's degree of leverage (DL) can be calculated as

$$DL = DFL \times DOL = \frac{EBIT + Fixed\ Costs}{EBIT - Total\ interest\ expense}.$$

The application of leverage for financial institutions is well defined by the regulatory framework set out by the Basel III framework that will also be discussed in further detail in Chapter 3 on asset-liability management. Leverage creates risk for an institution when it does not perform well and becomes particularly relevant during an economic and financial downturn. After the Global Financial Crisis (GFC), regulators eventually introduced the leverage ratio and heavily curbed its applications for globally systemic financial institutions.

2.2 FINANCIAL VALUATION

Financial valuation uses static information from financial analysis and derives the value for a business or entire institution. The focus of this second step stone is to introduce different valuation methods by translating an accounting into an economic view and moving from a static to a dynamic framework. There are different ways in establishing an entity or equity value. As outlined previously, the estimation of cash flows remains challenging for financial institutions and with it the application of the widely used discounted free cash (DCF) model. Often a DDM is used in combination with different multiples where the price-to-book ratio has a particular meaning for the analysis of a bank. The economic value added (EVA) methodology, on the other hand, can be applied to capital allocation mechanism as it is further discussed in Chapter 3 on asset-liability management. We need to keep in mind that banks are a compilation of different businesses usually organised across retail and consumer banking, corporate and investment banking, wealth and asset management, and other distribution businesses for financial products (e.g. investment, insurance, and pension products) of third parties. Each of them requires a separate analysis and valuation of their key business segments. In addition, banks are highly levered institutions which makes their valuation sensitively dependent on macroeconomic factors changing economic circumstances.

2.2.1 Valuation methods and principles

The value of a business is defined as the economic profit or the profit minus all costs of the business, including the cost of capital. There are static and dynamic valuation methods to establish this value. Core to a consistent valuation methodology though is the combination of different methods to a comprehensive decision framework which then also makes the value comparable to the institution's peer group (often in a so-called precedent transaction analysis). The banking business has specific particularities which require the adjustment of the standard models.

The definition of value

The common standard of value is established in a fair market. A fair market is defined by the arm's length principle by which an asset or business changes hands between parties that are independent and willing to transact on an equal footing with regard to their knowledge and information of the relevant facts. The fair market principle implies a cash price at an arm's length between the transaction parties. There are different terminologies applied which includes intrinsic or fundamental, external, or third-party valuation. Most important, the value of an asset and business enterprise is an expression of its entire capital structure which further distinguishes the enterprise from the equity value. Valuation models that measure the business's entire value available to all investors, including equity and debt holders, are summarised under the entity approach. Models that estimate the value after funding capital, working capital, and debt financing needs apply the equity approach. Exhibit 2.5 illustrates the relationship under fair value considerations.

The different methods of the entity and the equity approach are to be considered when different valuation methodologies are applied. Financial institutions who engage in lending and other risk transfer activities allocate defined levels of equity capital in accordance with the risk of those activities, further specified by specific requirements

Equity value = enterprise value (EV) of the firm − market value (MV) of debt

EV = equity value + debt + minority interests + preferred shares − total cash − cash equivalents, and

Equity value = market price of shares outstanding times the share price.

Exhibit 2.5   Equity value under fair value considerations

set out by the regulators. There are different equity-like instruments that can be used for a write-off in case of a loss. Chapter 3 covers those instruments in further detail. Debt, on the other hand, is defined by client deposit and other arrangements that can be seen as raw material to fund the risk-taking activities. Capital is therefore more narrowly defined as equity which makes the equity approach the predominant factor in establishing the value of the business and entire institutions. This applies to all static as well as dynamic models.

Static and dynamic methods

There are static and dynamic methods to establish a valuation. The static methods follow an accounting methodology by using metrics from financial statements and comparing them to market prices: for example, price-to-book and price-earnings ratios. As we will further elaborate, capital in financial institutions or banking settings is narrowly defined as equity. All static metrics or multiples, therefore, need to be selected from this perspective.

Dynamic methods are all based on the economic principle of discounting the value to be received in the future by a discount rate appropriate to the business risk of the firm's operations and the risk of extracting the value. The value of a business is hence calculated by forecasting the future contribution components of the value and by discounting these components back to present value at the appropriate required rate of return. The discount rate is equal to the sum of the risk-free rate and the different risk premiums inherent to the firm's positioning and operations. It remains crucial to realise that the appropriate discount rate differs according to the capital holder's perspective. By applying a weighted average of the different cost of capital, for example, equity versus debt holders as it will be further outlined later, the formula estimates the discounted value available to all capital suppliers. Formally, expressed as

$$V = \sum_{t=1}^{\infty} \frac{CC_t}{(1 + WACC)^t},$$

where V = value, CC = contribution component, t = time, and $WACC$ = weighted average cost of capital.

There are three main models under the dynamic method which can be further applied to a banking environment. The DDM expresses that value of equity capital through the payout cash flows of a firm, that is, the dividends. It is the base but also a special case of a cash-flow model. The discounted cash flow models approximate the value of a business by means of free cash flows, that is, the cash flows that are generated by a firm's business operations and that do not need to be reinvested to continue the operations at their current levels. The analysis can be further enhanced by applying a leveraged buyout (LBO) model that further incorporates the application of debt instruments in the valuation methodology. The residual income (RI) is also a commonly used estimate for the value. It is defined as the amount of earnings made during the period that exceeds the one required for investor returns. The EVA valuation methodology, developed by Stern Stewart & Co., is a commercialised application of the residual income method.

Dynamic methods are more sophisticated valuation models that incorporate a dynamic view on economic reality. DCF methods in particular have become the industry standard in valuing companies. For banks and other financial institutions where finance decisions are inherently part of the business model, operations cannot be valued separately from interest income and expenses since these are the main categories of a bank's core operations. As we will further elaborate, it is therefore necessary to value cash flow to equity and not an average measure of cost of capital. Dynamic valuation methods know two main input factors, the free cash flows (FCF) and the weighted average cost of capital (WACC).

Free cash flows

The free cash flow is the core input factor for all dynamic methods. There are different methods to calculate the FCFs. Very detailed ones in accordance with the cash flow statement as outlined previously and more general application/proxy such as the one proposed by Thomas Copeland, Fred Weston, and Shastri Kuldeep with which the free cash flow can be calculated as shown in Exhibit 2.6.

EBIT is used as a starting point and then adjusted for tax expenses and noncash items of the income statement due to the fact that discounting expected free cash flows are valued prior to interest expenses from debt payments. The explanation to this lies in the second component of the WACC which directly considers the interest rate expenses.

Earning Before Interests and Taxation (EBIT)

./. Tax expenses

Net operating profit less adjusted taxes (NOPLAT)

+ Depreciation and amortisation

./. Gross Investments

Free cash flow,

where gross investments = changes in capital expenditure (CAPEX) + changes in net operating working capital (OWC) + changes in other asset-liabilities

---

Exhibit 2.6   Free cash flow computation

If the free cash flow is derived from the cash flow statement for valuation purposes, it is required to adjust by the interest expenses. IAS 7 allows the flexible classification of interest expenses as operating, investing, or financing cash flows. We previously suggested that for a banking business, it should be part of the operating cash flow given it is part of net revenues. This is consistent with the previously established view that equity is the dominant form of capital for a financial institution. Therefore, when the free cash flow is estimated for a banking business, EBT should be used. EBT minus the actual cash tax expenses for the year will then lead to net operating profit less adjusted taxes (NOPLAT) which further should be discounted with costs of equity only.

The residual income (RI) method, better known as EVA, follows a similar methodology. In accordance with Bennett Stewart, it uses a cash-based input factor, called net operating profit after taxes (NOPAT), which is further derived as shown in Exhibit 2.7.

The different conversions transform the accounting values from balance sheet and income statement into a cash-flow based valuation model (i.e. the economic view of a dynamic model). The operating conversion includes all the noncash items from the income statement such as depreciation and amortisation. The funding conversion subtracts the interest expenses. The tax conversion addresses the difference between the accrued tax expenses and the taxes paid. Finally, the shareholder conversion incorporated the elements of dividends and share buybacks.

NOPLAT and NOPAT should not be confused. NOPLAT is used to calculate the free cash flow in an indirect format for the DCF method. NOPAT, on the other hand, is a cash-oriented component for the value under the EVA methodology. Both methods, DCF and EVA, eventually depend on the free cash flow but they start their assessment from a different perspective. The discounted cash-flow method (DCM) is from the beginning purely cash driven whereas the EVA starts from the accrual perspective and converts its accounting methodology into a cash-oriented framework. Exhibit 2.8 discusses this relationship in further detail.

Weighted Average Cost of Capital

In an entity-driven valuation methodology, the cost of capital is expressed by thereby an arithmetic average of the equity and debt components of the cost of capital. It is called

---

Earning before interests and taxation (EBIT)

./. Tax expenses

+ Operating conversion

+ Funding conversion

+ Tax conversion

+ Shareholder conversion

Net operating profit after taxes (NOPAT)

Exhibit 2.7   Net operating profit after taxes (NOPAT)

The difference between NOPLAT and NOPAT can be explained through the application of operating income and EBIT.

NOPLAT = EBIT − taxes on EBIT + change in deferred income taxes

NOPAT = Operating Income × (1 − tax rate)

EBIT equals operating income as long as there is no nonoperating income. Operating income can therefore be transferred to EBIT by subtracting nonoperating income and vice versa.

Assuming operating income = EBIT, *which derives that*

NOPAT = NOPLAT − change in deferred income taxes[4].

NOPLAT factors in explicitly changes in deferred taxes that are counted inside the formula whereas in NOPAT, changes in deferred taxes are directly adjusted in the other accounts on the asset-liability side.

We can therefore conclude that FCF is equal to

NOPAT + depreciation +/− changes in asset-liability accounts,

which equals to

NOPLAT + depreciation +/− changes in asset-liability other than deferred taxes.

Exhibit 2.8   The derivation of NOPLAT and NOPAT

the weighted average cost of capital (WACC). It is calculated as the weighted average of the rates of return required by each of the capital supplier and can be applied as a discount and capitalisation rate. Used as weights are the proportions of each capital source to the firm's total market value:

$$WACC = \left(\frac{MV(equity)}{MV(firm)}\right) \cdot c_{equity} + \left(\frac{MV(debt)}{MV(firm)}\right) \cdot c_{debt}(1 - t),$$

where MV = market value, c = cost of capital, and t = taxes.

The required rate of return of equity is an expression of the cost of equity capital (c_{equity}). It can be estimated with the application of an asset pricing model such as the capital asset pricing model (CAPM) or the arbitrage pricing theory (APT). Both models are more formally discussed in the next section on financial modelling.

The CAPM estimates c_{equity} through

$$c_{equity} = R_f + \beta(R_{Benchmark} - R_f),$$

where R_f = risk-free rate, β = Equity beta, and R = simple returns.

---

[4]Deferred taxes are reported taxes on the income statement that were not actually owed nor paid to the taxing authority. Taxes payable, on the other hand, refers to taxes that were reported for a period and are due to the taxing authority for the respective period and for which the actual payment has been delayed into the next accounting period.

The required rate of debt capital (c_{debt}) can directly be measured by interest rate expenses. Together with tax expenses for the variable taxes, they can be taken directly from the income statement.

Firms are valued by discounting expected free cash flows prior to debt payments at the WACC whereas equity is valued by discounting cash flows to equity investors at the cost of equity. As we previously outlined, debt payments for financial institutions cannot easily be identified which makes it difficult to estimate free cash flows. Therefore, the equity approach remains predominant in valuing financial institutions. This applies to the static method such as selecting the right multiples such as price-to-earning or price-to-book ratios as well as to dynamic methods where the DDM and an equity-focused DCF or EVA are applied.

2.2.2 Valuation models and techniques

There are series of valuation models such as the DDM, DCF, and LBO models that we are going to cover in further details. The EVA model is an alternative model that finds its specific application in the capital allocation of banks to a concept called economic profit (EP).

Dividend Discount Model

The equity value, that is, the value of a single stock, can directly be determined with the constant growth dividend discount model. The constant growth or Gordon DDM assumes a constant growth rate. Formally, this leads to

$$P_0 = \frac{D_1}{c_{equity} - g},$$

where P = Stock price, D = Dividend, c_{equity} = cost of equity, and g = growth rate.

For the valuation of equity, the discount factor, that is, the cost of equity capital that is nothing less than the required return for equity capital, is determined by the return on equity that can be estimated with the CAPM. The growth rate is approximated with a constant growth rate of the dividends that is equal to the growth rate of net income. The growth rate is bounded to the growth rate of net income because if it is not equal dividends will at some point in the future either be bigger than the net income (higher) or become zero (lower). Overall economic growth bounds the growth rate of an institution, or the firm would be at a certain stage in the future bigger than the whole economy. The sustainable growth rate (SGR) represents the maximum rate of growth that an institution can sustain without changing the capital structure through additional equity or debt. It involves maximizing revenue growth without increasing financial leverage. Through the DuPont equation, the SGR can be expressed as

$$SGR = r \times ROE,$$

with r = the retention rate and ROE = return on equity.

For the relative valuation of equity, the price-earning-ratio of a stock offers interesting information. With the dividend discount model, it can then be derived by dividing the dividends through the earnings. This leads to

$$\frac{P_0}{E_1} = \frac{\frac{D_1}{E_1}}{c_{equity} - g} = \frac{dividend\ payout\ \text{rate}}{c_{equity} - g},$$

where E = earnings.

Finally, we get

$$\frac{P}{E} = \frac{1 - b}{c_{equity} - g},$$

where b = retention rate, estimated from the operating income after taxes that is not distributed as dividends but reinvested in the production process, formally expressed as

$$retention\ rate = 1 - \frac{dividends\ declared}{operating\ income\ after\ taxes}.$$

To judge if the stock market in general, individual sectors, or stocks have an interesting valuation, the current price-earning-ratios have to be compared with their historical peers, the level of interest rates and the situation in the business cycle.

Discounted Cash Flow (DCF)

The DCM values the business with discounted free cash flows. When a DCM model is applied, the enterprise value (EV) can be separated into two periods. The first one is the present value (PV) of the periodic free cash flows during the explicit forecast period (T), defined as

$$PV_{Forecast} = \sum_{t=1}^{T} \frac{FCF_t}{(1 + WACC)^t}.$$

The second one is the continuing value (CV) which is equal to PV of the periodic free flows after the explicit forecast period of usually five years. It is the value of the expected free cash flows beyond this period. The CV eliminates the need to forecast in detail the company's periodic components over an extended period. It often accounts for a large percentage of the total enterprise value.

Furthermore, it is extremely sensitive to changes in the structure of the WACC. Usually the CV is calculated by means of a perpetuity formula that assumes that the company's periodic components will grow at a constant rate during the continuing value period, formally defined as

$$CV = \frac{FCF_{continuing}}{WACC - g},$$

where g = expected growth rate of FCF in perpetuity.

The CV value is usually applied after period five of the valuation. This means that in the first five periods, the periodic value, the WACC, and the growth rate are accurately estimated and then approximated by the perpetuity formula. In mathematical terms, this can be generalised to

$$EV = \sum_{t=1}^{n} \frac{FCF_t}{(1 + WACC)^t} + \left[\left(\frac{1}{(1 + WACC)^n} \right) \cdot \left(\frac{FCF_{n+1}}{WACC - g} \right) \right].$$

and $FCF_t = FCF_{t-1} \cdot (1 + g_t)$.

In case of a banking business, the free cash flow proxy would have deducted the interest rate expenses/debt payments and then discounted as the cost of equity, derived from the CAPM. However, we need to keep in mind that the volatile nature of banking cash flows may distort the outcome so additional considerations are to be incorporated. Formally, this can be expressed as

$$EQ = \sum_{t=1}^{n} \frac{ECF_t}{(1 + c_{equity})^t},$$

where EQ = equity value, FEF = equity cash flow, c_{equity} = cost of equity, and t = time.

Koller et al. further suggest a proxy for equity cash flow that may be applied alternatively for a short-cut assessment in the valuation of banking organisations. It is formally defined as

$$ECF = NI + OCI - \Delta B,$$

where ECF = equity cash flow, NI = net income or profit for the period, OCI = other comprehensive income (non-cash), and ΔB = change in equity (book value).

Leveraged Buyout

LBO analysis is the core analytical tool used to assess financing structure, investment returns, and valuation in leveraged scenarios. The same technique can also be used to assess refinancing and restructuring alternatives for corporate bond issuances. At the centre of a LBO analysis is the LBO model, a financial model that is constructed with flexibility to analyse a given target's performance under multiple financing structures and operating scenarios.

LBO

An LBO is defined as a debt-funded acquisition of a business or an asset. The management of a company or an investor (known as a financial sponsor) such as a private equity firm aims to invest a small amount of equity (relative to the total purchase price) and uses leverage through debt instruments to finance the remainder of the consideration paid to the seller. Through financial engineering, a financing structure is crafted that enables both the financial sponsor and debt investor to meet their respective investment objectives and return thresholds, while providing the target with sufficient financial flexibility and cushion needed to operate and grow the business. The financing arrangement may include secured (e.g. bank debt), senior unsecured (e.g. high yield bonds), and subordinated debt as well as other forms of mezzanine financing, derivatives, and other complex financial instruments.

In a management buyout, the management team aims to get control over the business and uses debt to fund the required capital. Financial sponsors' ultimate goal, on the other hand, is to realise an acceptable return on their equity investment upon exit, often through a sale or initial public offering (IPO) of the target. Debt has typically compromised between 60% and 70% of the financing structure with equity ranging for the remaining 30–40%. Historically, financial sponsors' hurdle rates have been in excess of 25%, but may be as low as 15–20% depending on the sector and the characteristic of the underlying asset.

The investment horizon is usually set for three to seven years, although in financial services such as insurance it can be longer given the nature of the business. The leverage arrangement is supported by the cash flow generation of the targeted business which enables the sponsor to contribute a small equity investment relative to the purchase price and achieve an acceptable return.

The use of debt financing further provides additional benefits through tax savings due to the tax deductibility of interest expense. Businesses with stable and predictable cash flows and a strong asset base generally represent attractive LBO candidates due to their ability to support larger quantities of debt. An appropriate LBO financing structure must balance the target's ability to service and repay debt with its need to use cash flow to manage and grow the business.

LBO model

LBO models have particular relevance in private equity or hedge fund settings in which the acquisition is treated as an investment. The acquisition must deliver an expected return on invested equity that meets a hurdle rate for the investment. The expected return on invested equity is measured by analysing expected internal rates of return (IRR). It represents the total return on a sponsor's equity investment, as a discount rate at which the net present value of cash flows equals zero. Formally, expressed as

$$0 = -EI_0 + \sum_{t=1}^{n} \frac{ECF_t}{(1 + IRR)^t}, \text{ where}$$

EI = equity investment, ECF = equity cash flow, IRR = internal rate of return, and t = time.

In addition to IRR, returns can be evaluated on the basis of a multiple of their cash investment. This metric is called cash return or cash-on-cash (CoC) multiple, and is calculated as the final value of the equity investment at exit divided by the initial equity investment. For illustration, a private equity firm contributes US$250 million of equity and receives equity proceeds of US$1 billion at the end of the investment horizon. The cash return or CoC then is 4x. For further reference on best practice, LBO investments usually are in a range of 2x–5x.

Key input factors such as financial projections, financing structure, and exit multiple allow the performance of a sensitivity analysis that produces a range of IRRs used to frame valuations for the target. Through this analysis, the buyer determines what he can afford to pay for the target while still realising an adequate return on its investment. The maximum purchase price for the target is established through applying specific leverage levels and equity return parameters. This develops a view of the equity and debt characteristics of a leveraged transaction at a given price and allows to calculate the minimum valuation for a company with regard to those parameters, and provides a floor valuation for the target. The price ranges will guide negotiations and bidding strategies by analysing the price the price that a competing bidder might be willing to pay for the target.

In application of the DCF methodology, an LBO model can be derived across five major steps:

1. Develop operating premises and projections for the target to arrive at EBITDA and available cash flow for debt repayment over a set time horizon. Again from a banking perspective an equity free cash flow will be used with EBTDA as starting point.
2. Determine key leverage levels and capital structure that result in realistic financial coverage and credit statistics.
3. Estimate the multiple at which the buyer is expected to exit the acquisition.
4. Calculate the IRR that quantifies returns on invested equity, and sensitize the results to a range of leverage and exit multiples, as well as investment horizons.
5. Solve for the purchase price that can be paid to meet the parameters. In case of a fixed purchase price, the model solves for achievable returns.

Joshua Rosenbaum and Joshua Pearl in chapter five of their book *Investment Banking* walk through the entirety of an LBO analysis across a well-defined template that further illustrates the individual steps of the IRR assessment. It would go beyond the scope of this book to further specify and detail a LBO model.

Economic Value Added and Economic Profit

The residual income method transforms an accounting valuation approach (static with accounting values) into an economic valuation model (dynamic with cash flows). Stern Stewart & Co developed the EVA valuation model which is a commercialised application of the residual income method.

It is derived as

$$EVA = NOPAT - (WACC \times NOA), \text{whereas}$$

$NOPAT$ = net operating profit after taxes, NOA = net operating assets, and $WACC$ = weighted average cost of capital.

NOPAT and WACC were covered separately in the previous section on input factors. The third component, the net operating assets (NOA), is equal to the invested operating asset. It can be expressed as

$$NOA = Total\ assets - non\text{-}interest\text{-}bearing\ current\ liabilities.$$

In the same principle as for NOPAT, NOA can therefore be derived from the book value of equity and then adjusted by four levels of conversion with the objective to move from the accounting value of the operating assets to the cash-flow-based, economic value. This incorporates all non-interest-bearing liabilities and makes adjustment for nonoperating assets, leasing, deferred taxes, brand, and goodwill. On an aggregated level, the firm's enterprise value is the sum of the periodic EVA, which is known as the market value added (MVA), defined as

$$MVA = \sum_{t=1}^{\infty} \frac{EVA_t}{(1 + WACC)^t}.$$

EVA can also be expressed as EP or economic spread (ES) which is a function of the ROIC. Formally, this is expressed as

$$EP = EVA/NOA, \text{which leads to}$$

$$EP = (NOPAT/NOA) - WACC, \text{or}$$

$$EP = ROIC - WACC.$$

In case of a banking business with equity as its dominant form of capital, which leads to the removal of interest expenses in the calculation of NOPAT, all debt elements in case of NOA and the application of costs of equity only,

$$EP = return\ on\ equity\ (ROE) - costs\ of\ equity\ (c_{equity}).$$

Banks with high capital consumption have been applying an attributed equity measure, called return on attributed equity or ROAE. It weights multiple internal and external factors in the calculation of a performance measure such as the two main capital constraints, that is, common equity T1 ratio as an expression of risk-weighted assets (RWA) and the leverage ratio as expression of the leverage-ratio exposure (LRE). Formally, the metric can then be defined as

$$EP = ROAE - c_{equity}.$$

This concept will be further discussed as capital allocation mechanisms in Chapter 3 on asset-liability management.

Valuation synthesis across methods

Valuation models can be very sensitive with regard to their input factors and may lead to a range of results across different methods. Through the combination of static and dynamic valuation models and application of an average or respective weights, a synthesis and more stable results can be attained. Historical costs, represented through the book value of an asset and business, can be the starting point for an intrinsic valuation, followed by the analysis of the replacement costs and the fair value assessment through a cash-flow model. Precedent transactions within the peer group of the business gives interesting comparable to the intrinsic outcomes of a valuation methodology. It is designed to reflect current market valuation based on prevailing market conditions and sentiments. Exhibit 2.9 illustrates the average valuation as synthesis of different valuation methods.

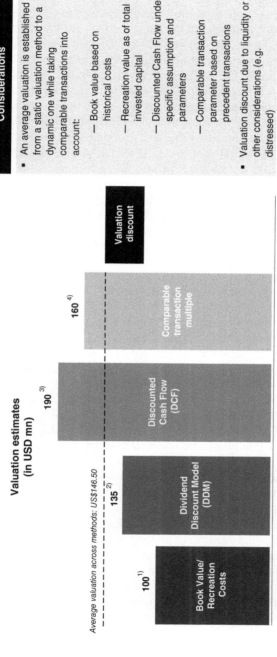

Exhibit 2.9 Valuation synthesis across methods

Trading multiples and respective proxies allow the comparison of similar transactions within a defined peer group. There are series of multiples available, and the application of the right valuation metrics vary by sector. From a financial institution or banking perspective, there are two major multiples that we want to discuss in addition to previously introduced ROIC, ROE, and ROA. These are the equity value multiples such as price-earnings (P/E) and price-to-book ratio (P/B). The price-earnings (P/E) ratio is calculated as current share price divided by diluted EPS. It is a very widely recognised and reported trading multiple. The calculation is usually based on forward-year EPS as investors are focused on future growth. Businesses with higher P/E than their peers tend to have higher earnings growth expectations. The price-to-book ratio to compare a business's market to book value is obtained by dividing price per share by book value per share (BVPS). The P/B ratio reflects the value that market participants attach to a company's equity relative to its book value of equity. The book value is equal to the net asset value of a business, calculated as total assets minus intangible assets and liabilities. It is an accounting measure based on the historic cost principle and reflects past issuances of equity, augmented by any profits or losses, and reduced by dividends and share buybacks. A business's market value, on the other hand, is a dynamic, forward-looking metric that reflects a company's future cash flows.

P/B ratio provides a valuable reality check for investors seeking growth at a reasonable price and is often looked at in conjunction with return on equity (ROE), a reliable growth indicator. Due to accounting conventions on treatment of certain costs, the market value of equity is typically higher than the book value of a financial institution, producing a P/B ratio above one. Under certain circumstances of financial distress, bankruptcy, or expected plunges in earnings power, a financial institution's P/B ratio can dive below one. Because accounting principles do not recognize brand value and other intangible assets, unless the company derived them through acquisitions, companies expense all costs associated with creating intangible assets immediately. Post GFC, many European banks such as Deutsche Bank, Santander, or Society General traded way below a price-to-book ratio of one. Closely related to the P/B ratio is the price to tangible book value (PTBV). The latter is a valuation ratio expressing the price of a security compared to its hard, or tangible, book value as reported in the company's balance sheet. The tangible book value number is equal to the company's total book value less the value of any intangible assets. Intangible assets can be items such as patents, intellectual property, and goodwill. This may be a more useful measure of valuation when the market is valuing something like a patent in different ways or if it is difficult to put a value on such an intangible asset in the first place.

In case of a distressed scenario with potential risk of liquidation of the business, an overall discount or adjustments needs to be applied. Reasonable expectations are developed as scenarios are outlined for a recovery value. This can be very tricky with financial institutions in particular during a fire-sale scenario. An appropriate adjustment to the discount and capitalisation rate may be enough or a market comparison may point to a more extreme outcome. This is more an art than a science and often crucially dependent on the negotiations between the capital providers.

2.3 FINANCIAL MODELLING

Through financial modelling, we are moving from valuing an individual business to pricing a tradable asset in a capital market equilibrium. The economic view of the financial decision framework is further broken down in a rigorous quantitative representation of individual asset price dynamics. A set of assumptions and hypotheses about future outcomes are translated in a quantitative methodology with which asset price behaviour and inherent risks can be assessed. On the one hand, this methodology is required to successfully perform financial analysis and valuation in an adaptable decision framework. On the other hand, asset prices are fundamental value drivers for financial institutions. A thorough understanding is required. The following section establishes the mathematical fundamentals of modelling asset price dynamics and behaviour across the three main areas of financial modelling, namely risk and return, asset pricing, and contingent claim analysis. The fundamental role of risk in will then be further discussed in Chapter 3 on asset-liability management.

2.3.1 Risk and return

The fundamental properties of risk and return are the base for financial modelling where stochastic processes are applied with the normal distribution as core assumption.

Return properties and premises

For the modelling of asset-price dynamics, the relations between asset prices (A_t), simple return (R_t), and continuously compounded return (r_t) are to be assessed. Simple returns on an asset between the dates t and $t+1$ are defined as a simple one-period return

$$R_t = \left(\frac{A_{t+1}}{A_t}\right) - 1,$$

and the average simple return of n subperiods is the geometric average of the individual simple n-subperiod returns (j)

$$\overline{R} = \sqrt[n]{\prod_{j=1}^{n}(1 + R_j)} - 1,$$

which expresses the multiplicative relation between simple period returns. This relation is equal to the absolute price change or drift of an asset over time. Because of this multiplicative effect, simple periodic returns as well as the underlying asset prices are lognormally distributed.

A continuously compounded return, on the other hand, is defined as being the natural logarithm of the simple period return, which leads to

$$r_t = ln(1 + R_t) = ln\left(\frac{A_{t+1}}{A_t}\right).$$

The average continuously compounded return is the arithmetic average of the individual continuously compounded n-subperiod returns (j), equal to

$$\bar{r} = \frac{1}{n}\sum_{j=1}^{n} r_j,$$

which is an expression of stationarity for the first, the mean, and the second moment, the standard deviation of the distribution.

In continuous return calculations, a multiplicative operation is converted into an additive operation by using the natural logarithms. A continuously calculated return is therefore defined as the natural logarithm of the absolute price change (drift) of an asset, which implies that in accordance with the central limit theorem of statistics, continuously calculated returns are normally distributed. Mathematically, this relation can be expressed by

$$r = ln\left(\frac{A_{t+\Delta t}}{A_t}\right) = ln(A_{t+\Delta t}) - ln(A_t) = \Delta\, ln(A) \sim N\left(\mu \cdot \Delta t, \sigma\sqrt{\Delta t}\right).$$

As we will further elaborate, normally distributed returns calculated in continuous time are a fundamental property and premise in modelling asset price behaviour.

Risk properties and premises

Risk is defined by the uncertainty of the asset returns which is measured through volatility. Mathematically, volatility is measured by the standard deviation of the asset returns. The standard deviation is nothing else than as a measure of the dispersion defined as the square root of the variance of the asset return, given by

$$\sigma = \sqrt{\frac{\sum_{t=1}^{T}(R_t - \mu)^2}{T}} = \sqrt{\frac{\sum_{t=1}^{T}(r_t - \mu)^2}{T}}, \text{where}$$

σ = volatility, μ = mean, and T = time.

However, the standard deviation shown here is a theoretical measure only as it assumes that entire population of returns are available in the calculations. This implies that the entire distribution of data that describe the population is available and the mean is clearly defined. This is never the case when real statistical data (such as financial market data) are applied because there is only a subset of the relevant data (equal to the entire dataset) available. When dealing with financial data, a sample variance measure is to be used. Mathematically, it is given as

$$\sigma = \sqrt{\frac{1}{T-1}\sum(R - \bar{R})^2} = \sqrt{\frac{1}{T-1}\sum(r - \bar{r})^2}.$$

The formula for both the population and the sample standard deviation is nearly the same. The crucial importance lies in the use of $\bar{R}$ and $\bar{r}$ instead of μ as the mean for the entire population can only be approximated. Furthermore, for the population standard deviation, one divides by the size of the population that is equal to the number of observations (T = days for the number of observations). For the sample standard deviation, the term is divided by the sample size minus 1 ($T - 1$). In accordance with the law of large numbers, using T only would result in an underestimation of the population variance, especially for small sample sizes. This systematic understatement causes the sample variance to be a biased estimator of the population variance. By using the sample size minus 1 ($T - 1$) instead of the sample size (T) in the denominator, the underestimation is compensated and the sample standard deviation is an unbiased estimator of the asset return uncertainty.

When it is assumed that the historical returns are a good approximation for the expected return (μ), the standard deviation (σ) is expressed as

$$\sigma = \sqrt{\frac{1}{T-1} \sum (\mu - \overline{\mu})^2}.$$

To make the risk of an asset comparable, the standard deviation is an annualised measure. This implies that

$$\sigma = \sqrt{t} \cdot \sigma_t,$$

where $t = n$ = number of observations.

For instance, a monthly standard deviation of 2.2% is to be multiplied with the square root of 12 (=3.46) and is therefore equal to 7.62%. A daily standard deviation of 0.6% is to be divided by the square root of 252 (=15.87) as an expression of the trading days. That is equal to 9.52%. As we will further cover at the end of this chapter, asset price volatility should not be underestimated. In particular stock market volatility is on historical average between 15 and 20%. The value for single stocks ranges from 20 to 40% per annum and can jump substantially higher in case of a market dislocation.

Market efficiency and its mathematical properties

Following the market efficiency hypothesis, historical information such as past price movements and other available financial data do not affect asset prices and cannot be used to predict their future direction. All currently available information is reflected in asset prices and past information has no relationship with current market prices, while information diffusion about future outcomes is unpredictable. This is a fundamental premise of market efficiency in financial modelling. Accordingly, the evolution of asset prices can be described by discrete or continuous stochastic processes, known as the discrete random walk or the continuous Brownian motion, which is based on two mathematical properties. The Martingale property describes a complete set of information for market-traded financial asset prices while the Markov property further defines the independence of the price increments of financial assets as a result of information diffusion.

Martingale property

More formally, an informationally efficient market is modelled by a family of probability spaces (Ω, F, P). Ω is a set of outcomes ($w_1, \ldots, w_T$) called the sample space. F represents the process of information filtration. P is a probability measure defined by Ω and F. Public information revealed to market participants over time is modelled by a sequence of progressively finer partitions (F) that defines a specific outcome or state of nature (w). Therefore, the asset value (A) is equal to the pay-off outcome (w) that is a result of the relevant information filtration in the respective state of nature. As a result, a probability measure can be defined. This probability measure might be subjective on an individual basis. However, due to the assumption of rational expectation, it becomes objective with respect to the probability distribution at an aggregated market level. In an informationally efficient market, the fair value of the asset is always revealed.

The fair value of an asset is the fundamental value that reflects the potential economic profits of an asset. It is defined as the discounted stream of future income. In an informationally efficient market, the market-traded price should therefore be equal to the fair value of an asset. On average, the fair value results in a conditioning equilibrium value. For an individual investor, there are no price or signal incentives to incorporate individual or additional information with extra pay-off potential. This means, however, that all information is publicly available and equally accessible for all market participants. Market efficiency requires that market participants are unable to make arbitrage profits on the basis of public information. A price process that meets this condition is information efficient. This leads to the Martingale property of financial modelling, which states: Tomorrow's asset price is expected to be equal to today's price, given the asset's entire price history. Mathematically, this leads to

$$P\left(A_{t+i}\middle|A_t,\ldots,A_1\right) = P\left(A_{t+i}\middle|F_t\right),$$

under the assumption that the information sequence $F_0,\ldots,F_T$ will coincide with the value function of the asset (A).

The price of each asset is the best estimate possible based on the current set of information. This can mathematically be expressed by conditional expectations, applied to the random process of information filtration (F). A pair (w, F), in which the outcome (w) is adapted to F, is then called a martingale for a specific point in time t, given by

$$E\left(w_t\middle|F_t\right) = w_t.$$

When the outcome (w) is expressed in the asset value, then it becomes

$$E\left(A_t\middle|F_t\right) = A_t.$$

This conditional expectation is usually expressed as the sum of discounted income streams under a given probability measure. Asset prices behave like martingales in a very small trading interval Δt. Although the martingale property places a restriction on the outcome of expected returns in the short run, it does not account for long-term risk in any way.

Markov property

The asset price is the conditional expected price of tomorrow's prices, given the set of information (F) is available. Due to the application of the martingale property, asset price processes can be expressed as a Markov chain. A Markov process is a sequence of random variables in which knowledge of the past is totally irrelevant for any statement concerning the state of the outcome w_{t+1} when $i > 0$, given the last observed value w_t. The conditional distribution of w_{t+1}, given $w_0, \ldots, w_T$, depends only on w_t. This means that the information filtration available at time t is obtained by observing the price process A until t and that no further information about future price increments can be extracted. More intuitively, the conditional probability distribution of future asset values, conditional on time t, depends only on the current value of A. Value changes are completely dependent on future information diffusion. The present value of the asset price is the only variable relevant for predicting the future. The history of the variable and the way the present has emerged out of the past are irrelevant which is consistent with the weak form of market efficiency. This implies that asset prices are random and hence not predictable. If asset price changes result from information diffusion only, the price drifts must be independent, which further implies that return patterns and asset price drifts are uncorrelated.

Stochastic processes and the normal distribution

In accordance with market efficiency and its mathematical properties, the fundamental stochastic process that is applied in financial modelling is the random walk. A random walk describes a binomial random process that consists of a sequence of discrete steps of fixed length. Random walks have interesting mathematical properties that vary greatly depending on the dimension in which the walk occurs and whether it is confined to a lattice. For financial modelling, a random walk refers to a discrete setting where its binomial distribution describes an uptick in the asset price (a price increase)

$$\Delta A(t) = A(t + \Delta) - A(t) = +a\sqrt{\Delta}$$

and a downtick (price decrease)

$$\Delta A(t) = A(t + \Delta) - A(t) = -a\sqrt{\Delta},$$

where $\Delta A(t) =$ change in the asset price during the fixed time interval Δt.

The pay-off outcome (w) of the asset value (A) with respect to time (t) that can therefore be defined by a sum of random variables:

$$w_t = A_t = \widetilde{w}_0 + \ldots + \widetilde{w}_t, t \in T.$$

These random variables as an expression of the pay-off outcome ($\widetilde{w}$) are mutually independent as it is assumed that the random variables only change due to new available information as outlined previously. Therefore, a random walk follows a binominal distribution if

$$\Delta A_t = +a\sqrt{\Delta} = p$$
$$\Delta A_t = -a\sqrt{\Delta} = (1 - p)$$

with the first and second moment of

$$E[\Delta A_t] = p(a\sqrt{\Delta}) + (1-p)(-a\sqrt{\Delta}), Var[\Delta A_t]$$
$$= p(a\sqrt{\Delta})^2 + (1-p)(-a\sqrt{\Delta})^2 - [E[\Delta A_t]]^2.$$

If information efficiency is assumed and the Martingale property holds, then

$$E(\Delta A_t) = E(\widetilde{w}_{t+1}) = 0.$$

This implies that there is a 50% chance of either an up-tick or a down-tick at any time (t), so that the transition probability (p) is

$$p = \frac{1}{2}.$$

The binominal distribution that describes the random price behaviour converges into a normal distribution if the amount of realisations (n) of the independent, equally distributed random variables that describe the price and return behaviour of assets (expressed as a constant risk premium Δ) is increased and finally becomes continuous. Beginning with $t_o = 0$, in the immediate future, the asset value (A_t) has only two possible values

$$A_0 + n\Delta = A_0 \pm a\sqrt{n\Delta},$$

with probability p and $1 - p$ respectively. If $p = 0.5$ and $\Delta > 0$, then $A_0 = 0$ in a short-term perspective. As $n \to \infty$, $A(n\Delta)$ may take an infinite number of values and hence becomes continuous. According to the central limit theorem, the distribution of $A(n\Delta)$ approaches the normal distribution as $n\Delta \to \infty$. Then, for a fixed Δ and a "large" n, the distribution of $A(n\Delta)$ can be approximated by a normal distribution with mean 0 and variance $a^2 n\Delta$. The density function will be given by

$$g(A(n\Delta) = w) = \frac{1}{\sqrt{2\pi a^2 n\Delta}} e^{-\frac{1}{2a^2 n\Delta}(w)^2}.$$

A technical advantage of continuous time is that a complicated random variable gets a very simple structure in a continuous setting. The stochastic process that models continuous price changes is a generalised Brownian motion[5], which has a geometric

---

[5]In financial modelling, both terms, Brownian motion (named after the Scottish botanist Robert Brown, 1773–1858) and Wiener process (named after the American mathematician Norbert Wiener, 1894–1964), are used widely and congruently. According to the initial mathematical assumptions, we can distinguish between the standard and the geometric Brownian motion (or Wiener process). The latter is an expression of a mathematical generalisation of the continuous-time stochastic process described by the generalised Brownian motion/Wiener process that is often called the Itô process (named after the Japanese mathematician Kiyosi Itô, 1915–2008).

diffusion due to the multiplicative effects of the return structure. The stochastic element ($\widetilde{w}$), which reflects the randomness of the price behaviour, can be expressed as a standard normally-distributed random variable (dN), which leads to

$$\Delta \ln A = \mu \Delta t + d_N \sigma \sqrt{\Delta t}, \text{ where } d_N = \frac{\Delta \ln A - \mu \Delta t}{\sigma \sqrt{\Delta t}}$$

and

$$\frac{\Delta A}{A} = \alpha \Delta t + d_N \sigma \sqrt{\Delta t},$$

where

$$\alpha = \mu + \frac{1}{2}\sigma^2.$$

The standard normally distributed random variable therefore follows a standard Brownian motion with $dN \sim N(0, \sigma)$. The term $\mu \Delta t$ is the expected value of the asset return. The parameter μ is the normally-distributed expected rate of return per unit of time. $\alpha \Delta t$ is the expected return per unit of time, which is lognormally distributed, and σ is the volatility of the asset price in continuous time. For simple returns that reflect periods smaller than one year, the approximation of the normally distributed return structure seems to be fair. For longer periods, this assumption is no longer valid, because there are multiplicative effects between the individual simple-period returns. Simple returns understood as their absolute price changes (drifts) in percent are lognormally distributed, whereas continuously compounded returns are normally distributed.

Intuitively, the drift transformation shows the relationship between lognormally distributed discrete returns (for more than one year), asset prices and normally distributed continuous returns. Mathematically, the drift adjustment $\frac{1}{2}\sigma^2$ between the lognormally distributed drift (α) and the normally distributed drift (μ) can be explained by applying Itô's lemma. Itô's lemma is a way of calculating a stochastic process, followed by a function of the variable from the stochastic process and the variable itself. By using the natural logarithm ($\ln$), the exponential function of an instantaneous change can be derived. Applying Itô's lemma leads to

$$d \ln A = \frac{1}{A_t}dA_t + \frac{1}{2}\sigma^2 A_t^2 \frac{1}{A_t^2}dt + 0 = \frac{1}{A_t}dA_t - \frac{1}{2}\sigma^2 dt,$$

which proofs that an instantaneous drift follows

$$\frac{A_t + \Delta t}{A_t} = e^{\left(\alpha - \frac{1}{2}\sigma^2\right)dt + \sigma dB_t}.$$

The normal distribution is a fundamental premise in modelling asset price behaviour in particular with regard to derivatives pricing and contingent claim analysis.

2.3.2 Asset pricing

The estimation and modelling of returns are based on a market equilibrium as another core assumption of financial analysis. This section derives a market equilibrium with its properties.

Asset allocation and risk premiums

In a simplified setting of a financial decision framework, there exists a risk-free and risky asset that exhibit different characteristics. Asset allocation aims to balance risk versus reward by shifting between a risk-free and risky asset. The difference or excess between the risk-free and the risky asset is called the risk premium. It is a form of compensation for investors who are willing tolerate the additional risks over the risk-free rate. Each asset has a positive premium that fully reflect the risks related to potential economic profits and hence future income streams. The fundamental risk premium is assessed by the risk-utility function and by specific measures of risk aversion which differs across investors.

The first objective investors face in an asset allocation decision is towards the level of uncertainty they are comfortable with. As we discussed, uncertainty is expressed by volatility. In a very basic didactic setting, the volatility of the diversified baskets depends on two macroeconomic variables, earnings, and consumption which reflect the risk of an investment in an asset or a basket of assets. In an asset allocation decision, an investor must decide how much to save and how much to consume. In the basic equilibrium described by the Fisher Separation theorem, the marginal utility loss of consuming a little less today and buying a little more of a return given asset should equal the marginal utility gain of consuming a little more of the asset's pay-off in the future. If price and pay-off do not satisfy this relation, the investor should buy either more or less of the asset. This leads to the simple and fundamental concept of financial valuation. The asset's price should equal the expected discounted value of the asset's pay-off, using the investor's marginal utility to discount the pay-off. This relation can be formally introduced by the following equation, which is known as the duality of the stochastic discount factor and the asset pay-off. Given by

$$A_t = E_t(m_{t+1}, w_{t+1}) \ and \ m_{t+1} = f(data, parameters),$$

where A_t = asset price, E_t = conditional expectation operator corresponding to the information available at time t, w_{t+1} = asset pay-off at time t, and $t + 1$, $m_t + 1$ = stochastic discount factor.

The pay-off rate of a risk-free asset is only a transformation rate between present and future consumption. This implies that there is no uncertainty in the pay-off outcome. It reflects the time value of money only without any other risk compensations. However, corrections of risks to asset prices (as an expression of uncertainty in the pay-off outcome) should be driven by the covariance of asset pay-offs with marginal utility. This duality of the pay-off outcome and the stochastic discount factor can be expressed as

$$(1 + R^f_{t,t+1})E_t[m_{t+1}]w_t = E_t[m_{t+1}, w_{t+1}],$$

where $R_{ft,t+1}$ = risk free rate from t to $t + 1$.

If there is no uncertainty, the risk-free asset can be expressed by the standard present value formula:

$$A_t^f = \frac{1}{1 + R_{t,t+1}^f} w_{t+1}.$$

Riskier assets are valued by using a risk-adjusted discount factor ($1/R$) that reflects the random elements of the future pay-off outcomes. The asset-specific risk correction is generated by the correlation between the random components and the common discount factors m, given by

$$A_t = \frac{1}{1 + R} E_t(w_{t+1}).$$

Risk refers to the uncertainty of future events that endanger a positive outcome. It is the random outcome that leads to a specific risk and return structure. Financial assets require, therefore, a specific market risk premium that reflects the correlation between the uncertainty of future pay-offs and the common discount factor m over the risk free market rate. The risk-free rate, however, has no uncertainty that might put the future pay-off at risk. It does not correlate with any existing risk factor. The fundamental question in financial valuation is what constitutes the stochastic factors that might endanger future pay-off states and hence future consumption. Each market participant has different risk preferences which then equalise on an aggregated market level in a perfect setting, objectively reflecting the true nature of the underlying risk of the asset. Whether we use a one-risk-factor model such as the CAPM or more-risk-factors models such as the APT for pricing individual assets, the underlying assumption is always one of an arbitrage-free setting of the perfect-market equilibrium.

Arbitrage-free settings of perfect and complete markets

Through a financial instrument an asset becomes tradeable. Financial instruments usually get subsumed under the term securities, referring to debt and equity securities as well as derivatives. Securities define the legal structure for the risk transfer between investors and producers, representing an intertemporal shift of consumption to financing and other productive activities in an open market. The risk preference of each investor shapes the selection and optimal combination of securities in a portfolio context. For an individual investor this may be shaped by their life situation and current wealth and as well as their personal attitude towards risk. For an institutional investor such as a pension fund or insurance company, institutional and regulatory requirements such as the coverage and solvency ratio shape those preferences and the institution's overall risk tolerance. Securities are traded in capital markets. In financial modelling, these markets follow two arbitrage-free settings of the perfect and complete markets.

Perfect market paradigm

The perfect market paradigm defines a market in which the number of buyers and sellers is sufficiently large, and in which all participants are small enough in relation to the market, so that no individual market agent can influence the prices of a security. This implies an equilibrium of supply and demand, a condition that is more likely to occur if assets are traded homogenously through regulated securities (e.g. publicly listed stocks at an exchange). In such a perfect market, there are no frictions or any costs for portfolio construction.

Complete market paradigm

In the analytical framework of the state preference theory, the uncertainty about a portfolio of securities' future value is represented by a set of possible state-contingent pay-offs. A complete market is further defined as an ecosystem where every pay-off of a security can be constructed from or replicated through a portfolio of existing market securities. From a modelling perspective, the number of unique linearly independent securities is equal to the total number of alternative states of nature in such a complete market. Complete markets are therefore markets in which additional financial instruments (known as derivatives) allow replicating a unique state of value. The state preference theory introduces the property of a pure security that either pays one or nothing at the end of a period given that a specific state occurs. Every state and pay-off have a unique price which implies an arbitrage-free setting. Pure securities allow the logical decomposition of market securities into a portfolio of pure securities, and every market security may be considered a combination of various pure securities. As illustration, there are four securities with the pay-offs *(1,1,1)*, *(1,0,0)*, *(0,1,1)*, and *(0,1,2)*. Three among the four are linearly independent state-contingent pay-offs, and with these three states the market is complete. On the other hand, three securities with the pay-off *(1,1,1)*, *(0,1,1)*, and *(1,0,0)* exist but no other security can be traded. In this case, there are three securities and three states of natures but not a complete market since the pay-off of one of the securities is just the sum of the pay-offs of the other two securities. The three securities are not linearly independent. In such an incomplete market, not every possible security pay-off can be constructed from a portfolio of existing securities. These existing securities will have a well-defined price but any possible new security is not spanned by these securities and will not have a unique price as an arbitrage-free mechanism to clear the market.

It takes linear algebra to obtain the pure securities with a unique price from an arbitrary complete set of traded market securities. However, once we know how to form them, it is easy to replicate any other security from a linear combination of the pure securities. Pay-offs can be fully replicated but there is one unique price for each security. If the requirements of the perfect market paradigm are further fulfilled, then any return patterns can be created through portfolio construction. This eventually means that in a perfect and complete market, the implicit price of a pure security can be derived from the traded market securities and how the prices of other market securities can be developed from the implicit prices of pure securities. A capital-market equilibrium requires that market prices be set so that supply equals demand for each individual security. An arbitrage-free setting conditions can be defined for this equilibrium where any combination of securities with the same state-contingent pay-off must be priced identically. Otherwise, there would be an arbitrage to buy the securities with the lower price and sell the ones with the higher prices. This condition is called the single-price law of markets and represents an arbitrage-free setting in a fully functioning capital market environment.

Market equilibrium

To attain a capital-market equilibrium, investor preferences must match the underlying risk and return profile of an assets. Portfolio construction, on the other hand, allows in a perfect and complete market to replicate a desired return profile. Return is a pure function of risk. The higher the risk, the higher the expected return of an asset or portfolio of assets. The minimum variance portfolio (MVP) defines the locus of a risk and return combination offered by a portfolio of risky assets that yield the variance for a given return. Variance is the square of the standard deviation which measures the volatility of an asset as an expression of risk. The variance of a portfolio of two assets A_1 and A_2 can be expressed as

$$VAR(R_P) = w_1^2(VAR\ R_1) + w_2^2\ (VAR\ R_2) + 2\ w_1\ w_2 COV(R_1, R_2),$$

where w = weights, R = simple returns,
while
COV is the covariance is a function of the correlation ρ, defined as

$$\rho = \frac{COV(R_1, R_2)}{\sigma_{R_1}\sigma_{R_2}},$$

which leads to $VAR(R_P) = w_1{}^2(VAR\ R_1) + w_2{}^2\ (VAR\ R_2) + 2\ w_1\ w_2\ \rho\sigma_1\sigma_2.$

Uncorrelated assets have a correlation of zero whereas perfectly correlated assets have a correlation of one. Through the correlation effect, the risk (measured by the variance or standard deviation) of a combination of two assets usually is lower than the risk of a single asset.

The MVP allows the construction of efficient frontiers by combining assets in minimising the variance that leads to a given return. A utility-maximising portfolio can now be found where the marginal rate of transformation between risk and return along the minimum variance opportunity set equals the marginal rate of substitution that reflects the investor preferences. Naturally, an efficient set or so-called efficient frontier of mean-variance choices from any investment opportunity set will be selected for which a given variance or standard deviation offers a higher mean return. The two-fund separation property further defines that each investor has a utility-maximising portfolio that is a combination of the risk-free asset and a portfolio of risk assets, determined by the line drawn from the risk-free rate of return tangent to the investor's efficient frontier of risky assets. If investors have homogenous beliefs, then they all have the same linear efficient set that is called the capital market line (CML). It provides a simple linear relationship between the risk and return for efficient portfolio of assets, mathematically defined as

$$E(R_P) = E(R_M) = R_f + \frac{E(R_M) - R_f}{\sigma(R_M)}\sigma(R_P),$$

which leads to a market equilibrium between supply and demand. The slope of the CML, formally defined as

$$\frac{E(R_M) - R_f}{\sigma(R_M)} \sigma(R_P)$$

represents the market price of risk or market risk premium[6].

For individual assets, the security market line (SML) enables us to calculate the reward-to-risk ratio for any asset in relation to that of the overall market. Assuming the market efficiency hypothesis applies, the risk of an individual asset is a linear expression of its risk which is measured by its risk sensitivity, expressed by beta (β). β represents the systematic risk which includes the different types of risk that may affect the performance of an asset, including macroeconomic factors and events that cannot be neutralised through diversification. Mathematically, it is defined as

$$\beta = \rho \frac{\sigma(R_i)}{\sigma(R_m)},$$

for which ρ = correlation between asset a_i and the market m.

SML illustrates the relation to expected return and systematic risk and shows how the market must price individual assets in relation to systemic risk which cannot be diversified. Therefore, when the expected rate of return for any asset is deflated by its β coefficient, the reward-to-risk ratio for any individual asset in the market is equal to the market reward-to-risk ratio, equal to

$$\frac{E(R_i) - R_f}{\beta} = E(R_M) - R_f.$$

The market reward-to-risk ratio is effectively the market risk premium as defined previously and by solving for $E(R_i)$, the CAPM is obtained by

$$E(R_i) = R_f + \beta(E(R_M) - R_f).$$

The fundamental theorem of the CAPM states that the individual risk premium equals the market premium times β. A beta of less than one indicates the risk of asset is lower than the market risk. A beta equal to one indicates the risk of an individual assets is equal to the overall market risk. A beta of greater than one indicates an asset's risk greater than the market risk.

A key determinant of beta is financial leverage, that is, the level of an institution's debt compared to equity which is an expression of the capital structure. Given that financial institutions are highly levered and tend to be much more homogenous in terms of capital structure, it may make sense to use an average levered beta for a peer group of comparable firm and not the bottom-up for the firm being analysed.

---

[6]In performance evaluation, it is also known as the Sharpe ratio.

To calculate the leveraged beta, we need to know the unlevered beta and the debt-to-equity ratio of assets, expressed through

Levered beta = unlevered beta $\times$ *[1 + (1 − t) (Debt/Equity)], for which t = tax rate.*

Accordingly, beta demonstrates that expected equity returns can be increased through financial leverage while the cost of equity increases with financial leverage as the financial risk of an institution increases respectively. The capital structure remains an important factor in establishing the cost of equity. Capital management and structuring will be more extensively discussed in Chapter 3 on asset-liability management.

Asset pricing models

Within the established market equilibrium, the previously introduced CAPM determines the market price for risk and the appropriate measure of risk for a single asset. It shows that the equilibrium rates of return on all risky assets are a function of their covariance within the market portfolio. A second important equilibrium model that is more general than the CAPM is called the APT. It states that any return of a risky asset is a linear combination of various common factors that affect asset returns. The CAPM can be shown as a single-factor specific case of the APT whereas the multifactor application makes the APT model more general.

To start with, the CAPM can easily be modified by additional factors such as a size premium (S_i) and specific risk premiums that encompasses any additional and uncaptured risk of an asset or a business. The most famous application of such modification was through Eugene Fama and Kenneth French from 1992 which establishes a three-factor model, defined as

$$E(R_i) = R_f + \beta_{\mathrm{mod}}(E(R_M) - R_f) + \beta_s SMB + \beta_h HML + \alpha,$$

for which β = modified beta factor given there are two additional factors SMB = Small Minus Big and HML = High Minus Low. SMB refers to the market capitalization and HML to the book-to-market ratio as they measure the historic excess returns of small caps over big caps and of value stocks over growth stocks.

According to the APT, equity returns for asset *j* that can further be broken down in individual risk factors or sensitivities *n* across statistically relevant risk premiums, formally expressed through

$$E(r_j) = r_f + \beta_{j1} RP_1 + \beta_{j2} RP_2 + \ldots + \beta_{jn} RP_n,$$

for which E = expectations, r_f = risk-free rate, B_{jn} = sensitivity, and RP = risk premium.

The asset price should equal the expected end of period price discounted at the rate implied by the APT model. If asset prices diverge, arbitrage should bring it back into line with the expectations derived by the model as originally proposed by Stephen Ross in 1976. The APT differs from the CAPM in that it is less restrictive in its assumptions.

It assumes that each investor will hold a unique portfolio with its own particular array of betas, as opposed to the identical market portfolio described by the CAPM. The CML represents a single-factor model of the asset price, where beta is exposed to changes in value of the market. One of the core challenges of the APT is that the selection and the number of factors to use in the model is ambiguous. Academic literature usually quotes three to five selected factors but those factors differ substantially from market to market and do not seem to be empirically robust over time.

2.3.3   Contingent claims

The derivation of the closed-form Black-Scholes-Merton formula was a substantial breakthrough for financial modelling. It allowed the quantification of complex, nonlinear financial instruments within a comprehensive framework. Technically these instruments are referred to as contingent claims. Financial options are such contingent claims. The value of such an option depends on the price of one or more underlying assets and contractual rights of its owner to take certain actions under specified conditions. A call option constitutes the right to buy and a put option the right to sell at predefined conditions. These conditions are defined by the exercise and strike price during any time up to maturity (for American options) or at expiry only (for European options). Chapter 3 on asset-liability management covers under its section on financial engineering the different types of options in further details. Objective of this section is to cover the fundamental properties of contingent claim analysis with its core concept of risk neutrality. It allows to extend our decision making framework by incorporating nonlinearity into it. Options and other forms of derivatives find their most natural application in risk transfer and management such as hedging. They may also increase exposure through leverage or design specific return targets through pay-off structures. At the same time, contingent claim analysis represents another important tool for financial modelling and can further be applied in financial analysis and valuation through probability assessments and real option methods.

Pricing framework

The pricing of contingent claims often refers to the Black-Scholes-Merton formula as the holy grail of option pricing. In its derivation, a series of ideal market assumption for the asset and the contingent claim are made. Firstly, the short-term interest rate is known and constant through time. Secondly, the price of the asset follows a random walk in continuous time with a variance rate proportional to the square of the asset price. Thus the distribution of possible asset prices at the end of any finite interval is lognormal. The variance rate and as an expression of the volatility is constant. Thirdly, the asset pays no income or has any other form of distribution. Fourthly, the contingent claim is European, meaning that it can be exercised only at maturity. Fifthly, the perfect market assumption holds that there are no transaction costs in buying or selling the asset or its contingent claim. Furthermore, it is possible to borrow any fraction of the price of a security to buy or to hold it, at the short-term interest rate. Finally, there are no penalties to short selling. A seller who does not own a security will simply accept the price of the security from a buyer and will agree to settle with the buyer on some future date by paying him an amount equal to the price of the security on that date.

The Black-Scholes-Merton formula defines the price of an option as

$$G(A, t) = AN(d_1) - Ke^{T-t}N(d_2), \text{ where} \tag{2.1}$$

$$d_1 = \frac{ln\left(\frac{A}{K}\right) + \left(r + \frac{1}{2}\sigma^2\right)(T - t)}{\sigma\sqrt{T - t}}, \text{ and} \tag{2.2}$$

$$d_2 = d_1 - \sigma(T - t),$$

for which G = [call] option, A = asset, $T - t$ = time horizon, σ = standard deviation, N = normal distribution, and K = strike price with d = confidence interval.

The following sections will derive this formula across different paths and will discuss the core concepts that are relevant for financial modelling such as the fundamental partial differential equation (FPDE), risk neutrality, and the difference between closed-form and numerical solutions.

Fundamental Partial Differential Equation

The FPDE remains the core of the analytic framework for contingent claims and option pricing theory. There are two derivations for the FPDE. The classic one from Black-Scholes-Merton that is based on the works of Fisher Black, Myron Scholes, and Robert C. Merton. The second derivation applies modern methods of stochastic calculus that is known as Martingale transformation which directly leads to the risk neutrality theorem. It is based on the works of Michael Harrison, David Kreps, and Stanley Pliska. The FPDE further allows the derivation of the risk sensitivities of an option known as the Greek. The following section emphasis the economic reasoning behind the derivation of the FPDE and less the accuracy of the math underlying it.

Black-Scholes-Merton derivation

Although Fisher Black and Myron Scholes in their groundbreaking paper from 1973 refer in their derivation of the FPDE to Robert C. Merton who later calls their line of argument "red herring", the Black-Scholes-Merton differential equation can easily be established by a few formal steps. To derive the FPDE an ingenious argument is applied. With a full replication of the option position, done by investing a specific amount Δ in a risky stock position that is financed by a risk-free credit position, the stochastic part of the price process of the underlying can be eliminated. The following section demonstrates the intuition behind this derivation.

Let the drift of the asset price (A_t) follow a geometric Brownian motion with

$$dA_t = \alpha dt + \sigma A_t dB_t,$$

$$\text{where } \alpha = \mu + \frac{1}{2}\sigma^2.$$

With the application of Itô's lemma, a stochastic differential equation (SDE) can be derived for the option value (G), mathematically given as

By plugging

$$dA_t = \alpha dt + \sigma A_t dB_t$$

into this equation and rearranging terms, we further obtain

$$dG \left(\frac{\partial G}{\partial A_t} \mu A_t + \frac{\partial G}{\partial t} + \frac{1}{2} \sigma^2 A_t^2 \frac{\partial^2 G}{\partial A_t^2} \right) dt + \frac{\partial G}{\partial A_t} \sigma A_t dB_t.$$

With the full replication of the option position (G) through an asset position (A) and a risk-free asset position (B) a perfect hedge is attained:

$$dG = \Delta dA_t - dB_t$$

and

$$dB_t = \Delta dA_t - dG = -dG + \frac{\partial G}{\partial A_t} dA_t.$$

The perfect hedge is therefore mathematically defined as

$$dG = d\Pi = r\Pi dt = rGdt = -dG + \frac{\partial G}{\partial A_t} dA_t,$$

where Π = value of the replication portfolio and r = short-term risk-free rate.

The risk-free hedge is achieved and the stochastic element of the standard Brownian motion (B_t) can be eliminated. When we assume that through the full replication of the option position (a perfect hedge), the expected drift is equal to the risk-free rate (equal to the hedging costs) so that $\alpha = r$. The result is the FPDE, given by

$$\frac{\partial G}{\partial t} + rA_t \frac{\partial G}{\partial A_t} + \frac{1}{2} \sigma^2 A_t^2 \frac{\partial^2 G}{\partial A_t^2} = rG.$$

The characteristic nature of this equation is that it does not involve any variables that are affected by the risk preferences of investors. If risk preferences do not enter the equation, they cannot affect its solution. Any set of risk preferences can therefore be used when valuing options. It can therefore be very simply assumed that all investors are risk neutral which is called the risk-neutral property of finance. The formal derivation of the FPDE therefore implies that receiving random payouts from the option is equivalent to receiving the proceeds from the hedging strategy that allows the full replication of the derivative by its underlying asset, on which the option is written. In case of risk-neutrality, the expected return on all assets is the risk-free rate. The derivative position becomes redundant in the sense that the option does not add anything new to the market and that no economic benefits can arise. Yet the entire theorem is based on the assumption that the asset on which the option is written can be used for hedging through a perfect hedge with an expected return as an expression of the hedging costs that is equal to the risk-free rate.

Martingale transformation

An alternative derivation of the FPDE can be obtained by means of a direct application known as the Martingale transformation or change of measure. To avoid arbitrage in this setting, a risk-neutral density is applied. The mean of this risk-neutral density must satisfy the restrictions of the Martingale property that simply states that the price of an option is given by regarding the expectation of its pay-off with respect to a risk-neutral density and the discounted expectation at the risk-free rate. In this framework, the price of the underlying asset is equal to its traded value. More formally, the expected pay-off under risk-neutrality is nothing else than the discounted value of option where the discount rate is the risk-free rate, defined as

$$G = e^{-rt}\widehat{E}(C_t),$$

which leads to

$$\widehat{E}\left(\frac{dG}{G}\right) = rdt,$$

where $\widehat{E}$ = pay-off-expectation under risk-neutrality.

Michael Harrison, David Kreps, and Stanley Pliska show that the same argument can be applied by converting the discounted derivative asset into a Martingale, which is done by switching the driving Brownian motion to a new process with the associated probability measure Q. This transformation constitutes the first and the second fundamental theorem of finance.[7] The first fundamental theorem relates the notion of no arbitrage to the existence of an equivalent martingale measure. The second fundamental theorem relates the notion of market completeness to the uniqueness of the equivalent Martingale measure. To get from a risky to a risk-free state with no risk premiums, the probability measure needs to be changed. Under some conditions, it is possible to derive and find an equivalent probability measure Q, so that the equality

$$E^Q[e^{-rt}A_t \mid A_u, u < t] = e^{-ru}A_u$$

satisfies the Martingale property.

The application of the Girsanov theorem allows the transformation of a sub-Martingale into a Martingale, which is in its economic interpretation equal to the transformation of a risky state with its true price dynamics into a risk-neutral state. Formally, the geometric Brownian motion

$$\frac{dA_t}{A_t} = \alpha dt + \sigma dB_t$$

---

[7]See Michael Harrison and David Kreps's paper from 1979 on "Martingales and Arbitrage in Multiperiod Securities Markets" in the *Journal of Economic Theory* and Michael Harrison and Stanley Pliska's publication from 1981 on "Martingales and Stochastic Integrals in the Theory of Continuous Trading" in Volume 11 of *Stochastic Processes and Their Applications*.

that describes the asset return is transformed in

$$\frac{dA_t}{A_t} = \hat{\alpha}d_t + \sigma dW_t,$$

where $\hat{\alpha}$ = modified drift.

With the new probability measure Q, this is defined as a standard Brownian motion with $N(0, \sigma)$. The drift α in d_t becomes zero as one switches the driving error term in the geometric Brownian motion, B_t, to a standard Brownian motion, W_t, with the probability distribution Q where

$$\frac{dA}{A} = \alpha d_t + \sigma d\left[B_t - \left(\frac{\mu - r}{\sigma}\right)t\right].$$

The driving part of the Brownian motion has been eliminated and the normal distribution can be applied.

The term $\left(\frac{\alpha - r}{\sigma}\right)$ defines the standardised risk premium that has previously been defined as the market price of risk. Adapting the original driving process B_t (geometric Brownian motion) according to the historical or true statistical probability (P) leads to a risk-neutral process W_t with the Martingale probability Q, so that

$$W_t = B_t - \theta \cdot t,$$

where θ = market price of risk.

Finally, to get the risk-free state, the price drift (μ) must be modified. This leads to

$$\hat{\alpha}(A_t, t) = \alpha(A_t, t) - \theta_t \sigma(A_t, t),$$

which finally results in

$$\hat{\alpha}(A_t, t) = r.$$

If we neglect the original value of the asset position (At), the modified drift $\hat{\alpha}$ becomes equal to the continuously calculated risk-free rate (r). Hence, when risk-neutrality is assumed, the FPDE is satisfied. Risk neutrality is an elegant or more simple way to solve the FPDE. The FPDE can further be used to describe the dynamic hedging procedure with the replicating portfolio, which is mathematically defined as

$$\frac{\partial G}{\partial t} + rA_t\frac{\partial G}{\partial A_t} + \frac{1}{2}\sigma^2 A_t^2\frac{\partial^2 G}{\partial A_t^2} = rG.$$

The pay-off structure of the underlying has no impact whatsoever as the FPDE is only an expression of dynamic hedging. The FPDE can therefore be applied to all different underlying assets that are dependent on the asset price (A) and the time-to-maturity (t). The FDPE is therefore nothing else than the characterisation of the arbitrage-free price of a contingent claim. This insight is fundamental in the final step of the derivation of a pricing formula for options but it knows many solutions, corresponding to all different derivatives that can be defined with the asset price (A) as the underlying variable. The particular derivative that is obtained when the FPDE is solved depends on the boundary conditions of the pay-off of the contingent claim that are applied. These specify the values of the derivative at the boundaries of possible values of A and t. In the case of a European call option, the key boundary conditions are

$$G = max(A - X, 0)$$

when $t = T$.

In the case of a European put option, it is

$$G = max(X - A, 0)$$

when $t = T$.

These boundary conditions are applied when a closed-form solution is derived and when simple numerical procedure exists. The original derivation of Black-Scholes (1973) used an application of the heat-transfer equation of physics to solve the FPDE and attain the world-famous analytical or closed-form solution. Robert Merton and Myron Scholes won the Nobel Prize in Economics in 1997 for pioneering a formula for the valuation of stock options. Fischer Black unfortunately died in 1995 and was not awarded the Nobel Price as it is not recognised posthumously.

The Greeks

The FPDE allows to describe the hedging mechanism of contingent claims across a group of risk sensitivities, known as the Greeks. The FPDE allows to express their relationship as

$$\Delta r A_t + \Gamma \frac{1}{2} \sigma^2 A_t^2 + \Theta = rG,$$

where Δ = Delta, Γ = Gamma, and Θ = Theta.

The following section focuses on the Greeks individually as a risk measure and discuss the formal as well as intuitive relationship between them. Keep in mind that in the Black-Scholes-Merton framework, it is implicitly assumed that volatility and interest rate remain constant. Vega and Rho which measure volatility and interest rate sensitivities are not part of the FPDE. The role of Vega which measures the sensitivity of volatility is covered separately in the upcoming section on implied volatility.

The delta (Δ) is defined as the rate of change of the option price with respect to the price of the price of the underlying asset. It is the slope of the curve that relates the option price to the underlying asset price. Expressed mathematically, delta is the partial derivative of the call price with respect to underlying asset price

$$\Delta = \frac{\partial G}{\partial A}.$$

For a European call option on a non-income-paying asset, it can be shown from the Black-Scholes formula that

$$\Delta_C = \frac{\partial C}{\partial A} = N(d_1).$$

For a European put option on a non-incoming-paying asset, it can be shown from the Black-Scholes formula that the delta is given

$$\Delta_P = \frac{\partial P}{\partial A} = \Delta_C - 1 = N(d_1) - 1.$$

The value of the delta ranges from -1 to 0 for a put option and 0 to 1 for a call option. An at-the-money option has a delta value of approximately 0.5, which means that the option premium will rise or fall by half a point with a one-point move up or down in the underlying asset. This also means that the option has a probability of 50% that it will be exercised. A call option has a positive delta and a positive relationship to the price of the underlying. If the underlying asset rises, so does the premium of the call, provided there are no changes in other variables such as implied volatility and time remaining until expiration. To remain delta neutral, a long position in a call option should be hedged by a short position in the underlying asset. A short position in a call option should be hedged by a long position in the asset. The delta of a put option is negative, and the premium falls when the underlying rises and vice versa. A long position in a put option should be hedged with a long position in the underlying asset, and a short position in a put option should be hedged with a short position. Furthermore, the delta tends to increase as the option gets closer to expiration for near- or at-the-money options. It is not constant but changes with the price movements of the underlying asset and it is also subject to changes in implied volatility.

The rate with which the delta changes is measured by the gamma (Γ). It is the first derivative of the delta and measures the rate of change of delta with respect to the price of the underlying asset. It therefore measures how much delta changes following a one-point change in the price of the underlying asset. Mathematically, it is defined as the second partial derivative of the option value with respect to the asset price:

$$\Gamma = \frac{\partial^2 G}{\partial A^2} = \frac{N'(d_1)}{A\sigma\sqrt{t}}.$$

The gamma measures the curvature of the relationship between the option price and the underlying asset. It is positive for a long position because of the convexity of the curvature for a long position either in a call or put option and negative because of the concavity of a short position. From the put-call parity we know that the Gamma for a call and a put option must be identical, so that

$$\Gamma_P = \Gamma_C.$$

If gamma is small, delta changes slowly. Adjustments to keep a portfolio delta neutral need only be made relatively infrequently. However, if gamma is large in absolute terms, delta is highly sensitive to the price of the underlying asset and it becomes quite risky to leave a delta-neutral portfolio unchanged for any length of time. Gamma is highest when an option gets near the money or in general for at-the-money option. It tends to be smallest for deep out-of-the-money and deep in-the-money options.

The theta (θ) is the rate of change of the option value with respect to the passage of time when all else remains the same. Equivalently, it measures the rate of change of the option value with respect to a decrease in the time-to-maturity of the option, the rate of decline in the time-premium resulting from the passage of time. It is referred to as the time decay of an option. In other words, an option premium that has no intrinsic value but only a time value will decline at an increasing rate as expiration nears. Mathematically, the theta is defined as

$$\Theta = \frac{\partial G}{\partial t}.$$

Applying the Black-Scholes formula, the theta of call option is given as

$$\Theta_C = \frac{\partial C}{\partial t} = -\frac{A\sigma}{2\sqrt{t}}N'(d_1) - rXe^{-rt}N(d_2),$$

whether the theta of a put option is defined as

$$\Theta_P = \frac{\partial P}{\partial t} = -\frac{A\sigma}{2\sqrt{t}}N'(d_1) - rXe^{-rt}(1 - N(d_2)).$$

Theta for a long position is therefore usually negative because as time passes, the option tends to become less valuable. This is always the case for plain-vanilla European calls and for American call and put options. An exception to this rule is a deep in-the-money European put option on a non-income-paying asset or an in-the-money European call option on a currency with a very high domestic interest rate. In these cases, the value of the European put decays upward in value. Theta is highest for at-the-money option as the intrinsic value of the option is zero and the time decay has its largest impact. For the same reason, theta can be very high for out-of-the-money option if they contain a lot of implied volatility. Theta will increase sharply in the last few weeks of trading and can severely undermine a long option holder's position, especially if the implied volatility is on decline at the same time. For a deep-in-the-money option, the sensitivity to term-to-maturity therefore decreases as the options moves in-the-money. The sensitivity increases as you move out-of-the-money. Double the term-to-maturity can easily double, triple, and quadruple the value of the option if it is well out-of-the-money. When gamma is positive, theta tends to be negative and vice versa. The hedging sensitivity increases as the time value of the option decreases and the sensitivities decreases as the theta as an expression of the time-to-maturity increases.

The different Greek measures allow neutralising the option position individually in terms of their exposure to the underlying risk variable. However, the mechanisms are more complex and are interrelated. An option can be replicated and therefore hedged by a certain amount (delta) in the risky asset (A) and another position in the risk-free asset (B). This is called the replicating portfolio. More formally, this leads to

$$G = \Delta A + B,$$

$$if \ G = call \ option, then \ \Delta > 0 \ and \ B < 0,$$

$$if \ G = put \ option, the \ \Delta < 0 \ and \ B > 0,$$

$$where \ G = option, \Delta = Delta \ and \ B = risk - free \ asset.$$

In case of a call option, a long position in the replicating portfolio that is equal to a long position in the asset is financed through a risk-free asset. In case of a put option, a short position in the replicating portfolio that is equal to a short position in the asset and the received capital is then invested in the money market (i.e. the risk-free asset). If a financial institution sells a call option to a counterparty, it is synthetically short the underlying and will buy the underlying to delta hedge the position. If a financial institution buys a call option from a counterparty, it is synthetically long the underlying and will sell the underlying to delta hedge the position. If it sells a put option to the counterparty, it is synthetically long the underlying and needs to sell the underlying to hedge the position. If it buys a put option from the counterparty, it is synthetically short the underlying and need to buy the underlying to delta hedge the position. As an example consider a long position in a call option that is delta hedged by a short position in the replicating portfolio. If the asset declines in value, the delta declines and the required position of the trader in the risky asset decreases. The trader must lend the risk-free asset from money markets and buy back the amount of the risky asset. The opposite is true for a short position in the call option or a long position in the put option.

Implied volatility

Volatility is a measure of the variability of asset prices. It is a critical input factor in contingent claim analysis and knows two forms. The realised volatility is calculated from historical returns as we covered earlier in this chapter. Implied volatility is derived from traded option prices and reflects the market's expectations of future volatility. It depends on the strike price as well as on the tenor of the option and is multidimensional. The Vega (v) is the rate to change of the value of the option with respect to the volatility of the underlying asset, mathematically defined as

$$v = \frac{\partial G}{\partial \sigma} = A_t \sqrt{t} N'(d_a).$$

Vega tells us approximately how much an option price will increase or decrease at the level of implied volatility. If Vega is high in absolute terms, the portfolio's value is very sensitive to small changes in volatility. If Vega is low in absolute terms, volatility changes have relatively little impact on the value of the portfolio. A long position in an option always has a positive Vega as the option holder gains if volatility increases. A short position, on the other hand, always has a negative Vega as the writer of an option gains when the volatility falls. Vega can increase or decrease even without price changes in the underlying asset because implied volatility is the level of expected volatility. Vega can increase from quick moves in the underlying, especially if there is a big drop in the stock market. Vega falls as the option gets closer to expiration.

In option pricing theory, there is only one implied measure of volatility for an underlying asset at a given moment in time. Hence, a graph showing implied volatilities versus exercise prices should be horizontal. The observed pattern, however, is u-shaped and widely known as the volatility smile. The volatility smile reflects a plot of an option's implied volatility being a function of its strike price. The u-shape implies that the volatility is lowest for at-the-money options and that it progressively becomes higher as the options move either in the money or out of the money. The smile form usually applies to foreign currency options, whereas the volatility structure of equity options is more like a skew. Volatility decreases as the strike price increases, and the volatility used to price an option with a low strike price is significantly higher than the one used to price a high-strike price option. There are various explanations for why the volatilities exhibit a skew or smile structure. The most common explanation, to which many risk managers refer to, is the ideal assumptions of the Black-Scholes-Merton framework. Almost every one of these assumptions such as lognormally distributed asset prices, homoskedasticity of the return structure (implied in the constant volatility assumption), or frictions in the perfect market assumption may have a major impact. In most markets, returns appear more leptokurtic than it is assumed by normally distributed asset returns (that is equal to lognormally distributed asset prices). More intuitively, market forces seem to price in this leptokurtic shape that is nothing less than an expression of extreme event risk such as a stock market dislocation. It therefore reflects investors' fear of market crashes or price spikes. Furthermore, the volatility smile may also refer to relative supply and demand mechanism in financial market that will further be covered in the next section on financial stress.

In addition to volatility smiles and skews, implied volatilities used to price at-the-money options depend on the maturity of the option (also called tenor). This is known as the term structure of volatility. Expectations of a rise in volatility will increase when volatility is low and vice versa. Volatilities also tend to be mean-reverting. Thus, the shape of the volatility structure depends on the tenor of the option. Volatility has therefore a clear term structure, which depends on the time value of the underlying state of the market. The state of the market refers to the state of the economy in general (expectations) or, in a short-term and more specific setting, to the state of trading (liquidity). This shape can be increased, inverted, and/or show extreme forms at the short or long end of the maturity structure. In most cases, the volatility structure becomes less pronounced as the option maturity increases. Combining the volatility structure with the time-to-maturity of the options leads to a three-dimensional structure known as the volatility surface. Analyses of volatility structures have often been carried out by using three-dimensional volatility matrices.

Numerical methods

In addition to the closed formula Black-Scholes-Merton formula that was introduced at the beginning of this section, there are a series of numerical methods with which the price of a contingent claim or option can be calculated. The methods are based on the modelling of a stochastic process of the underlying assets while applying a respective pay-off structure for the option that is expressed by the boundary conditions. The boundary conditions are dependent on the type of options and different for European, American, and all generations of exotic options. The following section provides a brief overview of numerical methods with focus on the widely used binominal trees with its different model specifications.

Binominal trees are based on diagrams that represent different possible paths of the underlying over the life of an option. For most options, the underlying assumption

is that the stock price follows a random walk. In each step, there is a certain probability of moving up by a certain percentage and a certain probability of moving down
by a certain percentage. As the time steps become smaller and smaller, leading in the
limit to a continuous time setting, the asset prices follow a lognormal distribution and
their continuously calculated returns a normal distribution. As we covered earlier, this
is a direct application of the central limit theorem, a key concept of probability theory which states that the sum of independent random variables tends toward a normal
distribution even if the original variables themselves are not normally distributed. The
normal distribution can therefore be applied to various problems involving other types
of distributions.

The most general approach for binominal trees is referred to as CRR which stands
for Cox, Ross, and Rubinstein who published the method in 1979. If we suppose that an
option lasts for time T and that during the life of the option, the asset price can either
move up from A_0 to a new level, A_0u where $u > 1$, or down from A_0 to a new level, A_0d,
where $d < 1$. The percentage increase in the asset price when there is an up movement is
$u - 1$ and the percentage decrease when there is a down movement is $1 - d$. Depending
on the type of option, we can assume a pay-off g_u if the asset price moves up to A_0u,
and g_d if the asset price moves down to A_0d. If a portfolio of assets consists of a position
in Δ assets and a short position in one option G, we can calculate in application of the
risk neutrality principle the value *of* Δ that makes the portfolio riskless. If there is an up
movement in the asset price, the value of the portfolio at the end of the life of the option
is $A_0u\Delta - G_u$, and the other way around if the asset price moves down to $A_0d\Delta - G_d$,
which equals to

$$A_0u\Delta - G_u = A_0d\Delta - G_d$$

and

$$\Delta = \frac{G_u - G_d}{A_0u - A_0d}.$$

Under risk neutrality, the present value of the portfolio is $(A_0u\Delta - G_u)e^{-rT}$ while the
cost of setting up the portfolio is $A_0\Delta - G$ which leads to

$$(A_0u\Delta - G_u)e^{-rT} = A_0\Delta - G.$$

Substituting Δ with its components above and simplifying, the equation for the
expected pay-off (p) of the option (G) becomes

$$p = \frac{e^{rT} - d}{u - d}.$$

This option pricing formula does not involve the probabilities of the stock price
moving up or down as the option is not valued in absolute terms. Its value is calculated
in terms of the price of the underlying asset. In accordance with the previously introduced Martingale and Markov properties of finance, the probabilities of future up or

down movements are already incorporated into the asset price and do not need to be taken into account again when valuing the option in terms of the underlying asset price. If p is the option's expected pay-off, then the value of the option today is its expected pay-off discounted at the risk-free rate which is again the application of the formerly introduced risk-neutral valuation principle. Putting this all together means that value of the option (G) can be calculated as

$$G = e^{-rT} (pG_u + (1-p)G_d),$$

while simulating the underlying asset price in accordance with u and d which are reflecting the expected price drift of the asset in %. To model a binominal tree in practice with the objective to represent the underlying asset's price movements, the parameters u and d are chosen to match the price volatility of the asset. Mathematically, this leads to

$$u = e^{\sigma \sqrt{\Delta t}},$$

and

$$d = e^{-\sigma \sqrt{\Delta t}}.$$

The parameters p, u, and d describes so far, have been chosen in the formulation originally proposed by John Cox, Stephen Ross, and Mark Rubinstein (CRR method). There are several alternative methods available such as the equal-probability approach proposed by Robert Jarrow and Andrew Rudd. Based on the assumption that over a small period of time, the expected mean and variance of the applied binomial model will match those expected in a risk neutral world, they propose to set

$$p = \tfrac{1}{2},$$

which leads to

$$u = e^{\left(r - \frac{1}{2}\sigma^2\right)\Delta t + \sigma \sqrt{\Delta t}},$$

and

$$u = e^{\left(r - \frac{1}{2}\sigma^2\right)\Delta t - \sigma \sqrt{\Delta t}}.$$

There are a series of other approaches and methods available that includes the extension of a binominal to a trinominal tree which go way beyond the objective of the chapter of this book. Furthermore, there are finite difference methods which solve iteratively different equations that the contingent claim satisfies. In today's world of option pricing, Monte Carlo simulation is the most sophisticated and common method use for derivatives pricing. It is a similar approach as previously described where the underlying asset price is simulated through stochastic processes and then used to find the discounted expected option pay-offs. Its application is almost mandatory in case the pay-off is dependent on several underlying variables such as time or the underlying's price history.

2.4   FINANCIAL STRESS

In the previous section on financial modelling, we assumed perfect and complete market conditions which lead to a series of fundamental mathematical properties for financial decision making. If those assumptions are in place, capital markets are in equilibrium and a stable asset-pricing framework can be applied. Financial market history paints a different picture though and exhibits regular patterns of market dislocations, financial stress, and systemic crises. Those phenomena cannot be explained by the conventional framework of financial modelling but only through the introduction of demand and supply mechanisms in the broader analytical framework of financial decisions.

The following section introduces the cycle of financial stress and liquidity risk and with them a framework for assessing market dislocations and banking crises. It applies supply and demand economics in combination with dynamic system theory and macro-history in establishing an analytical decision framework. We distinguish between market dislocations and banking crises. Both are financial crises in the definition of the academic literature that defines broadly a variety of situations in which some financial assets suddenly lose a large part of their nominal value. Some of them such as the Great Depression from the 1930s and the GFC from 2008 may lead to a full-blown banking crises. Others such as the stock market crashes from 1987 and the bursting of the technology, media, and telecommunications asset bubble from 2001 are pure market dislocations that left the banking system unaffected. Market dislocations may be trigger a broader financial crisis which includes the banking system but as a single event that requires much less government interventions and overall system stabilisation.

2.4.1   The cycle of financial stress

Financial stability is a property of a perfectly functioning financial system. It is essential for an economic growth environment. A stable financial system is in a position to absorb shocks endogenously via self-corrective mechanisms, preventing adverse events from disrupting the real economy or spreading over to other financial systems. Any financial shock and imbalances are dissipated and the perfect market equilibrium prevails. At the same time, without financial stability, asset prices may deviate significantly from their intrinsic values, financial institutions constrain lending, and creditors struggle in fulfilling their payment schedule. Financial stress, on the other hand, is a situation of supply and demand imbalances where the system is no longer in a position to absorb exogenous and endogenous events. Market dislocations are often followed by broader system crises that may trigger bank runs. From analytical perspective, it remains difficult to model these effects and dynamics as they fundamentally challenge the mathematical properties of the perfect and complete market equilibrium. New information may trigger an initial response but the endogenous or internal dynamics accelerate as the system aims to find its new equilibrium. Prices tend to overshoot and the corrective mechanisms can often not be halted without an external intervention of policy makers. Financial history exhibits on a regular basis stress and crises such as in modern times the great bank run of 1907, the great crash of 1928 followed by the Great Depression in the 1930s, the Latin America crisis of the late 1980s, the Asian crisis of 1997, the collapse of the tech bubble in the early 2000, and the most recent GFC of 2007–2008.

Most important remains the question if these developments and effects can be modelled analytically outside of the conventions of modern asset pricing. In his book *Big Debt Crises*, Ray Dalio introduces the notion of a cycle to the analysis and proposes the use of logically driven series of events that (re-)occur in pattern. A historical perspective replaces a quantitative methodology. We follow this approach and establish a cycle of financial stress while incorporating elements of a similar framework by Ben Bernanke, Timothy Geithner, and Henry Paulson in their book *Firefighting*. The cycle of financial stress distinguishes between seven phases, starting with an early stage (1), bubble (2), stress (3), dislocation (4), banking crisis (5), economic recession and depression (6), and resolution (7).

In the early stage phase of the financial stress cycle, different forms of innovation (technological, financial, social, . . .) followed by a period of strong economic growth triggers lead to the use of debt leverage. Borrowed money is chasing business expansion and new growth opportunities. Given the early stage, balance sheets are healthy with low debt burden which allows for the broad application of financial leverage and innovative funding tools. During the bubble phase, price increases accelerate with debt levels rising faster than incomes. The leverage produces strong asset returns and growth. This environment leads to a positive wealth effect as the rising net-wealth often paired with higher incomes increases the lending capacity of borrowers. Prices tend to overshoot and move away from their intrinsic value and historical references. The rationale of the price development is explained by new ways of productivity gains and forms of endogenous growth. Usually, central banks start to warn about price exaggeration such as the then chairman of the Federal Reserve board Alan Greenspan with his quote on "irrational exuberance" on 5 December 1996 in the running to the tech bubble.

During the dislocation phase, external events or endogenous shocks trigger feedback loops of asset sales with the effect that prices correct towards their intrinsic value. Demand and supply are out of balance and states of illiquidity result in market dislocations and price divergences to the intrinsic value of an asset. During these tense market conditions, the stress dynamics become self-sustaining through shortening of the investment horizon and the negative wealth effect. To assess these dynamics, we will introduce a comprehensive model for market dislocations. A banking crisis usually is a result of tense market and funding conditions that exasperate in panic and bank runs and eventually lead to the demise of financial institutions that undermines the entire system. The management of the impact on financial institutions is core to our analysis. A following section will also be dedicated to a historical perspective on banking crises and the common factors that can be established. The last two phases of economic recession and depression and resolution though is less the concern and focus of this book, and we would like to refer to the memoirs and combined works of policy makers such as Ben Bernanke, Timothy Geithner, and Henry Paulson or of the former Governor of the Bank of England Mervyn King, as well as the publications of academics in particular the work of Carmen Reinhart and Kenneth Rogoff.

2.4.2 Liquidity risk

Conventional financial modelling assumes perfect liquidity and hence no frictions due to differences in supply and demand. Liquidity though is an expression of supply and demand mechanisms in imperfect and incomplete markets. Financial decision making knows two forms of market liquidity, asset and funding liquidity. Both forms impact asset prices and constitute the term knows as liquidity risk. As a result of the GFC, the Basel committee introduced with Basel III a series of requirements and metrics to address liquidity issues on bank balance sheets. These regulatory requirements will further be covered in Chapter 3 on asset-liability management. The following section focuses on the mechanics of liquidity risk and the underlying supply and demand principles that lead to the previously defined financial stress cycle. It follows Philippe Jorion in distinguishing asset and funding liquidity and their duality, establishing an applicable definition of liquidity risk.

Asset liquidity

Asset liquidity, often also called market liquidity, relates to the liquidation value of financial instruments. The liquidation value might differ significantly from the current mark-to-market value, depending on the price sensibility of the asset or the specific liquidity situation in financial markets. The value of an asset can be utilised only through the liquidation of its position so that the marginal utility of an investor depends heavily on it. Asset liquidity refers to the time and costs associated with the transformation of a given asset position into cash and vice versa. It defines the marketability of assets, the time involved in the process of liquidation, and the liquidity price impact of these actions. Formally, this can be expressed by the asset-liquidity-price-ratio, defined as

$$L = \frac{\Delta N}{\Delta A},$$

where L = liquidity, N = notional amount of assets traded in the market and A = asset value.

The asset-liquidity-price-ratio is defined as the notional amount of the traded asset that has to be traded in the market to drive down the asset price by one point, which should be a positive number. This number is written from a market participant's standpoint. If some notional is sold to the market (change in notional is negative), then the price will go down (change in price is also negative) and vice versa. The liquidity number derived is a practical way to describe how trading affects the market. Traders usually have a good idea of what that number could be and how much one should trade to move or not move the market. If asset liquidity tends to be small, the notional amount of assets traded, which is the same as the asset supply, gets full pricing power and develops a perfect price impact.

Asset illiquidity arises when transactions cannot be conducted at prevailing market prices because of the size of the position relative to normal trading lots. In a liquid market, market participants can rapidly execute large-volume transactions with no or at least a small impact on prices. Liquidity costs may be negligible for such positions when marking to market provides a proper liquidation value. In contrast, illiquid markets are characterised by high volatilities of spread, quote depth, and trading volumes. The unwillingness to trade may be a result of specific events that lead to one-way situations in pro-forma efficient markets (based on information efficiency). These events are not related to economic fundamentals and are, hence, not conditioned on the fair values of assets. Such events are called liquidity events. A liquidity event reflects the conditioning equilibrium between supply and demand. Illiquidity stands for a disequilibrium in supply/demand, which implies an imbalance or dislocation in the marketplace. Moreover, supply and demand reveal the match (liquidity) or divergence (illiquidity) in expectations that condition the economic equilibrium. Liquidity (L) should, therefore, be treated as an expression of the economic equilibrium between supply (S) and demand (D). The mechanics are outlined in Exhibit 2.10.

The traded notional amount that moves prices beyond their intrinsic fair values is called the liquidity price impact. It results in a state of illiquidity. A liquidity event may have a negative price impact when supply exceeds demand. The majority of market participants will prefer to be on the sell side, and no one is willing to buy the asset. A liquidity event may have a positive price impact when demand exceeds supply. The majority of market participants will prefer to be on the buy side of the market, and few will be willing to sell the asset. However, a positive liquidity price impact usually has limited economic value as resulting capital gains can either be realised at any time or can be replicated by other financial instruments.

Funding liquidity

Funding liquidity refers to cash that an institution must face to meet its payment obligations. It deals with cash resources as well as potential cash requirements and implies a formal default risk when the institution runs out of it and/or is unable to raise additional funds. In the accounting literature, several funding liquidity ratios have been developed to assess potential internal cash and refinancing risk. Measuring funding liquidity involves the examination of the asset-liability structure of the balance sheet of an institution. It compares potential cash demand with the available asset supply of

---

If $S > D$, then $L \geq 1$; *illiquid trading environment.*

If $S \leq D$, then $L \leq 1$; *(very) liquid trading environment.*

In terms (numbers) of the previously introduced asset-liquidity-price-ratio, this leads to

$\Delta N = L \cdot \Delta A$, *so that*

If $L \geq 1$, then $\Delta A \geq \Delta N$, *the asset supply gets full price impact; even a small notional amount traded has a large price impact,*

If $L < 1$, then $\Delta A < \Delta N$; *the notional amount only develops a small price impact,*

If $L \rightarrow O$; *the asset supply has no price impact whatsoever.*

Exhibit 2.10   Liquidity mechanics and supply and demand

equivalent instruments. The Counterparty Risk Management Policy Group (CRMPG) evaluates funding risk by comparing the amount of cash available with respective payment requirements. It defines the funding liquidity ratio through the potential decline in the value of asset that may lead to cash flow needs, such as

$$Funding \ liquidity \ ratio = \frac{cash \ equivalent}{potential \ decline \ in \ value}.$$

Together with asset liquidity, funding liquidity constitutes the liquidity risk.

The duality of asset and funding liquidity

Liquidity risk is defined by the duality of asset and funding liquidity. Margin requirements, collateral agreements, leveraged trading positions, market-making as well as trading behaviour endorse funding liquidity, which may enforce an unwanted liquidation of assets. In situations of financial stress, the correlation between asset and funding liquidity leads to a systemic liquidity risk in form of a vicious liquidity cycle that implies large price volatilities. The association between asset and funding liquidity illustrates the complexity of the liquidity risk that is the result of the interaction between the two types of risk. Marking-to-market has been primarily developed to control credit risk. The problem is that such a procedure creates an additional cash flow risk because of margin calls that may force the institution to liquidate certain holdings at depressed prices, thereby creating asset liquidity risk.

Liquidity risk is a function of the uncertainty between the current unrealised value and the future liquidated value of an asset. Exogenous liquidity risk results from external economic factors that lead to a liquidity event and price impact with a specific state of illiquidity. Endogenous liquidity risk depends on individual liquidations of asset positions which, because of the size of the trading positions, lead to an intertemporal risk of the price process. The exogenous form of liquidity risk is common to all market players while the aggregated market behaviour is unaffected by actions of individual participants. During financial stress, however, exogenous liquidity might be affected by the joint action of all market participants. Endogenous form of the liquidity risk is specific to an asset position. It varies across market participants, and their movements affect the exposure of any participant. It reflects the price impact triggered by the execution of an individual trade for a given asset. It is mainly driven by the size of a position. The larger the size, the greater the risk. In tense market conditions, the exogenous liquidity risk becomes endogenous at an aggregated market level.

2.4.3   Market dislocations

Exogenous states of illiquidity result in market dislocations and price divergences regarding the theoretical fair value of an asset. A set of negative information has reached the financial system. It can be understood as an external shock that is changing market perceptions. During financial stress, this newly available set of information acts as a catalyst only. Once financial losses reach beyond a trigger point, the stress dynamics becomes self-sustaining. Markets dislocate until a new equilibrium can be found. Market dislocations are a supply and demand phenomenon and, as we previously outlined, an expression of liquidity adjustments. They lead to dynamic allocation mechanisms at an aggregated market level as a result of the increased risk aversion, the shortening of the investment horizon, and the negative financial impact on the wealth positions of the participants. The following discussion describes these dynamics.

Analytical framework

Richard Bookstaber introduces in his assessment of the liquidity crisis cycle three stages of market dislocations. The first stage is the trigger stage with a first loss due to external shocks or continuously diminishing expectations that trigger the initial price impact. The aggregated selling behaviour decreases asset demands and thus the liquidity in the market. Market prices tend to overreact when they converge towards the theoretical fair value, given there is a new set of available information (F). The second stage is the one of liquidation. Due to the external shock, dynamic allocation mechanisms and funding requirements of margin calls, collateral requirements and convex pay-off strategies lead to large asset sales. The price behaviour develops dynamically. The urgent need of aggressive liquidation becomes the core problem as soon as this critical trigger point is reached. Markets dislocate until they reach a new equilibrium and price point. The third stage is the one of technical rebound where long-term value investors start buying assets. The market prices readjust to their perceived (new) fair values, given that there is an indicative set of information available showing the economic profit potential as a discounted future income stream. With these three stages, market dislocation and financial stress can be assessed across a consistent framework.

These dynamic behaviours can be modelled in a simplified market structure with four classes of participants. The first class, noise traders, trade on short-term information. Their trading behaviour is not of common interest as long as it has no aggregated effects on the market as a whole. However, trading on rumours and taking short-term profit positions can have trend-supporting as well as destabilising effects on the financial system. The second class, securities dealers and their execution traders, perform voluntered market making and act in their liquidity function as supply-informed investors. Dynamic price investors as the third class follow convex pay-off strategies to protect their equity base such as pension funds and insurance companies. Their asset and liability structure, the legal and regulatory constraints of their trading environment, and the individual risk capacity of their business strategy demand capital preservation. They protect their capital by an extensive use of derivatives to hedge their positions. Although dynamic price investors view their asset allocations with a long-term perspective as a result of their funding obligations and liability structure, in a short-term perspective they orientate themselves on current market prices only. They are to be understood as uninformed investors, because in tense conditions they observe the asset price (A_t) only and ignore any signals and information regarding asset supplies and/or fair values. They may become price sensitive as a result of a decreased risk capacity and an increased need of funding liquidity. Finally, there are long-term value investors, who view the fundamentals of the asset price behaviour with a clear long-term perspective. They are price-informed investors with a sustainable risk capacity for large price movements and stress dynamics, as it is assumed that their long-term wealth position will not be affected.

Dynamic asset allocation

With the objective to manage their risk exposure, market participants follow three systematic strategies that lead to dynamic asset allocations. Core objective of these strategies is to get some sort of risk insurance in portfolios, intending to eliminate their exposure to market risk when the portfolio's value approaches a specified risk-tolerance floor. They are in turn willing to hold a substantial market risk when their portfolio's value is above the floor and lose the ability when the value is at or below the floor. The floor is set by an institution's risk capacity as a minimum level before the existence of the risk entity is endangered. For most financial institutions, the floor is defined by their liability structure and solvency profile.

Stop-loss strategies are the most rudimentary forms of these systematic strategies and can be characterised as a crude form of portfolio insurance. They are designed to overcome the uncertainty of the downside risk associated with trading positions. The stop-loss price triggers are defined by the risk-tolerance floor, and the sell transactions are executed when the value limits of the strategy are reached. Stop-loss strategies were widely used in the 1920s in order to hedge market risk or at least to lock in paper gains across a stair structure. The formation of the stair-structure might have contributed to the negative price dynamics of the stock market eruption in 1929. Although stop-loss trading is of a certain static nature, it has no directly observable ex-ante costs of implementation. It should, therefore, not be confused with static portfolio insurance.

Portfolio insurance is a more sophisticated risk instrument, which can be implemented either statically or dynamically. Static portfolio insurance uses options combined with linear instruments. Buying index call options combined with money market instruments (or holding cash) or index put options combined with risky asset positions provide the insurance holder with a capital guarantee. At an aggregated market level, the use of traded options has the advantage of the hedging amount being public information with an ex-ante anticipation of potential liquidity-related price dynamics. Dynamic portfolio insurance, on the other hand, uses a dynamic trading strategy in risk-free securities (cash or money market) and a risky portfolio (usually implemented via index futures) to synthesise the convex pay-off structure of a European put protection. The idea, initiated by the introduced Black-Scholes-Merton framework, shows that under the assumption of a perfect market, returns of any option can be replicated by an appropriate trading strategy that dynamically generates insured portfolio values. With dynamic portfolio insurance, there are no traded options needed to achieve insured portfolio values. The hedge amounts of dynamic portfolio insurance are nonpublic information and ex-ante nondeterminable, as they depend on the price behaviour. This implies an enormous liquidity risk in a market that is dynamically evolving during financial stress.

Value-at-risk (VaR) has become the risk management standard since the regulatory endorsement of the Basel framework by the 1990s. The concept will further be discussed in Chapter 3 on asset-liability management. VaR is a simple but transparent risk measure that allows aggregating different sensitivities across risk factors and asset classes.

It is defined by the maximum loss over a certain target horizon, so that there is only a low, prespecified probability that the actual loss will be larger. By controlling market risk, VaR aims to protect the equity base and the underlying capital. The target VaR is determined by the individual risk capacity of the entity. By signalling that the critical VaR is reached, risky asset positions are liquidated to adjust to the appropriate risk levels. If several institutions follow the same indicators of their risk management systems (which must be assumed given the regulatory requirements), not only the application of the risk methodology is standardised but also the risk behaviour. The standardised risk perception results in an aggregated risk behaviour, which has a market impact similar to the one of positive dynamic feedback trading. During market eruptions with large volatilities, VaR induces and enforces the liquidation of asset positions, which potentially exacerbates the stress dynamics and market dislocations.

Dynamic feedback loops

In case of an external shock, acting as trigger event, dynamic asset allocation leads to feedback loop with the potential to dislocate financial markets. To further illustrate the dynamics, we need to distinguish between negative and positive feedback trading. Negative feedback traders buy assets when prices are falling and sell assets when prices are rising. They act contrary to the market, which provides liquidity and stabilises asset prices. Positive feedback traders, on the other hand, sell assets when prices are falling and buy assets when prices are rising. They are trend-supporting, which has dynamic effects on asset prices and leads to a liquidity shock. The difference between positive and negative is purely dogmatic and depends on the state of trading, on the investors' preferences, and their risk capacities. A trader can be a positive feedback trader in one asset and a negative feedback trader in another. Asset liquidity, however, is an aggregated function of positive and negative feedback trading. Liquidity is provided when financial markets are dominated by negative feedback trading. Markets become illiquid when they are dominated by positive feedback trading. In a liquid market, negative feedback traders outweigh positive feedback traders, market price fluctuations are reduced, and liquidity does not dry up in the wake of an external shock. Liquidity is at risk of drying up when positive feedback traders become more important in relation to negative feedback traders. Financial market liquidity collapses when the number of positive feedback traders outweighs the number of negative feedback traders. Trading positions can no longer be liquidated at their fair values. The results are price discounts and higher transaction costs.

Dynamic price investors aim to protect their capital base via futures and options markets which are extremely price sensitive. The faster asset prices drop due to negative expectations of further downturns the more hedging strategies are implemented. These hedging activities (π) within convex pay-off strategies depend on current asset prices (A_t). $\pi(A_t)$ denotes the asset supply related to such convex pay-off strategies. The strategies are implemented dynamically and depend on the state of trading and hence the asset price (A_t) itself. The supply of assets from these strategies is therefore a known function of the asset price and can be mathematically modelled as a decreasing differentiable function of A_t. It is a net demand of dynamic price investors is given by

$$D = \pi(A).$$

The liquidity price impacts of the hedging strategies will be fully transmitted to the real underlying securities because the financial institutions that provide the derivative positions will always follow a market-neutral strategy. If the financial institution has a specific trading position because of a specific long or short position, it will continuously take an offsetting position to neutralise its exposure and hence become delta neutral. We assume that securities dealers in a specific asset position have an initial trading position (m) and that this position is more or less constant in normal market conditions. For reasons of simplicity, we further assume that one and the same institution takes the role of the securities dealer for both the derivatives and the underlying assets. The value of the securities dealer's position is given by the initial amount in the fundamental asset and in the delta-neutral asset position, which will continuously be adjusted, mathematically expressed as

$$D = m + \pi(A).$$

During financial stress, continuous activities of hedging strategies lead to path dependency of prices, which is further enforced by noise trading. Noise traders act on short profit opportunities, which can be trend-supporting and which encourages liquidation. Securities dealers will transmit the price impact of their hedging activities to the spot market of the underlying asset. In the trigger and liquidation stage, all three classes act as positive feedback traders and no one is willing to buy assets, which implies an oversupply in assets and thus a large risk of liquidation. These activities turn into a vicious cycle that will be stopped only when the total amount of risky assets in the portfolios is sold. The only investors that are willing to buy asset positions and thereby provide liquidity to the market are the long-term value investors. Because of the divergence of the market-traded asset price from its fair value, long-term value investors see a profit opportunity that should pay off in the long run. After strong waves of asset-selling, there are usually technical rebounds, because market-traded asset prices have diverged from their fair values. The long-term profit opportunity in the divergence in fundamentals should justify the risk positions. Once markets have turned, noisy traders will buy assets on short-term profit opportunities. Finally, dynamic value investors will have to increase their quotas in risky asset positions to get them in line with their long-term asset allocations.

The negative capital effect

During financial stress, the sudden need for funding liquidity as well as the decreased risk capacity demand an adjustment of the long-term asset allocation and its risk exposure. This may result in a price collapse at aggregated market levels when certain trading situations become unsustainable. The negative capital effect occurs when dynamic price investors suffer losses and liquidate some of their positions in response to their reduced risk-bearing capacity. Negative stress dynamics undermine the goals of a long-term asset allocation for investor classes that have a short-term risk exposure such as margin requirements or other forms of payment liabilities. Other technical liquidity restrictions are mainly enforced by legal and regulatory constraints (e.g. solvency ratios as defined by regulations such as Solvency II), the accounting system (e.g. mark-to-market requirements as defined by IFRS 9), and the discussed risk management methods. The dynamics of the technical liquidity constraints result in the notion of the negative capital effect. The negative capital effect defines the forced liquidation of asset positions due to negative price dynamics and an increase in price volatility. As a result of the negative capital effect, the risk capacity decreases, the point of endangerment is reached, and risky asset positions must be liquidated.

The more the capital positions of dynamic price investors decline with the negative price dynamics, the more risk averse they become in their trading behaviour. As their capital position declines towards a certain point of endangerment (e.g. a minimum solvency ratio), price dynamic investors become continuously risk-averse, which reaches infinity when their capital position gets close to zero. The point of endangerment represents a trigger point that questions the sustainability of the trading position. In risk management terminology, it reflects the maximum VaR and the minimum risk capacity of dynamic price investors. When the minimum risk capacity is reached, the fulfilment of payment liabilities and future consumption become endangered and asset positions must be liquidated. Short-term trading or long-term asset allocation decisions become unsustainable. To prevent their capital position from reaching the point of endangerment or becoming negative, dynamic price investors will use the liquidity provided by long-term investors to liquidate their risky positions. The state variable which constitutes the equilibrium of the asset market and from which the price pressure develops during negative price dynamics (stress) is the aggregated capital position of the dynamic price investors (W). The negative dynamics are enforced by the level of noise trading (γ). To explain the dynamics between the point of endangerment (ψ), capital (C), and the inherent price shock, we follow the mathematical interpretation of Sanford J. Grossman[8] that applies a partial differential equation formally expressed as

$$dr = \mu(\psi, C)dt + \sigma_A(\psi, C)dz_u + \sigma_\gamma(\gamma, C)dz_u,$$

where dr = excess return in continuous time, μ = expected return, σ = standard deviation, dt = level of uncertainty, ψ = point of endangerment, W = wealth position, A = asset price, and γ = level of noise trading.

The level of uncertainty in the negative asset price dynamics arises from the negative capital positions as price dynamic investors see their asset positions declining towards the point of endangerment. These negative dynamics are further enforced by the momentum trading of noise traders. Because of the negative dynamics, investors' preferences become biased towards risk-free assets. In these situations, there is no rational reason to buy assets, as the institutional factor prices have a downward bias. The uncertainty suddenly becomes so strong that future developments can no longer be judged. The tremendous increase in the implied volatility of option prices is generally an indicator for uncertainty in price dynamics and hedging activities. As a result, asset prices become path dependent to the point where the divergences in relation to the fair values become so large that the excess returns justify changing momentum strategies and buying the assets as a short-term trading opportunity.

Technical liquidity constraints of institutional and individual liquidity constraints of private investors can lead to dynamic allocation behaviour and hence market dislocations. To protect their capital base, dynamic price investors follow convex

---

[8] See Sanford J. Grossmann's publications from 1988 in the Journal of Business "An Analysis of the Implication for Stock and Future Price Volatility of Program Trading and Dynamic Hedging Strategies" and in the Journal of Portfolio Management "Insurance Seen and Unseen: The Impact on Markets".

pay-off strategies. The larger the price drop, the more aggressive their hedging and risk mitigation activities. This is a result of an increase in risk aversion when the point of endangerment is reached and the required risk capacity of a sustainable asset allocation is no longer assured. In such situations, liquidation is the only strategy to preserve the individual capital base and to guarantee a sustainable asset allocation. The negative capital effect shows that not all asset price volatility is explained by fundamentals, that conditional correlations between asset returns are not necessarily constant, and that variations in correlations are not explained by information filtration only.

2.4.4 Systemic crises

Market dislocations can quickly evolve to a systemic crisis through broader panic in the financial system. Liquidity problems may lead to a full-blown banking crisis, transmitting dislocations in supply and demand to a mismatch of assets and liabilities via the balance sheets of financial institutions. Given their role in the financial system, banks are exposed and very sensitive towards the broader dynamics in the financial system. Systematic banking crises are an important subset of financial crises in which all banking activities are getting impacted and restricted. Given the importance of the financial system for the broader economic system, the collapse or potential collapse through panic and bank runs at systemically important financial institutions is an important cornerstone in the evolution of the world history's most severe financial and economic crises. Economic downturn and depressions have usually coincided with the collapse of the banking system. The financial literature further distinguished between currency crises and sovereign defaults, illustrated by the dynamics of the Asian crises of 1997–1998, although both of them impact and are impacted by the dynamics of banks' balance sheets, eventually leading to the collapse of the financial system. In modern history, there has been a series of banking crises that have been systemically important for the financial and broader economic system and may have even affected the outcome of world history. They can be used as case studies with the objective to extrapolate common factors from a macro-historical perspective, using past events to determine root causes and patterns through a comparison of proximate details while establishing a financial decision-making framework as core objective of this chapter. The objective is to use historical analysis to enhance the models of economic and financial theory when the limits of the mathematical properties are reached.

The anatomy of historical crises

This following section assumes that the macro-historical processes of financial crises repeat themselves in explainable and tangible ways. We selected four historical banking crises from the United States to illustrate how banking crises evolve as part of broader financial turmoil. The objective here is to establish another decision layer for business transformation and value creation. Since the end of the Civil War in the second part of the 19th century, the United States has been at the front end of economic, financial, and technology development and become by far the world's largest economy. The four selected crises allow to describe the impact of market dislocations and how financial volatility evolves to a broader panic and bank run. The complexity of currency and foreign debt dynamics can be neglected given the size and structure of the US economy which is often an important part of financial crises in particular in emerging markets (e.g. Mexican peso crisis or the previously mentioned Asian crises of the 1990s) but also in Europe (e.g. the Scandinavian banking crises of the 1990s). This approach allows us to conclude on the evolutionary role of those crises for today's financial system.

The bank panic of 1907

The bank panic of 1907 is a classic case of how deteriorating market liquidity and falling depositor confidence can lead to a bank run. The increased public scrutiny in unregulated trust companies triggered a run on them, followed by a broader mistrust in the banking system. The crisis eventually led to the development of the Federal Reserve System (Fed) in 1913 after a comprehensive framework of monetary policy and reform in the banking system was shelved for more than five years.

The crisis occurred during a period of six weeks in autumn 1907. The trigger was bankruptcy of two minor brokerage firms, F. Augustus Heinze and Charles Morse, after a failed attempt to buy up shares of a copper mining firm resulted in a run on banks associated with them. The contagion further spread to trust companies that were already under high public scrutiny. The Knickerbocker Trust Company, New York City's third-largest trust, was unable to withstand the run and failed in late October. Initially, the panic was centred in New York City but it eventually spread to other economic centres across the United States. Without an established central bank system, leading financiers such as J.P. Morgan and John D. Rockefeller had to step in and provided vital liquidity. It was ultimately quelled when the federal government provided over US$30 million in aid, and J.P. Morgan and others continued orchestrating deals to bring confidence and liquidity back to the financial markets.

Great crash and depression of 1929–1936

The Great Depression of 1929–1936 was a worldwide economic downturn that began with the great crash on 24 October 1929 known as Black Thursday after the decade of the roaring twenties that followed World War I. Although it originated in the United States, the Great Depression caused drastic declines in output, severe unemployment, and acute deflation in almost every country of the world. Its social and cultural effects were staggering, especially in the United States, where the Great Depression represented the harshest adversity faced by the Americans people since the Civil War. It may also have been a root cause for the ascension of Adolf Hitler and the Nazi regime to power in Germany which led to the outbreak of World War II in Europe.

It is a great case study to illustrate how market dislocations and the unwinding of leveraged asset position can lead to a sharp economic downturn and widespread financial despair, following a period of innovation, optimism, wealth excess, and overproduction in agriculture and rapidly expanding industrial production during which the economy grew by over 40%. The developments started as in early September when the London Stock Exchange (LSE) was sent into a tailspin after the collapse of the Hatry group. On Black Thursday, share prices on the New York Stock Exchange collapsed by 11% at the opening bell on large trading volumes. The deleveraging and restrictive policy responses led to the most devastating economic conditions across the United States, accompanied by bank runs and economic contractions. With his New Deal, President

Franklin D. Roosevelt proposed a fundamental reform of the economic and political structure in combination with a strong fiscal program. The economy recovered slowly in a volatile fashion until World War II erupted in Europe and the world moved into another period of political and economic uncertainty.

The US savings and loan crisis of the 1980s and 1990s

The savings and loans crisis (S&L crisis) in the United States took place from 1986 to 1995 during which the Federal Savings and Loan Insurance Corporation (FSLIC) closed almost 300 banks and the Resolution Trust Corporation (RTC), a specially created asset management company, resolved over 700 institutions additionally. The S&L crisis led the cornerstone and principles for modern bank resolution and the management of distressed assets. An S&L association is a financial institution in the United States that accepts savings deposits and makes mortgage, car, and other personal loans to individual members. In European countries, their mostly know as cooperatives and building societies. S&L went through a boom and it became part of the American dream to have one's own house and property, accelerated with several domestic spending programs of President Lyndon B. Johnson's "Great Society" programs. Inflation picked up in the 1970s, further accelerated by the high military expenses of the Vietnam War and the oil price shock. At the same time, the S&L industry was deregulated, leading to relaxed business, financing, and lending conditions combined with fraudulent behaviour of some participants.

In 1979, the Fed under chairman Paul Volcker raised its discount rate aggressively in an effort to bring the inflation down. S&Ls faced a completely changed financing conditions. They previously had issued long-term loans at fixed interest rates that were lower than the interest rate at which they could borrow. Furthermore, the S&Ls had the liability of the deposits which paid higher interest rates than the rate at which they could borrow. The industry could no longer attract adequate capital to continue its operations and became insolvent. Rather than admit to insolvency, the lax regulatory oversight allowed several institutions to invest in highly speculative investment strategies such as junk bonds. This had the effect of extending the period where S&Ls were most likely insolvent. These adverse actions also substantially increased the economic losses for the S&Ls than would otherwise have been realized had their insolvency been discovered earlier.

The Global Financial Crisis of 2007–2015

The GFC crisis began in the summer of 2007 with the collapse of the subprime mortgage market in the United States that led to the close-down of several specialised purposed vehicles (SPV), followed by strong market volatility. With the collapse of the investment bank Lehman Brothers on 15 September 2008, these dynamics developed into a global banking crisis. As this book covers in all details, it led to a completely changed business environment and competitive landscape driven by regulations and technology change.

To understand the origins of the GFC, we need to go back as far as the 1980 when a wave of deregulation began in the United Kingdom, Europe, and the United States. The Big Bang of 1986, effected by British government under Margaret Thatcher, made London the international hub for financial innovation through derivatives trading, securitisation, and other complex financial instruments. The initiatives to support the US mortgage market under President Bill Clinton's administration through the government-sponsored enterprises (GSE) Fannie Mae, the Federal National Mortgage Association (FNMA), and Freddie Mac, the Federal Home Loan Mortgage Corp (FHLMC) built the base for the boom in subprime mortgage, further supported by securitised and exotics products (e.g. collateralised debt obligations [CDO]) that were developed by the banking industry. Financial institutions invested in these products and took excessive risks which led to a global boom in asset prices until the sharp price depreciation and market dislocation that started in 2007. The bankruptcy of Lehman Brothers in September 2008 was followed by substantial bailouts and other supportive monetary as well as fiscal policy programmes to prevent a possible collapse of the world financial system. Nevertheless, the global economic downturn led to the European debt crisis which impacted the banking system in Southern European countries in particular, threatening the existence of the Eurozone.

Macro-historical conclusions for financial decision making

Financial crises are preceded by a time of economic excess triggered by technology and financial innovation, often accompanied by broader social and cultural change. The bank panic of 1907 was preceded by the Gilded Age during which monopolies like Standard Oil dominated the economy, and led to the concentration of wealth among select individuals. The great crash and depression followed the decade of the roaring twenties subsequent to World War I. Similarly, the periods before the S&L crisis and GFC were characterized by loose fiscal or monetary policy and high profitability in the financial sector.

These economic booms are accompanied by heavy borrowing and leverage which may lead to an asset bubble that usually lasts for a surprisingly long time while all warning signs are ignored. If leverage goes unchecked, financial stability becomes increasingly fragile with huge dependence on asset price levels. Both before the great crash and GFC, there were fundamental beliefs that financial stability was high in unprecedented ways as historical quotes from Irving Fisher and Alan Greenspan illustrate. As the financial system deleverages, corporate and individual balance sheets come under substantial pressures, leading to defaults. These waves of defaults undermine the balance sheets of financial institutions which can trigger bank runs and lead to systemic crises. The events in 1907 and in the 1930s led to closure of banks whilst in more recent times, central banks and government authorities stepped in to stabilise the system. It may have been a God-given sign (or Alan Greenspan's magic touch) that with Ben Bernanke, a former academic with core interests in the great depression, was appointed shortly before the GFC to chair the Fed. The Fed as well as the European Central Bank responded with aggressive monetary stimulus from lowering interest rates to quantitative easing. Broader asset reliefs and resolution programs were initiated, and the G20 proposed a fundamental regulatory reform. In general, the aftermath of a crises is dominated by new regulatory and financial policy in a political attempt to reform the financial system structurally and deal with broader social and economic fallouts. The 1907 bank run led to the creation of the Fed while the recession of the GFC prompted new reforms like Basel III. These mechanisms intend to protect the broader public from a financial meltdown and hinder the big banks from taking unreasonable risks.

RESOURCES AND FURTHER READING

Ahamed Liaquat (2020). *Lords of Finance: The Bankers Who Broke the World*; The Penguin Press.

Alber, Robert Z. and Charles P. Kindleberger (2015). *Manias, Panics and Crashes: A History of Financial Crises*; Palgrave Macmillan.

Bernanke, Ben (2015). *The Courage to Act*; W.W. Norton & Company.

Bernanke, Ben, Timothy F. Geithner and Henry M. Paulson (2019). *Firefighting—The Financial Crisis and Its Lessons*; Penguin Books.

Bookstaber, Richard (2017). *The End of Theory—Financial Crises, the Failure of Economics, and the Sweep of Human Interaction*; Princeton University Press.

Chancellor, Edward (1998). *Devil Take the Hindmost. A History of Financial Speculation*; Farrar, Strauss and Giroux.

Cochrane, John N. (2001). *Asset Pricing*; Princeton University Press.

Copeland, Thomas, J. Fred Weston and Kuldeep Shastri (2014). *Financial Theory and Corporate Policy*; Pearson.

Dalio, Ray (2018). *Big Debt Crises*; Bridgewater.

Damodaran, Aswath (2012). *Investment Valuation*; Wiley.

Ferguson, Niall (2012). *The Ascent of Money: A Financial History of the World*; Penguin Books.

Geithner, Timothy F. (2014). *Stress Test*; Broadway Books.

Goetzmann, William N. (2016). *Money Changes Everything: How Finance Made Civilization Possible*; Princeton University Press.

Graham, Benjamin and David Dodd (2008). *Security Analysis*; McGraw Hill.

Ingersoll, Jonathan E. (1987). *Theory of Financial Decision Making*; Rowman & Littlefield.

Jorion, Philippe (2006). *Value at Risk: The New Benchmark for Managing Financial Risk*; 3rd Edition, McGraw-Hill.

Jorion, Philippe (2013). *Financial Risk Manager Handbook*; Wiley Finance.

Karatzas, Ioannis and Steven Shreve (2001). *Methods of Mathematical Finance*; Applications of Mathematics #39, Springer.

King, Mervyn (2016). *The End of Alchemy—Money, Banking and the Future of the Global Economy*; Little Brown.

Koller, Tim, Marc Goedhart and David Wessels (2020). *Valuation*; Wiley.

Lowenstein, Roger (2014). *When Genius Failed: The Rise and Fall of Long-Term Capital Management*; Random House.

Malkiel, Burton G. (2019). *A Random Walk Down Wall Street*; W.W. Norton & Company.

Neftci, S. H. (2002). *An Introduction to the Mathematics of Financial Derivatives*; 2nd Edition, Academic Press.

Paulson, Henry, Jr (2010). *On the Brink*; Business Plus.

Pignataro, Paul (2013). *Financial Modeling & Valuation*; Wiley.

Reinhart, Carmen M. and Kenneth S. Rogoff (2009). *This Time Is Different*; Princeton University Press.

Rosenbaum, Joshua and Joshua Pearl (2013). *Investment Banking*; Wiley.

Ruetschi, Joerg (2005). *Liquidity in Financial Markets: Theory and Application in the Swiss Securities Market Structure*; Haupt.

Ruttiens, Alain (2013). *Mathematics of the Financial Markets*; Wiley Finance.

Stewart, G. B. (1999). *The Quest for Value*; HarperCollins.

Taleb, Nassim N. (1998). *Fooled by Randomness: The Hidden Role of Chance in Life and in the Markets*; Penguin.

Taleb, Nassim N. (2008). *The Black Swan: The Impact of the Highly Improbable*; Penguin.

CHAPTER 3

Asset-liability Management

The transfer and management of risk are the fundamental value drivers of the financial industry. Balance-sheet strength and risk management are the key capabilities of a successful financial institution model. Asset-liability management (ALM) is the discipline within financial institutions to manage and optimise the balance sheet with its funding requirements, as well as managing and mitigating risk and respective exposure. It is usually organised as a separate function within the finance and risk department and works across the lending and trading activities. This chapter discusses the transfer of risk with its core principles and pricing fundamentals. It covers the discipline of financial engineering with the implications for risk and capital management as well as regulations. The introduction of different financial instruments and their innovative journey over the last 20 years provide the background to understand the regulatory environment that emerged after the Global Financial Crisis (GFC) under the umbrella of the Basel accord.

3.1 RISK TRANSFER

Risk transfer is the fundamental concept and core function that drives financial institutions. Risk by itself can be defined in various ways and often refers to the uncertainty of an outcome. Our working definition focuses on the probability of an event that allows one to quantify the compensation for transferring risk between parties. The following section applies this definition and develops a framework to price and transfer risk across business functions.

3.1.1 Principles of risk-taking

Financial institutions are defined by their risk-taking capabilities with its core functions of lending and credit underwriting, securities trading, and marketing as well as asset management. Risk-taking is shaped by economic, regulatory, and accounting requirements and their underlying constraints. Behind each risk-taking activity, there must be a sound capital base. The type of risk taken has to be fundamentally understood, which can be attained by assessing the right price and understanding the different sensitivities around it. The price of risk must be transparently reflected in management and accounting systems, following the requirements of a consistent mark-to-market valuation. This allows active management of the risk with available financial instruments as the underlying risk-taking assumptions may change.

Lending and underwriting consist of the activities of origination, risk analysis, pricing, underwriting, risk management, and workout. Origination refers to the client interaction of bringing a financing opportunity to a financial institution. The steps of risk analysis, pricing underwriting, and risk management are part of the risk-transfer process that are covered in this chapter. Recovery is part of a workout and is covered in Chapter 5 on turnaround and transformation. The quantitative and qualitative analysis that drives the risk-taking decision is called credit scoring. It is further defined by the lending policies that are set in accordance with the risk appetite and profile of a financial institution. Traditional lending has been disintermediated through direct lending by alternative players such as hedge and private equity funds, insurance companies, and securitisation. This has been a result of higher capital requirements that have constrained credit underwriting from the traditional banks. Technology innovation, driven by machine learning (ML) and applied analytics, has led to substantial efficiency gain in lending and underwriting as will be further discussed in Chapter 4.

Securities trading and marketing enclose the activities of buying and selling financial instruments such as cash and derivatives products, raising funding, and managing risk. It incorporates making a market for those instruments, actively taking and positioning risks while facilitating client transactions across fixed income, currency, commodity, and equity products. Asset management is a broad term that includes the professional management of various asset classes in order to meet specified investment objectives such as specific return targets, liabilities matching, and portfolio diversification, depending on the individual requirements of institutions or private individuals. It is often used in reference to the investment management of collective investment funds (also called mutual funds in the United States), endowment funds, and other institutional arrangements. Private wealth management, on the other hand, refers to private client money.

Specialty finance refers to specific situations in transferring risk across project, object, commodities finance, and other specialised operations. Project finance is a method of funding in which the lender looks primarily to the revenues generated by a single project such as infrastructure, both as the source of repayment and as security for the exposure. Object finance refers to the acquisition of usually capital intensive physical assets such ships, aircraft, and fleets for which the cash flow generated by the assets has been pledged to the lender. Commodities finance refers to short-term lending and finance arrangements of reserves, inventories, and receivables of exchange-traded commodities where the exposure will be repaid from the proceeds of the sale of the commodity. However, the term specialty finance is applied broadly today, referring to asset-based lending, supply chain finance, factoring, and invoicing that have now become more accessible to a broader base of participants due to technology advancements. The term is used not only in specialised lending but also insurance and other risk-transfer businesses. Chapter 7 discusses the increasing importance of specialty-finance businesses in the post-GFC financial system.

3.1.2   The pricing taxonomy of risk

There are different types of risks which can be classified in accordance with their underlying asset classes as macro and micro risks. Macro risks are interest-rate, currency, and commodity exposures as they are driven by macroeconomic and political events.

Micro risks such as credit and equity are driven by entrepreneurial risks on a microeconomic level. Many investment banks organise their risk-taking businesses accordingly. Credit and equity traders, for instance, sit together to make sure that no arbitrage opportunities remain unassessed.

The relationship between credit and equity risk is well understood and documented in academic literature as we covered previously in Chapter 2. To establish a taxonomy remains crucial to understand the different components of a respective risk exposure which builds the base to price risk in the right format. Later in this chapter under the Basel framework, we further discuss the classification of credit, market, liquidity, and funding risk in accordance with the respective regulatory methodology. The following sections develop a consistent framework for the quantitative assessment of risk, following a macro and micro taxonomy. The focus remains on core or conventional risk factors in banking and trading books, consisting of interest rate, foreign exchange (FX), commodity, credit, and equity risk. Each form of risk needs to be classified with its underlying component understood with the objective to establish a coherent framework to price it.

Interest-rate risk

Interest-rate risk describes the risk that arises from fluctuating interest rates. Whilst it can be defined as the most fundamental form of financial risk, it is the most challenging one to manage. One challenge is that there are many different interest rates, such as deposit, prime, treasury, interbank borrowing and lending, and swap, in any given currency. Although these rates tend to move together, they are not perfectly correlated. The yield curve or term structure of interest rates provides the base for this analysis in describing the interest-rate environment across the term structure with its different rate levels. With the different rates across maturities, there are many variables, and their movement and correlation to each other have to be considered. The liquidity preference theory states that long-term rates tend to be higher than those predicted by expected future short-term rates. The term structure may invert though when a steep decline of interest rates is expected.

For banking businesses, the management of net interest income margin (NIM) is a key risk management activity. NIM is similar to the gross profit margin at nonfinancial institutions and measures the excess of interest income generated (i.e. the interest received) over the amount of interest paid, relative to the amount of interest-earning assets. It is usually expressed as a percentage of the earning of a loan in a time period and other assets minus the interest paid on borrowed funds divided by the average amount of the assets on which it earned income in that time period. It is the role of the ALM function within the bank to ensure that the NIM remains stable through time. The financial instruments introduced in the following section provide the tool set to manage the risk. Before providing the tool set to manage interest rate risk, the underlying rates and benchmarks as well as the valuation, pricing, and risk metrics need to be thoroughly understood.

Interest-rate benchmarks

There are a variety of different interest rates depending on currencies, financial systems, and respective customs. With the application of derivatives instruments, underlying price reference or benchmarks became crucial elements of the financial system. The following section provides an overview of the respective interest-rate references.

Government and central bank rates

Government interest rates (or short government rates) are the rates that investors earn on government securities such as Treasury bills and bonds in the United States, Gilts in the United Kingdom, Bunds in Germany, and OATs in France. These rates are based on the instruments that are used by governments to borrow in their own currency. It is usually assumed that there is no or a very limited chance that a government will default on an obligation denominated on its own currency, and government rates are usually referred to as risk-free rates.

The Overnight Indexed Swap (OIS) rate is a swap where the legs are based on the geometric average of overnight unsecured lending between banks in the government-organised interbank market where banks with excess reserves lend to banks that need to borrow to meet reserve requirements. The effective rate on a particular day is the weighted average of the overnight rates paid by borrowing to lending banks on that respective day. In the United States and hence for the US dollar (USD), the overnight borrowing rate is known as the Federal Funds rate (Secured Overnight Financing Rate), in the EU for the Euro (EUR) as Euro Overnight Index Average (Eonia), and in the United Kingdom for Pound Sterling (GBP) as Sterling Overnight Index Average (Sonia). An OIS is an IRS where the periodic floating payment is generally based on a return calculated by the compounded rate of the overnight rate in respective currency. Accordingly, an OIS allows overnight borrowing and lending to be swapped at a fixed rate for a period of time, for example, one month, three months, and so on. This fixed rate is known as the OIS rate.

OIS rates have the advantage that they are set off the federal funds effective rate, which is an overnight rate based on a volume-weighted average of trades that occur each trading day through the major brokers. OIS is also considered to be less risky than the corresponding interbank rate (London Interbank Offered Rate [LIBOR]) because there is limited counterparty risk. For illustration, LIBOR is set once a day by the British Bankers' Association (BBA), which publishes the rate after asking 16 member banks how much it would cost to borrow from each other in a range of currencies. The Federal Reserve, on the other hand, uses the one-month OIS rate to set the minimum bid level when it lends cash to banks through its term auction facility. The latter gives market participants a better idea of where the lending and borrowing level between banks is and it is a market-traded price.

The LIBOR–OIS spread is the difference between LIBOR and the OIS rates. The spread between the two rates is considered to be a measure of health of the banking system. It is an important measure of risk and liquidity in the money market and considered to be a strong indicator for the relative stress in short-term money markets. A higher spread is an indication of a decreased willingness to lend by major banks, while a lower spread indicates higher liquidity in the market. As such, the spread can be viewed as indication of banks' perception of the creditworthiness of other financial institutions and the general availability of funds for lending purposes. The LIBOR–OIS spread has historically averaged around 10 basis points (bps). However, in the midst of the GFC after the default of Lehman Brothers in October 2008, the spread spiked to more than 360 bps, exhibiting the seriousness of the credit crunch and the overall risk to financial stability.

London Interbank Offered Rate

The LIBOR is a daily reference rate based on the interest rates at which banks offer to lend unsecured funds to other banks in the London wholesale money market, the so-called interbank market. LIBOR will be slightly higher than the London Interbank Bid Rate (LIBID), the rate at which banks are prepared to accept deposits. During 1984 it became apparent that an increasing number of banks were trading actively in a variety of relatively new market instruments, notably interest-rate swaps (IRS), currency options, and forward rate agreements (FRA). Whilst recognizing that such instruments brought more business and greater depth to the London interbank market, it was felt that future growth could be inhibited unless a measure of uniformity was introduced. In late 1984, the BBA established various working groups that eventually culminated in the definition of a standard for interest settlement rates, a predecessor of LIBOR. It soon after became the market standard.

As of January 1986, LIBOR fixings started and provided a new reference benchmark for the decades to come. LIBOR is often used as a rate of reference for GBP and other currencies, including the USD, EUR, Japanese Yen (JPY), Swiss Franc (CHF), and many others. It is published by the BBA after 11 a.m. each day, London time, and is a filtered average of interbank deposit rates offered by designated contributor banks, for maturities ranging from overnight to one year. There are 16 contributor banks and the reported interest is the mean of the eight middle values. The actual rate at which banks will lend to one another will, however, continue to vary throughout the day.

Since the outbreak of the GFC, Libor has been called into question since the Bank for International Settlements stated that some lenders may have understated borrowing costs to hide their true financial situation. Criminal investigations in LIBOR manipulation by several large financial institutions followed. Market participants started to use alternative measures for borrowing costs and a series of reforms were initiated by regulators. After years of back and forth, the Financial Conduct Authority announced in July 2017 that the benchmark will be phased out by 2021 and alternative OIS-based reference rates are being set up for the different currencies.

Valuing interest-rate instruments

The price of an interest-rate instrument is simply the present value of its future cash-flow stream, discounted at the required rate of return that is called the yield to maturity (YTM). The following sections cover the yield curve with its respective specifications and pricing principles.

Yield-to-maturity

The YTM is defined as the internal rate of return (IRR) earned by an investor who buys the instrument today at the market price, assuming that it is held until maturity and that all coupon and principal payments are made on schedule. It is equal to discount rate at which the sum of all its future cash flows, that is, the return that equals coupons and principal to its current price. It is a blend of the risk-free rate (i.e. a government rate) and credit spread of the specific instrument. The YTM is often given in terms of annual percentage rate but more often specific market conventions are followed. Day count convention determines how interest accrues over time for a variety of interest-rate instruments. For example, it defines the amount when a fixed-income instrument is sold between interest payment dates, the seller is eligible for some fraction of the coupon amount. The day count convention calculates the number of days between coupon payments and determines the amount transferred on payment dates and also the accrued interest for dates between payments. It is used to quantify periods of time when discounting a cash flow to its present value. The International Swaps and Derivatives Association (ISDA) in particular has worked to standardise the terminology across different markets. The year is counted as 360 days or 365 days while fractions of a year may be counted as a number of days that can be based on the actual (ACT) number of days, or on full months of 30 days plus actual number of days for a fraction of a month. Money-market instruments are usually calculated ACT/360, swap rates 30/360, and US Government Treasury Bonds ACT/365 while EUR Government Bonds are ACT/ACT.

Yield curve

Any fixed-income instrument such as a government or corporate bond is to be seen as a package of cash flows. Each cash flow can be viewed as a zero-coupon instrument, with the maturity the date that the cash flow will be paid and the maturity value equal to the cash. The value of the instrument is then equal to the total value of all zero-coupon instruments whilst the value of each zero-coupon instrument is determined in turn by discounting its maturity value at a rate that is unique to that zero-coupon instrument. To value a fixed-income instrument, we need to determine zero-coupon rates across the different maturities which constitute the yield curve. To value default-free cash flows, theoretical basic rates for different maturities are required. These basic or spot interest rates constitute the yield curve and as we discussed are zero-coupon rates. They fluctuate with macro- or microeconomic developments only and are, in risk terminology, an expression of pure interest-rate risk.

The yield curve is the graphical depiction of the relationship between the yield to maturity on securities of the same credit risk and different maturity. The basic/spot rates should be derived from highly rated government securities because these instruments are generally perceived as being free of credit risk. In theory, there can be any yield curve derived for zero-coupons as well as coupon paying bonds with different credit ratings. In the United States where a very liquid Treasury market exists, the yield curve can be constructed from the maturity and observed yield of Treasury securities because Treasuries reflect the pure effect of maturity alone on yield, given the market participants do not perceive government securities to have any credit risk. In a process called STRIP, coupons are removed from a bond and then the separate parts are sold as a zero-coupon bond and an interest-paying coupon bond. However, there are only a few, very illiquid zero notes and bonds available whilst transaction costs can make it impossible to use STRIPS. The yield curve is therefore either derived from zero-coupon rates of traded zero-coupon bonds or approximated by mathematical methods such as bootstrapping. These methods allow the construction of the theoretical basic/spot curve from observed yields-to-maturity that do not exist in reality.

Bootstrapping describes the methodology for deriving the zero-coupon forward and spot yield curve from the prices of a set of interest-rate instruments with coupons such as bonds and swaps. It is an iterative process in which yields are solved recursively by using prices of instruments to receive specific spot rates (s) when the same instruments are valued using the entire curve across maturities. Some European government bond markets are not very liquid so that on-the-market swap rates (z) are used for bootstrapping. For further illustration, we are using the on-the market swap rate as the fixed leg of the swap is equal to a coupon-paying par bond so that the swap rate approximates the yield and coupon of a very liquid par bond. This is formally described as

$$d_1(1 + s_1) = 1,$$

which leads for the two-year swap rate to

$$d_1 \times s_2 + d_2 \times (1 + s_2) = 1,$$

and n-year swap rate to

$$d_1 \times s_2 + \ldots + d_n \times (1 + s_n) = 1.$$

More generally, this can be expressed as

$$d_t = \frac{1 - \left(s_t \times \sum_1^{T-1} d_t\right)}{1 + s_t},$$

whereas d = discount factor and s = spot rate which is equal to z = swap rate.

Another widely used mathematical method for yield-curve approximation is cubic spline interpolation which reduces the effects of overfitting. There are a number of different yield-structure models proposed in the academic literature such as the ones with normally distributed rates of Ho-Lee, Hull-White, and Heath-Jarrow-Morton; the one with lognormally distributed rates of Black-Derman-Toy; and the widely used equilibrium models of Vasicek, Cox-Ingersoll-Ross, and Longstaff-Schwartz.

Forward rates

The forward curve applies the same bootstrapping methodologies, taking into account the different forward rates across the yield curve. From the spot and previously defined zero-coupon rate curve, we can infer implied forward rates of the term structure, which are rates that start at a future date and make an investor indifferent between the two alternative investments on the yield curve. Market participants can observe forward rates and implied expectations easily, which allows a dynamic view on the future movement in interest rates. Let us consider the one-year and two-year spot rates to illustrate the dynamics. An investor has the choice to lock in a two-year investment at the two-year rate observable today or to invest for a term of one year and roll over at the future one-year rate prevailing in a year. Assuming risk neutrality (i.e. as previously outlined, there is no risk premium), we can expect from return calculations that the two alternatives will give the same pay-off, formally defined as

$$(1 + s_2)^2 = (1 + s_1) \times (1 + E[s_{1,1}]).$$

$E[R_{1,1}]$ is the one-year rate expected in a year, which can be defined as the one- to two-year forward rate $f_{1,2}$ from

$$(1 + s_2)^2 = (1 + s_1) \times (1 + f_{1,2}).$$

The term structure is said to be unbiased if the expected future interest rates equivalent to the forward rates computed from observed market prices of the instrument formally expressed as

$$E[s_{1,1}] = f_{1,2}.$$

The t-period spot rate can be expressed as a geometric average of the zero-coupon rates and the forward rates, defined as

$$(1 + s_t)^t = (1 + s_1) \times (1 + f_{i;1,2}) \times \ldots \times (1 + f_{i;t-1,1}),$$

For which $f_{t,t+1}$ is the forward rate of interest prevailing now (at time i) over a horizon of t to $t + 1$.

Forward rates represent mathematically the breakeven yield for each point on the curve at some point forward in time, defining the opportunity costs of an investment. As the rates can be effectively locked in at zero cost, they are said to capture market expectations in accordance with the unbiased expectation hypothesis. As outlined previously, this hypothesis states that forward rates are the best forecast of future spot rates. However, empirical studies have shown that forward rates are not a good predictor of future interest rates in reflection of market consensus rates. Accordingly, market participants refer to implied forward rates as breakeven and/or hedgeable rates as the cost of carry can be locked in today.

Term structure

The structure of yield curve knows three forms of expression. When the spot rate curve as the pure term structure is flat, the zero-coupon rate curve is identical to the par yield curve and the forward yield curve. The yield as an IRR is independent of the coupon payments. If the term structure is upward sloping, the forward rate curve implies a time premium over maturity. The received coupon payments can be reinvested at a higher rate over maturity which leads to a higher price of the coupon bond than of the zero-bond. The effect is known as the mathematical coupon effect. If the term structure is downward sloping, the forward rate implies a time discount over the maturity. The received coupon payments can be reinvested at a lower rate over maturity. This leads to a lower price of the coupon bond than of the zero-coupon instrument.

Risk metrics

As any other asset class and related financial instruments, interest-rate securities have a series of metrics to measure their risks. They are called duration and convexity. Duration is a linear approximation of the price risk while convexity incorporates a higher derivation through measuring the curvature that describes the relationship between the price of an interest-rate security such as bonds and its YTM.

Positive and negative convexity

As outlined previously, the price of an interest-rate instrument is simply the present value of its future cash-flow stream, discounted at the required rate of return, the YTM. When the YTM changes, the present value of the instrument's cash flow (consisting of coupon and notional payments) are calculated using the changed yield as a new discount rate. If the discount rate goes up, the present value of the future cash flows and hence the price goes down and vice versa. There exists a negative or inverse relationship between the price of an interest-rate instrument and the YTM. Bond prices and yield move in opposite directions. Due to its mathematics, this relationship is not linear but convex. These instruments also exhibit reinvestment risk which describes the opportunity cost that coupons have to be reinvested at a lower yield when the interest rates change.

Non-callable instruments such as a straight bond exhibit positive convexity. This means that prices go up faster than they go down. In a low-interest-rate environment, prices rise at an increasing rate as yield falls. At high interest-rates, prices fall at a decreasing rate as yield rises. The positive convexity has a clear impact for the price volatility of a non-callable bond. For small changes in yield (less than 50 bps), the magnitude of the percentage price changes is equal whether the yield increases or decreases. For large changes in yield (more than 50 bps), the magnitude of the percentage change depends on whether the yield increases or decreases. The percentage price decrease associated with a given increase in the yield is less than the percentage price increase associated with an equal decrease in the yield. This also explains why a higher derivation of the risk such as the convexity measure is used to measure large shifts in the interest-rate structure. The magnitude of the percentage price change on a fixed-income instrument for a given change in interest rates is *ceteris paribus* (all other things being equal) also dependent on the coupon rate, the term-to-maturity, and the initial yield. Firstly, the lower the coupon of the instrument, the greater the price volatility and vice versa. Secondly, the longer the term-to-maturity, the greater is the price volatility. Finally, the lower the initial yield, the greater is the price volatility.

Callable instruments for which the issuer has the right to retire the bond prior to maturity at some specified call price exhibit negative convexity. Negative convexity describes the state when yields falls, they do so at a decreasing rate as the rate of the increase in the price of the instrument will start slowing down and eventually level off. This price-yield behaviour is due to the fact that the issuer has the right to call the bond.

Duration measures

The duration of interest-rate instrument represents the weighted average time until its cash flows are received. It can also measure the instrument's price sensitivity with respect to a unit change in yield or percentage change in price for parallel shifts in the yield structure. These two applications of the duration measures make the use of the term confusing. The former is called the Macaulay duration, and the latter Modified duration. Macaulay duration is a time measure with units in years and only be applied for instruments with fixed cash flows. The concept of Modified duration, on the other hand, measures the percentage rate of change of price with respect to its yield. It can be applied to interest-rate instruments with nonfixed cash flows and may therefore be applied to a wider range of instruments than the Macaulay duration. The Macaulay and Modified duration are almost equal in value. A standard 10-year coupon bond will have Macaulay duration somewhat but not dramatically less than five years and from this we can infer that the price sensitivity expressed by the Modified duration will also be somewhat but not dramatically less than 5%. The longer the maturity of an interest-rate instrument, the larger its duration.

The Macauley duration (DMac) can be described as the present value-weighted time to maturity. The DMac is between zero and the maturity of a vanilla interest-rate instrument (e.g. a regular bond with fixed coupons c_t at times t_i) and is equal to the maturity in case of single payment at maturity (e.g. a zero-coupon bond). It measures how long the bond holder has to wait for the cash flow of the instrument. More formally, it can be described as

$$DMac = \sum_{i=1}^{n} t_t \frac{PV_i}{B},$$

whereas $PV = PV_i$ is the present value of the ith coupon and principle payment and B = market price of the instrument (B stands for bond as most common instrument).

The Modified duration (DMod) further measures price sensitivity with respect to the instrument's yield. It is an adjusted version of DMac, accounting for changes in YTM, formally expressed as

$$DMod = \frac{DMac}{\left(1 + \frac{y}{n}\right)},$$

for which y = YTM and n = number of coupon periods or compounding frequencies per year.

DMod determines the changes in an instrument's price for each percentage change in yield, which can be formally described as

$$DMod = -\frac{1}{B}\frac{\Delta B}{\Delta y},$$

and the corresponding price change of the instrument (ΔB) is then equal to

$$\Delta B = -DMod B \Delta y.$$

DMod is often also referred to as dollar value change (DV01) or basis point value (BPV). It can also be measured in absolute monetary terms of the respective currency of the interest-rate instrument, which is then known as Dollar duration ($D\$$). $D\$$ measures the actual changes in the instrument's price to its yield (versus the proportional changes in price to its yield for *DMod*), defined as

$$D\$ = -\frac{\Delta B}{\Delta y}.$$

Effective duration (DE), on the other hand, is applied for instruments with an embedded optionality such as callable bonds. It takes into account that expected cash flows fluctuate with interest-rate changes, and the option may be executed. The ED is estimated using *DMod* across different price levels, calculating the expected price change for an instrument when interest rates rise by 1%. For its calculation, it is assumed that an instrument with embedded options behaves like one without any optionality, which is the case when exercising embedded options would offer no additional benefit to the investor. Formally, it can be expressed as

$$DE = -\frac{P_1 - P_2}{2P_0\Delta y},$$

where P_0 = original price, P_1 = price if the yield were to decrease by 1%, P_2 = the price of the bond if the yield were to increase by 1%, and Δy = the estimated change in YTM used to calculate P_1 and P_2 *respectively*.

Finally, key rate duration (KRD) is the extension of the duration concept by applying sensitivity to shifts of different parts of the yield curve. Key rate durations might be selected with respect to zero-coupon rates often with maturities of 1-month, 3-month, 6-month, 1-year, 2-year, 5-year, 10-year, 20-year, and 30-year, depending on the currency. The method allows assessment of the sensitivities of the curve towards specific price points and provides a more comprehensive picture over respective shifts of the curve.

Convexity measure

All the duration measures capture exposures to small changes in YTM. It is a linear approximation of the previously described mathematically more complex convex relationship between price and yield. The estimate can be made more accurate by factoring in the instrument's effective convexity. For larger changes in YTM, the instrument's price behaves differently as there is more curvature in the relationship with the YTM. The convexity measure (C) is defined as the weighted average of the square of the time to the receipt of cash flow, formally expressed as

$$C = -\frac{1}{B}\frac{\delta^2 B}{\delta y^2},$$

which leads to a second order approximation to the change in the price, defined as

$$\Delta B = -\frac{\delta B}{\delta y}\Delta y + \frac{1}{2}\frac{\delta^2 B}{\delta y^2}\Delta y^2, \text{ and}$$

$$\Delta B = -DMod\Delta y + \frac{1}{2}C\Delta y^2.$$

Foreign currency risk

Foreign currency or exchange (FX) risk refers to the risk of fluctuations in currencies. It is also known as currency risk or exchange-rate risk and describes the possibility that the value of an asset may decrease due to changes in the relative value of the involved currencies. FX risk can be expressed through the interest-rate parity equilibrium which is a no-arbitrage condition under which investors will be indifferent to interest rates available in two countries. Given foreign exchange market equilibrium, the interest-rate parity condition implies that the expected return on domestic assets (i_D) will equal the exchange rate-adjusted expected return on foreign currency assets (i_F). Investors then cannot earn arbitrage profits by borrowing in a country with a lower interest rate, exchanging for foreign currency, and investing in a foreign country with a higher interest rate, because of gains or losses from exchanging back to their domestic currency at maturity. Formally, this can be expressed as

$$E_t(S_{t+n}) = S_t \frac{(1 + i_D)}{(1 + i_F)},$$

for which $E_t(S_{t+n})$ = expected future spot exchange rate at time $t + n$, n = number of periods into the future from time t, S_t = current spot exchange rate at time t, i_D = interest rate in domestic country, and i_F = interest rate in another foreign country or currency area.

In financial market history, there is evidence that the equation generally holds, though not with precision owing to the effects of various risks, costs, taxation, and ultimate differences in liquidity.

Commodity risk

Financial hedging and speculations found its origins in commodity prices for raw materials to manage price movements in agricultural societies. Commodities are distinguished among five broad classes. There is energy which includes oil, natural gas, and heating oil; industrial metals with aluminium, copper, nickel, and zinc; precious metals with gold, silver, platinum, and palladium; and finally agriculture and livestock. Each of these five commodity classes have a defined role within the production process and the business cycle of an economy. Commodities risk is therefore a function of economic growth and development as well as their availability and scarcity. With economic growth and development, demand for commodities increases and is to be matched by respective supply. The supply has to be guaranteed through production and inventory of the commodities. The production of some commodities remains challenging as they are exhaustive, less accessible, and require specific infrastructure and transportation. Other commodities can be exploited and processed flexibly within a certain time frame and without regional constraints. Storage and inventory costs further drive commodities prices. To conclude, each aspect of commodity supply can be brought down to availability and scarcity. With increasing economic development and growth, availability and scarcity dominate the equilibrium between demand and supply and hence the tradable prices of commodities. The factors of economic prosperity such as population growth, industrialisation, and urbanisation are drivers of the demand of commodities.

Commodities represent an instrument of diversification to traditional financial risks such as interest rates, credit, and equities and an alternative tool for risk management in particular to hedge macroeconomic risk. Financial assets tend to perform best when economic conditions are worst and the potential for improvement is highest. They tend to perform worst when the economy is strong and there is the greatest potential for negative surprises. Commodities, in contrast, are more directly tied to the current economic conditions and traditionally generate their best returns in periods of global overheating with strong inflationary growth as a result of it. The price cohabitation between financial assets and commodities results in a low or even negative correlation between these asset classes and offers a natural diversification effect in managing financial risks. The main reason for this is attributed to event risk that is inherent in commodities prices. This event risk arises from significant price spikes that historically come from supply shocks such as shortages in production and inventories with positive price effect. As a function of the event risk, the statistical distribution of commodity returns is positively skewed and exhibits fat tails. The shape of the distribution reflects the positive price spikes of commodities if a supply event happens. The same event that causes shortages in commodities tends historically to decrease prices of financial assets.

Commodity futures investments can be implemented through commodity indices. There are several widely known commodity indices available that provide broadly diversified exposure to commodities. S&P GSCI, formerly known as the Goldman Sachs Commodity Index or just GSCI, is based on 24 physical commodities and applies a production weighted scheme using a five-year average of the production input. The GSCI is a momentum-based index because increasing prices cause the commodity to have increasing weight in the index. The Bloomberg Commodity Index (BCOM), originally launched as the Dow Jones-AIG Commodity Index (DJ-AIGCI), applies liquidity considerations reflected by the amount of trading in the respective commodity contract with actively weighting and rebalancing once a year. No single commodity class represents more than 33% and no single commodity represents less than 2% or more than 15% of the index. In the extremes the DJ-AIGCI is a contrarian-based index as it sells good performing commodities and buys underperforming ones to rebalance to weight limits of the index. There are several others such as Rogers International Commodity Index and Reuters/Jefferies CRB Index that follow similar principles.

Credit risk

Credit risk describes the risk of default that may arise from a borrower failing to make required payments. This includes the loss of principal and interest, disruption to cash flows, and increased costs of collection. It is linked to the probability of default as function of a credit event which is defined as an event when a counterparty defaults on its debt obligations. The probability of default finds its expression in the credit spread which is defined as the spread over which a risky asset with a given probability of default (e.g. a corporate bond with default risk) trades over a risk-free asset (e.g. government securities for which it is assumed that there is no default risk). Credit risk may arise outright through lending arrangements such as a corporate loan and a mortgage but it may also arise from the possibility that a counterparty in derivatives transactions may default. Collateral such as the pledge of property and equipment, securities, and cash is often used to mitigate the impact of respective credit exposures. Rating agencies such as Moody's, S&P, and Fitch provide information on the long-term creditworthiness and credit quality. The standardised approach (SA) for credit risk of the Basel framework uses these published ratings to assess the capital requirements while the internal rating-based allows financial institutions to use their own internal ratings. This is in particular important as many small and midsize companies do not have an official credit rating from a rating agency. Internal ratings are then used to estimate probability of default (PD) involving profitability and balance-sheet ratios.

Credit risk components

Probability of default (PD) describes the likelihood of a credit event. A credit event is an event in which debt is not repaid as agreed and falls into default. If we assume that there is no recovery value following default and the PD is expressed in continuous time, then the investor should be indifferent between the expected proceeds of risky corporate and risk-free government bond, equalising to

$$(1 - PD)e^{(r+cs)t} = e^{rt},$$

where PD = probability of default, r = risk-free rate, cs = credit spread, and t = term-to-maturity. All calculations are in continuous compounding.

Rearranging terms, the PD can then be expressed as

$$PD = 1 - e^{-rt}.$$

The recovery rate (R) is the extent to which the principal and accrued interest on defaulted debt can be recovered. It is expressed as a percentage of face value and represents the value of an asset when it emerges from default or bankruptcy. It can vary widely, as they are affected by a number of factors, such as instrument type (e.g. seniority), specific corporate issues, and the overall macroeconomic conditions. The recovery rate enables calculation of the loss given default (LGD) which is defined as the loss estimate in the event of default, formally expressed as

$$LGD = 1 - R.$$

If we assume a given recovery value, the PD equalises to

$$PD = \frac{1 - e^{-rt}}{1 - R},$$

where R = recovery rate.

The exposure at default (EAD) measure the potential amount that can be lost under default. Such amount is often unknown in advance.

Edward Altman developed in the 1960s the Altman Z-score, based on accounting ratios and a statistical technique called discriminant analysis to predict the default of companies. The Z-score applies five accounting ratios:

- X_1: working capital/total assets
- X_2: retained earnings/total assets

- X_3: earnings before interest and taxes/total assets
- X_4: sales/total assets
- X_5: market value of equity/book value of total liabilities

The original Z-score was developed for publicly traded companies in the manufacturing space and is defined as

$$Z = 1.2X_1 + 1.4X_2 + 3.3X_3 + 0.999X_4 + 0.6X_5.$$

If the Z-score was greater than 3.0, the company was considered unlikely to default. If it was between 2.7 and 3.0, there was a rationale to be on alert. Everything below 1.8 was considered to be of high default probability. The Z-score is an alternative measure to PD.

Credit spreads

The credit spread (cs) is a function of the PD and can be derived as follows:

$$cs = yield\ of\ credit\text{-}sensitive\ asset - yield\ of\ default\ free\ bond.$$

cs is a function of PD and can be expressed as the spread to default probability conversion rule that is defined as

$$PD = \frac{cs}{(1 - R)}.$$

If cs is the difference between a corporate and a government bond yield, it is simply referred to as the credit spread. If this spread is the difference between the swap rate and government bond yield along the different maturities, it is called the swap spread (zs).

Credit benchmarks

There are several credit indices available as benchmark and underlying reference of credit markets. Credit indices that are derived from credit default swaps (CDS) have standardised contracts and shared characteristics. Investors can trade these indices and transfer risk respectively. CDX indices contain North American and Emerging Market companies and are administered by CDS Index Company (CDSIndexCo) and marketed by Markit Group Limited. iTraxx is the brand name for the family of credit default swap index products covering regions of Europe, Japan, and non-Japan Asia. The iTraxx suite of indices are owned, managed, compiled, and published by International Index Company (IIC), who also license market makers. Both indices together form a large sector of the overall credit derivative market.

The most widely traded indices are the iTraxx Europe index and the CDX North America Investment Grade, composed of the most liquid 125 CDS referencing investment grade credits. HiVol is a subset of the main index consisting of what are seen as the riskiest 30 constituents at the time the index is constructed. Crossover is constructed in a similar way but is composed of 45 subinvestment grade credits. The indices are constructed on a set of rules with the overriding criterion being that of liquidity of the underlying CDS. The constituents of the indices are changed every six months, a process known as rolling the index. Maturities are 3, 7, and 10 years, whilst the Crossover trades only at maturities of 5 and 10 years. These indices are tradable instruments in their own right, with predetermined fixed rates and the prices set by market demand. Official pricing is collected on-behalf of the index providers on a daily basis by polling the trading desks at banks that are licensed market makers. The most liquid indices also have a weekly tradable fixing calculated in a similar fashion to the LIBOR fixings process. The tradable fixing is often used as a reference price for calculating payments of other structured credit instruments.

The CMBX reflects a group of indexes made up of 25 commercial mortgage-backed securities (CMBS) from the past two years with five subindices: AAA, AA, A, BBB, and BBB-. The CMBX indexes are an expression of the current state of the commercial mortgage market. The CMBX indexes are rolled over every six months. Trading in the CMBX tranches is done over the counter by a syndicate of large investment banks. The LCDX is a specialized index of loan-only CDS covering 100 individual companies that have unsecured debt trading in the broad secondary markets. The LCDX is traded over the counter and is managed by a consortium of large investment banks, which provide liquidity and assist in pricing the individual credit default swaps.

Equity risk

Equity risk refers to the risk of holding equity in a particular investment such as the stock of a company. We covered its properties such as volatility, risk premium, and forms of systemic and idiosyncratic risks extensively in Chapter 2 under financial decision making and add it here to complete the risk assessment from a micro perspective. Applying the arbitrage pricing theory (APT) allows for dissection of equity return for stock j that can be broken down in individual risk factors or sensitivities n across statistically relevant risk premiums, mathematically defined as

$$E(r_j) = r_f + \beta_{j1}RP_1 + \beta_{j2}RP_2 + \ldots + \beta_{jn}RP_n,$$

for which E = expectations, r_f = risk-free rate, B_{jn} = sensitivity, and RP = risk premium.

The concept is applied in particular on the portfolio level which allows one to hedge the individual risk premiums through tailored financial instruments. The art of managing risk and developing respective solutions is often referred to as financial engineering, which is the topic of the following section.

3.2 FINANCIAL ENGINEERING

Financial engineering is usually defined as the discipline of solving financial problems through developing new and innovative solutions. It is the science of financial instruments, responsible for financial innovation that has invented modern instruments such as swaps and more exotic forms of derivatives. It applies quantitative tools from financial modelling to devise these instruments and predict what types of risks are presented, how such instruments will perform, and whether a new offering in the financial sector would be viable and profitable in the long run. Financial engineering facilitates the risk transfer and establishes the building blocks for it. As a discipline, it lost much of its glamour and status, being made responsible for the origins and effects of the GFC. It remains, however, crucial in transferring and managing risk across individual balance sheets and markets. This section focuses on how to manage balance sheets with different financial instruments and how to mitigate the risk of financial innovation.

Financial instruments were previously introduced in Chapter 2 as the mechanism with which financial assets become exchangeable and tradeable. They are monetary contracts between parties defined by a legal structure within which they can be created, traded, modified, and settled. IFRS 7 and 9 define a financial instrument as "any contract that gives rise to a financial asset of one entity and a financial liability or equity instrument of another entity". They can either be cash or derivative instruments, pure monetary value in form of cash, evidence of an ownership interest in an entity (equity), or a contractual right to receive or deliver cash (debt). Cash instruments are instruments whose value is determined directly by the markets. They can be securities, which are readily transferable, and instruments such as loans and deposits, where both borrower and lender have to agree on a transfer. Derivatives, on the other hand, are instruments which derive their value from the value and characteristics of one or more underlining entities such as assets or investable indices. There are exchange traded and over the counter (OTC) from a broad range of futures, swaps, options, and securitised products. Derivatives transactions are usually agreed on a template of ISDA, the ISDA master agreement. There are two basic forms of the master agreement. One is for single jurisdiction and currency and another for multiple jurisdiction/currency. ISDA master agreements are generally combined with a schedule to set out the basic trading terms between the parties. Each subsequent trade is then recorded in a confirmation which references the master agreement and schedule. Specific collateral requirements are further outlined in the credit support annex (CSA) that supplements the ISDA schedule.

3.2.1 Cash instruments

Cash instruments are directly traded in markets and can easily be converted in cash. They are usually classified across asset classes such as loans, bonds, and shares. The following section will discuss these instruments briefly while physical assets such as property and infrastructure are not covered. It further is to be noted that capital market financing is much more common in the United States than in Europe, and as a result the most common form of funding for most corporations remains traditional bank lending.

Loans

There are different forms of loans. A secured loan is a loan in which the borrower pledges some asset as collateral. A mortgage loan is a very common type of loan, used by many individuals to purchase residential property. The lender, usually a financial institution, is given security, a lien on the title to the property, until the mortgage is paid in full. If the borrower defaults on the loan, the bank would have the legal right to repossess the house and sell it, to recover sums owing to it. Collateral can be more broadly defined as any property pledged such as cash, equipment, stock, inventory, and receivables that has been promised to the lender in the event of a default. It entails a security interest that defines the creditor's right (attachment) and notifies third parties (perfection). When a lender has a specific interest in a certain property upon default, it is considered to be a secured creditor with a security interest. A security interest is given notice through possession, control, or filing a financial statement in case of a default.

Unsecured loans are not secured against the borrower's assets. These may be available from financial institutions under many different packages such as credit card debt, personal loans, bank overdrafts, credit facilities or lines of credit, corporate bonds, and peer-to-peer lending. Interest rates on unsecured loans are nearly always higher than for secured loans because an unsecured lender's options for recourse against the borrower in the event of default are severely limited, subjecting the lender to higher risk compared to that encountered for a secured loan. An unsecured lender must sue the borrower, obtain a money judgment for breach of contract, and then pursue execution of the judgment against the borrower's unencumbered assets (i.e. the ones not already pledged to secured lenders). In insolvency proceedings, secured lenders traditionally have priority over unsecured lenders when a court divides up the borrower's assets. Thus, a higher interest rate reflects the additional risk that in the event of insolvency, the debt may be uncollectible.

Term loans are offered by traditional lenders and usually carry a fixed interest rate, with a principal amortisation over a fixed period of time and sometimes have a balloon payment at maturity. Revolving loans do not have a maturity date and it is anticipated by the counterparties that the loan will be renewed at maturity. Its purpose is to cover business seasonality, working capital needs, and special projects. Asset-based loans are based on company assets in a secured format. They are easier and faster to finance since the lender does not have to analyse and project the profitability of the company going forward. Factoring loans are not loans in the traditional sense but are contracts through which a third party is buying receivables at a discount which creates an initial benefit of immediate cash from the sale of the receivables. They can be structured nonrecourse which means that the third party assumes all responsibilities for collecting. In a recourse agreement, the selling company remains responsible for collection. Leveraged loans are loans, arranged by a syndicate of banks, to companies that already have substantial debt on their books and/or have a poor credit rating/history. They are significantly riskier than traditional loans and, as such, lenders typically demand a higher interest rate to reflect the greater risk. There are four main areas of application of leverage loans. In general, it is used to fund daily operations in particular in the area of asset financing. It is further used for corporate finance strategies to refinance the existing debt of the company and to recapitalize a company's balance sheet. Leveraged loans are commonly used to support a leveraged buyout, which is a specific merger and acquisition transaction that is often applied by private equity sponsors and hedge funds.

Although a loan agreement document is unique for each transaction, they contain some common provisions and have a more or less standardised structure, consisting of:

1. Definitions
2. A description of the loan and borrowing mechanism
3. Guaranties

4. Collateral
5. Conditions precedent
6. Representations and warranties
7. Financial and nonfinancial covenants
8. Defaults
9. Remedies

A loan guarantee is usually used to obligate a third party to repay all or some of the debt if the borrowers fail to do so. Covenants can permit a lender to compel or restrict a borrower's actions, review material changes in a borrower's business, and monitor a borrower's finances over the life of a loan. The noncompliance with informative, affirmative, negative, and financial covenants may trigger the default against the borrower under the loan agreement.

Bonds

Bonds are securities that reflect indebtedness of the issuer to the holders. The issuer owes holders debt and is obliged to pay them a coupon or interest and repay the principal at a later date, termed the maturity date. Bonds are a contractual right to receive or deliver cash, usually defined as very heterogeneous instruments with different maturities, coupons, issuers, and capital structure considerations. Bonds have a specific maturity unless they are perpetual such as Consols while the most common types are government and corporate bonds. There are many others like short-term commercial papers or securitised collateral debt and/or loan obligations that follow the same principles. Some bonds in particular in the United States are listed whereas most of them remain nonlisted and even do not have a public issuance but are placed privately. Covenants monitor the borrower's (in case of a loan) and issuer's (in case of a bond) finances over the life of a loan. It is common to use the term in primary reference to financial covenants such as tangible net worth, debt-to-worth ratios, or earnings before interest, taxes, depreciation, and amortisation (EBITDA) requirements. However, covenants reflect more than just a financial view and can compel borrowers/ issuers to restrict their actions across several dimensions such as information provision, which can affirm or prohibit certain actions.

Mezzanine capital

Mezzanine capital is a hybrid form of finance that has features of debt and equity. It occupies space between those two asset classes and is either structured as subordinated debt or preferred equity on an institution's balance sheet. It is subordinate in priority of payment to senior debt but ranks senior to equity. They are usually unsecured unless there is a bankruptcy remote entity with some collateral specifications. Mezzanine financing has been growing on an accelerated basis, fuelled by activities in acquisition financing and leveraged buyouts. For financial institutions, it covers a very specific part with specific subordinated instruments that are very clearly defined by the regulatory framework. The topic will be covered in further detail under the section on capital management.

Equity capital

Equity capital is shareholder capital that reflects through a certificate (stocks) owner-ship interest in an entity. Stocks of large companies are usually traded over organised regional exchanges that follow specific legal requirements and are heavily regulated. Privately held corporations often have a small group of shareholders with most of them taking an active role in running the company. Many have shareholder agreements in place that define specific rights and transfer restrictions. Stocks as an instrument were covered extensively in Chapter 2.

3.2.2 Forwards and futures

Forwards and futures are linear instruments that allow a market participant to buy and sell assets at a future time for a certain price. Futures contracts are traded on an organised exchange across standardised terms. By contrast, forward contracts are privately customised agreements between two counterparties. Both instruments follow specific mechanisms and pricing methodologies.

Forwards

A forward is a nonstandardized and customised contract between two counterparties to buy or sell an asset at a specific future time at a price agreed on at the time of conclusion of the contract. The price agreed upon is called the delivery price, which is equal to the forward price at the time the contract is entered into. The price of the underlying asset is paid before control of the instrument changes. Formally, the forward price (F) to be paid at time (T) is defined as

$$F = S_0 e^{(r-q)T},$$

for which S = spot price of the asset at time 0, r = risk-free interest rate and q = cost of carry.

The costs of carry depend on the underlying asset and can be the dividends, storage costs, and convenience yield. In contrast to futures that are listed at exchanges and follow specific requirements such as margining, forwards are traded OTC. Forwards typically do not have interim partial settlements such that the parties do not exchange collateral securing the party at gain, and the entire unrealized gain or loss builds up while the contract is open. However, a forward can be customised and specified to include mark-to-market and daily margin calls. A forward rate agreement (FRA) is one of the most common applications of forward contracts. It is a cash for difference derivative contract between two counterparties parties with an interest-rate index or benchmark as its underlying. It specifies through a fixed rate, notional amount, selected interest rate index tenor, and maturity date.

Futures

Futures are standardized forward contracts for which the underlying asset is usually a financial instrument and/or a commodity. The contracts are agreed at regulated futures exchanges, which act as a marketplace between buyers and sellers. To mitigate the counterparty risk, the exchange applies margining and the exchange of collateral during the contract. The first futures contracts were negotiated for agricultural commodities and then later for natural resources such as oil. Financial futures were eventually introduced in 1972 and have played an increasingly large role in the overall futures markets. The original use was to mitigate the risk of price or exchange rate movements by allowing parties to fix prices or rates in advance for future transactions. Futures also offer opportunities to speculate. Today financial futures are available for interest-rates instruments (e.g. bonds), a currency pair, or equity index. The following section covers the main financial futures individually and briefly touches on the basics of commodities futures. The pricing methodology is based on the forward price while applying the margining requirements and the interim exchange of collateral in accordance with the exchange requirements.

Interest-rate futures

Interest-rate futures are based on an interest-bearing instrument as the underlying asset. There are short-term interest-rate (STIR) futures such as the Eurodollar futures and contracts based on long-term government bonds such as the Treasury-bond futures. We will cover both instruments in more detail while also addressing the issue of the convexity adjustment to illustrate the impact of margining requirements of standardised instruments. The government-bond futures contract is based on any government bond such as Treasury bond in the United States that has more than 15 years to maturity on the first day of the delivery month and is not callable within 15 years from that day it can be delivered.[1] Treasury-bond futures have a cheapest-to-deliver function which allows the party with the short position to choose to deliver any bonds within the defined criteria. At any time during the delivery month, there are many bonds that can be delivered. They vary widely as far as coupon and maturity are concerned. The party with the short position can choose which of the available bond is cheapest to deliver.

When a particular bond is delivered, a parameter known as its conversation factor defines the price received by the party with the short position. The quoted price applicable to the delivery is the product of the conversion factor and the most recent settlement price. For each contract for which the delivery is US$100 000 face value of bonds, the face value of the bond for the party who receives it is calculated as

$$Settlement\ price \times Conversion\ factor + Accrued\ interest,$$

while the cost of purchasing a bond is

$$Quoted\ bond\ price + Accrued\ interest$$

The cheapest-delivery bond is the one for which

$$Quoted\ bond\ price - (Settlement\ price \times Conversion\ factor).$$

---

[1]This section follows the Chicago Board of Trade terminology and methodology.

Because of the cheapest-to-deliver option, it is difficult to determine an exact theoretical futures price for a government bond contract. However, if we assume that the delivered bond and delivery date are known, then the income of the government bond futures contract is also defined, and the future price at time 0 (F_0) related to the spot price (S_0) is defined as

$$F = (S_0 - I)e^{rT}.$$

STIR contracts, on the other hand, vary, but are often defined on an interest-rate index such as three-month sterling or US dollar LIBOR. One of the most popular interest-rate futures contracts is the three-month Eurodollar futures.[2] It has standard delivery months of March, June, September, and December for up to 10 years in the future. The settlement price is usually defined as *100 − interest rate* on the specific date where the Eurodollar futures is designed so that 1 bps move in the futures quote corresponds to a gain or loss of US$25 per contract.

The Eurodollar futures contract is similar to an FRA whereas a convexity adjustment is to be considered between forward and futures prices due to daily margin payments. If there is a correlation between daily futures prices and interest rates, one party to a futures contract will tend to receive margin payments on days when interest rates rise and make margin payments on days when interest rates decline. On average, the party will invest the margin payments it receives at interest rates that are higher than those at which it finances the margin payments it makes. The counterparty will experience the opposite situation. This should cause a divergence in forward and futures prices. The effect should increase with the maturity of contracts and their standard deviation.

For STIR such as the Eurodollar futures, this effect is exasperated. Not only do the forward rates they are linked to correlate highly with the overnight rates at which margin payments would typically be financed or invested, but there is an issue with how the margin payments are calculated. An FRA exhibits convexity. Its market value rises more for a given decline in the forward rate than it would decline for the same sized rise in the forward rate. If this were also true for Eurodollar futures, this convexity effect would partially offset the margining effect. The specifications for Eurodollar futures set the daily margin payment at US$25 per basis point move in the futures rate which deprives the contracts of the convexity exhibited in FRAs. Eurodollar futures rates can therefore diverge from corresponding forward rates. This effect is called the convexity bias on which the pricing has to be adjusted.

For short-dated Eurodollar futures (12–18 months), the effect is hardly noticeable, a basis point or less. For longer-dated futures, the convexity bias can be more pronounced, causing Eurodollar futures rates to exceed corresponding forward rates by 10 bps or more at the longest maturities. The actual magnitude further depends on the level and volatility of interest rates. To approximate the effect, the following formula is applied

$$Forward\ Rate = Futures\ Rate - \frac{1}{2}\sigma t_1 t_2,$$

---

[2]We hereby follow the methodology applied on the Chicago Mercantile Exchange.

where σ is the standard deviation of the underlying interest rate, t_1 is the time (in years) until maturity of the futures contract, and t_2 is the time (in years) until maturity of the underlying loan. The approximation assumes both the futures and forward rates are continuously compounded.

Prior to the early 1990s, traders were not considering the convexity bias. Eurodollar futures were used to hedge interest rate swaps, which were priced using Eurodollar futures rates as if they were forward rates. This caused swap rates to be higher than they should have been. The situation started to change during the early 1990s, as awareness of the convexity bias spread. Financial models were developed which took the convexity bias into account whenever swaps were priced or hedged with Eurodollar futures. Eurodollar futures are still widely used for hedging swaps and other interest-rate derivatives, but convexity bias has rendered Eurodollar rates as poor benchmark for pricing other instruments. The LIBOR-swap curve eventually replaced the Eurodollar rates as a benchmark before it had been questioned given the market manipulation scandal post GFC.

Other futures contracts

In accordance with this framework, the mechanisms of other futures contracts on foreign currency, commodities, and equities can be described. A foreign currency has the property that the holder of the currency can earn interest at the risk-free interest rate prevailing in the foreign country. If r_f is the value of the foreign risk-free interest rate when money is invested for time T, then the future can be priced as

$$F = S_0 e^{(r-r_f)T}.$$

The price of a commodities futures is a function of the storage costs (u) which can be treated as a negative yield on an annualised basis. Given the potential shortage and scarcity of supply of commodities, the users and end consumers of commodities may feel the benefits of immediately holding a commodity physically which is known as convenience yield (y). If u as the storage costs per unit are in constant proportion of the sport price (S), then the futures prices (F) can be defined as

$$F = S_0 e^{(r+u-y)T}.$$

Due to financing costs expressed through the risk-free interest rate (r) and storage costs (u), spot prices of financial assets are typically below their futures price. As many commodities are difficult to store and can usually not be borrowed, they exhibit a convenience yield (y) that pulls the futures below the spot price. This situation in which the futures curve exhibits a decreasing shape, that is, spot prices trade below futures prices, is called backwardation. Inversely, Contango describes a situation when the futures curve has an increasing shape.

As investments in commodities would give the investor a physical position in the underlying commodity with the respective storage and inventory responsibility, they are usually implemented via futures investments. The return of commodities investments, that is, the commodity indices that we discussed earlier, can therefore be attributed to three return components: changes in the spot price of the underlying commodity, the roll return of the futures investments, and the collateral return of the collateral posted to fulfil the margin requirements of futures exchanges. While the spot return is an expression of the underlying price movements, roll return depends on the shape of the futures curve of the commodity. As the futures prices tend to converge to the higher spot level, backwardation results in positive roll returns for commodities investments that are executed via futures. An additional return is provided by the shape of the futures curve even if commodity spot prices do not trend upwards. In Contango, rolling futures lead to costs and go along with negative roll returns. The collateral that is posted to fulfil potential margin requirements collects an interest rate which is often referred to as the collateral return.

Equity futures are based on the main stock indices such as the S&P 500 and the EuroStoxx 50 and regional or sector-specific indices. A stock index can be regarded as the price of an investment asset that pays dividends that are received by the holder of the stock composites of the index. If it is assumed that the dividends provide a known yield (d) rather than a known cash income, than the price of equity futures can simply be defined as

$$F = S_0 e^{(r-d)T}.$$

3.2.3 Swaps

Swaps have been one of the most important innovations of modern finance, and their standardised applications shows their wide acceptance today. In its simplest form, a swap consists of an agreement between two counterparties to exchange streams or sequences of future cash flows over a certain time period. Out of this simple definition, there comes a variety of instruments such as asset, interest rate, foreign exchange, and cross-currency and equity swaps. The following section provides an overview of the different types of swaps with their applications.

Asset swap

An asset swap is the exchange of cash flows produced by a bond for another set of economically equivalent cash flows. It is usually a combination of a bond or a loan and an interest rate or cross-currency swap. An asset swap allows customising coupon payments, facilitating yield enhancement, creating assets that are not available in the marketplace, or changing the interest-rate sensitivity of the portfolio of assets, without actually trading these securities. Its main advantage, however, is the delinking of duration, currency, and credit risk. This allows the repacking of an investment either into a form that is more consistent with a lender's funding structure or into a form that will represent a more attractive package to be sold to investors. There are several customised structures of asset swap available that can be classified in three categories under true-asset swaps, par-asset swaps, and yield-to-yield asset swaps. For these structures, it is crucial to understand that in an asset swap the underlying asset such as a bond or loan is from the point of view of default independent. The investor who buys a bond and uses asset swaps is still exposed to credit risk as the issuer of the bond may default. The swap component of the asset swap remains binding even if the client sells the security or if the underlying credit worsens or defaults.

The par asset swap is the most common type of asset swap. The investor buys the bond at the dirty price and receives upfront the difference between the dirty price and the par value (100%) if the price is higher. He pays upfront the difference between the par value (100%) and the dirty price if the price is lower. The end result is that the investor effectively pays par for the asset and receives fixed or floating interest payment on a par notional in return. In a true-asset swap, the investor buys the bond at the dirty price and there are no upfront cash flows. The investor pays through full bond coupons (including the first coupon payment) into the swap and any other payments made on the bond and in return receives fixed or floating on a notional of 100% x dirty price. At maturity, the investor either receives par from bond redemption or receives the difference of the dirty price minus par from the swap (or pays absolute value if the difference is negative). In a yield-to-yield asset swap, the investor buys the bond at the dirty price and enters into a plain-vanilla current coupon swap to the maturity of the bond. The initial swap payments may be a stub if there is a short first period. Notice that there are no upfront or backend payments associated with the vanilla swap and that the current coupon rate on the swap is very unlikely to be the same as the coupons on the bond.

In total return swaps (TRS), the underlying asset, referred to as the reference asset, is usually an equity index, loans, or bonds. This is owned by the party receiving the set rate payment. These instruments allow the party receiving the total return to gain exposure and benefit from a reference asset without actually having to own it. TRS allows one party to derive the economic benefit of owning an asset without putting that asset on its balance sheet and allows the other party, which does retain that asset on its balance sheet, to buy protection against loss in its value. High-cost borrowers who seek financing and leverage are natural receivers in TRS. Lower cost borrowers, with large balance sheets, are natural payers. Reverse swaps involve the sale of the asset with the seller then buying the returns, usually on equities.

Interest-rate swap

There are different forms of IRS available that allow market participants to gain and hedge exposure in accordance with their individual objectives.

Plain-vanilla IRS

In a plain-vanilla IRS, the fixed-rate payer agrees to pay the counterparty fixed interest-rate payments at designated dates for the life of the contract. This is referred to as the payer-position as the fixed rate is paid. The counterparty, who agrees to make interest payments in a floating reference rate and receives the swap rate, is called the fixed-rate receiver. This is a receiver position as the fixed rate is received. In a LIBOR-in-arrears IRS, the floating rate side is set at the end of the reset period instead of the beginning and the rate is applied retroactively. A vanilla swap sets the rate in advance and pays later whereas an arrears swap sets and pays later. A forward-starting swap is a vanilla swap in which two counterparties can agree to exchange cash flows at a predetermined future date and then agree to another set of cash flow exchange for another date beyond the first swap date.

The floating leg usually has been, by market convention, the LIBOR rate[3] with its daily fixing for a specific time frame (1 up to 18 months). The fixed rate is called a swap rate and is a par rate. As the name suggests, a par rate refers to a par bond. A par bond is a bond that trades at par, which implies that the YTM is the same as the coupon rate. The one-year swap rate (z_1) of a plain-vanilla swap with a six-month LIBOR rate can be calculated as the weighted geometric average between the 6-month LIBOR rate at present and the 6- to 12-month implied forward rate of the current LIBOR curve. For illustration,[4] this means

$$z_1 = \left(\left(1 + Libor_6 \cdot \frac{days}{360} \right) \cdot \left(1 + f_{6,12} \cdot \frac{days}{360} \right) \right) - 1,$$

where z_1 = 1-year swap rate, $Libor_6$ = 6-month London Interbank Offered Rate (Libor), and $f_{6,12}$ = 6 to 12-month Libor forward rate.

This swap rate plays a very important reference role in international financial markets as basic rate. Although US treasury markets are very liquid, government instruments in Europe are not very frequently traded. Therefore, the swap rates constitute an approximation of the theoretical basic rates, which should by definition be free of credit risk and hence an expression of pure market risk. They constitute a basic refinancing rate and have represented in that sense a benchmark rate for the costs of capital. This is why a large number of fixed-income securities use interest-rate swaps as the key benchmark for pricing and hedging. The swap spread can pose a challenge for asset-liability management when the discount rate for the liabilities is a government rate but the only available instruments are swaps. This often applies to long-dated liabilities where only swap instruments are available in certain currencies. The swap rate is often a reference point for systematic liquidity issues in financial markets. An increase in the swap spread reflects a regime switch in supply and demand between the default-risk free government and the swap market. The swap rate is mainly seen as a banking lending rate (base rate) and as an expression of the basic financing rate (cost of capital) of the corporate sector. The relative liquidity of these two markets depends mainly on flight to quality and the respective convenience yield of government securities. During financial stress, investors sell risky securities for the benefit of the ones with the smallest forms of risk exposure. Although swaps are the most liquid securities, they involve substantial transaction risks because of the complexity of their generic structure,for example, potential mispricing, difficulties in execution, or other forms of counterparty risk. Therefore, rational investors prefer the simplicity of government instruments with a short maturity, which guarantee them capital preservation. In such market situations, the convenience yield of government instruments becomes large, which makes government securities more attractive than swaps. Furthermore, government instruments allow financing over special rates in the market for retro purchase agreements (REPO). Through REPO, a holder of government securities can borrow at rates that are usually

---

[3]The floating leg of a swap could be any short-term rate or cash market instrument. However, the LIBOR rates with their different currencies have been the market standard.
[4]We ignore differences between the day count conventions of the bond market (swap rate) and the ones of the money market (LIBOR). The formula is for illustration only.

below LIBOR—using government instruments as collaterals. This creates incentives for government securities and swaps are sold for government securities. The swap spread increases accordingly, and sometimes dramatically such as during the Russian crisis of 1998, the systematic financial stresses of 2003, and the GFC of 2007–2008.

Constant maturity swap

The constant maturity swap (CMS) is a variation of a plain-vanilla IRS. A CMS is a floating-rate swap whose interest rate is based on a floating interest portion that is reset periodically according to a fixed maturity market rate (such as the plain-vanilla swap rate) of an instrument with a duration extending beyond that of the swap's reset period. The fixed rate of a plain-vanilla IRS is therefore no longer fixed but reset periodically with the respective value of long-term capital-market rate (e.g. five-year USD swap rate). In a CMS, there is not only one leg with a floating rate such as LIBOR in IRS but two legs with floating rates. LIBOR and the periodically reset floating rate that is linked to a long-term capital market rate. To sum up, the periodically reset interest rate with reference to a capital-market rate is nothing else than a swap rate with a longer duration rather than LIBOR. The other leg remains generally LIBOR. A CMS is similar to a series of differential interest-rate fix (DIRF) in the same way that a plain-vanilla IRS is similar to a series of FRAs. The CMS is priced in a similar way to a plain-vanilla IRS. Its price is reflected in the premium or discount paid on the constant maturity leg of the swap. This premium or discount is close to the weighted average implied forward differential between the constant maturity defined and LIBOR over the life of a transaction. Nevertheless, the present value of the forward differential must be taken into account which means that the convexity bias also has its effect in CMS pricing.

A CMS is exposed to changes in long-term interest rate movements as it is initially priced to reflect a fixed-rate product with maturities between 2 and 10 years in duration but adjusted with each reset period. The fact that there is a major divergence between the maturity of the swap and the reference rate gives rise to interest-rate structure risk but simultaneously opens up the opportunity to make substantial price gains if the yield curve changes. The prime factor for a CMS is the shape of the forward implied yield curve. A long position in a CMS is beneficial if the yield curve is normal or positive that is up-rising. With a positive yield curve, it is expected that the periodically reset floating rate increases in value over the maturity. A steepening yield curve partly leads therefore to significant price gains. An inverted or flat yield curve, on the other hand, is less beneficial because it can be expected that the periodically reset interest rate will decrease over maturity. A flattening or an inversion of the yield curve leads to falling bond prices, and significant price losses are possible in particular if there are extraordinarily fundamental or quick changes in the structure of the interest-rate landscape. The receiver of the periodically reset floating rate, which is based on a long-term capital market rate, profits when the yield curve steepens in a way that is equal to a widening of the difference between the long-term capital-market and the short-term money market rate. The payer of the periodically reset floating rate benefits from the flattening in the yield curve. That is the case when the difference between the long-term capital market and short-term money market rate decreases.

Foreign exchange and cross-currency swaps

A foreign exchange (FX) swap is a simultaneous purchase and sale of identical amounts of one currency for another with two different maturities. It is a combination of spot transaction with an offsetting forward transaction. The FX swap has two transaction legs, usually a spot and forward transaction that are executed simultaneously for the same quantity and therefore offset each other. However, it is not uncommon to trade a forward-forward FX swap where both transactions are for different forward value dates. The FX swap allows sums of one currency to be used to fund charges designated in another currency without acquiring foreign exchange risk. It permits companies that have funds in different currencies to manage them efficiently.

A cross-currency swap, on the other hand, is an agreement between two parties to exchange interest payments and principal denominated in two different currencies. Interest payments and principal in one currency are exchanged for principal and interest payments in another currency. A cross-currency swap is structured as plain-vanilla IRS. However, the currencies of the two legs are different and there usually is an exchange of principal at the beginning and at maturity whereas the principal amounts are chosen to be approximately equivalent using the spot foreign exchange rate at the time the swap is initiated. All cross-currency swaps are combinations of an IR and a basis swap. A basis swap is decomposed into two basis swaps of an arbitrary currencies against USD LIBOR as base currency. The market quotes the basis swap as USD three-month LIBOR flat versus three-month LIBOR + basis of another currency. This basis separates the interest-rate risk between two currencies and is a function of supply and demand between paying and receiving the respective currency against USD LIBOR. More technically, the market quotes the basis as an expression of a specific currency against the demand and supply situation of cash balances in USD.

Credit default swaps

In a CDS, the buyer of protection pays the seller for an insurance against a credit event or default of an underlying debt position. The payment usually is in the form of a fixed fee paid regularly over 5 or, less commonly, 10 years. It is often expressed as an annual percentage or spread of the national amount of protection. It is measured as a premium over the risk-free interest rates. The simplest form of CDS is a single-name instrument referring to only one company. CDS can be traded that makes to transfer the risk between capital market participants.

The ISDA defines eight credit events as bankruptcy, downgrade, merger, restructuring, obligation acceleration, cross default, failure to pay, and repudiation. A credit event initiates the (contingent) payment made by the protection seller, that is, the protection leg. By triggering the settlement of related CDS instruments, the credit event changes the nature or risk of the payments of the reference obligation. A settlement can be done physically with a partial settlement of the contract. It can also be transacted with a cash settlement where the seller of the protection pays the buyer only a proportion of what it would pay in a physical settlement. Defined as a percentage of 100% less the value of the bonds set by the auction process (a proxy for the recovery rate), this avoids the need for delivery of actual bonds.

Through the estimation of a given set of default probabilities, we can calculate the fair premium for a CDS. The expected PV of the stream of CDS premiums over time can be calculated as

$$PVS = s_N \sum_{j=1}^{N} t_{j-1,\,j} d_j PS_j,$$

where PVS = expected present value of the stream of CDS premiums, s_N = CDS premiums rate per annum for an N-year CDS, $t_{j-1,j}$ = length of time of period j (expressed as a fraction of the year), d_j = discount factor for period j, and PS_j = probability of survival through period j.

If a default occurs in period j, the expected PV of default payout will be defined as

$$(1 - R)d_j PD_j,$$

where R = recovery rate and PD_j = probability of default through period j.

As a default can occur in any period, the cost of default is the sum of the expected PV of the payout over time such as

$$PVD = (1 - R) \sum_{j=1}^{N} d_j PD_j,$$

where PVD = expected PV of the cost of default over time.

In a fairly priced CDS, expected present value of the stream of CDS premiums (PVS) must equal the expected PV of the cost of default over time (PVD), leading to

$$s_N \sum_{j=1}^{N} t_{j-1,\,j} d_j PS_j, = (1 - R) \sum_{j=1}^{N} d_j PD_j.$$

Rearranging this expression, the fair premium s for the CDS can be determined as

$$s_N = \frac{(1 - R) \sum_{j=1}^{N} d_j PD_j}{\sum_{j=1}^{N} t_{j-1,\,j} d_j PS_j,}.$$

Within this framework the probability of default can either be estimated through historical or model-based analysis, or a bootstrapping methodology can be applied where the PD is derived from market traded spreads. CDS basis represents the difference in spread between CDS and bonds for the same debt issuer and with the same or similar maturities. More formally it can be defined as

CDS basis = CDS spread − bond spread.

The CDS-bond basis is defined as the difference between the CDS premium and the bond spread, with either the asset swap (ASW) spread, z-spread, or option-adjusted spread (OAS). The z-spread is the most common spread measure compared to the CDS premium and is defined as the spread added to swap rates required to match the bond price. Another frequent spread convention, the ASW, measures the additional spread on the floating leg off a par swap required to match the value of the bond's fixed coupon stream and current price. The two spread measures are usually close together and differences can be largely attributed to the bond's premium or discount to par. Basis trades capture the difference between cash and synthetic demand on a name while minimizing exposure to credit risk. This transaction is implemented through buying a bond and buys credit default swap protection on the same credit. The basis trade owner collects the bond coupon and pays the premium on the CDS until the trade is unwound, maturity, or a credit event. It is called negative when the credit default swap spread trades tighter than the bond spread of the same credit. It involves buying a bond-obligation usually with a fixed coupon and buying protection on the same obligor which the bond is deliverable at a similar maturity. The opposite applies for a positive basis. Investors may pick up a spread, without taking on additional default risk on the underlying credit.

Equity swaps

Equity swaps can be classified as vanilla, dividend, and variance swaps. In the following section, we provide an overview of these different swaps with the objective to understand the implications for managing balance sheets of financial institutions.

Vanilla equity swap

An equity swap is a swap for which payments on one or both sides are linked to the performance of equities or an equity index. Equity swaps are therefore exchanges of cash flows in which at least one of the indices is an equity investment (i.e. equity index or single stock). Equity swaps are applied to avoid or decrease taxes, obtain leverage, or enjoy the returns from ownership without actually owning equity (e.g. the stock). There are many reasons to use equity swaps, some of which come from the motivation behind index trading. Equity might be applied for a financial institution that has a very large position in a single stock. It can swap the stock performance to the performance of broader equity index and get further diversification and or manage specific tax and regulatory requirements. Equity swaps are further used for index trading. For illustration, a financial institution promises to deliver the return of the EuroStoxx 50. Instead of buying the 50 stocks that comprise the index in their exact proportions, the bank can enter swap in which it pays some money market return (LIBOR + spread) in exchange for receiving the return on the index for a period of five years with monthly payments.

Dividend swaps

When financial institutions started issuing high volumes of equity derivative products at the end of the 1990s, they were increasingly exposed to dividend risk. In an equity derivative products such as plain-vanilla options, exotics, or structured products, the cumulative dividends until maturity have to be estimated. As there is little consensus on how to estimate or model dividend risk, banks often prefer to hedge their dividend risks fully or partially via dividend swaps. Dividend swaps enable financial institutions and investors to take a view on the dividends that will be paid by an underlying stock or equity index in a predetermined period. Market expectations can be measured and traded in the form of implied dividends. The swaps give exposure to the difference between the market-implied dividends at initiation of the contract and the realised dividends at maturity. Single-stock dividends are usually traded per share and in the dividend currency. Index dividends, on the other hand, are traded in exposure per index point. The contract period is usually one year.

In a dividend swap, there are two legs. For the fixed leg, the dividend buyer commits to pay the prevailing market-implied level multiplied by the desired exposure (per currency or index point) whereas for the floating leg, the counterparty commits to pay the realized dividend level at the end of the period multiplied by the exposure per point. If a dividend swap is unwound before maturity, the present values of fixed and floating legs are exchanged. Neglecting counterparty credit risk, the fixed leg of a dividend swap at initiation is equal to the present value of the market-implied dividends while the floating leg is equal to the present value of the expected dividends. To avoid arbitrage opportunities, the present value of the market-implied dividends should equal expected dividends adjusted for risk when the transaction is initiated. Market-implied dividends will usually be lower than expected dividends as the discount rate of the floating leg will include a risk premium for the expected dividends. There is no cash flow at the initiation of the transaction. Usually there is an initial margin requirement for which the amount depends on the exposure taken, the maturity of the swap, and if it is reset annually. Additional maintenance margin requirements might be applicable.

Variance and volatility swaps

Variance swaps were among the first instruments that offered risk managers a straightforward vehicle for achieving long or short exposure to market volatility. Although it is classified as a swap contract, it is fundamentally an option-based product with properties similar to those of options. The variance swap is a contract in which two parties agree to exchange cash flows based on the measured variance of a specified underlying asset during a certain time period. The variance swap is equal to a forward contract whose pay-off is based on the realised variance (i.e. volatility) of an equity index. On the trade date, the two parties agree on the strike price of the contract. This is called the reference level against which cash flows are exchanged and the number of units in the transaction is specified. The profit and loss of a variance swap is a direct function of realized volatility versus the swap strike level.

Variance swaps were originally engineered to be a substitute for traditional option-based volatility strategies such as straddles or hedged puts. The major setback when options are used is that once the underlying stock index moves, the former delta neutral trade is no longer delta neutral and has to be rehedged. The profit and loss of a delta-neutral option position maintained until expiration reflects the aggregate gamma capture from hedge rebalancing netted against the premium paid for the option. As we covered previously, gamma itself is a complex function of time, volatility, and moneyness, and the profit and loss are subject to inherent uncertainties. There are also volatility swaps with similar functions to a variance swap. A volatility swap has a linear pay-off, whereas a variance swap has nonlinear, convex pay-off. Because of the gamma effect, variance swaps are easier to price and hedge. This means positive for a long position and negative for a short position. A variance swap is therefore easier for the dealer to hedge because it can be replicated by a static portfolio of options. The volatility swap, on the other hand, requires a convexity adjustment to compensate for the requirement to dynamically rebalance the options hedge.

3.2.4 Options

The following section discusses different types and generation of options as nonlinear derivatives. Starting with standard plain-vanilla options, this section discusses more exotic structures where usually one specific model is applied. The hedging of exotic options such as barrier and multiasset options led to substantial losses during the GFC. A basic understanding is required from a balance sheet and asset-liability management perspective. This section focuses on describing the instruments while applying the framework of contingent claim analysis that was established in Chapter 2.

Vanilla options

Vanilla options can be classified as European and American options. A European option may be exercised only at the expiration date of the option, that is, at a single prede- fined point in time. An American option, on the other hand, may be exercised at any time before the expiration date. An American option is usually more expensive than a European one. For European call options, there is an important relationship called the put-call parity. It describes the relation between the price of a European call and put option when they have the same strike price and maturity date. The put-call parity is formally defined as

$$A + P_E = B + C_E \text{ and } B = K \cdot e^{-r \cdot t},$$

where A = value of risky asset, P = value of European put option, B = risk-free bond position, C = value of European call option, r = continuously calculated risk-free rate, T = time of expiration, and K = exercise price.

Within the put-call parity, convex pay-off strategy is defined as

$$A + P_E \text{ and } B + C_E \text{ which implies that } \Delta = \frac{\partial G}{\partial A} > 0 \text{ and } \Gamma = \frac{\partial^2 G}{\partial A^2} > 0.$$

Concave pay-off strategy, on the other hand, consists of

$$A - C_E \text{ and } B - P_E \text{ which implies that } \Delta = \frac{\partial G}{\partial A} > 0 \text{ and } \Gamma = \frac{\partial^2 G}{\partial A^2} < 0.$$

where G = value of option.

Convex strategies are often referred to as capital-protected pay-off strategies. While they provide a protected capital base, there remains the unlimited participation in the price up-potential. Their pay-off structure is a long call option. Concave pay-off strategies provide a premium due to the short option positions but have unlimited loss potential. Their pay-off strategy is similar to a short put option. The standard assumption in contingent claim analysis of the lognormal distribution of the asset price implies that asset prices are positively or right skewed in their distribution. This is nothing else as an expression of the limited liability structure of holding the asset or can be seen as a function of the limited downside potential. Because of the skewness, the pay-off potential for a call option is therefore higher than for a respective put option. However, the skewness implies also that the final price of the asset is more likely to end up below the strike price than above. A call option has thus a bigger pay-off potential than a respective put but a lower probability of achieving it. The put option has a smaller pay-off potential than the call but a higher probability of achieving it. The bigger pay-off and the smaller probability of the call option exactly match the smaller pay-off but higher probability of the put option. It follows that for at-the-money options, a call and put option have under risk neutrality the same expected pay-off and hence the same value.

A key insight from risk-neutral option pricing and the implied density with the Martingale probability Q is that out-of-the-money European calls reflect conditions in the upper-tail of the risk-neutral distribution. Out-of-the-money European puts reflect conditions in the lower tail. Symmetric risk-neutral distributions imply equal prices for out-of-the money European calls and puts, where skewed distributions create systematic divergences. The x% skewness premium is defined as the percentage deviation of x% out-of-the-money call prices from x% out-of-the-money put prices. It should be directly related to the skewness of the risk-neutral distribution. The simple Black-Scholes-Merton assumption of lognormally distributed asset prices with a constant volatility[5] implies that the risk-neutral distribution is roughly symmetric and slightly positive skewed. This allows the definition of the following property regardless of the maturity of the options

$$0\% \leq SK(x) \leq x\%,$$

for which $SK =$ skewness and $x =$ amount divergence in percentage.

Out-of-the-money options, x% out-of-the-money calls should trade at a slight 0% to x% premium over the correspondingly out-of-the-money puts if any of the standard distributional hypotheses of the Black-Scholes-Merton framework is assumed.

Exotic options

The first generation of exotic options include Bermuda, barrier, or digital option. At a later stage, options on multi-underlying assets appeared such as option on basket and rainbow structures. A second-generation of exotic options appeared at the end of the last century such as complex path dependent options and options on nonlinear underlying assets. This section provides an overview of the available instruments and the risk considerations for financial institutions' balance sheets.

Time-dependent options

Time-dependent options are options that include contract features that are determined at some time after the initiation of the contract. A Bermuda option permits the

---

[5] As described by the Brownian motion.

holder to exercise on certain specific dates on or before maturity. It lies between a traditional European option and an American option. Because of this feature, the value of a Bermuda option is greater than that of a European but less than that of an American option.

A forward-start option is the advanced purchase of a put or call option that will become active at some specified future time. It is essentially a forward on an option, only the premium is paid in advance. The underlying asset and time-to-maturity are specified at that inception of the option. The strike price is determined when the option becomes active. Typically, it is set at-the-money based upon the value of the underlying asset at that time. Alternatively, it can be set a predetermined percentage in-the-money or out-of-the-money. Forward-start options are therefore nothing else than an option that will start at some time in the future. A practical but less obvious example of forward-start options are employee incentive schemes.

A cliquet option (also called ratched or reset option) is a series of consecutive forward-start at-the-money options where the strike price is set in accordance with the underlying price behaviour. The first is active immediately. The second becomes active when the first expires and so on. Each option is struck at-the-money when it becomes active. The effect of the entire instrument is of an option that periodically locks in profits in a manner somewhat analogous to a mechanical ratchet. The expected value of a cliquet option is calculated by generating the implied forward volatility curve. The cliquet premium is then nothing else than the present value of the premiums for the option series.

$$C_c = \sum_{t=1}^{T} C_N e^{-rt_n}.$$

The number of reset periods (n) is determined by the buyer in advance. More resets make the option more expensive. A cliquet call is always more expensive than a straight at-the-money call.

Path-dependent option

Some exotic options are path dependent. Their terminal value (at exercise or expiration) depends upon the value of the underlying asset, not only at that time but also at prior points in time. In this sense, the option's terminal value depends upon the price path taken by the underlying asset over the life of the option. The pricing and the hedging mechanisms are typically more difficult for path-dependent options. Asian option has a pay-out at maturity that is a function of the average underlying prices (either arithmetic or geometric) over some designated period during the life of the contract rather than the price of maturity. It is an option whose pay-off is linked to the average value of the underlying asset on a specific set of dates during the life of the option. It is often also called average option with two basic forms. An average rate option (or average price option) is a cash-settled option whose pay-off is based on the difference between the average value of the underlying asset during the life of the option and a fixed strike. An average strike option is cash settled or physically settled. It is structured like a vanilla option except that its strike is set equal to the average value of the underlying asset over the life of the option. Both forms can be structured as puts or calls. Exercise is usually European, but it is possible to specify early exercise provisions based upon an average-to-date. Both forms of Asian options are less expensive than the plain-vanilla option.

A barrier option is a path-dependent option that has one of two features. A knock-out feature causes the option to immediately terminate if the underlying asset reaches a specified barrier level. A knock-in feature causes the option to become effective only if the underlying asset first reaches a specified barrier level. There are eight flavours of barrier options comprising European puts or calls having barriers that are up-and-out, down-and-out, up-and-in, and down-and-in. The option premium of a barrier is always paid in advance. Because of the contingent nature of the option, they tend to be lower than for a corresponding plain-vanilla option. Because barrier options are less expensive, they are often used to reduce transaction costs in market situations where the buyer either believes the chances of the option hits the knockout level are small or high for the knock-in level. This probability crucially depends on the volatility and its expectations of the underlying asset. If a barrier option fails to exercise, the seller may pay a rebate to the buyer of the option. Knockouts may pay a rebate when they are knocked out, and knock-ins may pay a rebate if they expire without ever knocking in. This decreases the loss to the option holder. The rebate can be paid at the knockout event that is at expiry (not deferred) or at the defined time-of-maturity (deferred).

There is no clear relationship between volatility and the option value in barrier options. On the one hand, an increase in volatility also increases the value of a barrier option as it increases the probability that the option ends in-the-money. On the other hand, the increase in volatility increases the probability that the trigger (barrier level) will be reached and the option ceases to exist in case of a barrier knockout option or begins to exist in case of a barrier knock-in option. These two effects are crucially dependent on the strike and barrier level and may compensate each other. It is therefore referred to the strike level effect and the barrier level effect. The closer the price of the underlying asset is at the strike level, the more dominant the strike level effect becomes. The closer the price of the underlying asset is at the barrier level, the more dominant the barrier level effect becomes. For a knockout barrier structure with a reasonable probability that the barrier level will be reached, an increasing term-to-maturity and volatility increase the probability that a barrier option will be knocked out. This makes the option cheaper. The holder of the knockout option is short volatility and long the time value. The opposite is true for knock-in structure where an increasing term-to-maturity and volatility increase the probability that the barrier option will be knocked-in. This makes the option more expensive. The holder of the knock-in option is long volatility and is short the time value.

Multiasset option

A multiasset or multifactor option is an option whose pay-off depends upon the performance of two or more underlying assets. A basket option is an option whose pay-off depends on the value of a portfolio or basket of underlying assets. As the diversification effect implies, the value of the basket option will be less than the sum of a set of options on each of the components of the basket. A European basket option can be valued with two approaches: firstly, with Monte Carlo simulation by assuming that the asset follows correlated geometric Brownian motion processes. Secondly, by calculating the first two moments of the basket at maturity of the option in a risk-neutral world while assuming the value of the basket is lognormally distributed at that time.

A quantity adjusting option (quanto) or cross-currency option is cash settled while having an underlying asset denominated in one (foreign) currency but settles in another (domestic) currency at a fixed exchange rate. Essentially, a quanto has an embedded currency forward with a variable notional amount. It is the variable notional amount that gives quantos their name. Quanto options have both the strike price and underlying denominated in the foreign currency. At exercise, the value of the option is calculated as the option's intrinsic value in the foreign currency, which is then converted to the domestic currency at the fixed exchange rate. Pricing a quanto option entails modelling both the underlying asset and the exchange rate, as well as the correlation between them. The lower the correlation between the underlying asset and the foreign exchange rate the cheaper is the option. The higher the difference between the two volatilities, the more expensive is the option. This price behaviour can be explained by the hedging mechanism that consists of a dynamic replication processes in both the underlying asset and the foreign exchange forwards. The correlation between the two affect the issuer's profit and loss which is reflected in the option value.

Interest-rate options

Although options on interest rates are nothing other than call (caps) and put (floors) option, their terminology is slightly different and needs a basic understanding when structuring them. So is the most common type of a cumulative option (a series of call options with an identical strike level that is called the cap level), the interest-rate cap. An interest-rate cap pays off if the average interest rate at the rollover dates of a firm's debt is greater than a specified cap rate. In an increasing environment, this allows, for instance, international corporations to hedge their interest rate expenses. A swaption, on the hand, is an option and therefore the right to enter into a swap transaction.

Caps and floors

An alternative to this linear hedge strategy of an anticipated rise in interest rates would be to buy an option that provides interest-rate protection. A call option on a FRA, for example, provides the right, but not the obligation to buy a FRA on the date when the borrowing rate was fixed. If interest rates had risen above the strike rate by then, the option would be exercised, and this would cap the borrowing rate at the strike level. A put option on an interest-rate future would have the similar effect. Caps are options designed to provide insurance against the rate of interest on an underlying floating-rate note rising above a certain level, the cap level. It is thus nothing else than a series of call option on the rate or put options on the respective zero bond. It can be used to create an upper limit on the cost of floating-rate liabilities. It guarantees the rate charged on loan will be the minimum of the prevailing rate and the cap rate. Interest-rate caps can best be understood by first considering a floating rate note where the interest rate is reset periodically. A cap is a package of single caplets over a certain time period. It is not usual to include the first interest period because the interest rate for the first period is already known so that an option on the first period would have no value. The exposure period for a caplet starts when the cap is purchased and finishes on the interest-rate reset date of one of the borrowing periods. Each caplet covers one protection period. The protection period for caplet corresponds to one of the interest-rate periods of the underlying borrowing and is normally 3, 6, or 12 months long. Floors protect the overall rate of return associated with a floating-rate asset. The interest-rate floor provides a pay-off when interest rate on the underlying floating rate note falls below a certain rate. Analogously to interest-rate caps, an interest-rate floor is a package of put options on interest rates or a portfolio of call-options on zero-coupon bonds. A floor is a package of single floorlets. If interest rates fall through the floor of the LIBOR rate on any reset date, the relevant floorlet will be exercised against the seller, who must pay the difference between the prevailing rates and the floor rate. From an investor view, the floor provides an investor's protection of falling floating interest coupon paying.

The combination of selling a floor at a lower strike rate, and buying a cap at a higher strike rate, is called a collar. The holder of a collar is usually a representative from the liability side of the balance sheet (corporations, firms with financing needs) as the interest expenses can be locked in. The reverse combination of buying a floor at a lower strike rate and selling a cap at a higher strike rate is called a reverse collar. The holder of a reverse collar is usually a representative from the asset side of the balance sheet (institutional investors such as pension funds or insurance companies or the treasury department) that need to guarantee a certain return structure (minimum return). In a collar, by setting the cap rate at or below the borrowers' threshold of pain, and the floor rate high enough to bring in sufficient premium income, the collar can be tailored to provide a reasonable compromise between the interest-rate protection and cost. By juggling with the cap and floor rates, it is possible to create a zero-cost-collar, one for which is no premium to pay. Collars are popular tools for hedging interest-rate risk over an extended period because they provide protection against a rise in interest rate, and some benefit from a fall in rates. If the market traded interest rate exceeds the capped rate on the reference date, the seller of the cap pays the firm the amount above the capped rate. If the market rate is less than the floor strike rate, the firm pays the buyer the difference between the floor rate and the interest-rate level. The cap-floor-parity states that when the cap and the floor have the same strike price, there is pricing relationship between the three derivative instruments. Unless this pricing relationship is not held at every point, an arbitrage opportunity exists in these markets that could be used to emulate the characteristics of the overpriced instruments

Swaptions

The swap options or swaptions provide another financial engineering tool for handling interest-rate risk that offers long-term interest-rate protection. The underlying instrument is a plain-vanilla IRS. They give the holder the right to enter into a certain IRS at a certain time in the future. The expiry date is the date upon which the swaption may be exercised into the underlying swap. The strike price is the fixed rate (swap rate) of the underlying swap. Swaption premiums are normally, like those on caps and floors, quoted as a percentage of the notional principal and are paid up front. A swaption can be regarded as an option to exchange a fixed-rate bond for the principal amount of the swap.

A payer swaption is the right to pay the fixed rate in an IRS. In a long payer swaption, the investor bought a payer swaption which gives him the right to enter into a payer position in an IRS. He believes in an increasing interest-rate environment as the payer swaption will then be in-the-money and hence exercised. In a short payer swaption, the seller of the payer swaption sold the right for an option premium to the counterparty to enter into an IRS. When the option is executed, she is taking the receiver position in the IRS. Her view is on falling interest rates because then the payer swaption will expire worthless. A receiver swaption is the right to receive the fixed rate in an IRS. In a long receiver swaption, the buyer is long in a receiver position that protects from a falling interest-rate environment. In a short receiver swaption, the seller of the receiver swaptions sold the right to enter into the receiver position of an IRS. In that case, the buyer would end up in a payer position. The buyer's view is on higher interest rates because the swaption will then expire worthless.

An alternative to swaptions would be to enter into a forward-start swap or a deferred-start cap. However, the engineering costs of the instruments differ. The forward-start swap rate is considerably higher owing to the steepness of the yield curve. The cap premium is substantially more expensive than for the swaption, which highlights two very important distinctions between the products. For longer exposure periods, a swaption provides protection against movements in interest rates only during the initial exposure period. By contrast, the cap provides protection against interest-rate movements right up to the expiry date of the last caplet. Swaptions can be exercised only once, whereas a cap has multiple exercise dates (multiple exercise prices). That gives the holder a great deal of protection. For these reasons, caps include more time value than equivalent swaption.

Credit options

There are several forms of credit options. The two most common ones are credit default swaptions and credit spread options. Credit default swaptions are option to enter into credit default swap. They are usually European with option maturities and their premium is usually paid upfront. Their maturity ranges from one month to one year, and the swap maturity is typically 5 or 10 years. Similar to the terminology in interest-rate derivatives, a receiver option defined the right-to-receive the spread which is equal to sell protection. A payer option, on the other hand, is the right-to-pay the spread and equal to buy protection. Unless otherwise specified in the default contract, the buyer of the payer swaption can also exercise the option if the underlying credit has defaulted. The pay-off of credit spread options is linked to the difference between the spread and the predetermined strike. Pay-off to option buyer at maturity can only be positive. This is to be distinguished from a credit spread forward in which the pay-off is linked to the difference between two yields or prices. It can be positive or negative.

3.2.5 Securitisation

In the process of securitisation, a pool of assets is sold to a special purpose vehicle (SPV) that repackages the assets in new distribution forms to investors. Securitised products such as collateralised debt obligations (CDO) and correlation products played a central role during the GFC. They led to substantial losses on financial institutions' balance sheets that concluded in the broader market panic after the collapse of Lehman Brothers in September 2008. However, securitisation with its hedging and trading mechanics remain an important tool for the management of balance sheets and risk exposure in the area of credit risk.

Legal process

Securitisation of asset can be defined as a process of packing individual instruments, converting this package into separate classes of securities, and enhancing their credit and/or liquidity status in order to sell them to third-party investors. Because the newly created instruments are backed by a pool of collaterals rather than by the general obligation of the issuing entity, the new securities are called asset-backed securities (ABS). ABS is a broadly used term whilst CDOs are linked to debt securities.

The process of securitisation remains for all asset classes the same though. The SPV, an independent legal entity, is solely created to purchase the individual securities of the collateral and issue shares of the ABS. It has no other assets than the debt securities acquired from the security originator (servicer). It has no other liabilities than those associated with the issued securities to investors. The originator creates the individual securities of the pool of collaterals and services their legal obligations. Through a pass-through structure, the payments are directly distributed to investors. Through a pay-through structure, the payments are first collected and then redistributed by means of an active cash-flow management. The pool of collaterals and its cash flows are administered by the SPV.

Investors' potential risk is dependent on the performance of the underlying pool. A traditional securitisation is defined as a structure by which the cash flow from an underlying pool of assets is used to service at least two different stratified risk positions. They are called tranches and reflect different degrees of credit risk. The payments to the investors depend on the performance of the specified underlying exposures. A synthetic securitisation is defined through a similar structure with at least two tranches that reflect different degrees of credit risk. The credit risk of an underlying pool of assets is transferred, in whole or in part, through the use of funded or unfunded credit derivatives and/or guarantees that serve to hedge the credit risk of the underlying asset pool.

Collateralised debt obligations

CDOs are asset-backed securities from a diversified pool of one or more debt classes. They can further be classified according to the characteristics of the underlying debt securities in collateralised loan obligations (CLO) and collateralised bond obligations (CBO). In a conventional CDO, there is an originator that pools together a number of debt securities which are sold to the SPV as a bankruptcy-remote entity. A synthetic CDO applies derivatives within CDO structures, linking its performance to the incidence of default in a portfolio of CDS. The synthetic credit risk, defined as the default risk of the portfolio of CDS, is redistributed by allowing different tranches to take these default losses in a specific order. Standard CDS indices such as the iTraxx and CDX have spawned index tranches. These are standard, tradeable slices of CSD index contracts, each bearing a different level of credit risk. There further exist customised or bespoke tranches and single tranche CDOs. In a managed synthetic CDO, the customised tranche of the reference assets in the portfolio is managed by the issuer or an appointed third-party asset manager. A CDO squared is the CDO of CDOs in which the collateral is made up of a mixture of CDO securities of several subtranches of synthetic CDOs. Others apply capital protected structures such as Constant Proportional Portfolio Insurance (CPPI) and Variable Proportional Portfolio Insurance (VPPI), techniques that are way beyond the objective of this chapter.

The risk within this structure is redistributed across three tranches. An equity tranche assumes the first losses up to a defined detachment point. The mezzanine tranche takes the next losses is defined through its attachment point. Finally, the senior tranche takes all the remaining losses. The advantage of such a structure is that by changing the details of the tranche in terms of its attachment points, it is possible to customise the risk profile of a tranche to the investor's specific risk profile. The attachment point hereby defines the amount of subordination below the tranche. The higher it is the more defaults are required. The detachment point defines the maximum amount of losses the tranche will encompass. It is used to set the tranche size and is often called the exhaustion point. The tranche size, also called tranche width, is defined by the exhaustion point minus the attachment point. The wider the tranche for a fixed attachment point, the more losses to which the tranche is exposed. The first-loss or equity tranche is the riskiest and usually not rated, but investors long the risk of this tranche get the highest spread in return. It usually defines *0% to 3%* of the asset portfolio's subordination. The mezzanine tranche which is lower risk and usually defined by *3% to 6%* of the portfolio is paid a lower spread. Finally, the senior tranche spawns *6% to 100%* of the portfolio and offers the lowest AAA-rated risk and the lowest returns.

The correlation between the different tranches has an important role within these structures. If default correlation is high, assets tend to default together which makes the senior tranches riskier. Senior investors see the risk of their tranche increase with correlation as more joint defaults increase the probability of default for them. For very high levels of asset correlations, the probability of default is located in the equity and the senior tranche. The securities in the portfolio either all survive or default together. Thus, senior investors are short correlation. If correlation increases, senior tranches fall in value. Equity investors, on the other hand, are long correlation. When correlation goes up, equity tranches go up in value. Mezzanine investors are typically short correlation, although this very much depends upon the details of the tranche and the collateral. The mezzanine tranche's sensitivity to correlation is a function of its attachment point, the size and the underlying credit spreads. Investors can be long correlation by being either long the equity tranche or short the senior tranche. They can be short correlation by being either short the equity tranche or long the senior tranche.

Correlation products

Correlation products are based on redistribution of the credit risk of single name credits across a portfolio of different securities. The redistribution mechanism is based on the idea of assigning losses on the credit portfolio in a specified priority, with some securities taking the first losses and others taking later losses. This exposes the investor to the tendency of assets in the portfolio to default together what defines the default correlation. A basket default swap is the simplest correlation product available. It is similar to a CDS with difference that the payout is triggered by the nth credit event in a specific basket of reference entities. Typical baskets usually contain 5 to 10 reference entities.

In a first-to-default (FTD) basket, $n = 1$, and it is the first credit in a basket of reference credits whose default triggers a payment to the protection buyer. In return for assuming the nth-to-default risk, the protection seller receives a spread paid on the notional of the position as a series of regular cash flow until maturity or the nth credit event for the FTD basket, whichever is sooner. The advantage of an FTD basket is that it enables an investor to earn a higher yield than any of the credits in the basket. The reason for this is that the seller of FTD protection is leveraging the credit risk by increasing the probability of a loss by conditioning the pay-off on the first default among several credits. The basket spread can therefore pay multiple of the spread paid by the individual asset in the basket. The most an investor can lose is par minus the recovery value of the FTD asset on the face value of the basket. More risk-averse investors can use default baskets to construct lower risk assets such as second-to-default basket, $n = 2$. A credit event is triggered after two or more assets are defaulted. As such they are lower risk second-loss exposure products, which will pay a lower spread than an FTD basket. The higher n becomes, the lower is spread paid to seller of credit risk. The greater the number of credits in the basket, the greater the likelihood of a credit event and the higher the spread. Credit quality, maturity, and recovery rate all have an influence of the pricing of the basket default swap.

The default correlation between the different assets in the basket has an important impact on the pricing of a basket default swap. If we assume full independence with zero correlation during the entire life of a transaction, the basket spread should be equal to the sum of the spreads of the assets in the basket. Given that the assets in the basket are all independent from each other and never become correlated during the life of a transaction, the natural hedge for a basket investor is to buy individual CDS protection of each of the individual names to the full notional. If a credit event occurs, the CDS hedge covers the loss on the entire basket. On the other hand, if we assume 100% or maximum correlation and the FTD basket is triggered by one credit event only, it will be as risky as the riskiest assets and the FTD basket should be equal to the widest spread of the assets in the basket. As with increasing correlation the probability of default of the individual assets as well as their probability of surviving increases, the spread of FTD basket is smaller with high correlation than with low correlation between the assets in the basket. The hedging of correlation products is driven by several factors and must be adjusted dynamically which makes it complex in nature.

3.3 RISK MANAGEMENT

While risk-taking is at the core of the commercial model of a financial institution, its management is about making the right strategic and tactical decisions to control it enterprise-wide. Enterprise-wide risk management defines a comprehensive framework across methods, processes, and policies. Value-at-risk (VaR) provides the quantitative methods to assess the risk. In Chapter 2, we introduced the generic principles of financial risk and this chapter has discussed the price of risk across the different asset classes and financial instruments. The following section brings it all together and applies the concepts comprehensively in a consistent framework under the VaR umbrella.

3.3.1   Enterprise-wide risk management

Enterprise-wide risk management (ERM) includes the methods, processes, and policies used by financial institutions to manage risks and seize opportunities in line with their commercial model. By identifying and proactively addressing risks, institutions protect and create value to their different stakeholder groups. ERM provides a framework that typically involves identifying particular events relevant to the institution's business, assessing them in terms of probability and magnitude of impact, determining a response strategy, and monitoring process and respective policy framework. The ERM framework is also to be understood as a risk-based approach to managing the organisation, integrating concepts of internal control, accounting and reporting, data protection, and strategic planning. The quantitative framework is based on the different VaR methods. The regulatory requirements fundamentally define the ERM framework. Specific internal policies set global risk limits which are allocated to business units in a top-down process. This process must be consistent and comprehensive. The risk reporting, on the other hand, remains bottom-up oriented.

Three lines of defence

The three lines of defence method is an effective scheme for structuring the roles, responsibilities, and accountabilities with respect to decision making, risk controlling, and institution-wide governance. It defines how methods, processes, and policies are aligned throughout the organisation. The business lines in the front office make up the first line of defence and are responsible for identifying, measuring, and managing all risks within their scope of business. They are responsible for day-to-day risk management. The central risk function as part of the executive management supervises and enforces the risk discipline across the organisation. It ensures an independent assessment and management from the business lines and is responsible for the guidance and implementation of risk policies and monitoring their proper execution complying with documented risk policies. Most important is to establish a risk culture that is based on a transparent assessment of risk and a response framework that is enforced with great discipline by senior management supported by the respective policy framework. The third line of defence is the internal and external auditors who report independently to the senior committee representing the different stakeholder groups. The internal auditors' role is to provide an independent review of the effectiveness and compliance to risk policies of the processes. Corporate auditors on the other hand are designed to provide a reasonable assurance that the information provided is materially complete, accurate, and reliable and that employees action comply with corporate policies, standards, procedures, and applicable laws and regulations.

Risk function and organisational responsibilities

The risk function should be independently organised as part of the executive management, next to the finance function. The finance function and within it in particular the treasury and ALM departments have an important function in implementing risk management strategies through hedging and other financial transactions. Cross-divisional ALM committees should meet on a regular basis with cross-functional representation. To be effective in managing their risk exposure, financial institutions need to segment their activities in meaningful blocks for which the risk can be assessed and managed on an aggregated basis. If risk policies are properly defined, then risk limits can be set which allow to delegate and decentralise the risk accountability while an oversight remains in place. Risk processes include the identification, monitoring, and control of risk. Risk models serve for measuring and quantifying risk and provide input for the management processes and decisions. The different VaR models are a widely used measure and metrics in risk management.

3.3.2 Value-at-risk

VaR is the core quantitative method applied in risk management today. It was originally pioneered by JP Morgan through RiskMetrics in the late 1980s/early 1990s and is today the standard for risk measurement in treasury management, financial control, financial reporting, and calculating regulatory capital. It is the core methodology applied to assess market risk under the Basel framework as we further elaborate in the following sections. The risk factors applied as an expression of market risks are equity prices, foreign exchange rates, commodity prices, and interest rates across volatility, correlation, and higher moments of the probability distribution of skew and kurtosis for extreme value analysis.

The VaR method

VaR is defined as a threshold or loss value for which the probability of the mark-to-market loss over the given time horizon for an asset and/or a portfolio of assets cannot be exceeded given by a respective probability level. It is a function of two parameters, the time horizon T and the confidence level q. It can be calculated from the risk factors' statistical distributions of gains or losses during the time horizon T. There are different models to establish the distribution of the risk factors. It either can be estimated either parametrically or nonparametrically. Historical simulation takes events that occurred during a specific period as base of the distribution. Monte Carlo simulation, on the other hand, follows the standard assumption that continuously calculated returns (i.e. the logarithm of the return as outlined in Chapter 2 under financial modelling) follows a normal distribution. It generates series of random market scenarios drawn based on normal distribution of the returns. For each scenario, the profit (loss) of the portfolio is computed and an averaging mechanism applied across the outcomes. In the context of a portfolio representation with risk factors across the asset class spectrum, a variance-covariance approach is applied which is also often referred as delta-gamma VaR.

Standard parameters for VaR are 1% and 5% probabilities with one-day up to two-week horizons. However, other less standardised combinations are in use as well. In its basic application, normal market conditions and no liquidity impacts are assumed, which can be expressed as

$$VaR = [expected\ return - (q\text{-}sore\ of\ the\ confidence\ interval) \\ \times\ standard\ deviation)] \times value.$$

For illustration, let us assume the asset portfolio has a one-day 5% VaR of US$1 million. This means that there is a 5% probability that the portfolio will fall in value by more than US$1 million over a one-day period, that is, a loss of US$1 million or more on this portfolio is expected on 1 of 20 days.

Expected Shortfall and Conditional Value-at-Risk

Expected shortfall (ES) and/or conditional value at risk (CVaR)[6] further evaluates the risk factors in a more conservative way, focussing on the less profitable outcomes of the distribution. It measures the expected shortfall at the $q\%$ confidence level which is the expected return in the worst $q\%$ of the cases. q is set to be the expected loss of an asset and/or portfolio of asset values given that a loss is occurring at or below the q confidence level. Formally, this can be expressed as

$$ES_\alpha(A) = \frac{1}{1-\alpha} \int_\alpha^1 VaR_q(A)d_q,$$

for which the expected value of the tail of the asset prices (A) are events that occur with a probability lower than $1 - \alpha$.

This means that for high values of probability (q), ES ignores the most profitable but unlikely possibilities. For small values of q, it focuses on the worst losses. A value of q that is often applied in practice is 5%. We need to keep in mind though that q (even for lower values) does not assess the single most catastrophic outcome which needs to be assessed through extreme value analysis.

Extreme Value Analysis

Extreme value analysis (EVAN) assesses events with extreme deviations from the median of probability distributions. It studies the probability of events that are more extreme than any previously observed in a historical distribution. EVAN has found its broad application in finance and risk management in particular for assessing financial stress and market dislocations to build additional capital buffers with the objective to expect the unexpected. The method applies asymptotic distribution of extreme events that are rare in frequency and huge in magnitude with respect to the majority of observations. It tests different distributional assumptions for the data and applies them

---

[6]Sometimes also known and referred to as expected tail loss (ETL).

to the previously introduced VaR, ES, and CVaR calculations for the study of contagion and interdependencies across markets under conditions of stress. The discussion of the different calculation methods for EVAN is highly technical and would go beyond the objectives of this book.

3.4 CAPITAL MANAGEMENT

The management of capital is a core element of the banking business. Deposits and other funding arrangements can be seen as the input on the liability side that is used to fund the ongoing lending operations on the asset side. Capital is narrowly defined as pure equity as we previously discussed in Chapter 2. A definition that is further reinforced by the regulatory authorities who count equity or equity-like financing only as regulatory capital. During bail-in considerations, this narrow definition of capital becomes an open battle ground when even deposits may be considered as part of a write-down. The following section discusses these elements, starting with capital adequacy, structure, funding mix, and a capital-allocation mechanism that is based on excess-return considerations.

3.4.1 Capital adequacy

Capital adequacy is a core concept of ALM as it defines the core line of defence and pre-emptive protection in particular during financial stress. It constitutes the foundation of banking regulations aimed to make financial institutions more resilient, referring to the minimum level of capital absorbing potential losses. The higher the capital buffer against losses is the higher the protection against failure. This framework is implemented by the Basel accord that will be further discussed in the final section of this chapter.

3.4.2 Capital structure

A bank's capital is made up of share capital, reserves, and a series of hybrid capital instruments. Based on their characteristics, these instruments are categorised into Tier-one (T1) as well as Tier-two (T2) capital. Capital in the form of debt instruments is always subordinated because senior debt does not count as bank capital. Debt has to comply with specific regulatory guidelines in order to count as capital. In setting these guidelines, bank regulators are primarily concerned with the protection of depositors such that capital can be regarded as a safety net to absorb a certain level of unexpected losses without affecting the interests of depositors.

Core tier-one (T1) capital

Tier-one capital (T1) is a bank's core capital. The main components of T1 are ordinary shareholder equity, retained earnings, perpetual noncumulative preferred stock (T1 Preferred), reserves created by appropriations of retained earnings, share premiums, other surpluses, and minority interests. The equity and reserves element of T1 are often referred to as Core T1. The T1 Preferred elements are often known as hybrid instruments because they have a mix of both debt and equity features.

Hybrid tier-one (T1) capital

Hybrid T1 instruments are a specific type of subordinated bonds issued by financial institutions. Their interest can be paid on a fixed or floating basis but they are not collateralised or guaranteed. Hybrid T1 instruments are allocated to core capital in the balance sheet of the issuer. In the event of liquidation, they are subordinate to senior bonds, subordinated bonds, participation certificates, and silent participations. However, their claims rank before those of the common shareholders. As a main characteristic, they should be able to absorb losses before or instead of general debt holders. If they are preferred, the instrument must be perpetual but many regulators allow a limited step-up associated with a call after the 10th anniversary of the issue. Hybrid T1 instruments should not hold a noncontractual obligation to pay dividends or interest. The deferral of a coupon is usually at the option of the issuer, and deferred coupons or dividends are noncumulative only. To qualify from a regulatory perspective, hybrid T1 capital must meet a series of conditions such as indefinite maturity, combined with the issuer right to cancel at the earliest after five years, then followed at each coupon date. They can be cancelled only if sufficient funds are available for repayment. An interest payment may only be made if there are sufficient distributable profits available.

Contingent convertible capital

Contingent convertible capital (CoCo), also known as enhanced capital note (ECN), is a fixed-income instrument that is convertible into equity if a prespecified trigger event occurs. The concept of CoCo has been particularly discussed in the context of crisis management and was further endorsed by the Basel III Accord after the GFC. A CoCo is defined by its trigger and conversion rate. The trigger is the prespecified event causing the conversion process. The conversion rate is the actual rate at which debt is swapped for equity. It can be bank specific, systemic, or dual but it needs to ensure automatic and inviolable conversion. Since the trigger can be subject to accounting and/or market manipulation, a commonly used measure has been the regulatory measure of bank solvency. There are two main forms of CoCo. The equity conversion CoCos convert into equity below certain trigger level. Instruments issued by Lloyds Banking Group and Credit Suisse during the GFC fall in this category. Write-down Cocos involve partial write-down below a certain capital ratio. Instruments that were issued by Rabobank and UBS after the GFC follow this definition. However, there have been other features and additional structures. Some are reversible back into regular debt during a recovery event in case a certain capital ratio is reached or equity price goes above certain level. A well-known example of such an instrument was issued by Bank of Cyprus during the collapse of the Cyprian banking system.

Subordinated tier-two (T2) capital

There are two forms of subordinated T2 debt, called upper and lower T2 instruments. The main components of upper T2 instruments are perpetual deferrable subordinated debt. This includes debt convertible into equity, revaluation reserves from fixed assets, and fixed asset investments as well as general provisions. They are relatively standard in form and cheap for banks to issue. Through the introduction of Basel III, stricter definitions to the various forms of bank capital have been introduced. T2 capital instruments will be harmonised while T3 capital will be abolished completely. Only a maximum of 25% of a bank's total capital can be classified as lower Tier 2.

3.4.3 Funding mix

A bank's funding strategy has the objective to develop a diversified pool of funding instruments or sources which is called the funding mix. This funding mix provides protection against unexpected fluctuations while aligning the sources of funding with their respective use.

Deposit and saving accounts

Deposit and saving accounts form a stable funding base in accordance with a financial institution's operations and liquidity requirements. They are usually structured across different features such as maturities and optionality ranging from payment-driven current accounts to saving products such as fixed-term saving accounts or individual pension. Banks model behaviour of both assets and liabilities to assess balance sheet funding gaps. The behavioural modelling approach reflects the forward-looking macroeconomic outlook and captures customer rollover and optionality behaviour within a given set of asset and liability products. These projected behaviours are then used to set interest-rate levels and maturities and determine internally the charges and rewards for businesses for the use and origination of funds.

Wholesale funding

Banks often access a variety of sources of wholesale funds in multiple currencies, including those available from money markets, repo markets, term investors, and other financial institutions across different distribution channels and geographies. The pool of wholesale funding is usually well diversified by maturity, currency, product, and geography. The heavy dependency on wholesale funding of global financial institutions, in particular with regard to money markets, put the financial system on the brink during the GFC. In the United States, the reserve fund's price fell below one USD after the bankruptcy of Lehman Brothers in autumn 2008, an event which is known as breaking the buck. Breaking the buck occurs when the net asset value (NAV) of a money market fund falls below one USD which can happen when the money market fund's investment income does not cover operating expenses or investment losses. Investors subsequently fled the Reserve Fund because of the assets held with Lehman Brothers and caused a broader panic for money market mutual funds until the US government intervened. Today, a new legislation that supports money market funds through numerous provisions is in place.

Debt

Financial institutions issue private and public debt in order to maintain a stable and diverse funding mix by type, currency, and distribution channel. Secured and unsecured securities are to be distinguished. Secured funding provides an alternative source of term liquidity for financial institutions' balance sheet in several forms. ABS and covered bonds that are secured primarily over high-quality customer loans and advances, such as corporate loans, credit cards, and residential mortgage loans. Covered bonds are backed by residential mortgages. The exposure is covered in the full amount at all times during their term by mortgages (mortgages bonds) or public sector loans (municipal bonds). In the event of bankruptcy of the debtor, the pledgee has a prior claim before all other creditors on these coverage amounts for the purposes of settling the amount owing. Uncovered bonds, on the other hand, are bearer bonds. These bonds are solely guaranteed through the financial power of the issuer. Given their rank in the capital structure, they are often referred to as senior unsecured debt as these instruments take priority over other unsecured or otherwise more junior debt. Senior debt has greater seniority in the issuer's capital structure than subordinated debt. In the event of bankruptcy, senior debt must be repaid before other creditors receive any payment.

3.4.4 Capital allocation mechanism

As we discussed, for financial institutions, return on equity (ROE) is the crucial performance measure that further defines the capital allocation across different businesses, equal to

$$(Net\ revenues - Expenses)/Equity.$$

Several international banks such as Goldman Sachs and UBS have applied an attributed equity measure, called return on attributed equity (ROAE). It weights multiple internal and external factors in the calculation of a performance measure. UBS, for instance, equally weights its two main capital constraints such as its common equity T1 ratio with its common equity tier 1 leverage ratio, e.g. 50% x (13.7% x risk-weighted assets [RWA]) x 50% x (3.7% x leverage ratio exposure) and targets a 15% RoE in normal market conditions. Depending on capital requirements and the respective consumption/allocation, this may lead to a very diverse performance outcome across business lines. As in case of UBS, the outcome was heavily criticised by the analyst community.

As a result of the higher postcrisis capital requirements, many banks operated with single digits RoE way below their costs of capital which has historically been in the range of 10%–12%. Costs of capital in banking is crucially defined by an equity measure, understand as required market expectations that is derived through the Capital Asset Pricing Model as introduced previously in Chapter 2. The crucial question from a bank profitability perspective is if a return above its costs of capital can be achieved. This is represented by the economic spread between their prospective return on capital and their cost of capital. The latter is calibrated to the risk profile and capital structure of each business rather than by applying a group average. This can formally be expressed as

$$EP = Return\ of\ Capital - Costs\ of\ Capital,\ which\ then\ equals\ to\ the$$
$$Return\ on\ Attributed\ Equity\ (ROAE) - the\ Cost\ of\ Capital.$$

Any portfolio optimization should begin with an assessment of their economic profitability through maximising the economic spread of a financial institution's business portfolio. The analysis must further include the economic value of franchise connections such as revenue referrals, shared customers, scale efficiencies, brand considerations, and ultimately the ability to compete and grow in key markets.

3.5 THE BASEL FRAMEWORK

In response to deficiencies in financial regulation revealed during the GFC from 2007 to 2010, the Basel Committee on Banking Supervision developed a third version of the Basel accords, known as Basel III. Basel III, in accordance with the previously published accords of Basel I and Basel II, is a global regulatory standard on bank capital adequacy, stress testing, and market liquidity risk. It was agreed upon by the members of the BCBS in 2010–2011 and has been revised further since. The following section discusses the revised Basel framework with its methodology and core principles.

3.5.1 Historical context and development

The original Basel I accord was enforced in 1988 for credit risk with the Cook ratio which sets the minimum required capital as fixed percentage of assets weighted according to their credit quality. It aimed to keep the calculations simple for an easy implementation, and stipulated that the capital should be at least 8% of RWA. Under the Cook ration, the RWAs are calculated as product of the asset size (e.g. loan) with a respective risk weight and the risk weight dependent on the credit quality of the borrowers. The weight scale started from zero for sovereign counterparties within the Organisation for Economic Co-operation and Development (OECD), 20% for banks and municipalities within OECD countries, 50% for residential mortgage-backed loans, and up to 100% for nonpublic businesses. This approach is today known as the standardised approach as we further elaborate in the following sections. The available capital puts a limit to a financial institutions risk-taking capacities and requires raising new equity, liquidating assets, and/or taking risk-mitigation strategies to manage the limits. The original capital base included subordinated debt but equity represented at least 50% of the total capital base which was already referred to as T1 capital.

The 1988 accord was followed by capital regulations on market risk in 1996, amended in 1997. It allowed financial institutions to use models for assessing capital charges for market risk. The objective was to build a minimum capital buffer to provide protection against losses of value that could occur over the liquidation horizon of the asset. The regulation was based on and actively promoted the previously introduced VaR concept. The Basel II accord of January 2007, originally published in June 2006, revised the original regulation and considerably enhanced the credit risk regulations across stronger management practices and risk-sensitive capital requirements by using bank's own internal model for the credit assessment of the borrowers. It introduced the internal-ratings-based (IRB) approach, using as inputs for the risk weights the internal ratings of financial institutions. If internal ratings are not applicable, banks can continue to rely on the standardised approach as defined under Basel I with its fixed risk weights.

After the GFC, global regulators responded swiftly to the emerging issues such as liquidity, market dislocations, fair-value accounting, and overall solvency, given the pro-cyclicality and contagion that resulted in the global meltdown of asset prices and questioned the resilience of the banking system. The BCBS responded originally to the large losses with a collection of changes to the calculations of capital charges for market risk that has become known as Basel 2.5. The changes of Basel 2.5 were centred around the calculations of a stressed VaR, a new incremental risk charge (IRC), and a comprehensive risk measure for instruments dependent on credit correlation. The Basel III accord then comprehensively strengthens bank's capital requirements and introduces new regulatory requirements on bank liquidity, funding, and leverage. It further aimed to constrain leverage through defining the leverage rate exposure (LRE). The incoming requirements make a clearer and subtle differentiation between the banking and trading book and introduce a series of new laws and frameworks such as capital floors, standardised approach for measuring counterparty credit risk exposures (SA-CCR), or the credit value adjustment risk capital charge framework to immediately address the origins of the GFC.

As many of the new standards evolved beyond the original objectives outlined in Basel III, the entire set of new regulations is by now often referred to as Basel IV. Other authors refer to those components as the final form of the Basel framework. This final strand of regulations set a 72.5% capital floor for RWA and promoted an integrated management of market and credit risk in the banking and trading book. It further introduced a series of measures to promote the build-up of capital buffers in good times that can be drawn upon in periods of stress with the objective to reduce pro-cyclicality and promoting countercyclical buffers. Stress tests were designed to dampen any excess cyclicality of the minimum capital requirement. Exhibit 3.1 outlines the historical milestones of the Basel framework. The focus of this section is on capital requirements and how they shape managerial decision making.

3.5.2 Methodological framework

The capital methodology of the Basel framework is defined across three pillars. Pillar I outlines the minimum capital requirement. Pillar II shapes the supervisory review process for capital adequacy, and Pillar III defines market discipline with

1988	Basel I accord
1996–1997	Market risk amendment
1999–2007	Consultation on the Basel II accord
2007	Basel II accord (implemented in Europe)
2010	First publication of proposal of revised Basel III accord
2011	Revision to Basel II market risk framework
	Fundamental review of the trading book
2019	Basel III/IV implementation

Exhibit 3.1   Historical milestones of the Basel framework

regard to transparency and reporting requirements. In Europe, the Basel framework is implemented by Capital Requirements Directives (CRD) III, IV, and V; the Capital Requirement Regulation (CRR) I and II; the guidelines for the Supervisory Review and Evaluation Process (SREP); the Bank Recovery and Resolution Directive (BRRD) I and II; and Single Resolution Mechanism Regulation (SRMR) I and II as outlined by the European Banking Authority (EBA) as main authority.

Pillar 2

The Pillar 2 methodology is intended to ensure the firms have adequate capital to support the relevant risks in their businesses and to ensure firms have appropriate processes to comply with CRD IV. Pillar 2 addresses risks that are not adequately covered by the minimum capital requirement and to which banks may become exposed over a forward-looking planning horizon. It is also intended to encourage financial institutions to develop and use better risk management techniques under regulatory supervision in monitoring and managing their risk. The Pillar 2 framework includes an Internal Capital Adequacy Assessment Process (ICAAP) carried out by financial institutions to establish the additional capital required. This process in Europe is reviewed by regulators under the SREP.

Stress tests

Stress tests were introduced by Timothy Geithner as an instrument of financial stability in response to the lack of confidence in the US banking system during the GFC and has been promoting globally more forward-looking provisions in accordance with the existing Basel framework. Since 2014, stress tests have been conducted in Europe every second year under the supervision of the EBA. The objective of stress tests is to build capital buffers at the individual institution as well as the sector level during financial stress through which a broader macro-prudential goal of protecting the banking sector from periods of excess credit growth can be achieved. Requirements, already recommended under Basel II, to use long-term data horizons to estimate probabilities of default and downturn loss-given-default estimates have now become mandatory. Financial institutions must conduct stress tests that include widening credit spreads in recessionary scenarios. It leads to an improved calibration of risk models and the overall risk functions, which convert loss estimates into regulatory capital requirements.

3.5.3 Regulatory capital

The following section applies the previously defined elements of the capital structure in accordance with the Basel framework and discusses the different requirements from a regulatory perspective. It further covers Basel III's LRE and the more recently implemented additional capital requirements regarding the resolution of banks under the two "bail-in" arrangements by the Financial Stability Board (FSB), the BCBS and their counterparts at the EU level through the EBA. The two specific initiatives, Total Loss Absorbing Capacity (TLAC) and Minimum Requirements for own Funds and Eligible Liabilities (MREL), were both developed in this context. TLAC applies to global systemically important banks (G-SIBs), and MREL applies to all institutions within the scope of the European BRRD. TLAC is a standardised Pillar I minimum requirements expressed in RWA. MREL is a firm-specific requirement outlined as a percentage of total liabilities set by the respective European resolution authority.

Tier-one (T1) capital

Under the Pillar I of the revised Basel III accord, financial institutions must have a core T1 capital equal to 8% of RWA or face restrictions on paying bonuses and dividends. This is defined as

$$\frac{\text{Core T1}}{\text{RWA}} \geq 8\%.$$

In addition, a surcharge is applied as the biggest systemically important financial institutions (SIFI) have to carry an extra 1%–2.5% in capital for a total of up to 10.5% of RWA. The quality, consistency, and transparency of the capital base has been raised under Basel III. The predominant form of T1 must be common shares and retained earnings and is fully loss absorbing. There are several criteria for inclusion in T1 capital. The capital is fully issued and paid in, subordinated to depositors, general creditors, and subordinated debt of the bank. It is neither secured nor covered by a guarantee of the issuer or related entity or other arrangement that legally or economically enhances the seniority of the claim vis-à-vis bank creditors. Most of previously issued T1 securities and preference shares will not count as T1 capital under the new standards applied by Basel III.

The capital has to be perpetual with no maturity date and no step-ups or other incentives to redeem. It may be callable at the initiative of the issuer only after a minimum of five years provided that the financial institution has received prior supervisory approval, and the bank must not do anything which creates an expectation that the call could be exercised. The call cannot be exercised unless the called instrument is replaced with capital of the same or better quality and the replacement of this capital is done at conditions which are sustainable for the income capacity of the bank. Alternatively, the financial institution demonstrates that its capital position is well above the minimum capital requirements after the call option is exercised. Financial institutions must have full discretion at all times to cancel distributions, and all deferred tax assets (DTAs) must be deducted from T1 capital.

Leverage Ratio Exposure

The Basel III accord introduced a leverage ratio as supplementary measure to the risk-based capital framework of RWA, established under Basel II that we are going to cover in the next section. Basel III defines the rule for leverage as the ratio of core T1 capital to bank's total assets (with no risk adjustment) may not exceed 3%. The balance-sheet assets to calculate the leverage ratio are called the LRE. The LRE measure is based on gross exposures and naturally put a floor under the build-up of leverage. It represents additional safeguards against model risk and measurement error of the RWA framework, further endorsed by 72.5% output floor across the different risk categories.

Additional bail-in arrangements

TLAC was introduced by the global FSB at the end of 2015. It has been applied to G-SIBs as of January 2019 with the objective to have enough capital to pass losses to investors and minimise the risk of a government bailout. It is designed as a standardised Pillar I minimum requirement and expressed as a requirement based on RWA. G-SIBs are required to hold a TLAC amount of 16% in terms of RWAs or 6% of LRE measure. It will further increase to 18% of RWAs or 6.75% of LRE by January 2022. National regulators may interpret the requirements more strictly in their own jurisdictions. Instruments that count towards TLAC need to be able to be written down or converted into equity to recapitalise the entity as it goes through resolution.

Securities that are eligible to be held as TLAC include common equity, subordinated debt, and some senior debt. At least 67% of TLAC is equity whilst 33% can be filled with debt instruments. They must be unsecured liabilities with a maturity of at least one year. If a financial institution is a holding company or an operating company has an impact on its TLAC requirements contingent on its resolution plan. The FSB recommends that a significant foreign subsidiary should apply TLAC at the local level, equivalent to between 75% and 90% of what its stand-alone TLAC requirement would be. This is intended to provide incentives for home and host resolution authorities to cooperate in the event of the G-SIB's failure. Minimum requirements for own funds and eligible liabilities (MREL) have been enforced by the EBA. It applies to all institutions within the scope of BRRD that is further discussed in Chapter 6. It is defined as a firm-specific requirement and set by the responsible resolution authority as a percentage of total liabilities. Exhibit 3.2 describes the differences in further detail.

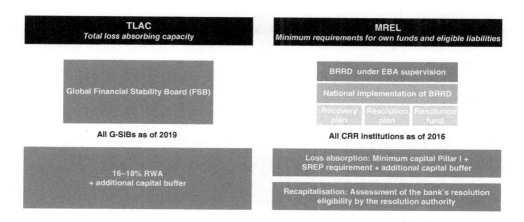

Exhibit 3.2   Comparison of total loss absorbing capacity (TLAC) and minimum requirement for own funds and eligible liabilities requirement (MREL)[7]

---

[7]Source: Dreke, Stefanie and Martin Wollinsky (2017). TLAC and MREL—Two initiatives, one goal in Neisen, Martin and Stefan Röth (2017). *Basel IV: The Next Generation of Risk Weighted Assets*; Wiley Finance.

3.5.4   Risk-weighted assets

The concept of RWA was originally applied to credit risk only under the Basel I Accord. It got today's importance and prominence through the Basel II Accord in the mid-1990s. It introduced through RWA a risk-weighted approach across the risk spectrum in determining capital requirements for credit, market, and operational risk. Standard models and internal models allowed financial institutions with different size and complexity of the business to apply a respective methodology. In this section, we follow the classic methodology introduced by the Basel framework across credit and market risks while liquidity and funding risks are discussed in a separate section.

Overarching principles

In accordance with its accounting terminology, the Basel framework distinguishes between the trading and the banking book. The trading book refers to assets held by a financial institution that are regularly traded and marked-to-market on a daily basis. The banking book, on the other hand, refers to assets on a financial institution's balance sheet that are expected to be held to maturity at historical cost and not required to mark-to-market. We further apply these two definitions across the treatment of the different risks categories. The entry point for the determination of capital requirements are five main asset classes. There is the sovereign asset class which includes government, central banks public sector entities, and development banks. Bank assets are explicitly specified by the regulation whilst insurance companies are treated as a corporate asset class. Corporate assets include all exposures of direct and indirect ownership interests in other corporations by a financial institution. Retail assets are characterised by a large number of small exposures to individuals such as mortgages or any other form of credit lines (e.g. credit cards, overdrafts, and consumer credit). Assets of small and medium-size enterprises (SME) are often considered as retail unless the lending arrangement is based on specific credit analysis.

Credit risk

Credit risk assessment was the core focus of the original Basel I Accord that was introduced in 1988 through the Cook Ratio and led to today's SA. From the early 2000s to shortly before the outbreak of the GFC in 2007, the revised Basel II Accord developed the IRB approach. As a result of the GFC, the reform under Basel III focused on credit risk in the trading book but then further followed up with introducing an output floor to close the gap between standardised and internal models under the more recent revision, now known as Basel IV.

Credit risk and its parameter estimation method

Credit risk is the risk of losses due to borrowers' default or deterioration of their credit standing. It has several components. Default defines the risk that borrowers fail to comply with their debt obligations which triggers a total or partial loss of an amount lent to a counterparty. It includes the risk of lost principal and interest, so-called exposure which leads to increased collection or workout costs. Various events potentially qualify as default such as delaying payments temporarily or indefinitely and bankruptcies. Exposure risk refers to the uncertainty with respect to the future amount that can be lost at the unknown time of default. The loss given default is the loss after the workout efforts. Credit risk also refers to the deterioration of a credit standing of a borrower which does not imply default but involves a higher likelihood of default. This is called migration risk. Recovery risk describes the uncertain value of recoveries under default. Recoveries depend on the seniority of debt, on any guarantee attached to the transaction, and on the workout efforts to the lender. Formally, the Basel framework applies the following parameter estimation method to model and quantify credit risk as

$$EL = PD \times LGD \times EAD, \text{while } RW = PD \times LGD,$$

for which EL = estimated loss, RW = risk weight, PD = probability of default, LGD = loss given default, and EAD = exposure at default.

The different risk components have been covered earlier in this chapter under the section on credit risk. RWA will be measured through the EL, and the charge is calculated as the capital adequacy ratio times the risk-weighted exposure. Under Pillar 1, the minimum capital requirements for credit risk are assessed by three main approaches, the SA and IRB approach which further distinguishes between the foundation and advanced approach. Exhibit 3.3 summarises the two approaches in more detail.

Standardised approach

The SA is used for banks that have no eligible credit rating system. It has remained in many countries the only approach that regulators have approved. Under the SA, financial institutions are required to use ratings from external credit rating agencies and specified risk weights as defined by the supervisory framework. All risk components are specified by the regulators. The Basel III accord originally did not target to

Approach	SA		IRB	
			Foundation approach	Advanced approach
Risk weight	External ratings		Provided by regulator	Internal estimates
Risk mitigation	Simplified as provided by regulators	Comprehensive internal estimates in accordance with regulatory specification	Provided by regulator	Internal estimates

Exhibit 3.3 Comparison of standardised approach (SA) and internal-rating based (IRB) approach[8]

---

[8]Source: Lang, Kristin, Friedemann Loch and Sebastian L. Sohn. TLAC and MREL—Two initiatives, one goal in Neisen, Martin and Stefan Röth (2017). *Basel IV: The Next Generation of Risk Weighted Assets*; Wiley Finance.

modify any elements of the SA but has been publishing consultation papers to address the increased criticisms. The regulatory risk weights are defined by asset class, that is, sovereign, banks, corporate, and retail. They range from 20% for AAA-AA rating up to 150% below the BB rating for the corporate asset class. Retail exposures are eligible for a top-down approach, which allows them to be treated as a pool rather than individually as for corporate exposure. The risk weight for general retail exposure is 75% while lending fully secured by mortgages on residential property is risk-weighted at 35%.

Internal-rating based approach

The IRB approach uses internal credit ratings assigned by a financial institution to all counterparties. The default probabilities are based on internal credit ratings and represent a conservative view of a long-run average throughout the cycle as annualised default probability. The total required capital is calculated as a fixed percentage of the estimated RWA and their applications subject to regulatory approval through local supervisors. The foundation and advanced IRB approaches are to be distinguished. Under the foundation internal ratings-based (F-IRB) approach, financial institutions can develop their own empirical model to estimate the probability of default (PD) for individual or groups of borrowers. This applies for nonretail portfolios only. F-IRB requires to use regulator's prescribed loss given default (LGD) and other parameters required for calculating the RWA. Regulatory recovery rates are prescribed as 55% for senior and 25% for subordinated debt. Under the advanced IRB approach, financial institutions are allowed to develop their own quantitative and empirical models to estimate PD, LGD, eEAD, and any other parameters required for calculating the RWA. For retail exposures, there is no F-IRB, and financial institutions are required to use either the SA or the advanced A-IRB approach in their measurement of RWA.

Credit risk mitigation

CRM defines the eligibility and methods of different credit risk mitigation techniques, namely funded and unfunded credit protection that can be applied to reduce capital charges. Common techniques are eligible collateral and credit guarantees. If recognised from a regulatory perspective, they impact the risk weights and LGD in a beneficial way. For collateral-based transactions, it is possible to offset a fraction of the exposure by a value assigned by the collateral. If securities are pledged as collateral, the value is adjusted by haircuts which are either defined by regulatory rules or based on financial institution's own estimates of collateral volatility. The rules maximise the gap between exposure and collateral value in order to take into considerations adverse market movements. For guarantees, the credit protection is recognised for third parties such as sovereign entities, public sector entities, banks with lower risk weight than the counterparty, and for other entities rated A- or better.

Securitisation framework

The BCBS published in December 2013 a revised securitisation framework that sets out the capital requirements for securitisation exposures held in the banking book.

It intends to address a series of shortcomings of the previous Basel II framework such as the heavy reliance on external ratings for traditional and synthetic securitisations as well as the difference of risk weights between highly rated and low-rated securitisation exposures combined with insufficient risk sensitivities of the underlying exposure. The revised framework introduces on a series of principles based on simplicity and look through with increased risk sensitivities through a more prudent calibration that is consistent with the underlying framework for credit risk. The securitisation exposure in the market portfolio have a specific risk, which is calculated as if they were in the banking book, and will further be covered in the following section under market risk.

The securitisation internal ratings-based approach (SEC-IRBA) is based on the capital charge for the underlying pool of exposures calculated under the IRB approach. In case the pool of underlying exposures is an IRB pool, the bank will be required to use the SEC-IRBA to calculate the capital requirements for the related securitisation exposure. If it is not possible to use the SEC-IRBA because of insufficient information on the underlying assets, the securitisation external rating-based approach (SEC-ERBA) is chosen, which is based on external credit ratings. If neither the SEC-IRBA nor the SEC-ERBA can be used, the securitisation standardised approach (SEC-SA) is applied as last resort. Under the SEC-SA, the calculation of the applicable risk weight will be based on the capital charges for the underlying exposures using the SA. In the event that none of these approaches are available, a 1250% risk weight is applied. All risk weights calculated under the SEC-IRBA, the SEC-ERBA, and the SEC-SA are subject to a floor risk weight of 15%.

Standardised approach for measuring counterparty credit risk exposure

The standardised approach for measuring counterparty credit risk exposures (SA-CRR) defines a comprehensive approach to measure counterparty credit risk associated with OTC derivatives, exchange-traded derivatives, and long settlement transactions. SA-CRR replaces both the current exposure method (CEM) and the standardised method (SM) with the objective to develop a risk sensitive methodology that appropriately differentiates between margined and unmargined trades. The SA-CCR retains the same general structure as that used in the CEM with two key components of replacement cost and potential future exposure. An alpha factor is applied to the sum of these components in arriving at the EAD. The EAD is multiplied by the risk weight of a given counterparty in accordance with either the SA or IRB approach for credit risk to calculate the corresponding capital requirement.

Market risk

The market risk regulation was originally introduced in 1996–1997 with a revision in 2011 after the GFC. The BCBS published in 2013 a consultative paper that has been the basis for the respective RWA treatment since.

Market risk and its parameter estimation method

Market risk is defined as the risk of losses due to adverse market movements depressing the values of on and off balance-sheet positions. The parameters fluctuating randomly are called market risk factors (m) which include the risks covered previously such as interest rate, foreign exchange, commodity, credit, and equity across different instruments. General and specific market risk factors are to be assessed separately. The Basel framework applies the VaR methodology as the underlying parameter estimation method for market risk. It can be measured under a standardised approach as defined by regulators and internal model approach in accordance with a financial institution's own proprietary specifications. At the same time, Basel III promotes more integrated management of market and counterparty credit risk as a response to the events of the GFC during which the capital buffer was not large enough to absorb the market-to-market losses of credit products. The revised framework for market risk provides incentives to strengthen the risk management of counterparty credit exposures, raise the capital buffers backing these exposures, and standardise OTC derivative contracts while moving their exposure to central counterparties.

Market risk in the trading book

The capital charge for market risk in the trading book is established across several components, defined as

$$Capital = m \times VaR + m \times Stressed\ VaR + Specific\ Risk$$
$$+\ Incremental\ Risk\ Charge\ (IRC).$$

The standard VaR charge for assets in the trading book applies a 99% q-confidence level over a 10-day time horizon. These specifications apply in the usage of internal proprietary market risk model, referring to the probability that losses are lower than VaR in absolute value, equivalent to the probability that the losses exceed the 1% q-confidence level. A multiplication factor between 3 and 4 is applied to the calculated VaR by the model with the objective to account for weaknesses in the modelling process and exceptional circumstances. A stressed VaR charge has been applied additionally since the revision to the market risk framework of 2011.

The specific risk charge is defined as supervisory percentage of exposures based on defined categories whilst unrated positions would receive an 8% capital charge outright while a less punitive application for liquid and diversified asset portfolios (applies in particular to equity). The IRC was introduced in 2009, in the middle of the financial crisis, as supplement and completion of VaR calculations for market risk. Its objective is to include the underlying default and migration risk, the widening of credit spreads, and the loss of liquidity for credit products in trading books, other than securitisation. It was left to the financial institutions how the IRC should be modelled, and the methodology of credit VaR can be used for deriving the IRC. As the IRC was proposed before the actual Basel III Accord from 2010, it is often referred to as a Basel 2.5 requirement. Under the fundamental review of trading book (FRTB), the IRC is getting replaced by the default risk charge. The comprehensive risk measure additionally incorporates specific and incremental risk measures from multiple defaults for securitised products in the correlation book. It is a specific risk charge for instruments dependent on credit correlation that is higher for resecuritisation than vanilla securitisation.

In 2013, the BCBS published originally as a consultative paper a comprehensive revision of the market risk framework that further became known as the FRTB. The FRTB rules were then published in early 2016 with an expected compliance deadline by the end of 2019, further endorsing a standardised treatment of market risk globally across stricter capital requirement. The FRTB addresses a number of major issues in a comprehensive assessment. A precise definition of the trading book outlines the new boundary between the trading book and banking book. The definition is based on instruments to limit the potential for regulatory arbitrage. The calibration of capital charges against default risk in the trading book will be more closely aligned to the banking book treatment. A new SA for all market risk areas to make it more risk sensitive and explicitly capture default and other residual risks. It remains the only method to assess the securitisation risk. The implementation of a new internal model approach (IMA) for market risk based on the previously introduced expected shortfall (ES) with a 97.5% q-confidence level that focuses on tail risk, varying liquidity horizons with constrained diversification and increased risk factor observability standards. Internal models will further attract regulatory scrutiny and stringent trading desk-level approval processes with more granular liquidity horizons and a new profit and loss (PnL) attribution and tests. There is an increased emphasis on stress testing, backtesting, and liquidity risk considerations.

Credit value adjustment

The treatment of counterparty credit risk in the trading book has further been enhanced with credit value adjustment (CVA) that incorporates the risk due to deterioration in counterparty's credit standards on the value of a derivative instrument. It strengthens the capital requirements for counterparty credit exposures arising from banks' derivatives, repo, and securities financing transactions. The CVA is the difference between the risk-free and risky value of a derivative trade. In it is calculated as CVA VaR, which is derived from the variation of credit spreads and added to the market VaR. It is further applied to collateral requirements that are outlined by the credit support annex (CSA). The CSA is a legal document that defines the terms or rules under which collateral is posted or transferred between swap counterparties to mitigate the credit risk arising from in-the-money derivative positions. It is one of the four parts that make up an ISDA Master Agreement.

Interest-rate risk in the banking book

The core market risk factor of the banking book is exposures to changes in interest rates, besides the SA-CRR that was covered under credit risk. However, it is not treated in the Basel framework as minimum capital requirement under Pillar I but as part of the enhanced supervisory process under Pillar II, that is, the ICAAP and the SREP. The BCBS considers financial institutions' internal systems as main tool for measurement of interest-rate risk in the banking book, and requires standardised interest-rate shocks as part of the regulatory monitoring. The VaR for assets in the banking book are calculated at a 99.9% confidence level on a one-year horizon. It takes into considerations the historical experience that it takes more time for credit events to materialise. If supervisors determine that a financial institution is not holding enough capital to commensurate with the interest-rate risk, they can require that the banks reduce their risk exposure or hold an additional amount of capital.

Operational risk

The framework of operational risk got introduced by the Basel II Accord and was revised in 2014 as part of Basel III by setting out a new standardised approach for its calculations, replacing the original basic indicator approach.

Definition and characteristics

Operational risk is defined as the risk of a change in value caused by the fact that actual losses, incurred for inadequate or failed internal processes, people, and systems, or from external events (including legal risk), differ from the expected losses. It further includes fraud, security, privacy protection, and legal, physical (e.g. infrastructure shutdown), environmental, and reputational risks. Contrary to credit and market risk, operational risks are usually not willingly incurred nor are they revenue driven. Moreover, they are not diversifiable and cannot be laid off. This means that as long as people, systems, and processes remain imperfect, operational risk cannot be fully eliminated. The Basel framework knows three methods to calculate capital charges: the basic indicator approach, standardised approach, and advanced measurement approach. The basic indicator approach is phased out and being replaced by the SA for operational risk.

Basic Indicator Approach and Standardised Approach

The basic indicator approach (BIA) is the simplest of the three approaches. It is based on the original Basel II Accord and only recommended for financial institutions without significant international operations. The BIA defines operational risk charges equal to the average over the previous three years of a fixed percentage of positive annual gross income. Figures for any year in which annual gross income is negative or zero should be excluded for the calculations. The fixed percentage, defined as α factor, is typically set at 15% of annual gross income. Under the SA for operational risk, financial institutions' activities are divided into eight business lines such as corporate finance, trading and sales, retail banking, commercial banking, payment and settlement, agency services, asset management, and retail brokerage. Within each business line, gross income is a broad indicator that serves as a proxy for the scale of business operations and thus the likely scale of operational risk exposure within each of these business lines. The capital charge for each business line is calculated by multiplying gross income by a beta (β) factor assigned to that business line. β serves as a proxy for the industry-wide relationship between the operational risk loss experience for a given business line and the aggregate level of gross income for that business line. The SA for operational risk is replacing the BIA on a going-forward basis.

Advanced Measurement Approach

Under the advanced measurement approach (AMA), financial institutions are allowed to develop their own empirical model to quantify required capital for operational risk which are subject to approval from their regulatory supervisor. Once the adaptation of AMA has been approved, a financial institution cannot revert to a simpler approach without supervisory approval. In order to qualify for AMA, a series of minimum requirements must be satisfied. The board of directors and senior management are actively involved in the oversight of the operational risk framework. An operational risk management system has been implemented that is conceptually sound and implemented with integrity. Sufficient resources are available to implement the operational risk measurement. Within the scope of AMA are internal loss data of a minimum five-year observation period, supplemented with external data that can be used to calculate the operational capital charges. The BCBS grants financial institutions several risk mitigation techniques that allow to decrease capital requirements.

Output floor

The output floor sets a floor in capital requirements calculated through internal proprietary models at 72.5% of those required under the SA. It is applied across all categories of RWA such as credit risk including counterparty credit risk and securitisation framework, market risk including CVA, and operational risk. The floor is a Pillar I requirement that was proposed under the Basel IV revision with the objective to remove inconsistencies and model risk in defining minimum capital requirements so they cannot fall below what is considered as an appropriate low level. Because of the potential impact of the floor on profitability and overall capital provision, the implementation is phased over a five-year period, starting with 50% in January 2022 increasing every year by 5% until it reaches 72.5% in its fifth year with a final increase of 2.5%. Under the Pillar III disclosure requirement, financial institutions have to publish two capital ratios: a first one under their internal proprietary approach and a second one that applies the 72.5% floor.

3.5.5 Liquidity requirements

During the GFC, several banks, including the United Kingdom's Northern Rock and the US investment banks Bear Stearns and Lehman Brothers, suffered a liquidity crisis, due to their overreliance on short-term wholesale funding from the interbank lending market. As a result of these events, global regulators under the G20 reform proposed new liquidity standards, the LCR and net stable funding ratio (NSFR), that were incorporated into the Basel framework. The LCR has been measured and implemented since 2011 with a full 100% minimum as defined under the standard by 2015 for G-SIBs and smaller banking organisations by 2019. The NSFR standard was initially proposed by the BCBS in 2010 and then amended in 2014 while banks had until 2018 to meet them. Over time NSFR calibration will be reviewed as proposals are developed and industry standards implemented. As we covered in Chapter 2, liquidity risk is the risk of a financial institution not to be able to raise cash when needed. There are two forms. Funding liquidity refers to the ability of borrowing for raising cash. It materialises when a financial institution is unable to borrow. Asset liquidity refers to cash raised from the sale of assets. It can create a vicious cycle when prices move against the asset holder while selling the asset. Extreme lack of liquidity results in the failure of an institution. The LCR and NSFR aim to address both forms of the liquidity risk. Banks have to keep enough cash and easy-to-sell assets to survive a 30-day market crisis and fund long-term assets with long-term debt.

Liquidity coverage ratio

The LCR addresses short-term liquidity risk by requiring banks to hold buffer of liquid assets to offset the risk from the loss of wholesale funding, partial deposits withdrawal, or other contingent liquidity risk. It applies to all banking institutions that have more than US$250 billion in total consolidated assets or more than US$10 billion in on-balance sheet foreign exposure. Banks are required to have a LCR of more than 100%, which means holding an amount of high-quality liquid assets (HQLA) that are equal to or greater than its net cash flow over a 30-day stress period. Formally, this can be expressed as

$$LCR = \frac{\text{Stock of HQLA}}{\text{Total net cash outflow over the next 30 calendar days}} \geq 100\%.$$

HQLA are cash or assets that can be converted into cash quickly through sales (or by being pledged as collateral) with no significant loss of value. A liquid asset can be included in the stock of HQLA if it is unencumbered, meets minimum liquidity criteria, and its operational factors demonstrate that it can be disposed of to generate liquidity when needed. The HQLA include only those with a high potential to be converted easily and quickly into cash such as cash, government bonds, or corporate debt. There are three categories of HQLA with decreasing levels of quality: level 1, level 2A, and level 2B assets. Level 1 assets can be included without limit and are not discounted when calculating the LCR. Level 2 assets cannot exceed 40% of the liquidity reserve with level 2A and level 2B assets have a 15% and 50% discount. Level 1 assets include balances at central banks, foreign resources that can be withdrawn quickly, securities issued or guaranteed by specific sovereign entities, and government issued or guaranteed securities. Level 2A assets include securities issued or guaranteed by specific multilateral development banks or sovereign entities and securities issued by government-sponsored enterprises. Level 2B assets include publicly traded common stock and investment-grade corporate debt securities issued by nonfinancial sector corporations.

Total net cash outflows are defined as the total expected cash outflows minus the total expected cash inflows during a stress scenario. The total expected outflows are determined by multiplying the outstanding balances of various categories of liabilities and off-balance sheet commitments by the supervisory rates at which they are expected to run off or be drawn down. Total expected cash inflows are estimated by applying inflow rates to the outstanding balances of various contractual receivables. The difference between the stressed outflows and inflows is the minimum size of the HQLA stock. Assume a financial institution has HQLA worth US$100 million and US$50 million in anticipated net cash flows over a 30-day stress period. It therefore has an LCR of 200% and meets the requirement under Basel III standard.

Net stable funding ratio

NSFR addressed structural liquidity risk. It is defined by available stable funding (ASF) over the required stable funding (RSF). The ASF is to be funded from debt longer than one year in remaining maturity. The RFS will remain on the balance sheet for more than a year. Formally, it can be expressed as

$$NSFR = \frac{Available\ amount\ of\ stable\ funding}{Required\ amount\ of\ stable\ funding} > 100\%.$$

Sources of available funding includes customer deposits, long-term interbank wholesale funding, and equity. Stable funding excludes short-term wholesale funding. The weights for longer term and structural term liabilities under the ASF are 100% of total regulatory capital that excludes T2 instruments with residual maturity of less than one year. It includes 95% of stable nonmaturity deposits and term deposits with residual maturity of less than one year provided by retail and small business customers; 90% of less stable nonmaturity deposits and term deposits with residual maturity of less than one year provided by retail and small business customers; 50% of funding with residual maturity of less than one year provided by nonfinancial corporate customers, multilateral and national development banks, and other funding with residual maturity between six months and less than one year not included in the other categories (this also includes funding provided by central banks and financial institutions); and 0% of all other liabilities and equity not included in the other categories, defined by liabilities without a stated maturity, derivative liabilities net of derivative assets, and trade date payables arising from purchases of financial instruments, foreign currencies, and commodities. Some of the weights for longer term or structural term assets under the RSF are as follows: 100% of loans longer than one year, 85% of loans to retail clients with a remaining life shorter than one year, 50% of loans to corporate clients with a remaining life shorter than one year, and 20% of government and corporate bonds.

3.5.6 Additional regulatory considerations of the G20 reform

Regulatory authorities introduced under the so-called G20 reform[9] series of policy measures which addressed the shortcomings of the precrisis ecosystem. In addition to the improved Basel capital framework, the structural reform addressed the separation of risk-taking activities such as trading businesses as well as the resolution of complex

---

[9]The G20 reform refers to the declarations of the G20 in landmark leaders' summits in London and Pittsburgh which listed specific commitments on financial regulatory reform.

banking organisation through defined recovery and resolution plans. The market infrastructure reform focused on counterparty risk and transparency through the introduction of centrally clearing, collateral, and reporting requirements. The jurisdictional authorities such as the EBA and the legislative bodies of the EU further developed and implemented the regulations in Europe. Chapter 5 on turnaround and transformation discusses the implications of both regulatory frameworks in further detail.

RESOURCES AND FURTHER READING

Bessis, Joel (2015). *Risk Management in Banking*; Wiley.

Cochrane, John N. (2009). *Asset Pricing*; Princeton University Press.

Coleman, Thomas A. (2011). *Practical Guide to Risk Management*; The Research Foundation of CFA Institute.

Copeland, Thomas, J. Fred Weston and Kuldeep Shastri (2014). *Financial Theory and Corporate Policy*; Pearson.

Crouhy, Michel, Dan Galai, et al. (2013). *The Essentials of Risk Management*; 2nd Edition, McGraw Hill.

Hull, John C. (2017). *Options, Futures and Other Derivatives*; Pearson Prentice Hall.

Hull, John C. (2018). *Risk Management and Financial Institutions*; 5th Edition, Wiley Finance.

Ingersoll, Jonathan E. (1987). *Theory of Financial Decision Making*; Rowman & Littlefield.

Jorion, Philippe (2006). *Value at Risk: The New Benchmark for Managing Financial Risk*; 3rd Edition, McGraw-Hill.

Jorion, Philippe (2013). *Financial Risk Manager Handbook*; Wiley Finance.

Lekatis, George (2016). *Understanding Basel III: What Is Different*; Smashwords Edition.

Neftci, S. H. (2002). *An Introduction to the Mathematics of Financial Derivatives*; 2nd Edition, Academic Press.

Neisen, Martin and Stefan Röth (2017). *Basel IV: The Next Generation of Risk Weighted Assets*; Wiley Finance.

Ruttiens, Alain (2013). *Mathematics of the Financial Markets*; Wiley Finance.

CHAPTER 4

Technology Management and Innovation

Technology management has been a critical success factor in banking and other financial services businesses. Often neglected from an investment perspective, the topic had up to the Global Financial Crisis (GFC) a shadow existence in many institutions, and this book would have most likely been written without this chapter. Only a few financial institutions such as Goldman Sachs and J.P. Morgan followed a different approach though in pursuing multiyear technology transformation programmes such as SecDB and Athena in response to specific business and operational requirements, in particular with regard to data analysis and management. The results have been impressive and got both firms a competitive edge in their respective business areas of global markets. SecDB is often quoted as the secret source that allowed Goldman Sachs to manage its balance-sheet exposure efficiently before and during the GFC. The centralised data pool provided crucial information in the daily marketing of the balance sheet to fair value, which seems to have given Goldman Sachs' finance department an early and sceptical view on the emerging issues in the US subprime mortgages market. Technology management and innovation are key capabilities of a successful financial-institution model.

Most other banks and in particular the global European banks relied on core systems that were often developed in the late 1970s and 1980s, leading to a patchwork of different system applications. These legacy systems provide stability but are inflexible to adapt to new requirements and add unnecessary complexity with time-consuming processes and high costs. After the GFC when revenues in many previously profitable areas collapsed and the cost–income ratios increased dramatically, the real operational costs of these outdated systems became transparent. After many rounds of business disposals and operational rightsizing, up to 75% of the incremental cost benefits were related to technology while investments of several billions of US dollars were required to modernise the platforms. Technology replatforming suddenly became a core focus in transforming and repositioning financial institutions.

At the same time, emerging technologies, often subsumed under the term "FinTech", created unseen momentum in innovation over the last 10 years. It seems that the previous emphasis on financial innovation switched to technology innovation as a result of the GFC. FinTech is the shortened version of the phrase financial technology and became a synonym for the initiatives of a dedicated start-up community that developed new services and solutions outside of incumbent financial institutions. Regulators and governments further supported the start-up community with testing platforms, known as sandboxes, and financial as well as political assistance. London in particular became a major hub where financial and technology talent were able to meet within an organised ecosystem. However, financial technology is more than this narrowly applied definition of FinTech that is associated with the start-up community and respective ecosystem. It is an industry-specific technology application that includes several building blocks from data management, artificial intelligence (AI) and machine learning (ML), robotic process automation (RPA), infrastructure, programming and software development, and distributed ledger technology (DLT).

The transformational impact of these different technology applications can further be assessed across the core functions of financial institutions. These include operational efficiency and performance improvement with emphasis on workflow solutions and application integration management as well as infrastructure with emphasis on data management and cloud computing. This is followed by augmented decision making which includes analytics and research, underwriting and lending, securities trading and marketing, investment advisory, and risk and capital management. And finally, technology-enabled or digital financial innovation has been in particular focused on crypto assets. These three areas form the core of the financial industry's change agenda. This chapter is organised accordingly, covering financial technology management, innovation with its four building blocks, and their transformational impact. During the entire chapter, we use a broad definition of FinTech, applying the abbreviation to the entire financial technology universe.

4.1   FINANCIAL TECHNOLOGY MANAGEMENT

Technology management is the discipline to align platforms and systems to the commercial and operational requirements of a business. Its objective is to ensure efficient and effective delivery of products and related services with the objective to gain a competitive advantage for its market positioning. It has a critical role in shaping the organisation and develop a roadmap for different system applications. It drives the commercial and operational agenda. Its importance has increased with the fundamental impact technology has had over any organisation. Innovation has always been a crucial part of the technology agenda and drives evolution from an organisational and structural perspective. Before we elaborate on this development further, the terminology of the different elements of technology management is to be clarified and substantiated.

4.1.1   Traditional role and innovation

Technology strategy outlines the long-term action plan to enable the realisation of the overarching corporate strategy through the available system architecture. It is outlined in a dedicated strategy document that must be aligned and approved by senior leadership and the business representatives. The technology infrastructure describes the collection of systems, the facilities and data centres on which the hardware and software are hosted. It allows data processing, and workflows can be automated through more advanced and sophisticated software solutions. Data are core to any financial services business, and the increased availability and capacity have been an opportunity, challenge, and threat at the same time. Security refers to measures taken to ensure that the business is protected against unauthorised access, use, modification, and destruction of data. This also includes any policy and initiatives taken against cyber security attacks.

The technology organisation is the function that delivers the services, including the development and maintenance of systems and infrastructure. In financial institutions, it supports many different areas in the front office and operations but most importantly the underlying data pool that facilitates the risk-transfer mechanism across the different businesses. Continuous development of technology is key as long as it is client centric and targets the efficient delivery of product and services.

In FinTech, as in any other form of industry-specific technology development, the innovation over the last 25 years has been dramatic and fundamentally transformed the operational possibilities in the design of distribution channels, processing, and new operating models. Operating models are repositioned in accordance with new forms of application and integration management that are well known in other industries such as consumer products (e.g. Amazon) and entertainment (e.g. Netflix) respectively. The relationships and partnerships with outside vendors and the value of customer data have had to be rethought through new models of open banking which has further been enforced by regulators. Outdated core systems are replaced by more standardised software applications while cloud computing completely changes data and infrastructure management. Open architecture allows the design of a new operating model with a more flexible application and integration of third-party vendors and the leverage of data analytics. Cloud computing (CC) further facilitates the central access of data across different functional agenda such as finance and risk management whereas distributed ledger technology (DLT) promises substantial gain in operational efficiency in particular in payments and settlement. There are substantial benefits for performance improvement, market differentiation, and new revenue opportunities through disrupting traditional distribution channels and breaking up traditional value chains. However, these developments may happen within the existing structure of the financial industry whereas specialisation in underserved client segments and lean delivery models remain core to the distribution through new players. Realising these benefits requires a thorough understanding of the underlying technology components, combined with specialised skill sets and consistent delivery methodology.

4.1.2 Targeted replatforming

Financial institutions' change agenda is fundamentally shaped by innovation which led to a dedicated discipline of technology replatforming. It replaces old with new systems while integrating the emerging technologies in the design of operational platforms. While profitability pressures drive the different change initiatives to increase operational efficiency and augment decision making, complex system architecture and large budget requirements have challenged the execution of a targeted replatforming agenda across the financial industry. Many financial institutions suffer under their inflexible legacy systems that are often more than 40 years old. These legacy systems made it difficult for financial institutions to adapt to the new customer and regulatory requirements imposed on them and to migrate away from their traditional technology solutions. Both the examples of Goldman Sachs's SecDB as well as J.P. Morgan's Athena have shown the multiyear investment horizon of such endeavour while many other banks have already abandoned their own large-scale replatforming initiatives. Changes to bank systems are cumbersome and expensive, requiring specific skill sets that are often scarcely available. However, these technical challenges are not the only reason why incumbent financial institutions have been slow in adapting to innovation. Political interests of individual business units, bureaucracy, and risk aversion to initiate change have been other major factors in slowing down the transformation agenda. The regulatory complexity such as requirements on operational risk are not supporting the change agenda.

At the same time, new players have started to establish themselves in payments, lending, and funding, reinventing the services provisions with a predominant focus on the retail segment. Most recently, new entrants have begun to move into corporate and institutional segment, disrupting analytical, advisory, and investment services that were in many cases dominated by a group of large established players. These FinTech companies are often portrayed as a principal threat to incumbent banks and the potential end of the traditional banking industry in a new, fairer, and more customer-centric world. However, when we move from pure technology service provision to actual client-facing services, many start-ups struggle to attract profitable customers and manage the regulatory complexity effectively. It remains an open question if the incumbents' market positioning remains untouched within their respective business areas or if new digital players can create commercially successful and sustainable service offerings. Most likely, the incumbents will consolidate and specialise to regain profitability with technology as a major driver of this transformation.

Many incumbents have responded to these challenges by setting up incubators, innovation centres/digital hubs, dedicated investment teams, and corporate venture capital (CVC) funds through which they bring the ideas and development of the start-up community in house. Santander's InnoVentures, BBVA's Propel Venture Fund, and SC Ventures Fintech Bridge are good examples of VC applications while Goldman Sachs Principal Strategic Investments (PSI) invested in successful FinTechs such as Kensho, Nutmeg, or Symphony in which it sees operational value for its businesses. PSI has been combined with other investing groups across GS and is today part of the GS Growth team. All major global banks including Citigroup, Deutsche Bank, UBS, and Credit Suisse have established their own incubators, innovation centres, and digital hubs in London, New York, Silicon Valley, and other major hubs across the globe. Several banks have set up their own digital banks such as RBS with Bo (consumer) and Mettle (commercial) or Goldman Sachs with Marcus. RBS later abandoned its efforts to build Bo. Other banks such as Deutsche Bank shelved similar plans before even implementing them. Financial institutions seem to be looking to start-ups to innovate and transform their commercial and operational models with the clear objective to preserve and defend their own positioning. All these efforts are driven by strategic or principal interests in changing and innovating commercial and operational models and need to be distinguished from typical venture capital investments that are usually driven by financial returns.

4.2   EMERGING TECHNOLOGIES

There are four major technology innovations that fundamentally impacted the commercial and operational models of the financial industry. Application programming interface (API), CC, AI, and DLT are changing the way financial institutions operate.[1]

---

[1] PSI has been combined with other investing groups across GS and is today part of the GS Growth team.

They represent core building blocks of financial technology innovation and are usually referred to as the emerging technology agenda that drives the industry transformation. These emerging technologies have been supported by the exponential improvements in computational power, data collection, storage, and connectivity (see Exhibit 4.1). API and CC, but also to some degree DLT, are of particular relevance from an operational perspective with regard to the design of operating models, technology platforms, and respective infrastructure and software services. AI has fundamentally been impacting decision making but also allows the automation of processes in particular with the support of robotics. Blockchain, a distributed ledger technology, is further shaping a new generation of technology-enabled financial innovation. The following section introduces these technologies. Their transformational impact is covered in a dedicated section later in this chapter.

4.2.1   Software and infrastructure

Innovations in software and infrastructure have accelerated over the last few years through API and CC solutions. They are fundamentally changing the operational platforms of financial institutions.

Application Programming Interface

API is a software and web development concept that has fundamentally changed the technology architecture of financial institutions. It represents a set of clearly defined methods of communication among various components that makes it easier to develop computer programs by integrating the underlying programming building blocks. API offers a simple way for connecting to, integrating with, and extending software systems. It is used for building distributed software systems whose components are loosely coupled. From a technical perspective, an API is a communication protocol and accepted set of rules between systems such as a server, websites, browser, desktops, or smartphone devices. This may be for a web-based application, desktop, operating system, database base, computer hardware, or a software library. It can take many different forms and often includes specifications for routines, data structures, object classes, variables, or remote calls. APIs are usually not visible on the surface and are directly called by other applications so they do not offer a user interface.

APIs drive connectivity and standardisation between third-party applications. It further facilitates the share of data between systems. This has led to new architectural design and business methodologies such as software as a service (SaaS). IT provides agility and flexibility to operating model design in particular with regard to the integration of third-party vendors and the management of client, transaction, and reference data. The new operating models have become known under the term open banking as they give customers a choice between different banking products and unlock customer data. APIs provide the mechanism to enable these open banking services between different providers. This allows financial institutions to focus on their core competencies and capabilities while being in a position to offer their clients a universal set of banking services. Within a typical banking technology architecture, software systems are typically isolated and the functionality of one system cannot be accessed from the other system.

	Software and Infrastructure	Artificial Intelligence	Distributed Ledger Technology
Description	• Standardised interaction protocols, application programme interface (API), allow third party and clients to interact with financial institutions' core systems • Interoperability enables agile workflow optimisation • Cloud computing offers new infrastructure solutions	• Machine learning facilitates information gathering, processing and analysis • Algorithmic decision making facilitates more accurate predictions and outcome	• Blockchain facilitates transparent and secure transactions between nontrusting parties • No central authority and intermediary • Bespoke contracts that can be individually designed
Impact	**Operational efficiency** • Connectivity • Accessibility of services • Leverage of platforms and systems • Core systems • Advanced workflow management • Robotic Process Automation under Artificial intelligence	**Augmented decision making** • Alternative data • Advanced analytics • Predictions • Algorithmic trading and investment advisory • Risk management and compliance	**Digital financial innovation** • Crypto assets • Decentralised finance

Exhibit 4.1 Emerging technologies in finance

APIs provide the opportunity to connect these separate software entities. They provide the capabilities which are essential for connecting, extending, and integrating software. By connecting software, APIs connect businesses with other businesses, businesses with their products, services with products, or products directly with other products.

Application interoperability and smart desktops have been one of the key technology developments for large-scale banking and capital-market businesses over the last few years. Its original focus was on the integration of web applications with other web applications. Open-system containers were developed over time with the objective to create a virtual desktop environment in which these applications could be registered and then communicate with each other. Interoperability has now evolved into full-service platform solution which include container support, basic exchange between web and web but also native support for other application types and advanced window management. A set of codified specifications for writing API, known as the FDC3[2] standards, is driving these developments under the umbrella of the Fintech Open Source Foundation (Finos). A growing number of financial institutions has worked collaboratively with technology vendors to accelerate this developments given the substantial potential to optimise the workflow. Cosaic with its Finsemble solution, OpenFin, as well as Glue42 are at the forefront of this movement.

At the core of the delivery is the customer experience through web-based applications, desktop, or any other form of client interfaces. The user experience (UX) reflects a customer's attitudes and individual perception about using a particular product, system, or service. It includes the different aspects of human–technology interaction, product ownership, and system experience. As illustration, the fictional institution challenger focuses on saving and investment products for high net worth individuals. It provides a platform for efficient onboarding and basic client services while specialising in tax-efficient saving accounts and the respective processing and servicing. Through an API-integration layer, challenger connects to a group of selected providers that further offer investment advice through a robo-advisor allocation mechanism and specific investment products to its clients. Everything is facilitated electronically and clients can access the services through webpage and mobile applications.

Cloud computing

CC is the on-demand network access and system resources availability to many different users over the internet. It is applied especially to data storage and computing power and has added completely new features to technology infrastructure and software applications. The availability of high-capacity networks, low-cost infrastructure, and storage devices as well as the widespread adoption of hardware virtualisation, service-oriented architecture, and autonomic computing has led to strong growth in CC in recent years. The technology enables financial institutions to dynamically scale their data storage, computational power, and bandwidth which leads to a huge advantage compared to previous solutions around data centre and server solutions. CC relies on the pooling and sharing of configurable computing resources to achieve economies of scale and coherence. These services of resources are provided by third-party vendors

---

[2]FDC3 stands for Financial Desktop Connectivity and Collaboration Consortium.

such as Amazon Web Services (AWS), Google Cloud Platform (GCP), and Microsoft's Azure without direct or active management by its users. When multiple users access the same virtual resources in the cloud such as software, storage, or virtual machines, those resources know multiple tenants. Multitenancy therefore is an important term that defines the pooling of resources to provide a shared, common service to each user. Elasticity at the same time describes the scaling of demand of the multiple tenants on the CC infrastructure.

Visualisation allows the pooling and scaling of resources across applications and servers in an elastic manner. Application virtualisation delivers an application that is hosted on a single machine to a large number of users. The end-user does not need to have high-grade hardware in order to run the application. Server virtualisation, on the other hand, uses common physical hardware (network, storage, and computing machines) to host virtual machines. Virtual machines can be installed with their own operating systems and their own different set of applications, which allows consolidation of large numbers of physical machines onto fewer physical machines with respective lower operating costs. Several cloud providers have open-source technologies and applications that can be flexibly integrated in the tailored offering of financial institutions.

CC distinguishes four deployment models. A private or enterprise cloud refers to a single organization protected by a firewall while public clouds are available to many organizations. Public CC services may be provided by computing resources anywhere in the world and can be accessed by anyone who has internet access. This has led to challenges with regard to data integrity as in particular financial institutions need to comply with strict regulatory requirements (e.g. privacy and data security laws). A combination of both private and public is called a hybrid cloud. A hybrid cloud is essentially a conglomerate of other types of clouds. It is mostly used when a cloud service needs to peruse computing resources from other clouds because its own resources are being utilised at full capacity. There are also community clouds which are a broader version of a private cloud. It supports communities that have common interests or shared concerns such as security requirements, data privacy, regulatory environment, business model, and needs of end users.

CC is associated with five service models across different levels of abstraction. Infrastructure as a service (IaaS) refers to services such as storing data and files in the cloud or using the cloud to transfer data. Platform as a service (PaaS) provides a computing platform solution complete with hardware and operating systems while the user specifies the software to use. SaaS provides an entire software solution via the cloud, that is, hardware, operating system, and respective software applications. Information as a service (INaaS) would in addition to the storage of the data (IaaS) provide the manipulation of data from a content perspective. Through business process as a service (BPaaS) an entire business function and/or process can be outsourced to a vendor. As we move from IaaS to BPaaS, the highest form of abstraction is attained. This means that each higher level incorporates the levels below.

The third-party vendors charge a pay-as-you-use model for its services which brings the overall operational costs down for technology, and allows to move from a capital expenditure (CAPEX) to an operating expenditure (OPEX) model in budgeting for each tenant technology requirements. Tailored compensation models may add further flexibility to managing technology costs across different operating models. CC allows financial institution to address the data fragmentation issue and outsource specific technology services from infrastructure through software. Core banking providers such as Temenos or IFS work with CC providers in offering SaaS solutions which then further allows implementation of an open banking operating model through integration layers.

4.2.2   Artificial intelligence

AI seeks to build autonomous machines that can carry out complete tasks without human intervention. AI has made significant steps forward in the digitisation and transformation of modern businesses. In financial services, AI has been broadly applied with early moves and contribution in particular in algorithmic-based decision making to assess and manage different forms of risk, price financial instruments, or execute trading strategies. Many of these algorithms have contributed substantially to the evolution of AI as a field by applying more advanced forms of ML. Most recently, due to performance and profitability issues, the focus has shifted to automate client interactions (e.g. onboarding) and operations as well as compliance monitoring and surveillance (e.g. fraud prevention). The expected increase in productivity could structurally reduce costs in financial institutions and address the ongoing performance issues. Before we discuss these applied topics of AI-enabled decision making and operating efficiency, a comprehensive definition of AI needs to be established. The following section covers the fundamentals of ML and RPA as a conceptual base with regard to the change agenda.

Machine learning

There are many and varied definitions of AI and the term is often interchangeably used with ML. However, the term AI should be applied broadly to the replication of human decision making and analytical capabilities which assumes a high level of human-like intelligence. ML in this sense is a specific application or key field of study of AI that uses models and algorithms for the analysis, manipulation, pattern recognition, and prediction of data. Under the term analytics, its objective is to discover useful patterns (relationships and correlations) between different items of data. As we further elaborate later, the rise of deep learning as a ML method is as close as technically possible today to a human-like form of AI.

Algorithms and ML models

Algorithms are mathematical procedures that allow one to interpret data in specific ways and create predictable output based on data patterns. As the name implies, ML is heavily supported by machine applications through computation. Although the speed and storage capabilities of computers have increased considerably over the last years, and ML algorithms have become more complex and sophisticated, computer or machine-based AI continues to fall short of true human intelligence. For human-like intelligence, often referred to as general intelligence that shapes learning and reasoning, there are additional elements required such as self-awareness, creativity, consciousness, and common sense that cannot be replicated via computer systems (at least at today's stage of development). The broader definition of AI must consider all forms of human intelligence and cannot restrict itself to specific tasks in the world of data science and computation on which ML is based. Professor Michael Wooldridge from the University of Oxford refers in his book *The Road to Conscious Machines* to precise recipes which can be followed by rote, which are to be distinguished from autonomous, general-purpose, human-level intelligence. Professor Max Tegmark further distinguishes in his book *LIFE 3.0* between narrow intelligence with the ability to accomplish a narrow set of goals and general intelligence with the ability to accomplish virtually any goals including learning.[3] Given the current development state and applications of AI modules, we refrain from using the word AI and focus on the ML terminology accordingly.

ML is underpinned by analytics through generating scores that drive decision making and subsequent actions. Descriptive analytics discover historical patterns to categorise data preferences while predictive analytics illustrate what actions should be taken based on predictions. Predictive models use large sample of historic and preprocessed data for new cases that are fed into the model in order to generate fresh predictions. Historical data are combined with algorithms to determine the probable future outcome of an event. Such models have made substantial progress through the advancements in computation and algorithm design. With linear models such as scorecards, decision trees such as classification and regression trees (CARTs), and artificial neural networks (ANNs), there are three main types of predictive models. ANNs represent the most sophisticated models today owing to their propensity to deliver more accurate predictions. They are based on an interconnected group of artificial neurons that uses computational models for information processing based on a connectionistic approach to computation. ANNs were inspired by communication nodes and information processing in biological system. Their computational models are loosely based on the structure of the human brain in accordance of how real neurons are connected. This allows replication of aspects of the brain's densely interconnected systems of neurons which define the process of learning through adjusting the strengths between theses connections. A typical ANN has anything from a few dozens to thousands if not millions of artificial neurons. Each of these artificial neurons falls into one of three categories. The first one is input units that are designed to receive various data inputs. The second is output units that provide the outcomes of the analysis, prediction, or decision. Finally, there are hidden units that provide the layers of connectivity between the input and output units. Information or data flow through the network between the input and output units across the hidden units that connect them in adjusting the weighting or strengths of the learning process. In most cases an ANN is an adaptive system that changes its structure based on the external or internal data that flows through the network

Advanced forms of ANN with multiple layers, called deep learning, are currently at the cutting edge of ML research and solve its most complex problems such as object identification, digital vision, and natural language processing (NLP). They are getting as close to human-like intelligence as possible and are today the fair proxy for a reference to AI. In deep learning, each layer learns to transform its raw input data in a more abstract and composite representation while deep refers to the number of layers through which

---

[3] Professor Tegmark even introduces the third form of universal intelligence with the ability to acquire general intelligence given access to data and resources.

the data are transformed. There are different deep learning model architectures such as feed-forward, recurrent, and convolutional neural networks that outline the path or chain across the different layers from input and output nodes. Feed-forward are the first and simplest type of ANN as the data move only in one direction. In recurrent ANN, mainly used for language modelling, data can flow in any direction and may propagate through a layer more than once. Convolutional ANN, mainly used in digital vision, have each neuron in one layer connected to all neurons in the next layer which makes the network fully connected.

ML methodologies can further be classified as supervised, unsupervised, and reinforcement learning. Supervised learning works with models that are being trained with data that have been structured and labelled manually by humans across clearly defined objectives. Unsupervised learning does not include instructions and labels, and the algorithms are free to identify their own structure, patterns, and grouping within the data, often without a targeted outcome. Reinforcement learning scores the performance of variations in a model against an objective to determine which models work best for a given dataset. The evolution of ML has accelerated dramatically over the last 15–20 years with computation and data availability as core drivers. There are many more different classes of models available, and new applications emerge on a frequent basis. With these developments, complexity has increased and with it costs in terms of resources, accuracy, and understanding of the models' output. Some model applications may even have become black boxes that are understood by only a small group of people. This leads to substantial model and operational risk that may raise further issues from a regulatory perspective.

Big data and decision analytics

Big data is a collective name that refers to the use of immense datasets for ML applications and respective computation power. It covers relevance, complexity, and depth of a financial institution's data that come from internal and external sources. Internal datasets are often propriety and nonpublic whereas external data are usually publicly available. To create a computer set-up that can learn, large datasets are required. Pattern recognition in a nondeterministic manner can happen only if the algorithm has access to a simple subset to make predictions of the dataset as a whole. Structured data are highly organised and can be codified, sorted, and searched in files. Most financial data such as accounting statements or transaction records are structured. Although structured data can be analysed with traditional computing techniques, the sheer amount of data today provides an operational challenge to almost any financial institution. The information value of structured data can much further be exploited in the decision making of any organisation which led to the emerging of big data techniques and the application of ML. Unstructured data, on the other hand, have no predefined model or organisation form. The individual data points have no clear and defined relationship with each other which makes it difficult to capture and organise them. Unstructured data can be found in emails, reports, news, social media, or any other form of written and oral communication. Specific forms of ML facilitate the process of interpreting unstructured data. They aim to accelerate this process and scale it to accommodate the enormous quantities of data involved while also enabling the identification of new and emerging patterns.

NLP is a branch of ML that facilitates the interactions between computers and human natural languages. This technology allows the identification, organisation, and analysis of large amounts of unstructured data from written or oral language samples. It applies the principles of linguistic structure and breaks down sentences into their elemental pieces to identify semantic relationships among them. In essence, it captures the raw data elements and processes them to decision analytics, often in the form of quantitative metrics such as scores. An applicant-dependent analysis is performed by the NLP on target and sentiment recognition. The algorithms detect the polarity of sentences within a range of positive, neutral, and negative on a respective target entity. The entity recognition may target company names but also influencers of a specific topics with regard to the company's situation and developments such as c-level executives and equity analysts. Sentiment data are an output of this process as they use large amount of language and evaluate its positive or negative connotation through a predefined event methodology. The event classification is shaped by key words that imply a specific attitude associated with statements made in the respective language. News and blogs can be analysed accordingly and establish a view on the sentiment of the statements in the text. A financial institution, for instance, can be evaluated with regard to the statements made in news and social media by influencers in terms of its environmental, social, and governance (ESG) agenda and respective sentiment scores calculated. Each ESG criteria will then define an event for the NLP mechanism to identify and analyse the available information feeds from numerous sources.[4]

The combination of NLP analytics with probabilistic optimisation leads to the development of effective forms of decision-making algorithms in financial institutions. Bayesian probability theory, for instance, allows the modelling of uncertainty in a sensible way by measuring unfamiliarity and enables appropriate subsequent decisions to be made under the respective circumstances assessed by the model through an underlying hypothesis. The probability for this hypothesis can be updated as more data become available in the process. This is called Bayesian inference, which allows the dynamic analysis of sequences of the same dataset. In the context of financial decision making, the Bayesian framework allows description of the collective behaviour of a stochastic variable such as an asset in a unified manner through underlying probability distributions. This enables the simultaneous assessment of risk and uncertainty. Unstructured data can therefore be collected and processed to a decision metrics before combining with traditional structured data through the implementation of an overarching ML algorithms that optimises the decision making. This approach has found its application in research, idea generation, and portfolio construction as we further elaborate in the upcoming sections on their transformational impact for financial decision making.

Robotic process automation and other process techniques

Robotics applies broadly to the application of physical, autonomous agents that behave intelligently. It encompasses all areas of ML as well as drawing heavily from other

---

[4]Andreas Pusch from YUKKA Lab provides in a dedicated chapter of the *AI Book*, an insightful overview of the topic.

engineering disciplines. In the case of financial institutions, it is mainly applied to the standardisation and automation of front-to-back processes through the concept of RPA. RPA is an emerging business process automation technology based on the notion of metaphorical software robots as ML workers. It allows an organisation to keep the value chain with its processes unchanged while automating it. RPA and similar techniques have now become an important contributor to the cost-cutting initiatives that have been pursued by many financial institutions.

Traditional workflow automation tools produce a list of actions to automate a task and interface to the back-end system using dedicated scripting language and internal APIs. RPA systems, on the other hand, develop the action list by watching the user perform that task in the application's graphical user interface (GUI) and then perform the automation by repeating those tasks directly in the GUI. Interactions with the GUI are getting automated and often do so by repeating a set of demonstration actions performed by a user. RPA allows data to be handled in and between multiple applications, for instance, receiving email containing an invoice, extracting the data, and then typing that into a bookkeeping system. Straight-through-processing becomes a norm for basic tasks and value chain initiatives. More advanced forms of ML such as advanced pattern recognition systems with self-learning capabilities can be deployed for more complex problem solving in these areas.

4.2.3   Distributed ledger technology

DLT is the parent technology behind blockchain, the technology that underlines the Bitcoin and Ether networks with their famous crypto currencies and digital tokens. The technology has found a broad application in financial institutions. It facilitates identity management, value storage, and back-office operations such as settlement. However, it is mainly known for financial innovation and speculation through cryptocurrencies such as Bitcoin and Ether. The section covers the basics of DLT with its blockchain design and the core technical components of cryptography, mining, and digital or crypto assets. The upcoming section in this chapter on the transformational impact further elaborates on the applications of blockchain technologies.

The DLT concept

DLT is based on a decentralised database. It is distributed across several nodes such as multiple computer systems and organisational units. The DL is a consensus of replicated, shared, and synchronized digital data with no central administrator or centralized data storage in place. The technology requires a peer-to-peer network as well as consensus algorithms to ensure that the replication across all nodes is undertaken. Every node will maintain the ledger, and if any data changes happen, it replicates and saves an identical copy of the ledger while updating itself independently. The primary advantage of this concept is the lack of central authority. When a ledger update happens, each node constructs the new transaction, and then the nodes vote by consensus algorithm. Once a consensus has been determined, all the other nodes update themselves with the new, correct copy of the ledger. Security is accomplished through cryptographic keys and signatures.

As a technology, DLT knows different concepts, which mainly differ in the way transactions are validated and stored. The most popular DLT concepts are blockchain, blockDAG (which stands for block directed acyclic graphs), and TDAG (which is an abbreviation of transaction-based directed acyclic graphs). These DLT concepts have different implementations that are specified by their designs. These implementations can be distinguished by specific features which are called DLT properties that are then further divided into DLT characteristics. Each DLT design has an individual configuration of DLT characteristics, which has to be a good fit for the requirements of a given use case. These requirements may be high scalability, high throughput, and a high level of anonymity. Our focus is on blockchain which is with very specific technology underpinning the most widely used form of DLT in financial services. Often the terms DLT and blockchain are used interchangeably although a rigorous technical application requires further specifications. These differences remains to be emphasised as DLT concepts are evolving further.

Blockchain technology

The blockchain system is today the most well-known DL design. In a blockchain, every node of the DLT has its own copy of the ledger. If someone adds a new transaction, all the copies of the ledger get updated automatically. The blockchain is a growing list (which explains the reference to chain) of records (so called blocks) that are linked using a mathematical mechanism know as cryptography. Each block contains the transaction data, a timestamp, and a cryptographic hash of the previous block.

Blockchain networks

As a concept or DL design, blockchain was invented by a person or most likely group of people using the name Satoshi Nakamoto in 2008 to serve as the public transaction ledger of the cryptocurrency bitcoin.[5] Bitcoin and the other well-known Ethereum network are specific implementations of blockchain. Bitcoin is written out as Bitcoin code, run by Bitcoin software which creates transactions containing data about Bitcoin coins that are recorded on the Bitcoin blockchain. Accordingly, the Ethereum network has its own cryptocurrency Ether, a multitude of tokens, and other related data that are recorded on Ethereum blockchain. Both networks follow the same blockchain principles but have different characteristics in their implementations.[6] We must therefore not only distinguish between DLT and blockchain but also emphasise the characteristics of the different blockchain networks. The next sections make for the sake of simplicity

---

[5]Henri Arslanian and Fabrice Fischer provide in chapter nine of their book *The Future of Finance* an interesting background view on the rise of Bitcoin while emphasising the objective of Satoshi Nakamoto's whitepaper to reduce the reliance on financial institutions. We must keep in mind that the whitepaper was published on 31 October 2008 less than two months after the bankruptcy of Lehman Brothers and with it the accelerated outbreak of the GFC. At the same time, the whitepaper never mentioned the terminology of blockchain.

[6]The upcoming section on the transformational impact will in addition discuss XRP which is the cryptocurrency on Ripple's XRP Ledger, an open-source, permissionless, and decentralised blockchain technology. XRP has a crucial role in the development of the payment sector.

general statements about the different blockchain although the rigorous technical specifications and applications may be different from network to network and in this sense from cryptocurrency to cryptocurrency.

> Blockchain is to be understood as a bunch of protocols (rules) that define and characterise its functioning. These protocols can best be articulated in a computer code which in turn can be compiled into a software that enacts those rules and makes them operate. This is how ownership is represented and recorded, what constitutes a valid transaction, and how participants can operate on the respective blockchain network.

A blockchain network can be public and permissionless or private and permissioned. A public and permissionless blockchain means that their list of transactions can be written to by anyone, with no gatekeeper to approve or reject parties who want to create blocks and participate in bookkeeping. Self-identification is not required to create blocks or validate transactions. In a private or permissioned blockchain, there is a controlling party or gatekeeper who allows participants to read or write to them. A private blockchain network requires an invitation and implement governing rules and restrictions in its participation. The Bitcoin and Ethereum blockchains are a public one but both codes can be run as a private network as well, starting a new blockchain with limited participants. This can be facilitated through modifying the code of the Bitcoin and Ethereum software solutions and creating private and permissioned networks that are not connected to the main public networks. Through the modification, the private coins, tokens, and smart contracts will no longer be compatible with the public ones. R3 consortium's Core, J.P. Morgan's Quorum, or Hyperledger Fabric by Linux Foundation are examples of private blockchains.

Cryptographic components

Transactions on a blockchain network apply a mathematical mechanism that is known as cryptography. Cryptography is the discipline of secure communications. The term comes from the ancient Greek words kryptos (hidden secret) and graphein (to write). It represents rules that are used extensively to protect data across communication protocols such as the internet and has had many different applications. Its most well-known use is the encrypted data exchange (encryption) that defines the process of encoding an information in a format that only authorised parties can access it. Although nothing on the Bitcoin network, for instance, is encrypted by default, the technology applies asymmetric cryptography with its public and private key schemes. Together with hashing and digital signatures, private and public keys are crucial technical components of blockchain transactions.

A public key is a mathematical procedure that is available for anyone to see the information while a private key allows decryption of specific communication protocols. The public key is mathematically derived from the private key to transport the information but the information can only be accessed through a private key. This is to be understood as a one-way street, that is, the private key enables the derivation of the public key but it is impossible for the public key to deduce the private key. On the blockchain networks, the public key is generated through different mathematically algorithms.

Bitcoin, for instance, uses an algorithm called Elliptic Curve Digital Signature Algorithm (ECDSA) to generate public keys while the private keys are just randomly chosen numbers for identification. Private keys are used to sign and authorise transactions to move Bitcoins across accounts. Bitcoin addresses, or accounts, are derivatives of the public keys and mint the respective coin in this process.

Digital signatures further prove account ownership and authenticate and validate transactions across the blockchain network. It allows network members who can see the public key to verify the holder of the associated private key without knowing the private key itself. As the signature is valid for a specific transaction, it cannot be manipulated without being invalidated. Cryptographic hashes are used as identifiers for transactions and blocks in order to link them in a chain which is a crucial part in the mining process. It is an algorithm that takes an input of any size and returns a fixed-length sequence of numbers that can be generated from any piece of data, but the data cannot be generated from the hash. Minor changes in the data structure will change the hash and immediately make it different. A network member uses the private key to sign the hash of the transaction which enables the identification of the signature as validation and proof of ownership. To further illustrate this process across the Bitcoin network, an electronic coin is a chain of digital signatures. Each owner transfers the coins to the next digitally by signing a hash of the previous transaction and the public key of the next owner and adding these to the end of the coin. A payee can verify the signatures to verify the chain of ownership through the hash which makes sure that the coin is not double-spent. Most blockchain networks operate in this way.

Mining process

In the context of blockchain design, mining is the process of validating by adding transactions to the existing blockchain ledger distributed among all members of the blockchain. It involves creating a hash of a block of transactions that cannot be easily forged, protecting the integrity of the entire blockchain. The mining process involves four variables: a hash of the transaction on that block, the hash of the previous block, the time of the transaction, and a random number called nonce. The miner will take the four variables and makes sure that output will meet the requirements of the applied cryptographic hash. In case of Ethereum's proof-of-work (PoW), the algorithm for the hash is called Ethash which works differently from the one for Bitcoin which uses a Hashcash algorithm. The main incentive for miners to include a transaction in their block is that members who choose to use a computer for mining are rewarded with new cryptocurrency for doing so. In case of Bitcoin, a bounty of 25 Bitcoins which has been agreed-upon by everyone in the network has been gradually decreased, halved with each 210 000 to currently 6.25 coins. In addition, the miner is awarded the fees paid by the members who send transactions.

Most blockchain networks apply a PoW mining schedule. PoW mining creates valid blocks by solving the algorithm of the hash which leads to the trusted and distributed consensus required for a blockchain transaction. It functions as a consensus mechanism. This is dependent on the computational cycle and hence the electricity use. The more blocks or coins are on the blockchain, the more complex is the computational cycle and hence the higher the electricity consumption. The more computer power is added to the network, the more difficult it is to solve the hash algorithm and with it the higher the electricity consumption. This adds a self-regulatory rule to a blockchain network. Although different technologies for mining have evolved quickly, the PoW has made the mining of Bitcoin and Ether expensive over time. In response, the Ethereum development roadmap plans to move from electricity-expensive PoW to a more energy-efficient proof-of-stake (PoS) mining protocol called Casper. Casper applies a mining concept than is not based on computational cycles but dependent on the number of coins held in the mining wallet. It will most likely be incorporated in a future release of the Ethereum software. PoS is not the only new mining schedule that is getting developed. There are many other such as proof-of-weight, proof-of-activity, and Byzantine fault tolerance.

Digital and crypto assets

Digital assets are assets that are created by a software and do not exist in physical matter. They are unique data items that are created or destroyed according to the rules articulated in the computer code that governs them. As we discussed, these rules are set by cryptography. We therefore often speak of cryptographically secured digital assets or crypto assets. All cryptocurrencies and coins fall under the categories of digital or crypto assets. Similar to any other asset, the ownership of these crypto assets can be passed from account to account. When these digital assets move from óne account to another they are all recorded on their respective transaction database which is the blockchain as the ultimate books and records. In this sense, it represents the universal understanding of the current status of all units of the digital asset.

Token

The term token is often used in a generic sense in reference to all digital assets. Technically, it simply represents a unit recorded on a blockchain. In a broad and universal definition, every digital asset may be a token and every token may be a digital or crypto asset. However, as the terminology is evolving, a narrower definition for token is emerging. On the one hand, there are coins such as Bitcoin, Ether, and Ripple's XRP that are tracked on the cryptocurrencies' respective blockchains. On the other hand, there are tokens that are usually issued during an initial coin offering (ICO) and tracked within smart contracts on any blockchain such as Ethereum as the most widely used. The term token can mean different things depending on the context in which it is used.

To provide a clear terminology, all cryptocurrencies are referred to as blockchain-native tokens. Native tokens have an intrinsic value by themselves that is not backed by an issuer or asset. Asset-backed tokens, on the other hand, are issued during an ICO and represent ownership of a financial or physical asset. They may have specific individual characteristics. Some tokens are fungible and are more or less replaceable by another. Others are nonfungible and each token represents something unique. Unlike cryptocurrencies, asset-backed tokens are usually issued by known issuers and guarantor who stand behind them. Asset-backed tokens are also called digital depository receipts (DDR) as they represent a claim on a custodian for a financial or physical assets. If the tokens represent claims to future products and service by the issuer of the token, they are further known as utility tokens. The detailed specifications of utility tokens are usually recorded through smart contracts on one of the blockchain networks.

Smart contracts

Smart contracts are computer protocols intended to digitally facilitate, verify, or enforce the negotiation or performance of a contract without third-party involvement. The implementations of smart contracts are based on the DLT concept and become trackable and irreversible today through blockchain networks. Several blockchains have implemented types of smart contracts with Ethereum as the most prominent representative. In a smart contract, many kinds of contractual clauses are partially or fully self-executing, self-enforcing, or both, which makes it very attractive in the use of financial instruments such as derivatives with specific cash flow and settlement specifications. An interest rate swap, for instance, could fully be based on a smart contract. At the same time, smart contracts aim to provide security that is superior to traditional contract law and to reduce other transaction costs associated with contracting.

4.3 THE TRANSFORMATIONAL IMPACT OF FINANCIAL TECHNOLOGY

After discussing the different technology components and building blocks, the following section covers the transformational impact of financial technology across three defined segments: operational efficiency, augmented decision making, and financial innovation. All of them fundamentally improved the performance of financial institutions while DLT added new layers to the financial infrastructure and digitised financial innovation.

4.3.1 Operational efficiency

Profitability has remained subdued in most financial institutions which is partly due to the inflexibility of the outdated and fragmented technology platforms used by many players. As business portfolios have decreased, operating platforms have also become disproportionately large. While technology innovation has brought new competitive pressures, it also provides incumbent banks with the opportunity to transform their own operating models fundamentally and renovate their technology platforms. These new technologies allow banks to replace their heavy core infrastructure with an open, flexible architecture, reducing their outsized cost bases and repositioning their businesses in line with their core capabilities. Technology innovation is not only enhancing customer experience, it is providing banks with an opportunity to complete their transformation journey and eventually regain profitability in the new postcrisis environment. From an operational perspective, there are three areas of major impact across open architecture model, core systems, and infrastructure.

Open architecture model

Since the establishment of the internet, API and CC have fundamentally changed the operating platform and technology stacks in financial institutions. An open architecture model summarises design principles across a group of core components that changes the operating models. It decomposes the value chain and separates the core platform from the service offering. In an open architecture model, API enables the access to large data pools, internal and external resources as well as regulatory compliant infrastructure, and allows the integration of best-in-class services from third-party providers. CC facilitates the consolidation and access of data across financial institutions which facilitates different service applications such as SaaS, PaaS, or banking platform as a service. An open architecture model allows financial institutions to focus on their core capabilities across customer management which includes onboarding, interactions, and compliance as well as risk transfer and management through assessing and managing the overall risk exposure. Exhibit 4.2 illustrates a generic open architecture banking model.

Regulators have established a framework for open banking and the respective management of data access and distribution. The Open Banking directive came into force in the United Kingdom on 13 January 2018 which forced Britain's nine biggest banks to release their data in a secure, standardised form, so that they can be shared more easily between authorised organisations online. It is part of European legislation known as the second Payment Services Directive (PSD2) which regulates the data exchange. PSD2 is counterbalanced by the General Data Protection Regulation (GDPR). GDPR is a regulation on data protection and privacy for all individual citizens of the EU and the European Economic Area. It aims primarily to give control over their personal data to individuals and to simplify the regulatory environment for international business by unifying the regulation within the EU.

Technology platforms can be built across different design principles. An in-house development model is based on internal resources for the development of integrated core banking system for booking and settlement of the full product suite. The software solutions will be developed in house by bank employees with the support of business partners. An integrated model relies on a commercial software vendor package that offers solutions for all administrative and core-business processes. The package will be customised to a financial institution's requirements during the integration phase. In a bank-in-a-box model, hosted solutions for integrated core banking systems and operations are offered by a third-party service provider. The service provider maintains the accounts through its own data centre while operations activities related to booking and settlement can be outsourced to other vendors. In a hybrid model, a financial institution acquires the best-in-class services for its various capabilities including the core banking system. The objective of the hybrid model is to select the best services that need minor customisation and integrate them to each other and to other internal and external peripheral systems. It may be at the core of an open architecture solutions.

Neo-banks (also called challenger banks in the United Kingdom) have implemented open architecture models over the last few years in different settings. They have been following a greenfield approach, either developing their technology platforms from scratch or applying standardised solutions of third-party software vendors. In a modular approach, multiple third-party providers are often combined to tailor the technology pack in accordance with the functional requirements of the commercial model. Others build their own core system and complement their offering with third-party vendors or apply very specific product solutions. The neo-banks Revolut and Number26 have been following a combination of greenfield and vendor solutions

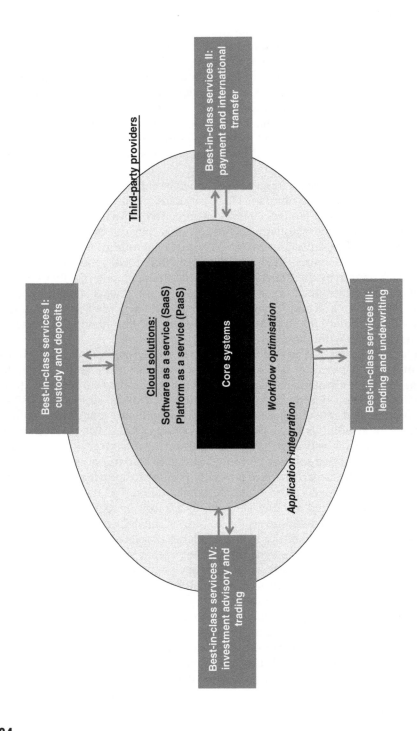

Exhibit 4.2 Open architecture banking model

in the build-up of their platforms. Other such as Monzo and Oak North focused more on third-party solutions before switching back to internal development initiatives. In any case, strategic partnerships are essential in establishing these neo-banking platforms. Many neo-banks started as pure disruptors but then increasingly worked with incumbent financial institutions which led in some cases to the acquisition of its platform (e.g. the sale of Simple to BBVA in 2014). As many neo-banks struggle with the successful commercialisation of their business model, this integration trend may accelerate as it allows incumbents to acquire a fully functioning platform in an effort to address their own technology challenges.

Several software providers have successfully established themselves with universal and modular solutions for core systems, replacing internally developed software applications that are in many financial institutions older than 20–30 years as minimum. The Swiss software vendor Temenos with its T24 system has achieved a strong positioning in particular in retail banking with focuses on mortgages. Avaloq, another Swiss software company, developed its offering originally in the wealth management space, and after an investment of the private equity firm Warburg Pincus in 2017 further aimed to extend its retail application suite. There are many other core banking systems such as Finastra with Fusion Essence, Infosys with Finacle, and Fiserv, or more emerging start-up providers such as Mambu, Thought Machine, and LEVERIS. Thought Machine is a company of former Google engineers that received an investment from Lloyds Banking Group in 2018, integrating different technology applications on one platform. The investment requirements to replace those core systems are substantial though and usually have a range of three to seven years with regard to their implementation and feasibility. They are core in establishing viable business models and bringing the financial industry back on a path of growth and profitability.

Open source programme languages such as Python and R, C++, and Javascript are facilitating these developments. Python is replacing COBOL which stands for common business-oriented language that was developed in the 1950s for business finance and administrative systems for companies and governments. COBOL is still widely used on mainframe computers of financial institutions' legacy systems and has in this sense still a major role in maintaining existing applications. Python was developed in the late 1980s and further revised in 2000 and 2008 through versions Python 2.0 and Python 3.0. It is an interpreted, high-level, general-purpose programming language that is available for many operating systems. It supports multiple programming paradigms across procedural, object-oriented, and functional programming, and follows language constructs and object-oriented approach to develop clear, logical code with emphasis on code readability. It is dynamically typed with a garbage collection system capable of collecting reference cycles. A global community of programmers develops and maintains CPython, an open source reference implementation that is in particular core for ML applications. C++, on the other hand, is an expressive language with which much more abstract elements can be implemented. It can be implemented on a low operational level from a programming perspective with the objective to influence operation codes that the program may never compile to actual software.

Financial infrastructure

The infrastructure in particular with regard to the payment sector has been the initial and probably most obvious entry point for FinTech innovation. The payment sector has been dominated by traditional financial institutions with a lack of competition, similar to capital-market infrastructure that was owned by a few global players together with often semipublic exchange organisations. Advances in robotics, software development, and DLT have led to new, innovative system applications.

Payment services

The payment industry that emerged during the 1950s was dominated by the large incumbent financial institutions; payment companies such as Diners Club, Visa, American Express, and MasterCard; and international debit card payment providers such as Maestro and Cirrus. With the rise of e-commerce, the industry went through a significant change in the 1990s. The launch of PayPal, a payment processor for online vendors and other commercial users, broke up this traditional value chain with core focus on online money transfers. During the next 15 years, technology innovation and advancement fundamentally changed the payment landscape. Higher specialisation led to substantial outsourcing from incumbent financial institutions to third-party technology vendors. Only a few players remained who have maintained the full-suite processing. To maintain efficiency and scalability, large-scale acquisitions followed such as the ones of Worldpay through Vantiv or of Six Payment Services through Worldline while private equity funds such Hellman & Friedman acquired Nets Group and a consortium of Blackstone and CVC bought Paysafe. Technology firms such as Google and Apple introduced their own payment solutions with their Wallet applications. Social networks such as Facebook and WhatsApp are further working on integrated payment platforms for its members.

Payment services are crucially important to financial institutions. They are the starting point of a typical customer journey, its most frequent interaction, and the cornerstone of a sticky relationship between the financial institution and its client. The payment value chain can be broken up in three main phases with merchant acquiring, transaction processing, and issuing services. The merchant acquiring phase covers the payment services provided to merchants and other business owners which enables them to execute electronic payment transactions through credit and/or debit cards while further receiving potential value added services (VAS) at the point of sales. The merchant acquiring is developed by financial institutions that service current and business accounts. Banks sign up merchants to accept payment cards, handle the transaction received from the payment networks and gateways, facilitate the authorisation requests, and bear the full risk of a customer's default or a nonfulfilment of the exchange of good and services.

During the transaction processing phase, the payment processor routes the transactions for authorisation while clears and settles them through national or international payment networks. The payment networks such as MasterCard, Visa, and American Express provide the infrastructure over which the transactions are processed. The infrastructure consists of a communication and payment network for transaction clearing and settlement. Merchant processing services refers to a broad category of services that enables a business to accept a transaction through a secure channel such as point-of-sales terminals and/or credit and debit cards payment processing systems. A payment gateway is an e-commerce application that facilitates the payment of transactions by the transfer of information between the acquiring bank or front-end processor and an electronic payment portal which can be a website or an application on a device. We need to distinguish between the acquirer and issuer processor. The acquirer processor opens merchant accounts and processes transactions on behalf of the acquirer while the issuer processor processes customer transactions on behalf of the issuer. Well-known payment processors are FirstData, WorldPay, and Square with different commercial and operational solutions.

Through card issuing services, the customer relationship is managed contractually from card authorisation to confirming future settlements. The issuer processor provides the services for card issuers, including account and customer interaction management, PIN code, cards, and the administrative tools such as confirmations and statements. Financial institutions, usually called issuer banks, are the typical issuers with extra branded cards relying on the account set-ups on their operational platforms. The operational platforms though are heavily dependent on third-party vendor solutions that have often been fully integrated in the technology stack. Open-loop payment platforms are solutions that link the customer's payment device directly to a credit or debit card. Consumers can use the device in the same way that they would use their card, subject to whatever terms and conditions the card issuer provides to the consumer. Apple and Google Pay have disrupted these markets with their digital wallet platforms and online payment systems, leveraging the existing payment networks but improving the respective services through new technologies such as near field communication (NFC) and one-click payments. Closed-loop payment solutions, on the other hand, allow consumers to preload funds into a spending account that is linked to the payment instruments such as cards or mobile devices. Customers can reload amounts during the event through a variety of mechanisms, including automatic top-up.

Peer-to peer solutions such as TransferWise in the United Kingdom have become in particular popular for international fund transfers. They can deliver money quickly with a transparent and flat fee structure, using a midmarket exchange rate. The neo-bank N26 has directly integrated their bank accounts with TransferWise. DLT and respective blockchain applications have further innovated payment such as Interbank Information Network (IIN), JP Morgan Chase's platform for cross-border currency transfers. Ripple is a real-time gross settlement system, currency exchange, and remittance network created by Ripple Labs Inc., a US-based technology company. It has been adopted by banks and payment networks as settlement infrastructure technology. Ripple is built upon a distributed open source protocol and supports tokens representing fiat currency, cryptocurrency, commodities, or other units of value such as frequent flier miles or mobile minutes. Its cryptocurrency XRP is further covered in a subsequent section.

Post-trade capital market services

Standardised software and blockchain-based solutions have helped to achieve harmonization, transparency, standardization, and efficiency across the trade life cycle and its value chain. Particular focus has been on the low-value added areas of onboarding/know your customer (KYC) and post-trade services that cover middle-office functions, reference data, and clearing and settlement functions. Core focus has been on automating processes and increases the straight-through-processing (STP) rate towards 100%. Third-party vendors such as Murex, Calypso, FIS, Finstra, and many others have been implementing software solutions that automate the functions across the value chain while more recently RPA added a new layer. Automation has been achieved for standardised cash and derivatives products for the liquid asset classes such as equity but struggles for tailored and more complex financial products (e.g. exotic derivatives) and most of the other asset classes such as rates, credit, and commodities. The tailoring of specific applications increases the implementation costs of third-party software solutions dramatically which led to the abandonment of several large-scale transformation projects at global institutions.

In response to the challenges, consortiums of several international banks have formed joint venture for reference data, KYC, and onboarding as well as collateral management which are often referred to as utilities, given their focus and origins in back office and infrastructure. The utilities either focus on data pooling that facilitates administrative tasks or focus on combined operational elements such as industry plumbing. Several technology infrastructure providers have been moving into this space, also operating outside of the regulated banking organisation as industry hold-ings. The pooling of operational and technology capabilities is executed as carve-out of entire platforms, tangible and intangible assets to a separate entity which can be co-owned by several banks or third-party players like technology companies and/or private equity funds. The services are then brought back through a long-term service level agreement (SLA) with the parent company. Several utilities have been set up by a bank consortium but then sold to a technology company in a second phase. Popular examples are the onboarding and KYC utility Clarient Global LLC that was sold to Thomson Reuters (today Refinitiv) and the collateral margin utility Blake that was sold to Arcadia Soft. Eventually the technology and infrastructure component is managed by a specialised nonbanking technology players.

DLT and blockchain applications have been implemented for settlement of secu-rities transaction. Australian Securities Exchange (ASX) has become the first major bourse to announce the adoption of blockchain technology with the assistance of Digi-tal Asset Holdings (DAH) while a group of financial institutions led by UBS Group has been developing a blockchain-based system, called the utility settlement coin (USC), to settle cross-border trades. JPMorgan Chase & Co. has further been working on a simi-lar token called JPM Coin. Several central banks engaged in pilot projects to develop the next-generation real-time gross settlement (RTGS) systems where payments are processed immediately between a central bank and the various clearing banks of the national payment system. The objective is to remove settlement and counterparty risk to increase speed and reduce financial, operational, and frictional costs. There has been a series of pilots for smart-contract application in particular for more complex derivatives products. Smart contracts allow completely new applications of derivatives contracts with complex, multifaceted payout features that can be fully automated. The Ethereum blockchain allows the facilitation of transactions that create smart contracts which are a small bit of general purpose logic that are stored on Ethereum's blockchain on all of the Ethereum nodes. When a smart contract is invoked, all the Ethereum nodes run the code and update their ledger with the results.

4.3.2   Augmented decision making

Decision making in financial institutions has been transformed by ML with core focus on data analytics and management. As we further explore in the following section, data-driven forms of ML have found application in research and analytics, credit-underwriting and lending, securities trading and marketing, investment advisory, and risk and capital management. Algorithmic methods allow the assessment of credit quality and pricing of financial contracts. Trading desks are using back-testing models and analysing the market impact of trading large positions. Hedge funds, broker-dealers, and other firms are using ML to find signals for higher (and uncorrelated) returns and optimise trading execution. In investment advisory, robo-advisors enable the automated decision making in specific asset management services and online financial planning tools that assist customers to make more informed consumption and saving decisions. Treasury teams are optimising scarce capital with ML techniques.

The core components that drive these ML applications start with the available data pool (input and capture) such as client onboarding as well as data processing. Efficient data pooling requires a central or consolidated database across the institution's different organisational units with their data streams. As we discussed previously, many financial institutions suffer under data fragmentation which impacts their abilities to deploy ML systems coherently across their businesses. This leads to a sensitivity to data quality issues and model dependencies. The scale of available data has been increasing exponentially over the last 20 years, and the information overload does not only overwhelm individuals but the entire organisation, impacting their decision making. ML adds value to decision making and data analytics through mathematical accuracy and objectivity which leads to unbiased results. At the same time, it leads to substantial efficiency gains and new insights. It can be applied across the entire spectrum of financial analytics from credit underwriting and investment analysis to risk management and surveillance.

Research and analytics

Large parts of the research and analytics working processes are in many ways rule based and standardised in accordance with well-defined frameworks and models. Through ML, many of these tasks can be automated. In a first stage, ML allows to read documents to extract important data and visualise information for readability. In a second step, it can further create models autonomously after observing the unstructured data and back-testing to learn from previous mistakes to improve accuracy. This step is often referred to as contextualising and has made a substantial way forward with the emerging NLP technologies. NLP models can provide deep insights in the news flow of traditional media, social media, and other relevant publications from research departments, corporations, and government authorities. This collection of unstructured data is often referred to as sentiment data and adds an additional layer of company and market intelligence to the traditional research process in financial institutions. Sentiment data are usually linked to an event methodology that is defined by a cluster of key words with which the publications are screened and analysed for their positive or negative context. In an academic setting, this process can be referred to as information filtration while propriety data from internal confidential documents (e.g. loan applications) and private markets need to be distinguished from publicly available news feeds. The scores represent tangible action points for financial decisions. In a third stage, they can further be combined with traditional financial data and then optimised through a probabilistic algorithm for which we earlier suggested the framework of Bayesian statistics.

These three stages allow a focus on the human tasks on the structuring of the model and interpretation of outcomes as well as the clear articulation with regard to results and their communication. Kensho, for instance, started to cooperate early with Goldman Sachs and other financial institutions in applying ML and analytics systems in particular to research through document scanning for key words and solving early stage analytical problems, applying NLP to gather and process large parts of unstructured data and commingling it with traditional, structured financial data. Other players in this space have developed their own often specialised datasets for topics such as ESG criteria, often working with the large information companies such as Refinitiv in case of MarketPsych or remain independent in case of RavenPack. However, alternative data are not limited to sentiment data but may include facial and voice detections, digital footprints, patent applications, lifestyle data, geolocalisation data, and many other datasets that give a competitive advantage in financial decision making.

Credit underwriting and lending

Lending and underwriting as any other risk-taking function defined the core of banking operations from origination, risk screening, pricing, and risk management. Behavioural data, using ML, neural network, and other advanced statistical techniques, have added new analytical tools to the underwriting process of incumbent financial institutions. The underwriting process has historically applied credit scores which in combination with Big Data and ML can estimate default probability more accurately. It allows detection of anomalies and understanding of complex patterns that may flag potentially troubling behaviour. Furthermore, unstructured data can be combined with historical financial data, which allows the validation of default probabilities while adding additional layers such as ESG criteria to the analysis. This can be applied more broadly to the use and integration of alternative data to augment the approval process. The alternative data sources may be applicants' payment history, shopping behaviour, management information system, and public comments. Many incumbents struggle with database and complex legacy processes that make credit applications cumbersome and long. Several neo-banking platforms are emerging that automate credit applications and combine it with ML algorithms while using payment histories combined with accounting and invoice management systems as crucial input factor for their credit models. This is getting applied in particular for smaller business where a large number of loan applications have to be processed. Some of these neo-banks such as OakNorth and Iowoca have made these services, mainly through cloud platform solutions, available as a licencing product for other financial institutions

Direct lending without any financial intermediary accelerated after the GFC as a result of the limited lending capacity of financial institutions and higher capital requirements. Peer-to-peer (P2P) lending got a lot of traction through new technology applications with companies such as Funding Circle and Zopa in the United Kingdom ad well as Lending Club, Prosper, and SoFi in the United States. All enabled through digital basis platforms, P2P lenders act as a facilitator to allow counterparts that are long on funds to find proper opportunities for direct lending that are short of funds, often individuals or corporations that struggle to get credit through the traditional banking channels. P2P lenders are not asking or do not get an interest rate spread but get paid an access, advisory, and transaction fee. To optimise their funding profile, the more sophisticated P2P lenders apply securitisation. However, the profitability of this commercial model remained below expectations and many traditional P2P lenders starting applying for a banking licence with the objective to deploy their own balance sheets. Amazon and other consumer platforms started to fund working capital requirements of their suppliers. The economic crisis during the coronavirus (COVID-19) pandemic further shifted focus of many P2P lending platforms as they started to deploy state-backed funding facilities in particular to the cash-strapped segment for small and midsize enterprises.

Securities trading and marketing

The trading of securities is now close to being fully electronic in particular for highly liquid asset classes such as equities and exchange-traded derivatives such as futures and options. An electronic trading and execution platform is a system interface to trade financial assets via a network of other financial institutions, market makers, and other participants such as institutional investors. These platforms can connect with a communication network, exchange, alternative trading system, crossing network, dark pool, or broker system and allow transactions to be executed from any location; they are in contrast to traditional trading via open outcry. Goldman Sachs established GSET, which stands for its electronic trading platform, after selling a majority stake in its electronic trading software business, REDI, to a consortium of investors. UBS created Neo, J.P. Morgan eXecute, Morgan Stanley MSET, and Credit Suisse AES (Advanced Execution Services).

ML is getting increasingly embedded in these electronic trading platforms, typically as a trading tool and support mechanism in areas such as market data, charting, news, account management, analyst research, and customized backtesting. It can also be used as a recommendation engine for trade execution where algorithms execute orders with the aim to minimise transaction costs and automate the process through trade algorithms. High-frequency trading applies sophisticated systems and technology applications to front-load execution and arbitrage. After a series of criticism and complaints, the regulatory response started limiting the impact on the price discovery mechanism while it remains an important matter to guarantee a price equilibrium. There have been several events, however, when price dislocations happened due to fast execution. IEX, which stands for institutional exchange, was created as a response to these developments. By adding a 350 micro-second delay to all incoming trade orders, IEX mitigates speed advantages of high-frequency traders.[7]

---

[7]Michael Lewis provides in his bestseller *Flash Boy* a more detailed account on high-frequency trading.

Investment advisory

Automated investment management and financial advice through robo-advisors, which have moderate to minimal human intervention, are digital applications that have become very popular post GFC. The term robo-advisor was first used by Richard Koreto in March 2002 in his contribution to *Financial Planning* magazine. The first robo-advisors were launched to the public in 2008 during the financial crisis with the objective to make professional investment services more broadly accessible. Through Betterment, robo-advisors became more popular in the marketplace in late 2010. Today, there are a variety of advisors from Wealthfront, Betterment, and FutureAdvisor in the United States and Nutmeg and Scalable Capital in the United Kingdom and continental Europe.

In a robo-advisor technology, the investment decisions are mainly quantitative, based on algorithms that apply financial and probabilistic theory. The mechanical rules are executed to automatically allocate, manage, and optimize assets. Fully automated and hybrid robo-advisors with some human interventions are to be distinguished. The algorithmic asset allocation is executed across the different classes and financial instruments from stocks, bonds, futures, commodities, and real estate. The investments are usually directed towards futures and exchange traded funds (ETF) because of their broad market representation on an index level and available market liquidity. Investors may choose between passive asset allocation techniques and active asset management styles, depending on their preferences. Robo-advisors started to implement ML technologies and Big Data to estimate risk and risk relations to implement investment strategies in accordance with a defined risk preference from conservative to balanced to high risk. Volatility-based asset allocation and minimum variance portfolios have become a major feature in the products of many successful robo-advisors.

Robo-advice brings formerly exclusive asset and wealth management services to a broader audience with lower cost compared to traditional human advice. The main difference therefore remains in the distribution channel. Consumers get direct access to portfolio management tools, in a similar way that they can obtain access to securities brokerage. This is a substantial step forward as the customer acquisition costs and time constraints faced by traditional human advisors have left many middle-class investors unable to obtain professional investment management services due to the minimums imposed on investable assets. Chatbots may be further applied for client interactions, onboarding, and basic advice to define the risk preference and initial asset allocation of a client. Kensho, for instance, developed a platform named "Warren" after legendary investor Warren Buffett to respond to financial questions posed in natural language. The form of automated advice is further to grow and with the development of ML technologies to become more sophisticated and broadly applicable across a comprehensive advisory platform.

Risk and capital management

In Chapter 3 on asset-liability management, we defined risk-taking and its management as the core function of any successful financial services business. It is a comprehensive element to all decision making while at the same time, an independent view and evaluation need to be established with regard to the risks taken, regulatory compliance, surveillance, and fraud detection. From a technology perspective, ML and predictive analytics through specific algorithm has further advanced the value-at-risk and regulatory methodology but in particular allowed automation of crucial functions across compliance, trade surveillance, and fraud detection. There are several providers in this space with specific services from cyber security such as Aponix and regulatory compliance such as Cordium and Throgmorton. Several incumbents such as banking giants HSBC and Citi have in particular invested in fraud detection with the support of ML-enabled tools and technologies.

Algorithmic applications and quantitative analysis in the assessment and management of risk have been popular since the early 1990s through the launch of RiskMetrics through J.P. Morgan, Fischer Black's and Robert Litterman's work at Goldman Sachs, or James Simons at Renaissance Technologies. It brought many new insights but has also standardised decision making which may add to market dislocations and financial disability during periods of market stress what was covered previously in the section on financial stress of Chapter 3. Many of the models are based on the value-at-risk methodology while ML and Big Data add further computation power to simulate asset returns and risk factors across more complex distribution and stochastic outcomes. MSCI Barra made the application of multifactor models standardised and more broadly available. NLP allows to integrate new forms of alternative data which can be further optimised in a portfolio and asset allocation setting by combining unstructured datasets with traditional financial data. As we elaborated, these developments are at an early stage and will further impact risk management as a discipline and methodology in the years to come. Several quantitative asset managers and hedge funds such as Two Sigma or Quadrature Capital have been at the forefront to develop AI solutions and integrate more complex forms of alternative data. However, the ambiguity and tail risks (unlikely extreme events with drastic consequences also referred to as Black Swans), as described in Chapter 2, remain unrecognised by algorithms unless the fundamentals shortcomings towards true human intelligence can be addressed.

4.3.3   Digital financial innovation

In Chapter 3, we covered financial innovation through the application of complex financial instruments. Post GFC, financial innovation mainly happened through technology innovation such as the establishment of cryptocurrencies that was originally initiated through the launch of Bitcoin in 2009. The following section aims to provide a view on the future of financial innovation, assuming technology as core driver of innovation, further discussing the different aspects of cryptocurrencies and their applications with decentralised finance (DeFi). The previous section on operational efficiency and performance improvement has already covered that impact of DLT and blockchain on payments and post-trade, back-office operations. The core of this digital innovation is the fundamental monetary concept of storage and transfer of value.

Cryptocurrencies

Cryptocurrencies and coins such as Bitcoin and Ether are based on the DLT design blockchain. As there are so many different applications with different rules and mechanisms across the broad universe of cryptocurrencies and coins, a generalisation of the theme becomes very simplistic. We therefore provide a brief overview of Bitcoin, Ethereum, and XRP with the respective commercial applications of tokens, ICOs, and smart contracts while keeping the differences between the cryptocurrencies in mind. There are many other types such as Cardano, NEO, Facebook's Libra, and hundreds of other cryptocurrencies.

Bitcoin

Bitcoins are digital or crypto assets whose ownership is recorded on the electronic ledger Bitcoin blockchain. All transactions are created and validated according to the Bitcoin blockchain protocol that sets the rules which govern the ledger. The Bitcoin blockchain is managed by a software such as Bitcoin Core running on computers that communicate with each other forming a peer-to-peer network. The ownership of Bitcoins is recorded on the respective Bitcoin blockchain which allows to identify the specific numbers of Bitcoins associated with an address. As the Bitcoin blockchain stores transactions and not balances, all the inbound and outbound transactions through the specific account get the current balance of any account.

As we previously discussed, the Bitcoin blockchain was defined by a pseudonymous Satoshi Nakamoto in a 2008 whitepaper. The concept and DLT design of blockchain are not mentioned in this publication. Satoshi core interest was not in the technological concept of a blockchain but rather on the monetary function of censorship resistant digital cash without any intermediating financial institutions. To achieve this monetary function, Bitcoin uses a PoW mechanism to ensure conceptually that anyone can add blocks to the blockchain a certain cadence without a central party coordinating access or providing permission. PoW creates a fair competition between block adders who compete to add blocks. This competitive computation process consumes a lot of electricity which has made the mining process of Bitcoin very expensive over time. Similar to the gold standard, this rule restricts the supply of Bitcoin and prevents at least in theory devaluation due to inflation from a monetary perspective. This is a Bitcoin-specific characteristic that is in line with Satoshi's initial objective to create an alternative and independent monetary system.

Bitcoin went through a volatile development, starting on 3 January 2009 when the first or genesis block was mined. Satoshi Nakamoto shortly after released version 0.1 of the Bitcoin software. This allowed people to review the code as well as download and run the software through which they became book keepers and miners. Several days later on 9 January 2009, a first Bitcoin payment was made on, and the first Bitcoin exchange was created. To put the price development into perspective, the bitcoin-based payment processor Coinbase reported in February 2013 that it sold over US$1 million worth of bitcoins in a single month at over US$22 per bitcoin. In 2017, Bitcoin passed US$10 000 and reached the high of US$19 783.21 on 17 December before collapsing spectacularly in the coming months. At the end of the writing period for this book in summer 2021, Bitcoin had a specular rebound surpassing US$50 000 for the first time with volatile up and down swings. However, there seems to be a broader acceptance of the cryptocurrency through professional and institutional money pouring into it. In late summer 2020, the hedge fund manager, Paul Tudor-Jones, a previous sceptic, confirmed that he had 1–2% of his assets in Bitcoin, emphasising its functions versus other stores of value. Tudor-Jones called it the great speculation for the digitisation of the global economy that has not stood yet the test in time such as gold for over hundreds of years.

Ether

Ether is the second most popular cryptocurrency. Ether is a token whose blockchain is generated by the Ethereum platform. Ethereum was proposed in late 2013 by Vitalik Buterin, a cryptocurrency researcher and programmer. It supports a modified version of Nakamoto consensus via transaction-based state transitions. Ethereum was split into two separate blockchains in 2016, following an incidence where US$50 million worth of Ether were stolen. There is a new separately launched version which became Ethereum (ETH) while the original one continued as Ethereum Classic (ETC). Ethereum provides the decentralized Ethereum Virtual Machine (EVM), an international network of public nodes on which the blockchain is run. It has an internal transaction pricing mechanism called Gas that functions as a price list for the miners depending on computational complexity. Gas is an additional characteristic with the objective is to allocate resources efficiently on the Ethereum network. Like Bitcoin, Ethereum is a bunch of protocols written out as code which is run as Ethereum software which creates Ethereum transactions containing data about Ether, recorded on Ethereum's blockchain. In contrast with Bitcoin, Ethereum transaction can contain more than just payment data, and the nodes in Ethereum are capable of validating and processing much more than simple payments. Such smart contracts have been invoked through Ether. Ether can be transferred between accounts and used to compensate participant mining nodes for computations performed. The system then went live on 30 July 2015 with 72 million premined coins.

XRP

XRP is a native cryptocurrency developed by Ripple which today is one of the largest coins by market capitalization. Ripple itself is a real-time gross settlement system, currency exchange, and remittance network created by Ripple Labs Inc., a technology company from the United States. Ripple relies on a common shared ledger, which is a distributed database storing information about all Ripple accounts. The network is managed by a network of independent validating servers that constantly compare their transaction records. Servers could belong to anyone, including banks and dedicated market makers. Ripple validates accounts and balances instantly for payment transmission and delivers payment notification with very little latency. All payments are irreversible, and there are no chargebacks. In contrast to other cryptocurrencies, the Ripple network created XRP at the beginning when it established itself. This has the advantage that all XRP were premined and shared out among key participants. As each XRP transaction needs to include a small amount of XRP as transaction fee, the coins are destroyed by block makers, and the total number of XRPs in circulation decreases with time. Today over 300 financial institutions are reported use its payment network, RippleNet, with payouts in more than 40 currencies operating in over 50 countries. The RippleNet members can settle transactions in three to five seconds, compared to days it could take in the traditional payment infrastructure.

In late December 2020 though, the Securities and Exchange Commission (SEC) sued Ripple Labs and its co-founders Christian Larsen and Bradley Garlinghouse for violation of US securities laws. The SEC claimed that Ripple should be treated as a securities offering and not a cryptocurrency. It was previously reported by the British Financial Times that Garlinghouse had admitted that, without sales of XRP, Ripple would be lossmaking. It was further made public that Ripple received legal advice as early as 2012 that under certain circumstances XRP could be considered an investment contract and therefore a security under federal laws. According to the SEC filing, its executives violated the disclosure of information in accordance with the legal requirements for a securities offering, and the company pursued illegal activities as far back as 2013. Ripple was able to raise at least US$1.38 billion by selling XRP without providing the type of financial and managerial information typically provided in registration statements and subsequent period and current fillings. Although the company is disputing the SEC's claim, the lawsuit led to high price volatility in XRP, leading to broader fears that the SEC would further clampdown on Ethereum and Ethereum-based crypto assets.

The SEC against Ripple is a good illustration about the uncertainty of government interventions and regulations around crypto assets until a stable legislative framework is established. Actions by regulatory and supervisory authorities had previously restricted Facebook's ambitious plans for the payment industry with its cryptocurrency Diem (formerly Libra) that was still in the process of being launched as of August 2021. At the same, the SEC investigation brings up again the question of the fundamental use of cryptocurrency as storage of value versus its speculative nature. The apparent strategy of Ripple's executives to sell XRP to keep its business afloat seems to follow the logic of a securities offering. Their actions together with the large price increases of XRP and other cryptocurrencies that were eventually created and held by a small group of insiders may show similar characteristics to previous financial bubbles in history. The concerns and actions of regulators is therefore understandable and justified. It remains to be seen if cryptocurrencies offer a real alternative to today's monetary systems that were established over centuries.

Cryptocurrency exchanges (CCE)

Cryptocurrency exchanges (CCE), also called digital currency exchanges, are platforms that facilitate the transactions of cryptocurrencies for conventional fiat money or other digital currencies. Similar to traditional exchanges, a CCE acts as a market maker and takes the bid–ask spreads as a transaction commission or simply charges a matching fee. The CCE can exchange cryptocurrencies through personalised wallets that may be backed by real-world commodities such as gold. Some of them even allow the conversion of cryptocurrency balances into anonymous prepaid cards which can be used to withdraw funds from regular ATMs. The largest and most well-known CCEs are Binance[8] and OKEX in Malta, Coinbase[9] in the United States, and Huobi in

---

[8] Binance is currently under investigation by the US Department of Justice and Internal Revenue Service on allegations of money laundering and tax offenses. In June 2021, the UK's Financial Conduct Authority (FCA) ordered Binance to stop all regulated activities.

[9] Coinbase completed successfully its initial public offering (IPO) in April 2021.

Singapore, but there are many other smaller platforms. In 2018, Intercontinental Exchange (ICE) launched the Bakkt project in cooperation with several corporate partners. The project builds a secure platform where global institutions can store, transact, and transfer digital assets through the Bakkt Warehouse and Bakkt Bitcoin Futures and Options contracts. Incumbent financial institutions such as Goldman Sachs and J.P. Morgan have set up dedicated teams but followed an on-and-off approach in engaging in trading crypto assets.

Several exchanges have faced operational and security challenges with the most famous incidence around Mt. Gox, the largest cryptocurrency exchange at the time.[10] In early 2014, Mt. Gox had to suspend trading, close its website and exchange service, and file for bankruptcy protection as a result of a large theft of several hundred millions of bitcoins out of the Mt. Gox hot wallet over time. Other cryptocurrency protagonists such as Michael Novogratz, a former Goldman Sachs and Fortress Investment Group executive and now chief executive officer of Galaxy Investment Partners, had to shelf their own plans to set up a CCE despite their strong beliefs in the future of crypto assets. Cameron and Tyler Winklevoss successfully founded Gemini, a CCE and custodian that allows customers to buy, sell, and store digital assets but has remained less successful in launching respective exchange-traded fund offerings. Regulators have remained slow in adapting to the different aspects of the crypto business and to come up with a globally coordinated approach. The current regimes differ from country to country and remain uncertain in many developed jurisdictions as regulators are still considering the right implementation framework. In Europe, for instance, several CCEs obtained licenses under the EU Payment Services and the EU Electronic Money Directives while the European Council and the European Parliament further announced that they will issue regulations to impose stricter rules targeting exchange platforms.

Decentralised finance

DeFi has become a broadly used term for experimental forms of finance that utilise smart contracts on distributed ledgers to perform financial functions. The DeFi ecosystem revolves around decentralized blockchain applications that provide similar traditional financial services but do not rely on central intermediation through financial institutions. Transactions are directly executed between participants, mediated by the smart contract programmes with Ethereum being the most frequently utilised one. The following section covers the most established applications and functions such as stablecoins, synthetic trading, and crowdfunding.

Stablecoins

Stablecoins are crypto-based assets that are linked to and redeemable in fiat money (i.e. different available currencies), commodities (e.g. precious metals such as gold), and any

---

[10]The name Mt. Gox stands for "Magic: The Gathering Online eXchange" and was originally founded in 2010 to trade Magic fantasy-based cards. It then handled up to 70% of the world's Bitcoin trading before it was hacked.

other underlying assets (e.g. basket of cryptocurrencies). The coins are usually issued by an independent third party and through the decentralised mechanism of the blockchain network with the objective to mitigate potential forms of counterparty risk. They can be traded on exchanges and are redeemable from the issuer at the conversion rate to take possession of real assets. The value of fiat-backed stablecoins is based on the value of the backing currency, which is usually held by a third-party regulated financial entity. USD Coin (USDC), which runs on different blockchain such as the Ethereum, for instance, is pegged to the US dollar. The value of commodity-backed stablecoins is fixed to one or more commodities and redeemable for such on demand.

The name stablecoin is misleading as it comes from the stabilisation effect of assets outside of crypto space and/or the combination of different assets to a lower volatility crypto assets. As stablecoins are backed by underlying assets though, they are subject to the same volatility and risk associated with the underlying pool of assets. The cost of maintaining the stability is the cost of storing and protecting the backing with an adequate level of reserves. The controversies around Tether, a USD-backed token issued by Tether Limited which was fined by the New York Attorney General for making false statements about its reserves, is a good illustration of the ongoing challenges for regulations and the wider issue of financial stability. At the same time, stablecoins are even getting considered by central banks as a tool of monetary policy. The Swiss central bank, SNB, reported in mid-2019 that it partnered with SIX group, the Swiss stock exchange operator, to work on a digital currency proof of concept. In early 2020, the SNB clarified its position and stated that it wanted to issue and run the digital currency itself, rather than use a third party. It quoted counterparty risk consideration as the main driver of its decision. In July 2021, the Treasury Secretary convened a committee of top US officials to discuss the growth of stablecoins and the associated risks. The group issued a statement that regulators expect to make recommendations on stablecoins in the months to come.

Synthetic trading

Different smart contracts applications facilitate the synthetic trading of assets, historically represented by derivatives contracts either traded at regulated exchanges or over the counter (OTC). Smart contracts replace traditional derivatives structures with their legal and collateral requirements. Synthetix, for instance, is a protocol for minting and trading synthetic assets on Ethereum. Synths are synthetic assets on the protocol that are designed to track the value of an asset, including foreign exchange such as the Japanese yen, commodities such as gold and silver, equity indices such as the Financial Times Stock Exchange stock index, and other cryptocurrencies. Uniswap is establishing a decentralized liquidity pool through an automated market maker (AMM) model. It allows traders to swap tokens without relying on a traditional order book. The AMM model relies on tokens that are always paired with Ethereum, ensuring there is always enough liquidity between any two tokens. Participants can add to or withdraw their funds at any time in exchange for trading fees in proportion to their share of the pool's liquidity. There are additional enhancements to liquidity provision through algorithmic allocation of token from providers such as Curve Finance and Balancer. Synthetic trading is still in an early stage but has huge potential for modernising trading infrastructure through more adaptable delivery mechanisms and liquidity provision. At the same time, the regulatory framework remains to be defined and clarified. Counterparty risk assessment and the prevention of fraud remain at the core of the regulatory agenda.

Crowdfunding

Crowdfunding has become a recent phenomenon, using the power of the internet where a company or specific project can be funded by raising small amounts of money from large numbers of people. The term crowdfunding is mostly used for platforms that raise equity capital. Well-known equity crowdfunding platforms are Seedrs, AngelList, CircleUp, and Fundable. The process itself is similar to an initial public offering (IPO) but through a web- and/or app-based platform that brings companies and investors together. Crowdfunding has allowed much smaller companies to raise capital while the formal process of an IPO requires size and track record. An ICO is the cryptocurrency equivalent to an IPO. Investors receive a blockchain equivalent to a share which is a cryptocurrency token. They are used by start-ups to bypass the rigorous and regulated capital-raising process required by financial institutions, and have become an advanced method for crowdfunding. Ethereum was an early pioneer with ICO in 2014, raising US$18 milion over a period of just over 40 days. Similar to IPOs which raise funds through selling shares in an open market, ICOs act as fundraising mechanism for companies through a token sale or generation event. The rationale behind this may be the creation of a new cryptocurrency or simply to get the funding for a commercial idea. Interested investors buy into the ICO either via fiat currency or with tokens from mainstream blockchain network such as Bitcoin and Ether. In exchange for the funding, investors receive a new token specific to the ICO.

When a start-up wants to raise money through an ICO, it usually creates a whitepaper on their respective project. The whitepaper outlines its objectives, the budget and payment requirements, the allocation of the tokens, and the schedule for the ICO campaign. As result of decentralization and a lack of regulation, ICOs are much more agile in terms of structure than classic IPOs. There are several variations with different characteristics. A company may set a specific goal or limit for its funding, which means that each token sold in the ICO has a preset price and that the total token supply is static. If the money raised does not meet the minimum funds required by the issuer, the money is usually returned to the investors and the ICO is deemed to be unsuccessful. Another variation has got a static supply of ICO tokens but a dynamic funding goal. The distributions of tokens to investors will be dependent upon the funds received. Other ICOs even have a dynamic token supply which is determined according to the amount of funding received. The price of a token is then static, but there is no limit to the number of total tokens. ICOs are a good example of how cryptocurrency innovation has added a new structural element to how capital can be raised in modern markets.

RESOURCES AND FURTHER READING

Arslanian, Henri and Fabrice Fischer (2019). *The Future of Finance: The Impact of FinTech, AI, and Crypto on Financial Services*; Palgrave Macmillian.

Biehl, Mattias (2015). *API Architecture*; API University Series–Volume 2.

Biehl, Mattias (2016). *API Design*; API University Series–Volume 3.

Bocij, Paul, Andrew Greasley and Simon Hickie (2018). *Business Information Systems*; Pearson.

Brookshear, Glenn J. and Dennis Brylow (2015). *Computer Science*; Pearson.

Guttag, John (2021). *Introduction to Computation and Programming Using Python*; The MIT Press.

Isaacson, Walter (2014). *The Innovators*; Simon & Schuster.

Kay, John and Mervyn King (2020). *Radical Uncertainty; Decision-making for an Unknowable Future*; The Bridge Street Press.

Lewis, Antony (2001). *The Basics of Bitcoins and Blockchains*; Mango Publishing.

Lewis, Michael (2014). *Flash Boys: A Wall Street Revolt*; W. W. Norton & Company.

Mougayar, William (2016). *The Business of Blockchain*; John Wiley & Sons.

Pusch, Andreas (2020). "Navigating a Sea of Information, News and Opinions with Augmented Human Intelligence," Chapter 4 of *The AI Book* by Susanne Chishti et al; John Wiley & Sons.

Ridley, Matt (2020). *How Innovation Works*; Harper Collins Publisher.

Ruparelia, Nayan (2013). *Cloud Computing*; The MIT Press.

Scardovia, Claudio (2017). *Digital Transformation in Financial Services*; Springer.

Sironi, Paolo F. (2016). *FinTech Innovation: From Robo-Advisor to Goal Based Investing and Gamification*; Wiley.

Tapscott, Don and Alex Tapscott (2016). *Blockchain Revolution*; Penguin.

Tegmark, Max (2017). *LIFE 3.0: Being Human in the Age of Artificial Intelligence*; Penguin

Warwick, Kevin (2013). *Artificial Intelligence*; Routledge.

William, Jacob (2016). *Blockchain*; Simple Guides.

Wooldridge, Michael (2020). *The Road to Conscious Machines*; Pelican Book.

Two

Repositioning Financial Institutions

P art II combines the managerial fundamentals to a comprehensive value creation and transformation methodology to bring financial institutions back to growth.

Turnaround and Transformation

A turnaround constitutes a situation in which a financial institution or one of its business units underperforms financially. It may be followed by the likely commercial failure in the foreseeable future unless short-term corrective actions are taken. This failure can imply the full spectrum from loss of the institution's competitive situation to financial woes, nonperforming and distressed assets, and insolvency which may lead to an unwind of the entire institution. In academic literature on corporate turnaround, a liquidity or cash crisis is often quoted as threshold for the use of the term turnaround. However, the term here is used much more broadly. It includes the spectrum of crisis, restructuring, and business transformation. This broader terminology is applied in this chapter.

Businesses either fail early in their beginnings or later in the cycle. The growth of mature businesses may become stagnant, and innovative forces[1] make the existing products, services, and distribution channels replaceable which undermines an institution's competitive position. The corporate life cycle of financial institutions is not that straightforward, given their complexity and crucial role in the economic cycle. High entrance costs and specific operational capabilities that have been built up over decades may lead to an ongoing competitive edge, further supported by the highly regulated nature of the business. However, the technology forces that were outlined in Chapter 5 may have changed these dynamics, if not the entire structure of the industry.

The Global Financial Crisis (GFC) led to a series of bank insolvencies while regulators intervened substantially in the process. After the bankruptcy of Lehman Brothers in September 2008, many global institutions were declared too big to fail although their balance sheets and business model were no longer viable. The complexity of the regulatory and legal arrangements to protect deposit holders prevented in many countries a broader market consolidation. The strong intervention from governments, regulators, and central banks prevented the immediate collapse of the global financial system but created large underperforming financial institutions. In Europe, several share prices have been continuously falling, resulting in price-to-book values way below one. Governments and regulators in Ireland, Spain, Greece, Portugal, and Italy created systemwide bad banks for removing toxic assets from balance sheets. Large global financial institutions such as UBS, RBS, Barclays, and Deutsche Bank created legacy or noncore units to unwind their distressed and nonperforming assets while shedding noncore businesses in strategic shifts to become more focused institutions. With the incoming higher capital requirements and leverage constraints of Basel III/IV,

---

[1]They are called destructive forces in the Austrian School of Economics.

the profitability of many businesses fell dramatically and many started operating way below their cost of capital. The previous growth area of fixed income, currencies, and commodities (FICC) in wholesale banking, for instance, was substantially impacted with revenue and profit losses of over 50%. As a result, many banks started to retreat and refocus their capabilities on their core business in their home markets.

To stabilise and resolve such situations, a turnaround mindset and transformation skill set are required. In most cases, the businesses need to be repositioned fundamentally. Turnaround means outright value protection with the objective to preserve a business. Transformation, on the other hand, initiates change to adapt to shifts in external requirements and systems. The objective is to bring a business back on a growth path. A well-managed turnaround usually includes the transformation of the business but a transformation does not necessarily mean a turnaround. Both areas can be incorporated in a broader value creation framework that we are going to discuss in the next chapter on value creation. Often after successful crisis management and phases of heavy restructuring, specific value creation is initiated to lead the business recovery, scale up, and even grow depending on the circumstances. Insolvencies, restructuring, and even transformation programmes are often perceived as heavy burdens, as they require businesses to clean up, abandon the past, and get a new orientation. This chapter is written accordingly. The entire turnaround process is outlined, and the principles of reorganisation and wind-down are introduced as an analytical and execution framework.

Most emphasis is put on the turnaround plan, applying a broad definition that shapes the financial restructuring, operational improvement, and business transformation for the long-term repositioning of financial institutions and their businesses. However, turnaround and transformation may also be seen as part of a natural journey of a business across the cycles of build-up, growth, stagnation, and destruction. It remains crucial to keep a value creation mindset and evaluate the value drivers on the journey during these cycles. Chapter 6 then provides a comprehensive framework for analysis, validation, and execution as part of a broader approach and management philosophy.

5.1 REORGANISATION AND WIND-DOWN

Turnaround and transformation are fundamentally driven by crisis, performance issues, and the need for change. It may eventually lead to a distressed situation with the risk of bankruptcy and insolvency. Bankruptcy and insolvency are defined as the state of being unable to pay outstanding obligations that may lead to the unwind of the financial institution. There are two fundamental applications that have today been reflected in the respective legislative framework. In the first one, reorganisation, a limited period of protection is provided for a company from its creditors to allow to develop a rescue plan. It allows an institution to emerge from formal insolvency and bankruptcy proceedings. In the second one, wind-down and liquidation, the company's assets are liquidated and the distribution of the proceeds to its creditors is executed. The latter usually does not involve the survival of the company, but the business may be carried out by someone else or a specific asset (e.g. technology) of the company may survive.

By nature, bankruptcy and insolvency have always been problem laden and heavily stigmatised in most societies. If someone went bankrupt in the 18th or 19th century, he or she may have been thrown in prison or even have lost an ear or other parts of the body. These draconian measures trace their roots to Roman and Napoleonic law and neglect the fact that any form of risk-taking may result in failure. Success and failure are part of the economic and corporate growth cycle. Every society that wants to encourage entrepreneurship has to allow risk-taking and, with that, failure as likely outcome. The United States and Europe have known different approaches to financial distress, reorganisation and restructuring, liquidation and wind-down, and insolvency proceedings. However, in recent years, a more agile approach and mindset found its way into European legislation. Because of its core function in the economic cycle and complex regulatory and balance-sheet requirements, the financial industry has developed its own rules though. The following section introduces the core concepts of reorganisation and wind-down across the legal frameworks in the United States and Europe. It then focusses on the recently introduced legislation that regulates bankruptcy and insolvency proceedings for the financial industry and banking and capital markets in particular. Exhibit 5.1 summarises the legal principles and their applications for financial institutions.

5.1.1 Legal principles

Participants in turnaround and restructuring situations need to know the legislative frameworks and applied principles in advance of the proceedings. It is instrumental to have an understanding of the legal concerns surrounding everyday activities when interacting with directors, management, employees, creditors, and the legal community. The legal uncertainty is getting mitigated and leaves the field to the economic solution on how to bring the viable business back on track to its future growth

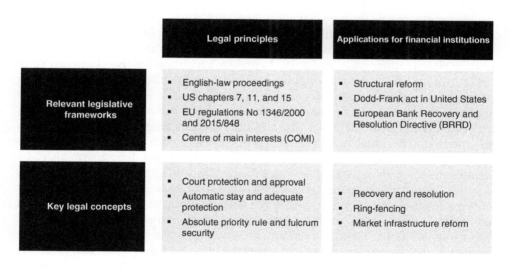

Exhibit 5.1 Reorganisation and wind-down of financial institutions

perspective. The objective of this section is to establish the fundamental concepts of today's legislative frameworks that separate reorganisation from wind-down and liquidation. It provides an overview of the core principles, looking at the legislation in the United States as global reference point and Europe with particular emphasis on international cross-border insolvency proceedings. The United Kingdom played a major role in developing and establishing this framework in Europe, even after Britain left the European Union (EU) in the meantime.

Relevant legislative frameworks

The harmonised legislation in the United States and Europe drive today's bankruptcy and insolvency proceedings on a global basis. In both laws the role of the two fundamental principles around court protection and fulcrum security are crucial. They will further be introduced.

United States

The United States with its entrepreneurial tradition in developing untapped territories has incorporated this fundamental principle of entrepreneurship deeply in its business customs. It has become today the global reference point for bankruptcy and insolvency proceedings. The US Bankruptcy Code is divided into nine separate chapters. The Chapters 1, 3, and 5 provide the provisions that generally apply to all bankruptcy cases. Chapters 7, 9, 11, 12, 13, and 15 are known as the operative chapters. Chapter 7 regulates liquidation, chapter 11 reorganisation, and Chapter 15 international cross-border insolvency proceedings. These three chapters are of particular relevance for the scope of this book. Chapter 9 on municipalities, chapter 12 on farming and fishing, and chapter 13 on lower-income individuals are less relevant from an operational perspective. Chapter 7 and chapter 11 cases are typically filed on a voluntary basis but under certain circumstances can be filed involuntarily against a debtor by a creditor. Cases under 9, 12, and 13 can be commenced only voluntarily by the debtor.

When filing chapter 7 for wind-down and liquidation proceedings, the business is typically closed immediately, and a court-appointed trustee administers the case from that point forward. The trustee will oversee and liquidate the assets of the business entity and then distribute the liquidation proceeds to the creditors after paying the administrative costs and other priority payments. At the end of the chapter 7 process, there is a discharge of any debts which is the base of a fresh start. Chapter 11, on the other hand, is available to business entities and individuals that aim to maintain control of their assets while establishing a plan to reorganise the repayment of its creditors. Its main objective is to provide debtors with a break from creditor collection activities (so-called automatic stay) which allows the opportunity to file and seek confirmation of a reorganisation. During the automatic stay, the debts are restructured and repaid in whole or in part. The debtor typically maintains control of its assets as a debtor-in-possession (DIP). In certain cases, owing to the complexity or bad-faith behaviour, an independent trustee is appointed by the bankruptcy court. During chapter 11 proceedings, the DIP has the ability to continue to operate its business in the ordinary course, subject to bankruptcy court oversight. A chapter 11 trustee, in contrast to a chapter 7 trustee, allows the business entity to continue the process of reorganising in an orderly manner. If certain requirements towards debt repayment are not fulfilled and or under specific circumstances such as gross negligence or mismanagement, the court may convert a chapter 11 into a chapter 7 case.

The origins of chapter 11 can be tracked back to the reorganisation of railroads, which could not be split and liquidated easily. In its basic tenet, chapter 11 gives companies the chance to sort out the future of its viable business under court protection from creditors. Chapter 11 is today widely regarded as the global standard for bankruptcy proceedings. It allows restructuring of troubled companies by protecting them from creditors, allows their management to stay in control until a reorganisation plan has been approved, and gives them the opportunity to continue borrowing money to keep the operations going. In addition, suppliers and customers cannot terminate contracts simply because of the chapter 11 filing. Most companies become insolvent, in a so-called cash-flow insolvency, because of their inability to meet debts as they fall due. The other common form is balance-sheet insolvency when assets are outweighed by liabilities. Chapter 11 allows addressing both forms of insolvency with the objective to keep the growth perspective of the viable business alive. It contrasts the outright liquidation of the business by terminating it or selling its assets to repay creditors. Chapter 11 therefore stands in contrast to chapter 7, which deals with liquidating companies outright and selling their assets to repay lenders.

Chapter 15 on international cross-border insolvency proceedings provides a mechanism for cooperation between the US courts and the courts in foreign countries. They act as secondary proceedings either to chapter 7, 11, or any foreign insolvency proceedings. The primary location will be typically the debtor's home country or main base of operations. Chapter 15 was created by the Bankruptcy Reform Act of 2005 and follows a similar concept as the centre of main interests (COMI) under the European regulations. COMI is a core element of the European regulation, and is based on an adoption of the model law on cross-border insolvency promulgated by the United Nations Commission on International Trade Law (UNICTRAL). UNICTRAL aims to respect and work with the differences in national bankruptcy proceedings laws but does not attempt to unify the legislation.

Europe

In Europe, liquidation and termination of ventures with the objective to protect creditors had been seen historically as the best answer to business failure. Following the introduction of cross-border insolvency regulations by the European Union in 2006, more flexible bankruptcy procedures have been put in place in several European countries. The United Kingdom has taken the leading role in developing and applying concepts in the spirits of the chapter 11 proceedings. Bankruptcy in the EU is primarily regulated through Regulation No 1346/2000 that was updated with Regulation 2015/848 in 2017. The system is based on the location of debtor's COMI where the company has its principal place of direction and administration. The court of the EU member state where the COMI is located has jurisdiction to open the main bankruptcy proceedings. The competent court must apply its national insolvency laws, and the effects of the proceedings are recognised EU-wide without formality.

There is the possibility for opening secondary proceedings, but they are restricted to the debtor's assets located in the respective EU member state. The legislation further contains coordination rules of main and secondary proceedings.

Through the European cross-border insolvency regulations, English-law proceedings have become an applicable solution for companies in continental Europe. This is done either by moving the companies' COMI to the United Kingdom or allowing English-law techniques of a scheme of arrangements to be imported domestically through incorporating them into local laws. Through Britain's 2002 Enterprise Act, financial restructuring can be achieved with only 75% of each lender class agreeing to its details. The legislation allows therefore the majority of creditors to prevail over the recalcitrant minority. Nevertheless, prepacked administration remains the most common form in which troubled companies are put into administration simultaneously with the efforts to sell the businesses to new owners.

The UK legislation sets out three main processes a debtor can use to commence a reorganisation. Company voluntary arrangements (CVA) is an agreement between an institution, its creditors, and shareholders in which the company's directors or an appointed administrator propose a reorganisation plan. This typically involves delayed or reduced debt payments and capital restructuring but mainly deals with the operational elements of a restructuring. Schemes of arrangement provide a mechanism enabling a company to enter into a compromise or arrangement with its creditors. Such schemes have been used in particular to effect a financial restructuring and are sometimes combined with a CVA or administration. Administration is a bankruptcy procedure that allows an institution to continue to trade with protection from its creditors by way of a moratorium. This may give the company sufficient breathing space to be reorganised and refinanced. While a company is in administration, it is controlled by an administrator, who must be a licensed insolvency practitioner (IP)[2]. To all effects and purposes, the power of the directors will cease while the administrator remains in office. The primary objective of administration is to rescue the company as a going concern. If the administrator comes to the conclusion that a better result will be achieved for the company's creditors by some other means, the institution may dispose assets or wind down completely. Liquidation in the United Kingdom, on the other hand, distinguishes between voluntary and involuntary liquidation. Voluntary liquidation knows different forms such as members' voluntary liquidation (MVL) in case the company is solvent and the directors are able to confirm this. If the company is insolvent, then there is the case of a creditors' voluntary liquidation (CVL). In both cases, shareholders pass a special resolution with a 75% majority to place the company into liquidation. In the case of involuntary or compulsory liquidation, creditors must apply to the court for a wind-down order. The most likely ground for this order is that the company is unable to pay its debts.

Many continental European countries have followed this framework and separated reorganisation from wind-down and liquidation which allows a more flexible application in case of bankruptcy. This development with the differentiation between outright

---

[2]A licensed insolvency practitioner is a regulated person in the United Kingdom who is authorised to act in relation to an insolvent company, partnership, or individual. Most IPs work in accounting firms.

liquidation and wind-down/reorganisation are core for operational restructuring and the establishment of a turnaround plan. Germany made substantial amendments to its Insolvency Code in 2012 and introduced protection proceedings under the "Schutzschirmverfahren". Switzerland separated the requirements of liquidation from reorganisation in 2014 and allows a more flexible application in which the reorganisation can be processed. Many other European countries made similar changes which allow today more flexible applications and provide the respective legal instruments to reorganise an institution under court protection from its creditors. What remains a notable difference in European legislation versus the US bankruptcy proceedings is the appointment of a trustee by the courts that oversee the reorganisation. The DIP concept of chapter 11 remains an exception rather than the norm in most European proceedings.

Key legal concepts

Court protection, automatic stay, and the fulcrum security are fundamental legal concepts and principles that must be understood from an operational perspective during a turnaround situation.

Court protection and approval

Clearly defined and transparent proceedings protected by the courts are the fundamental elements in the successful applications of reorganisations and wind-downs. Transparency and defined outcomes remain the keywords to resolve financial distress. Court protection has a crucial role in these settings as it outlines the legal framework and the standards to be adhered to. Furthermore, local customs and cultural differences can be taken into considerations by court rulings. For a successful restructuring, legal uncertainties must be minimised. Hence an effective application is possible only through a transparent process defined by court protection. Proceedings are commenced with the filing of a petition with the bankruptcy court. Companies that enter reorganization may continue to be run by their existing management sometimes with the oversight of a trustee and sometimes without. The plan that outlines the reorganisation has to be approved by the court. In chapter 11 bankruptcy proceedings, prepetition creditors are, for the most part, stayed from enforcement remedies. They do not receive payment of principal and/or interest while the company seeks to rationalize its business and formulate a plan of reorganization to restructure its balance sheet. A debtor may further pursue a nonconsensual confirmation of a turnaround plan via court decision. This form of restructuring is known as cramdown where the courts have the legal authority to impose a bankruptcy arrangement despite the objections of creditors. If a consensual restructuring cannot be attained, the institution can team up with the consenting creditors to arrange a prenegotiated or prepackaged plan that then gets forced on the opposing minority.

Court protection is in particular important for financial institutions as cash-flow insolvency may trigger the termination of outstanding financial contracts. Although in most legislation termination (ipso facto) provisions in contracts are unenforceable for financial institutions, the major documentations such as International Swaps and Derivatives Association master agreements with their credit support annex

(CSA) can terminate a transaction and/or lead to a liquidity event through triggering specific collateral requirements. The resulting cash requirements accelerated the price dynamics that led to GFC with billions of collateral outstanding. It drove the financial system at edge of collapse and led to the clearing requirements under the G20 reform in the aftermath of the GFC. Financial regulators have been granted bespoke powers to intervene in relation to the bankruptcy of financial institutions. This is important to mitigate the risks to financial stability and ensure consumer protection when these institutions are at risk of failing. In the United States, several regulatory entities like the Office of the Comptroller of the Currency, the Office of Thrift Supervision, and Federal Housing Finance Agency (FHFA) have been granted power to place financial institutions into receivership. Receivership is the concept to apply custodian responsibilities in cases where an entity cannot meet its financial obligations and becomes insolvent.[3] After heavy losses during the GFC, government-sponsored enterprises (GSEs) such as Fannie Mae and Freddie Mac were stabilised through receivership structures. At the end of September 2008, the Federal Reserve provided US$85 billion through a two-year loan to American International Group (AIG) to prevent its bankruptcy and the systemic collapse that may have followed. In return, the Fed took ownership of almost 80% of AIG's equity and received the right to replace management and veto power over all important decisions. Similar government interventions have been used in Europe to stabilise the financial system that are further covered in the dedicated section on the wind-down of financial institutions.

Automatic stay and adequate protection

Proceedings know the provision of automatic stay as defined in section 362 of the US bankruptcy code. It represents a breathing spell for debtors and is applied to all creditors, collections agencies, government entities, and individuals from pursuing debtors for amounts owed. The automatic stay precludes the initiation, commencement, or continuation of any manner any collection activity against the debtor or its property in case of a reorganisation or wind-down. The provision helps to protect equality of distribution among similarly situated creditors and puts them on a level playing field by preventing one creditor from seizing a debtor's assets before others have had the opportunity to do so.

Once an automatic stay goes into effect, creditors are unlikely to receive the full amounts they are owed. Instead, creditors will receive a proportional share of the bankrupt debtor's limited assets. The stay remains in place while the bankruptcy case is pending unless modified and terminated by the bankruptcy court. Creditors who

---

[3]With receiverships and assignment of the benefits of creditors (ABC), the US legislation provides two alternative methods to bankruptcy. ABC mainly is a method of liquidating an institution's distressed assets by the application of a trust format in accordance with state or common law. Receiverships can be initiated under federal and state law and knows a broader application not only driven by wind-down considerations but also oversight through a receiver who acts as fiduciary. Receiverships begins with one of the parties filling a lawsuit against the business and then filling a motion to appoint a receiver. It has been a successful instrument for government agencies to enforce their regulatory powers.

believe they have sufficient grounds can petition the court to lift the automatic stay so they can continue the collection process. There are certain circumstances under which the automatic stay terminates automatically or a certain relief of stay is granted for cause. Courts may condition further the automatic stay on the debtor providing adequate protection to its creditors. Such adequate protection may include periodic cash payments, sale or lease of debtor's properties, and the grant of additional or replacement liens with the objective to protect creditors from a loss in financial value.

Absolute priority rule and fulcrum security

In bankruptcy proceedings, there is a priority of interests and hierarchy in the right to get paid, that is, an order of payment among creditors and shareholders. Secured creditors come before unsecured creditors who in turn come before shareholders. As a result, senior creditors get paid in full before their juniors get anything. This is known as the absolute priority rule or liquidation preference. Secured creditors will be paid first to the extent of the fair market value of their collateral before any payments from the bankruptcy case. After the secured vendors are paid to the extent of the collateral, then the remaining claims are paid in a priority set, called classes, defined by the respective bankruptcy legislation.[4] This is particularly significant if the class of unsecured creditors is not paid in full and the class of equity holders beneath them in priority cannot retain their equity as a result of this.

Secured debt holders are in a position to shape the direction of the restructuring through controlling the cash collateral budget that may be required to fund operations. There are the first lien creditors on a defined set of assets for the cash collateral. Second lien creditors may provide incremental liquidity during a distressed situation which has been a common instrument for private equity sponsors and hedge funds in such lending transactions. One of the greatest advantages second lien lenders gain through a second lien structure is a seat at the negotiation table. On the other hand, there is a tier of creditors who will be only partially paid, which is often the case for unsecured debt. These claims that cannot be paid off in full or partially only are known as the fulcrum security. The fulcrum security is an important concept in the capital structure of a distressed company as it allows to control the company after a reorganisation. It represents the claim that is most likely to receive equity in the reorganised company after confirmation of a turnaround plan. It is the debt that is most likely to be converted into controlling equity for the lowest cost.

The purchase of the fulcrum security provides the maximum leverage over the approval of the debtor's reorganization plan. It can place an investor in a strong position

---

[4]A generic and abbreviated version of the order of claims (after secured creditors are paid to the extent of their collateral) may read as follow: first class consists of administrative expenses and claims of the ordinary course of the business during bankruptcy proceedings (post filing a court petition) which usually includes salaries, vendor services, and taxes required to operate the business; second class is defined by salaries and pension contributions earned within a specified period before bankruptcy; third class is prebankruptcy taxes; and fourth class is all other unsecured claims. All unsecured claims are often unsecured debt, nonpriority employment salaries and benefits, as well as trade creditors.

to control a restructuring situation by pursuing negotiations with DIP and its stake-holders. This is a direct result of the absolute priority rule which requires that senior creditors be paid in full before junior claims get anything. If a class of claimants is being only partially paid, then no one else is entitled to receive the equity of the reor-ganized institution unless the equity is bought with cash or all classes approve the plan respectively. So the group of these marginal or partially-in-the-money claims has a pre-sumptive right to the equity of the reorganized debtor. Distressed investors are targeting the fulcrum security as it will give them access to the situation and a role to play in the turnaround. It provides them with leverage over a turnaround plan because they are often the only class of claims that has a vote that matters with regard to control rights. Specific rules may apply (e.g. under chapter 11 proceedings) if creditors consent to per-mit the debtors to retain their equity interests or in case equity holders inject new capital as part of the turnaround plan. Both may lead to exceptions to the absolute priority rule and can change the payout and ownership structure accordingly. The term nuisance value defines the ratio of equity divided by subordinated debt. It is an important met-ric in the assessment of the opportunity. The ratio reflects an amount that a market participant is willing to pay to settle a claim not because it is valid or covered but it is considered to be worth that amount to control a company for reorganisation. Both con-cepts illustrate the importance of the capital structure in implementing a turnaround and the complexity the DIP face in negotiating with its stakeholders.

5.1.2   Reorganisation and wind-down of financial institutions

The chain reactions in the banking system in the aftermath of the implosion of Lehman Brothers remain a valuable lesson of the impact that uncoordinated bankruptcy and insolvency of a financial institution can have on financial stability and the overall economic environment. The reorganisation and wind-down of financial institutions have to follow specific requirements and instructions in accordance with a recovery and resolution regime that was refined by the structural reform after the GFC. Financial institutions therefore follow a specified legal framework in case of bankruptcy and insolvency that applies the outlined core principles but remains separate due to the balance-sheet structure and the potential implications from a wider system perspec-tive. Lehman Brothers Holding filed on 15 September 2008 for chapter 11 bankruptcy protection and administration in the United Kingdom which led to substantial market volatility and overall confidence loss in the financial system. The Fed followed suit and rescued AIG. It further brokered the acquisition of Merrill Lynch & Co. through Bank of America in the aftermath which then led to the US$700 billion bailout package "Troubled Asset Relief" programme. All these developments led to the initiation of a broader reform of financial regulation known as the G20 reform.

Under the new regime, all large bank holding companies in the United States are subject to a resolution regime defined under the Dodd-Frank Act. The regime is organised as a receivership process, controlled by the Federal Deposit Insurance Corporation and initiated by the Treasury Secretary and the Fed. This system will cover the large banks as well as the former investment banks, and many other important institutions with more than 85% of their activities in finance. In several European countries, different bailout regimes were applied for smaller regional banks during the

GFC which led to the creation of several resolution entities (often called bad banks) to resolve the situation on a systemic level. Some European regulators started to implement bail-in regimes which often led to losses of bond and in certain circumstances even to deposit holders that were outside of the deposit protection schemes established by the governments. The EU implemented a series of financial support measures in 2010 such as the European Financial Stability (EFSF) and the European Stability Mechanism (ESM), and developed a comprehensive regime for recovery and resolution called the Bank Recovery and Resolution Directive (BRRD) to harmonise the legal frameworks across the EU. For the international wholesale businesses[5] of global financial institutions that pursued risk-taking activities, ring-fencing requirements were implemented in several countries. The market infrastructure reform further specified the regulation of over-the-counter (OTC) derivatives which has been an important requirement for the large-scale trading businesses and a direct response to the origins of the GFC. The following section provides an overview over these specified laws. Chapter 3 previously covered the Basel framework and the crucial role of stress testing as part of these embedded regulatory frameworks.

Structural reform

After the GFC, regulatory authorities introduced as part of the G20 requirements the structural reform with its two major components recovery and resolution as well as ring-fencing. The following section focuses on the legislation in Europe while the core principles of the regulation can be applied universally on a global scale.

Recovery and resolution

The BRRD, established under the leadership of the European Banking Authority (EBA), a comprehensive regime for recovery and resolution. The United Kingdom, a EU member state at this stage, has been following BRRD and implemented it into UK law by a combination of Statutory Instruments made by the Treasury and Financial Conduct Authority as well as Prudential Regulation Authority (PRA) rules. Switzerland as a non-EU country introduced early its own "Too Big to Fail" regime for systemically important banks (S-IB) that further introduced ring-fencing, additional capital requirements, and the requirements of bank's recovery and resolution plans. The EBA developed a series of guidelines through the BRRD. They ensure a minimum set of tools and powers available to regulators mainly related to the planning to help the recovery of firms in financial distress, early intervention in the event of problems, the resolution of failed firms in a way that reduces costs to the public, and mitigation of the impact on the financial system. Governments and regulators prefer not to let a financial institution fail because large-scale bankruptcy could increase the likelihood of systemic problems that threatens financial stability. There are two resolution regimes that are used in distressed situations. Bailout involves the rescue of a financial institution by

---

[5]Wholesale businesses include capital markets, corporate and investment banking that are usually organised and pursued on an international level.

external parties, typically governments and central banks, using taxpayers' money for funding. In bail-in, the opposite of bailout, creditors, usually bond investors and deposit-holders, take losses through debt cancellation.

In Germany, several regional banks (Landesbanken) had to be bailed out by governments after getting caught up with exotic financial instruments during the GFC as part of an international growth strategy. West LB was closed down with some of its assets brought into Helaba, another Landesbank. Sachsen LB was folded into Landesbank Baden-Wurttemberg (LBBW) as part of a bailout package. The case that attracted most international attention was HSH Nordbank which got EUR €3 billion of fresh equity from its two state shareholders, Hamburg and Schleswig-Holstein, in combination of a EUR €10 billion risk shield for losses above a certain threshold. HSH Nordbank went to rounds of restructuring, reducing nonperforming assets and its headcounts gradually. The restructuring was dominated by scandals and political interferences on all levels. In another restructuring move several years later in 2016, the bank offloaded over EUR €6 billion of nonperforming loans (NPL), mainly shipping, onto its government majority owners which avoided its full wind-down. Finally, a consortium of private equity groups around Cerberus Capital Management and J.C. Flowers bought the bank in 2018 and renamed it Hamburg Commercial Bank (HCOB) after selling the bank's NPL portfolio to a special purpose vehicle at a price below its current book value.

In the United Kingdom, the British government established UK Asset Resolution, a state-owned limited company, to manage the assets of the two nationalised mortgage lenders, Bradford & Bingley and Northern Rock. Several large global banks such as Deutsche Bank, the Royal Bank of Scotland (RBS), Barclays Bank, and the two Swiss banks, UBS and Credit Suisse, transferred nonperforming assets and nonstrategic businesses to internal bad banks. The Swiss government and Swiss National Bank (SNB) had previously established a fund for rescuing UBS which after the collapse of Lehman Brothers was no longer able to sustain itself. Many of those banks eventually dumped the bulk of their commodities operation and fixed income business into an internal bad bank as part of their restructuring with the objective to greatly curtail their risk-taking activities and focus on the local business model and in case of UBS on international wealth management.

Southern Europe, in particular Greece, Spain, and Italy, were heavily impacted by the GFC and implemented large bailout programmes, supported by recapitalising programmes of the ESM. The financial crisis in Greece evolved in a local economic crisis which substantially impacted the large bank balance sheets through defaults on mortgage and business loans. The main cause for the crisis in Spain was a housing bubble fuelled by unsustainable economic growth rates and a lack of supervision of the local financial sector which was fuelled by exotic and long-dated financial products and scandal. When economic growth fell dramatically after the GFC, the Spanish banking sector slipped into a deep crisis. Bankia bank, the country's largest mortgage lender, was nationalized in May 2012 with a bailout package of over EUR €23.5 billion to cover losses from failed mortgages. In June 2012, the country received a EUR €100 billion package to stabilise its banking sector through the ESM which was further supported by the European Central Bank's Outright Monetary Transactions (OMT) program with unlimited purchases of short-term Eurozone sovereign debt. A few months later in autumn 2012, the European Commission approved the Spanish government's plan to shrink and restructure its three major Spanish banks, including Bankia, NCG Banco, and Catalunya Banc while selling Banco de Valencia. These measures included the loss-taking by investors in equity and junior debt of up to EUR €10 billion and the creation of its bad bank SAREB, a resolution entity to absorb up to EUR €45 billion of failed loans. We are further going to cover SAREB under the section on NPL. Italy's banking crisis evolved around the one of the world's oldest banks, Banca Monte dei Paschi di Siena (MPS) which was also the fourth largest Italian commercial and retail bank at this stage. The initial scandal and drama of MPS were followed a series of recapitalisations including several regional banks. Italy struggled to comply with the BRRD rules while it aimed to protect the bank's domestic investors who heavily bought bank debt in early parts of the recapitalisation.

Bail-ins attracted broader attention in 2013 after government officials resorted to this scheme in Cyprus. Uninsured depositors in the Bank of Cyprus with more than EUR €100 000 in deposits lost a substantial portion of their deposits but received in return shares of the bank. However, the value of these stocks did not equate to most depositors' losses. Portugal's central bank, Banco de Portugal, followed suit in late 2015 when it decided to bail-in senior bondholders of Novo Banco that previously was established under the recued plan for Banco Espírito Santo (BES). An international group of investors under the name of the "Novo Note Group" took legal actions against Banco de Portugal, stating that it unlawfully retransferred over EUR €2 billion of bonds from Novo Banco back to the bad bank which remained under its old name of BES.

Ring-fencing

Ring-fencing defines a terminology when risk-taking businesses such as propriety trading and other investment banking operations are separated organisationally and operationally from conventional business such as retail and commercial banking. Post GFC, ring-fencing was part of G20 requirements which can be seen as a moderate version of the Glass-Stegall Act, established in the 1933 during the Great Depression. In the United States, the rule, proposed by former Fed Chairman Paul Volker to restrict as part of the Dodd-Frank Act propriety trading operations of regulated banks in the United States, was successfully implemented. Similarly in the United Kingdom, a reform proposed by John Vickert ring-fences retail banking by separating retail and investment banking operations through creating separate legal entities and restricting derivative trading operations for the retail entities. It was formally introduced through the Financial Services (Banking Reform) Act of 2013. In the EU, a review chaired by Erkki Liikanen, governor of Finland's central bank, provided the regional proposal for restructuring big banks, with a twist on the trading restrictions of the US Volker rule and the UK Vickert reforms. It proposed a trading firewall and a series of other proposals to make bank safer and protect taxpayers, including measures to retain bonuses and take a tougher approach to the risk of property lending conducted by retail banks. The ring-fencing rules proposed require the spun-off of assets accounted for by trading into separately capitalised and funded subsidiaries. The proposal had not progressed since its original rejection in 2015, and was then finally withdrawn in 2018.[6]

---

[6]The proposal had been finalised under the regulation on structural measures improving the resilience of EU credit institutions.

In the United States, the Fed tailors its regulatory requirements for and supervision of foreign banking organizations (FBOs) to account for the size, complexity, risk profile, and financial activities of their US operations. Large FBOs with combined assets of US$50 billion or more are required to form an intermediate holding company (IHC) and comply with enhanced capital, liquidity, risk-management, and stress-testing requirements overseen by the Fed. Each large FBO is expected to ensure that the combined US operations and its core business lines can survive under a broad range of internal or external stresses. This requires financial resilience by maintaining sufficient capital and liquidity and operational resilience by maintaining effective corporate governance and risk management. Although it is not ring-fencing in the classic sense of the Glass–Steagall Act, it follows a regional approach to the same matter. In Europe, particularly the UK legislation followed suit, addressing the PRA's concern that troubled trading and investment banking businesses could be abandoned by the regulators in their home country. The regulations aimed to implement dedicated subsidiaries for such organisations, objecting to traditional branch structures of international financial institutions that were common up to the GFC.

Market infrastructure reform

Derivatives markets developed exponentially since the financial deregulation that started in the mid-1980s. They were a major growth driver of the international wholesale businesses of global financial institutions, while at the same time a major contributing factor in the evolution to the GFC. As a response to the GFC, the G20's market infrastructure reform focused on the regulation of OTC derivatives with the central purpose to manage and avoid systemic risk by increasing regulations on clearing and trading. The regulations further include requirements for reporting of derivative contracts and implementation of risk management standards. It established common rules for central counterparties and trade repositories with the objective of the legislation being to reduce systemic counterparty and operational risk and help prevent future financial system collapses. In Europe, the reform was implemented through the European Market Infrastructure Regulation (EMIR) with its three major requirements of reporting, risk mitigation, and clearing. These requirements directly address some of the core challenges that disrupted derivatives markets during the GFC.

EMIR requires that all entities entering into derivative contracts must submit reports to their corresponding trade repositories (TR), outlining each OTC trade. These mandatory reports must also include a unique transaction identifier (UTI), legal entity identifier (LEI), information on the trading capacity of the counterparty, and the market-to-market valuation of the position. Risk mitigation techniques defined by EMIR include timely submission of reports and confirmations of adherence to regulation by all counterparties, and open reconciliation and compression of portfolios. Other techniques include a new dispute resolution process, daily market reports and exchanges, and the public exchange of collateral between parties. Under EMIR, the European Securities and Markets Authority (ESMA) applies mandatory clearing obligations for specific OTC derivative contracts. The obligations require that such trades are cleared through central counterparties. The clearing regulation applies to financial counterparties such as banks, insurers, and asset managers, as well as nonfinancial counterparties such as corporates in OTC derivatives.

5.2 TURNAROUND PROCESS

The turnaround process for financial institutions describes the corrective actions management has to undertake to achieve the recovery from its challenges. This process, illustrated in Exhibit 5.2, is organised across four phases. The first or initial planning phase starts with immediate crises management to stabilise the situation and institution (phase 1). It is followed by the development of a strategic roadmap which in this context is called a turnaround plan (phase 2). The planning phase is followed by a broader reorganisation which includes the financial restructuring (phase 3), and the long-term oriented activities of operational performance improvement and business transformation to reposition the business (phase 4). If the turnaround process is unsuccessful, bankruptcy and wind-down may follow as a final phase of existence. The early focus on taking control while building or rebuilding stakeholder support is a crucial success factor of this process.

Crisis management and business transformation define the spectrum of turnaround activities with different recovery speeds and probable end-states. Crisis management aims to achieve business viability quickly while transformation aims to achieve high level of performance improvement and change over the mid- to long term. The scope of a business transformation programme does usually not encompass crisis management while it may lead to business transformation in a later stage, in particular if an institution faces structural issues. Many of the regional, systemic banks in Southern Europe had not only to deal with the immediate implications of the Eurozone crisis but more fundamentally with the viability of their business model given the structural challenges in Spain, Greece, Portugal, and Italy. In accordance with our applied definition of turnaround, the following sections aim to cover the full spectrum of immediate crisis response and the long-term positioning of a business. Maintaining open lines of communication across creditors, employees, and other stakeholders is imperative during a turnaround and transformation. The workforce may become demoralised when short-term concerns are not addressed while it is not advised discussing specific strategies outside of the team that execute them.

5.2.1 Crisis management

Shaun O'Callaghan defines a crisis as the turning point when assumptions about the future change and/or promises that were made will be no longer delivered. If we are applying this definition, we may reach the conclusion that the entire banking industry is in crisis with new dynamics threatening its current structure and long-term positioning. In the context of our turnaround framework, crisis management is the immediate response to a situation that threatens the existence of a financial institution. It focuses on the disposal of assets to repay outstanding obligations with the objective to avoid insolvency, the recapitalisation of balance sheets, and rapid business performance

	Crisis management	Turnaround plan	Financial restructuring	Operational restructuring

Activities	■ Assess situation and stabilise institution
	  – Understand magnitude of losses
	  – Ring-fence toxic assets
	  – Develop retention plan
	■ Address immediate funding needs
	  – Recapitalise
	  – Maintain solvency
	  – Tap into existing and new sources of capital
	■ Reorganise in accordance with legal framework
		■ Impact assessment and response
		  – Regulatory and capital requirements
		  – Technology innovation
		  – Competitive positioning
		■ Realign vision and mission to create long-term stability and value
		■ Define market positioning
		■ Identify capability system
		■ Optimise capital structure
		■ Optimise funding model
			■ Recapitalise
			■ Debt restructuring and relief
				■ Assess business portfolio along defined profitability targets and key performance indicators
				■ Separate core and non-core business
				■ Divest noncore business, and acquire core businesses
				■ Restructure organisation for future growth
				■ Simplify client and product portfolios
				■ Rationalise distribution channels
				■ Optimise cost base and align new business model and core operations
				■ Assess TOM
				■ Re-platform by integrating new technology solutions

Engagements	■ Situation analysis ■ Recapitalisation and funding plan ■ Market positioning	■ Strategic roadmap	■ Legal entity restructurings including recovery and resolution planning ■ Capital optimisation plan	■ Portfolio optimisation ■ Disposal programmes ■ Front-to-back transformation ■ Targeted re-platforming

Exhibit 5.2 Financial institutions' turnaround and transformation cycle

improvement initiatives to stabilise the crisis situation. The long-term repositioning of an institution and business is not the priority at this stage. The core objective is to retain and stabilise the troubled businesses.

Immediate crisis response

The core of the immediate response is to address the worsening cash position that may bring the entire operations to a halt when an organisation runs out of cash. Crisis management requires radical leadership to turn the situation around while ensuring stakeholder support. Financial institutions are crucially dependent on customer confidence and their trust in the institution's solvency. Without them a bank run may arise in its traditional format through queuing customers outside of a brick and mortal branch (in case of Northern Rock in the United Kingdom in 2007) or the wave of redemptions of hedge funds and other institutional investors from prime brokerage operations (in case of Morgan Stanley and Goldman Sachs in autumn 2008). During such a crisis, government and regulators have historically declared bank holidays to shut down destabilised institutions, guaranteed liabilities through dedicated bad banks, and nationalised operations.

The cost of financial distress can be substantial and in itself can lead to a vicious cycle that concludes in default and liquidation. The operating performance of a company declines if there is continuous uncertainty around financial matters and the firm's viability. Management gets distracted, working with regulators, creditors, and major shareholders. Customers and vendors lose trust, which in the case of financial institutions can be fatal. The existing or incoming management team has to move swiftly and take control with full conviction. By securing a short-term future for an institution or business, the management team creates a window of opportunity in which the rescue plan can be implemented. To rebuild confidence and trust with shareholders is a fundamental base for the stabilisation and long-term survival of the firm. This is achieved when predictability in operations is reinstalled through stable cash-flow predictions. Any form of financial restructuring, operational performance improvement, and long-term business transformation initiatives requires a stable situation. Lacking this, the strategy and future commercial model will not be viable.

Immediate crisis response in contrast to more long-term financial restructuring initiatives is by launching a series of cash generation strategies. Working capital can be reduced by liquidating current assets, improving interest and debt collection, and attracting additional funding such as DIP financing. This is also the reason why often a new finance director is introduced because of the critical importance of strong financial management in an immediate crisis response. In any case, the going concern of the business is to be ensured in accordance with the respective legal requirements or else the wind-down and liquidation proceedings will be initiated. The presumption of going concern for the business is based on the basic declaration of intention to keep operating its activities at least for the next year alive. It further assumes that the financial obligations can be met when they fall due. It means that the business has neither the intention nor the need to wind down and liquidate.

Zone of insolvency

The zone of insolvency refers to the state when an institution is at the edge of insolvency but has not yet become insolvent. When an institution operates in the zone of insolvency, the decisions of the board of directors and management will be closely scrutinised by the company's shareholders and stakeholders. Questionable decisions, behaviours, and fiduciary positions may lead to personal liabilities. The best protection is to continue to adhere to good corporate governance practices and discharge director's and officers' duties in good faith, through informed judgement based on all relevant, material information. It is further advised to get legal counsel and other qualified advisors involved to ensure compliance with respect to legal requirements. It may also require to get an independent assessment on the financial situation, the enterprise value and the institution's strategic options to maximise the value of all corporate assets. Detailed records of corporate meetings and the decision making process are to be kept and may become an important base to validate sound decision making and business judgement in such situations of crisis. Directors and managers should refrain from engaging in risky strategies that gives preferred treatment to certain parties. This includes preferential and fraudulent payments to themselves, any shareholder, or creditor. As we will further elaborate, the trust fund doctrine requires managers to act in the interests of all parties but in particular creditors if the company slips into bankruptcy. The entrepreneurial focus on creating shareholder value shifts towards protecting creditors while safeguarding the going concern of the institution in accordance with the turnaround plan.

5.2.2 Turnaround plan

Chapter 1 introduced under the section on strategic evaluation the concepts of roadmap and impact assessment which in case of a turnaround situation evolves in a turnaround plan. It outlines the immediate steps to stabilise the situation and all activities for a sustainable recovery. This involves a viable business strategy, supported by an adequate organisation and governance structure as well as a target operating model (TOM) that aligns the financial institutions' capabilities, products, and services with its market positioning. A turnaround plan defines the agreed course of actions with at least provisional stakeholder support for them. All assumptions, opinions, and recommendations must be substantiated by facts and analysis.

Process

A valid turnaround plan has to be comprehensive and addresses commercial, operational, and financial issues holistically. In contrast to a long-term turnaround plan, a rescue or crisis response plan outlines an immediate action list with core objectives to stabilise an institution and/or business in a crisis situation. A sustainable recovery requires at the same time to develop a sustainable competitive advantage. Stuart Slatter and David Lovett outline a group of key characteristics for a robust turnaround plan. It must address the fundamental problem of the turnaround situation, tackling the underlying causes rather than the symptoms. The plan must be broad and deep enough to resolve all of the mission-critical issues. At the same time, it remains core to focus on the key issues and identify the main leavers to stabilise and sort out the underlying causes of the situation. Radical change is required that is tackled through a fundamental and holistic plan.

As a credible turnaround plan may take some time to develop, a rapid initial assessment or diagnostic review must be undertaken as quickly as possible. The objective of a diagnostic review is to establish the true position of an institution from a strategic, operational, and financial perspective. It is followed by establishing the available options that allow the turnaround of the institution and business. It will determine if the business is viable and has a chance to survive in case of a crisis whilst the detailed and long-term turnaround plan is getting established. The previously introduced hypothesis-driven approach in application with rigorous financial analysis will provide in complex situations an efficient toolset to establish an initial view.

The diagnostic review usually includes a preliminary view of the management team and an analysis of the stakeholders' positions and support. Given the available time, the diagnostic review is high level and broad in scope. Only the identified core issues will be covered in-depth. The diagnostic review should combine recovery or insolvency analysis with the known elements of a conventional roadmap and can be seen as a high-level or first draft of a turnaround plan. A rescue plan in case of crisis may be nothing more than a diagnostic review when a business is running out of cash or time respectively. The threat of insolvency must be assessed during this process as the legal requirements may lead to a filing in case that the going-concern of the institution is no longer given. The balance-sheet test assesses if a company is insolvent when the fair market value of its assets is less than the sum of its liabilities (balance-sheet insolvency). The cash-flow test determines if an institution is insolvent if it is unable to pay its debts as they come due (equitable insolvency). The determination of whether a company is insolvent under these two tests is fact intensive and often heavily disputed.

Structure

A turnaround plan is to be compiled as written documents for key decision-maker engagement such as board members, shareholders, and other stakeholders. There is an open question if it should be shared with the parties in its entirety. In case of formal bankruptcy proceedings and the filing of a petition, this plan may have to be submitted to the court, outlining to the parties involved how a troubled company can successfully exit the current situation and pay its creditors. If the institution is insolvent, the fiduciary duties owed by directors and officers are extended to creditors. The trust fund doctrine may apply for which directors and officers are said to hold the remaining corporate assets in trust for the benefit of all creditors.

The turnaround plan may be organised across the following outline depending on the circumstances. Such a plan may have to satisfy in addition certain statutory requirements in case of formal proceedings as for example outlined in section 1123 of the US bankruptcy code. The structure of a turnaround plan looks as follows:

1. Executive summary and overview
   - Scope and objectives [mandate descriptions]
   - Summary of plan and major recommendations

- Definition of turnaround strategy
- Implementation considerations
2. Company background
   - Brief and high-level description of business, operations, and organisation
   - Strengths, weakness, opportunities, and threats (SWOT)
   - Key issues that are leading up to the current situation
3. Impact assessment and status quo
   - Overview of current actions
   - Heat map
   - Financial analysis which includes revenues and cost trends, capital, breakeven and contribution, market and competitive analysis
4. Liquidity management
   - Initial assessment
   - 13-week cash-flow plan
5. Financial forecast and request
   - Projected income statement
   - Projected balance sheet
   - Projected cash-flow statement
   - Financial and borrowing capacities
   - Financing and investment request
6. Tactical plan and implementation
   - Turnaround strategies with its key elements
   - Viable commercial model
   - Target operating model
   - Implementation roadmap
   - Tactical steps
   - Timeline and communication protocol

There always is an existential question if the turnaround plan should be implemented by a new or existing management team. The chief executive officer (CEO) and existing management team has the most sophisticated understanding of the business while their business judgment may be affected by crisis denial or suffer from crisis denial or a reality gap. To bring in a dedicated turnaround manager or chief restructuring officer (CRO) to assist the existing management team or replace the CEO as undisputed leader may be the right answer depending on the situation and the immediate crisis response. Ensuring trust and confidence of key stakeholder are key to any turnaround situation. These attributes are facilitated by the communication of the turnaround plan with regular updates on progress and further development. What remains for sure though is that rigorous project management is the key success factor for execution. A dedicated turnaround programme office should coordinate the initiatives and track and communicate progress across the organisation and stakeholders. Furthermore, an overarching steering committee consisting of the management team, board members, and key shareholder if not stakeholder should oversee the execution.

Communication

Internal and external communication remains key for the successful implementation of the turnaround plan. Core objective is to align stakeholders and banks with their funding line and keep the internal morale up with a clear vision and path for the turnaround. Throughout the turnaround process, there will be misinformation, rumours, and misunderstanding. Only frequent and clear communication will offset the negative forces likely to be at work within the institution and its broader ecosystem. This includes a broad range of communication instruments from internal information memorandum, targeted stakeholder communication, and press releases. It often makes sense to employ a communication agency that specialises in crisis and turnaround situations.

5.2.3   Financial restructuring

Financial restructuring is the process of reorganizing the balance sheet and capital structure. Its overall objective is to achieve a financial strategy that enables the company to implement the turnaround plan and fund the strategic repositioning while remaining solvent by meeting all its ongoing liabilities. Most important as a starting point, the management team needs to have a clear view of the financial position and an information system in place to control it and track the quantitative impact of all the different initiatives. This often requires the reduction of the number of authorised persons and the establishment of a strong central team. Financial restructuring aims to restore solvency both with regard to cash flow and balance sheet while aligning the capital structure and financing.

Cash-flow restructuring

Cash-flow restructuring aims to address immediate liquidity and cash-flow issues by managing working capital and disposing tradable assets. Working capital optimisation can be facilitated by reducing debtors and overdue payments, extending creditors, accelerating invoicing and fee realisation, applying asset finance by lending against specific balance-sheet assets as collateral, and refinancing by securing short-term funding. Cash-generating initiatives can also materialise through operational performance improvement. The management team has to establish a comprehensive view on the financial and business performance as some asset and businesses may be linked to an immense cash potential out of their operational capabilities.

The traditional concept of working capital can be applied to financial institutions only on a limited basis as they do not have typical current assets such as accounts payable and their main source of income is interest payments and fees. On the liability side, institutions such as banks typically rely on deposits and wholesale funding as a prime source for capital, often with an undefined term. More practically as indicator for a financial institution's cash-flow position is net interest margin (NIM). NIM measures how much a bank earns in interest compared to how much it pays out to its investors and depositors. Fees are a central income source but often depend on asset size and market developments, so specific predictions are to be made which often face a high level of uncertainty. Naturally, the disposal of balance-sheet assets and entire businesses become the core focus of a financial institution to manage its cash flow during stress situation. Banking institutions will also have access to central bank facilities and can pledge assets against liquidity. During the GFC, central banks set up short-term facilities and swap lines to manage the liquidity crunch. After the default of Lehman Brothers in September 2008, the two remaining pure-play investment banks, Morgan Stanley and Goldman Sachs Group Inc., converted into traditional bank holding companies to get access to the emergency facilities at the Fed. It ended an era of the classic Wall Street model where a group of independent brokerage firms were less regulated than traditional banks and enjoyed a higher profitability as a result of it. Post GFC, the revised Basel framework further introduced the liquidity coverage ratio (LCR) and the net stable funding ratio (NSFR) as minimum regulatory standards to ensure that banks maintain adequate levels of liquidity. The LCR and NSFR were discussed in a dedicated section of Chapter 3.

Balance-sheet restructuring

The main areas of a balance sheet that a business has to restructure include current assets and liabilities, long-term assets and liabilities, and equity capital. Debt and equity restructuring can further be distinguished while debt restructuring is more commonly used. Debt restructuring often requires the agreement of creditors when the characteristics of interest and principal payments are changed or converted in other financial instruments. The term workout describes a process that has the objective to reduce the indebtedness of a financial institution's balance sheet via the disposal of assets. It can be debtor led and hence controlled by the company's management or creditor led in case of financial institutions and under the deposit protection scheme heavily directed by regulators. In case of secured debt, the workout is a creditor-led process. On the other hand, workout defines a mechanism to maximise the potential recovered value coming from distressed or nonperforming assets such as a loan that is held on a bank's balance sheet. Post GFC, distressed and nonperforming assets became a major issue for the financial system. This began in the United States with its subprime mortgage exposures and then massively affected the banking systems in Southern Europe after the economic downturn.

Distressed and nonperforming assets

Distressed assets are assets with major financial difficulties, usually either in default or close to default. They have greatly devalued and are often traded below their intrinsic value due to the previously outlined liquidity effect. Nonperforming assets (NPAs) are a specific form of distressed assets that cease to generate income for the financial institution. It is often a loan or other form of credit facilities, referring to NPLs in which the interest and/or the instalment of principal has remained past due for a specified period of time. The Basel framework defines this time period as due for more than 90 days or the point in time from which there is reason to consider that these payments will never be made in full. NPL are the most common form of NPA and will be covered here in more detail.

NPLs have the risk to destabilise balance sheets by reducing core-tier equity through write-off of negative interest-rate margins. The bank has forgone interests on the asset side while continuing to pay interests on its liabilities. This eventually leads to solvency and liquidity issues, threatening the survival of the financial institution or the entire banking system, as it was experienced in many Southern European countries after the GFC. The Basel framework provides guidance with regard to the standards of measurement of NPLs and the treatment of specific characteristics such as the collateral. The EBA further published in late 2018 their final guidelines on management of nonperforming exposures (NPEs). These guidelines, which apply a threshold of 5% of gross NPL ratio as a trigger, aim to ensure that financial institutions have the adequate prudential tools and frameworks in place to manage effectively their NPEs and to achieve a sustainable reduction on their balance sheets. It has been targeted to address and finally resolve the substantial NPL issues in the EU.

In accordance with applied industry practice, several authors and regulators have proposed a holistic approach to NPL.[7] This framework established a portfolio view by aggregating the individual NPE, segmenting them by identifying the key drivers in line with their aggregated characteristics. Finally, it applies an active approach in managing the key drivers such as ticket size, vintage, presence of third-party guarantees, collateral, and other factors. In accordance with the respective solvency proceedings, actions on NPL can be taken in or out of court. Given the cumbersome and burdensome administrative processes in many European countries, out-of-court resolution initiatives have been pursued by many financial institutions. This may include a debt relief with partial write-off combined with financial advice to sort out the situation. Too many banks kept on refinancing interest and principal so that no impairment or any other financial implications have been taken. Many troubled financial institutions remained overwhelmed with the scale of the workout and the establishment of dedicated teams to manage the NPL exposure. Joint ventures between financial institutions and partnerships with third parties were formed as a result of this. Specific asset servicing and asset management solutions were developed by specialised providers. These providers offered the range from pure asset servicing to dedicated investment strategies with focus on realising the intrinsic value and taking the assets through bankruptcy and insolvency proceedings.

Asset management companies (AMC) consisting of multiple institutions were set up in several countries with the public purpose of addressing the large NPL issues. The government of Ireland established in 2009 the National Asset Management Agency (NAMA). The Hellenic Financial Stability Fund (HFSF) was established in 2010. The Spanish government created in 2012 SAREB which stands for Sociedad de Gestión de Activos procedentes de la Reestructuración Bancaria [Company for the Management of Assets proceeding from Restructuring of the Banking System]. Those structures were organised as AMC in separate entities that purchase the NPL from domestic banks at a substantial discount funded by government bonds. Italian banks, which had with over EUR €360 billion in gross book value (according to Banca d'Italia in 2015) the highest NPL issued in the EU, set up in 2016 a private equity fund, Atlante. The fund has been dedicated to purchase the junior tranches of securitised NPL while recapitalising the domestic banking system. Important to Atlante was the circumstance that the Italian government guaranteed the senior tranche of the securitised NPLs. The overall experience with such bad banks was mixed and more broadly impacted by turbulences and

---

[7]Claudio Scardovi's book *Holistic Active Management of Non-Performing Loans* is an excellent reference to the topic. Scardovi further provides a detailed framework on workouts to which we refer interested readers for a more detailed discussion of the topic.

bailout activities of the governments in these countries. However, AMC seem to have stabilised the immediate crisis situation. It remains now with banks and policy makers to follow through on the end-to-end repositioning and transformation of their respective banking systems.

Disposals

Financial institutions' assets and individual businesses may be disposed to gain access to liquidity and pay off immediately obligations that are due. A structured process is to be applied that allows optimisation of the disposals with the core objective to mitigate any long-term implications on the institution's strategic positioning. After conducting a portfolio review, the assets and/or business units are disposed over a certain time frame. After the GFC, several financial institutions created noncore units to facilitate these sales. Bankruptcy proceedings such as section 363 of the US code further outline the nonordinary course disposal of business assets, with notice and the court's permission, that are free and clear of all liens. The debtor typically seeks and obtains the bankruptcy court's approval and then proceeds with an auction. The auction, which can be private or public, is geared towards ensuring the maximum return to the bankruptcy estate.

The procedures may use a stalking horse which is a buyer who has proposed terms for the purchase of assets. The offer becomes the opening bid and sets the general parameters and floor that the other offers must exceed. It is a strategy to test the market in which an initial bidder chooses to make the first bid when assets or businesses are sold. The financial institution makes a list of possible bidders and chooses the highest. The selected bidder is offered many incentives such as breakup fees and reimbursement fees to make the auction more enticing. The bidder will be willing to offer a higher price for the assets of the company. Since the price of the highest bidder becomes the starting price of the auction, the chance for the institution to extract the highest value is greatly increased. Any incremental bid amounts will be in part determined by the value of the asset.

Recapitalisation

Recapitalisation is a type of financial reorganization that involves substantial change in an institution's capital structure. Recapitalisation may be motivated by a number of reasons. Usually, the large part of equity is replaced with debt or vice versa. In more complex transactions, mezzanine financing and other hybrid securities are involved. In Chapter 3 on asset-liability management several hybrid capital instruments were introduced that were further refined after the GFC. The refinancing is usually a two-stage process. One is short-term survival financing, followed by long-term financial reorganisation of the capital structure. The raising of new funding may involve additional debt, starting with existing lenders who can be persuaded that the best prospect of recovering their existing exposure is by the provision of further funds. New equity capital may be raised through right issues or specialised financial investors such as hedge funds and private equity that are focussing on turnaround situations. At the same time, a complete review of the banking arrangements needs to be undertaken. Financing is often crucially dependent on the communication of the turnaround plan.

Short-term survival financing

The short-term survival financing ensures that there is sufficient funding in place to enable the company to produce its business plan and to develop a refinancing proposal. The natural providers of funding are critical stakeholders who have all interest to keep the company afloat. In some circumstances, shareholders will also provide financial assistance although this can be a risky strategy as their support may lead to a reduction of the debt exposure. Balance-sheet items, crucial operating assets, and intellectual property have significant value as collateral for financing and provide an interesting base for short-term survival financing. Section 364 of the US bankruptcy code knows the concept of DIP financing. It is a specific form of financing that allows companies in administration to attract new funds by allowing these rank ahead of existing creditors. As we discussed previously, a DIP is an institution that has filed for a bankruptcy petition but remains in possession of the property upon which a creditor has a security interests (also called lien). In such financing facilities, lenders can get superior seniority and enhanced security that is not available outside the context of bankruptcy. The loans have to be completely paid off before the borrower can emerge from chapter 11 proceedings. This is known as super priority. Actively traded bonds are further common for DIP financing so bondholders have a crucial role in the restructuring process. This allows specialised distressed investors to buy the bonds in the markets and begin with the restructuring in accordance with the bankruptcy proceedings. Any proposed DIP financing is subject to court approval.

DIP financing can be attained in securities or loan format. DIP loans are typically asset based, revolving working-capital facilities put into place at the outset of chapter 11 to provide both immediate cash as well as ongoing working capital during the reorganization process. Perhaps most important, DIP financing helps the company restore vendor and customer confidence in the company's ability to maintain its liquidity. A priming lien can be granted only with the consent of the secured creditors who are being primed or if the court finds that these creditors are adequately protected despite the granting of the priming DIP lien. One reason secured lenders often consent to being primed is because the value of their collateral interest (and thus their recovery) will plummet unless new money is lent to the debtor to maintain operations and inspire vendor and customer confidence. Many DIP financings include a roll-up provision. In a roll-up provision, the prepetition lender agrees to provide the debtor with DIP financing if a proportion of the financing is used to pay off its prepetition lien. Essentially, the lender's postpetition loan pays off its prepetition ones. The reasons for this approach are the creation of super priority claims (e.g. administrative costs) or the resolution of lien issues, the reaffirmation of guarantees, and the closure of holes in loan documents. In addition to collateral and a super-priority claim, DIP loans are typically designed with covenants and other protections to permit the DIP lender a full recovery even if the debtor liquidates.

Long-term financial reorganisation of the capital structure

Mid- and long-term financing and refinancing initiatives focus on the commercial and operational requirements in repositioning an institution and its businesses. While taking into consideration all outstanding liabilities and the respective creditor ranking, a long-term financial reconstruction has the company's future prospects in mind. The objective of the long-term plan is a solvent balance sheet and ability to implement the turnaround plan. The refinancing solution has to be agreed with the major stakeholders. These negotiations can be tricky as there may be an inherent conflict between existing creditors and incoming distressed investors, or some creditors aim to improve their position unreasonably. Sometime a creditor standstill in complex multilender situations and moratoria with key suppliers have to be arranged.

As we outlined previously, creditors and shareholders most likely have different views. Debt holders aim to recover their loans with appropriate reward for providing risk support during the restructuring. Shareholders aim to retain the upside on any new capital going in whereas they are more willing to write off their entire investment. This can lead to tough negotiations between stakeholders in particular if there is a debt for equity swap that may impact the ranking. The negotiations are driven by each party's perception of the value of their best alternative to the negotiated position. Creditors would generally seek an equal ranking on converted debt to new equity injected, whereas the shareholders want to see a discount on conversion. In the context of a financial institution, the impairment of individual assets may fundamentally threaten the equity position so there is a clear incentive to delay those procedures. During the GFC, many banks reluctantly wrote down their subprime mortgage exposures to fair value which increased market uncertainty until the Fed and the US Treasury initiated a stress test for the systemically important institutions. The former US Treasury Secretary Tim Geithner outlines the rationale and further context to this approach in his autobiography "Stress Test".

5.2.4   Operational restructuring

Operational improvement covers the wide range of operational restructuring and business performance improvement. Business transformation refers to the mid- and long-term repositioning of a business. It can apply for a former restructuring situation where a business comes out of insolvency as well as an enterprise-wide performance improvement programme for institutions that are underperforming without the immediate risk of failure or insolvency. A financial institution may try to reduce costs or regenerate growth in regaining its performance ability. Employment considerations are extremely important in this section and need to be managed carefully with regard to its legal requirements. This may require compliance with notification periods to government agencies and employees in case a large number of employees are affected (e.g. mass layoff) or an operating unit is closed down. Furthermore, there are employment benefits and salaries that are protected by the respective laws and may need to be paid our ahead of unsecured creditors.

Rapid business performance improvement

A crisis situation requires a rapid business performance improvement. The same principles as outlined in Chapter 2 apply but they need to be implemented rapidly. This is done by focussing on the core levers that can be implemented quickly with immediate results. In crisis situations or financial stress, all focus is either on increasing revenues or reducing costs rapidly. Revenues can be increased by focussing the organisation on its core products and organise sales and business development efforts around it. Costs can be decreased by identifying unprofitable operations, product lines, and customer segments. Product and client portfolios often experience tails of unprofitability that need to be cut and realigned to the core revenue objectives.

Given the required speed, there is an inherent risk that too much gets done that may impact the long-term viability of the commercial strategy and business model. During the GFC, many financial institutions were forced to proceed with fire sales of assets and businesses to come up with liquidity mainly as a result of collateral calls. This led to a vicious cycle of limited liquidity and deteriorating credit quality. Cash remains king but the long-term implications of stabilisation decisions need to be carefully weighted with regard to survival versus the long-term positioning. When the immediate crisis situation is stabilised, the more management's focus can shift to operational improvement and business transformation in the spirits of long-term commercial and operational change.

Corporate renewal

Corporate renewal defines the strategy when a business needs to be changed fundamentally when its performance questions the model's long-term viability. It is defined by the commercial and operational transformation that starts with redefining and refocusing the institution on its core businesses and capabilities. As we previously covered in Chapter 1, the tool for implementing this objective is through portfolio optimisation and divestments/disposals while following the core strategic principles of coherence and best practice to establish a competitive market positioning. In a second step, the TOM needs to be aligned with this new commercial strategy. It provides the base for the planned operational improvements in which best-practice benchmarks are once again applied in a front-to-back setting. Front-to-back optimisation aims to apply technology replatforming with the objective to automate and streamline as much as possible. As previously covered, outsourcing and offshoring are core principles of this front-to-back optimisation framework.

The emerging technology agenda has led to new decision frameworks and operating models which have initiated a broader change and innovation agenda in banking and financial services. Given the ongoing profitability challenges and investment requirements, several large global banks created joint ventures (JV) for the infrastructure and technology stacks of their international wholesale businesses. Those JV were labelled as utilities and usually for low-cost or nondifferentiating services that were a critical but pure cost drivers for the client solution. A consortium of large wholesale banks created onboarding and reference data utilities that were later sold and operated by information and technology companies such as Thompson Reuters (today part of Refinitiv), Acadia Soft, and DXC.

RESOURCES AND FURTHER READING

Collins, Jim (2009). *How the Mighty Fall*; The Random House Group Ltd.
Depamphilis, Donald M. (2014). *Mergers, Acquisitions and Other Restructuring Activities*; Elsevier.

Epstein, David G. and Steve H. Nickles (2007). *Principles of Bankruptcy Law*; Thomson/West.
Geithner, Timothy F. (2017). *Stress Test*; Broadway Books.
Scardovi, Claudio (2015). *Holistic Active Management of Non-Performing Loans*; Springer.
Scardovi, Claudio (2016). *Restructuring and Innovation in Banking*; Springer.
Slatter, Stuart and David Lovett (1999). *Corporate Turnaround*; Penguin Books.
O'Callaghan, Shaun (2010). *Turnaround Leadership*; KoganPage.
Van Zwieten, Kristin (2019). *Principles of Corporate Insolvency Law*; Sweet & Maxwell.
Vance, David (2009). *Corporate Restructuring: From Cause Analysis to Execution*; Springer.

CHAPTER 6

Value Creation and Growth

T he financial industry has been following a defensive mindset in repositioning and reorganising its businesses. Driven by technology innovation, the mindset is slowly shifting towards organic and inorganic growth through a value creation focus. Value creation defines activities and their financial impact on stakeholders such as customers, shareholders, and employees. Its objective is to increase the worth of an entire business measured by tangible key performance indicators (KPI) or intrinsic value drivers. It became a widely used term since its introduction of the shareholder value approach and value-based management in 1990s, fundamentally driven by the work of McKinsey & Company.

Business operators with focus on creating shareholder value such as private equity firms and activist investors use value creation initiatives as a key tool set of their investment strategy. The concept of intrinsic value investing can be tracked back to the work of Benjamin Graham who became the intellectual mastermind behind Warren Buffet's Berkshire Hathaway, followed today by many activist investors such as Carl Icahn, Daniel Loeb, and Bill Ackman. This chapter provides a framework to structure value creation initiatives across the engagement life cycle of growth initiatives and high-impact situations while providing a quantitative methodology to measure them. Although both the business framework and valuation methodology can be used generically, it is specifically applied to financial institutions. The chapter links the concepts outlined in Part One on the managerial fundamentals with emphasis on their application in specific transactional settings, driven by growth through transformational merger and acquisition (M&A) and principal investments.

6.1 INTRINSIC VALUE

Value creation is a management philosophy with the goal to drive an institution's performance through its governance and culture. As its core outcome, value creation becomes first priority for management and employees in driving all company decisions while the form of value contribution needs to be defined through a measurable and comparable methodology. More narrowly defined, value creation focuses on the immediate financial impact of defined strategic and operational initiatives measured by a set of defined metrics and KPIs. This narrow definition finds its most common application in special and high-impact situations such as turnaround, transformational M&A, and greenfield build-ups for which a comprehensive value creation plan is required across the engagement life cycle.

Value creation and protection are natural stages of corporate development during the life cycle of a business and can be applied broadly to crisis management, restructuring, and growth as a management philosophy. At the end of a turnaround, an institution often moves back on a path of value creation with the objective to lead the recovery and growth of the business. In academic and management literature, the last phase of a turnaround is often referred to as stabilisation. It involves the continuing improvement of an institution's performance while the situation starts to normalise. The focus moves to profitable growth through focused marketing initiatives and enhanced efficiencies throughout the business. Scalability and growth get at the core of the value creation agenda as soon as an organisation emerges from situations of turnaround and transformation.

6.1.1   Growth initiatives

Growth is a central part of the corporate life cycle and is based on the successful scale-up and acceleration of a business. This can be achieved organically through scaling available internal resources or inorganically through M&A transactions. The concept of intrinsic applies to venture and organic growth initiatives such as the greenfield build-up and scale-up of a business as it does to M&A. Core focus in a growth environment is on scalability and acceleration of a business' value proposition with its product portfolio and its operational set-up represented by the institution's capabilities, technology, and products. Growth initiatives, which may include internal build-up or the external acquisition of specific capabilities, have to be clearly articulated. The concept of capability-driven strategy that was introduced in Chapter 1 provides a well-articulated framework for this analysis. A growth plan is to be established that follows the logic of a business plan and can further be specified through an investment memorandum (IM) that outlines the investment requirements.

A growth and business plan usually contains the following sections:

1. Executive summary
2. Introduction to the company with mission statement
3. Value proposition and in-depth overview of a proposed venture
4. Management structure
5. Industry background and market opportunity
6. Market and competitive dynamics
7. Commercial positioning across target segments
8. Operating model and technology capabilities
9. Marketing plan and commercial model
10. Financial overview
11. Execution plan with timeline and milestones

Such as plan can further be the base of an IM as we elaborate in the section on high-impact situations.

In today's environment, the growth accelerators of financial institutions are shaped by consolidating specific businesses while leveraging their existing core capabilities. Part of the challenge has been the scale and variety of the businesses that global financial institutions offer. Regulations have added additional complexity. Technology management and innovation play an important role in driving this set-up as we outlined in Chapter 4. As many financial institutions have had severe gaps in their technology capabilities, the focus shifted to principal investments and the acquisition of specific capabilities. These initiatives were accompanied by the replatforming to focus on scale and higher operational efficiency as we elaborated previously. Inorganic growth has an important role to play in executing this growth agenda. At the same time, financial institutions need to become more focused on their core businesses where the market positioning is clear and differentiating. Specialisation in the offering of product and services gives you such advantages.

6.1.2 High-impact situations and the M&A transaction life cycle

High-impact situations are defined by events that fundamentally impact the value of a business. This usually happens within a certain time frame and can be applied equally to events during a turnaround or transformational M&A situations. An alternative term for high-impact situations is special situations that are usually associated with distress or specific corporate events. A turnaround, for instance, is a special situation that focuses on value protection as we elaborated previously in Chapter 5. Transformational M&A, on the other hand, describes situations where investors buy a business with the objective to impact its intrinsic value creation. They buy to transform the business or to further build on it. Buy-to-fix combines the purchase of an institution or a carved-out organisational unit with the transformation and integration of the business. In buy-to-build, a business is bought to further grow and scale it, organically or through so-called bolt-on acquisitions.

These strategies are in particular common in private-equity investing. However, financial institutions also acquire businesses for strategic and operational objectives under principal investment considerations. Although in many ways similar to a regular transformation, the strategies also differ as the purchase is linked to an anticipated successful repositioning of the business ahead of the transaction. The success chances of this endeavour and the involved tasks need to be assessed in advance. A value creation plan is established to do so. It provides the framework outlining the specific levers before engaging in the transaction. It assesses the situation and provides a base for the decision making. To establish a view on value creation opportunities, we first need to understand the life cycle of a transaction. This life cycle, illustrated in Exhibit 6.1, is organised across several phases. It starts with idea generation, origination, and preparation that conclude in a deal strategy. It is followed by the offer process that then leads to the due diligence and execution phase. The negotiation steps to close the transaction usually happen in parallel to the due diligence. After closing the transaction, the implementation with its planning and harvesting phases kicks off. This last phase is covered separately under the section on value realisation.

Idea generation, origination, and preparation

Financial institutions as any other organisation, continuously look to further establish their market position and close the capability gap for their respective growth strategy.

Deal strategy & offer process	Due diligence (DD)	Deal execution	Planning	Harvesting

▪ Idea generation
▪ Market screening
▪ Target identification
▪ Evaluation and first assessment
▪ Value driver analysis
▪ Investment rationale
▪ Initial and nonbinding offer (NBO)
▪ Preparation for DD
	▪ Commercial DD
	▪ Operational and technology DD
	▪ Financial DD
	▪ Financial valuation
	▪ Predeal value creation plan
		▪ Negotiation
		▪ Legal documentation
		▪ Closing and completion
		▪ Price adjustments
			▪ Postdeal value creation plan and operational blueprint
			▪ Plan for day 1
			  – Urgent action list
			  – 100 day-implementation planning
			▪ Set up central programme management, i.e. separation/integration office and processes
				▪ Execution of urgent actions
				▪ Execution of 100-day plan
				▪ Detailed postdeal plan
				▪ Focus on business imperatives, operational issues, financial and management reporting
				▪ Extracting cash

Exhibit 6.1 Transaction life cycle

The investor community with private equity and activist investors at the forefront aims to buy specific businesses and transform them with focus on value creation and new growth dynamics. For both situations, there is a continuous need for ideas while identifying targets to execute on the objectives. Investment banks, specialised financial boutiques, strategic advisors, and accountancy firms have dedicated corporate finance teams to support idea generation and target identification. Most of them follow a top-down approach across industry trends, sector drivers, and specific company targets. This process is called idea generation and origination.

There may be a natural match with firms on the other side of the spectrum that aim to merge or sell themselves into a broader ecosystem and/or are looking for a change from a generational perspective. As we outlined previously, the IM or more formally offering memorandum (OM) is a document that summarises the proposition across defined segments such as an introduction to the company, market opportunity, commercial positioning and target segments, operations and technology capabilities, value creation plan and growth strategy, and financial overview. The IM is a direct expression of the business and growth plan, the investment requirements, and the rationale of a transaction. In addition to the IM, a vendor due diligence (VDD) report is often conducted in which an external party confirms the information in the IM and provides more granularity for upcoming investor and buyer discussions. From an operational or value-creation perspective, the firm needs to be prepared to be sold while the respected status quo, addressable issues, and planned activities are documented in a blueprint. A thorough documentation is a crucial preparation in any transaction. Legal and tax implications are often neglected in preparation or come up relatively late in the process which can delay the execution of a transaction. In distressed M&A situations during a turnaround and restructuring, time can be of essence, and the respective assessment is an important factor of the preparation.

Deal strategy and offer process

The execution of a transaction requires the definition of a roadmap which sets milestones and measure progress towards realisation. At the same time, the structuring of the transaction is an important element of the deal strategy which needs to incorporate the legal considerations across entities, tax implications, and regulatory requirements into the roadmap at an early stage. A value creation plan is to be added that outlines how to optimise and realise value across the different stages of the transaction life cycle. As we further elaborate in this chapter, a value creation plan follows a framework across commercial, operational, and financial optimisation which includes financial engineering and other technical dimensions. The combined roadmap is the base of the execution and value realisation strategy. It will be used to realise the value as the transaction moves forward from the offer, the due diligence, and the negotiation to the closing and execution phases. An initial view on valuation is established early in the process that then is refined as more information become available, applying different valuation methods. A deal principal is appointed who takes charge of the roadmap and implements the execution strategy with a dedicated deal team.

The offer process starts before the due diligence process when a buyer makes after an initial assessment a first offer in the form of a letter of intent (LOI). A LOI is also called a memorandum of understanding (MOU). It provides the necessary understanding of the deal needed to move forward in the process across the life cycle but remains nonbinding. It can be structured as a nonbinding offer (NBO) when a specific target is approached by a buyer or acquirer. The terms of the NBO are usually summarised in a term sheet (TS) or heads of terms.

The TS usually includes the following elements:

1. Transaction structure
2. Price considerations
3. Timeline with signing and closing date
4. Contingencies such as appraisals and specific documents
5. Agreement to sign a sales and purchase agreement (SPA) in the future
6. Expense arrangements that outlines that each party is responsible for their own costs
7. Financing considerations which often defines an escrow deposit
8. Agreement on confidentiality and exclusivity

The signing of the TS is typically the time when the negotiations kick off. At the same time, it outlines a framework for the negotiations process. It intentionally remains a high-level document that is going to be specified further in the sales and purchase agreement (SPA). The SPA becomes a legally binding contract to conclude the transaction. It finalises the terms and conditions and is the culmination of negotiation between the acquirer and the seller after performing due diligence and agreeing on terms. Although the transaction does not go into effect until closing the sale, the agreement allows both parties the assurance that they are bound by the terms included in the agreement. The agreement, therefore, memorialises the material terms of the transaction and provides a basis for the transaction upon closing.

As a framework, the SPA usually includes the following elements:

1. Legal names and details for the parties involved
2. Definition of terms used throughout the agreement
3. Summary of the transaction
4. Closing date and timeline
5. Purchase price and other considerations involved
6. Any allowable adjustments to the purchase price, payment terms, and liabilities assumed by each party
7. Representation and warranties made by each party
8. Postclosing rights and obligations of each party
9. Applicable law and dispute resolution protocol
10. Signature of all parties to the agreement

Due diligence (DD)

The due diligence (DD) process kicks in after the signing of the LOI. A DD is much more than a standard checklist of procedures in order to provide approval for a proposed deal situation. It is a fundamental assessment of a M&A situation. In its core methodology it investigates, analyses, and judges the commercial positioning, the business strategy, and the different aspects of the target operating model (TOM). It can be categorised in commercial, operation (and technology), and financial dimensions while running an integrated process across the DD dimensions. The DD process is often conducted by third-party advisors with specialist support that give an independent assessment and opinion as a decision base. This is because the buyer and investor need to confirm whether the target company is viable as a standalone business and/or explore the potential for adding value and synergy that could be gained from the target company and to successfully manage the postdeal integration. This more integrated approach enables the buyer to gain a more coherent view of the direction of the company, a holistic overall picture of the transaction opportunity, and the potential for growth and development. The DD is usually supported by a virtual data room (VDR) that provides access to the required documents. Interviews with key employees, suppliers, and customers are integrated part of the process.

Representations and warranties

Representations and warranties form the basis of a DD by describing the assertions that a seller and buyer make in a SPA. Both parties are relying on each other to provide a true account of all information and supporting documents to close the transaction. The seller's representations relate to the information that the buyer's valuation is based on. The seller ends up not only stating that all financial information provided is true and accurate but also delivering all information to support this statement. Essentially, representations and warranties provide an opportunity for the seller to disclose any potential issues with the company prior to completing the transaction. In addition to the disclosure in the VDR, often a separate disclosure statement is provided by the seller. The buyer's representations relate to the form of consideration being used to complete the transaction. If equity is part of the transaction consideration, then the buyer must represent that it is legally able to offer the shares (e.g. any restrictions through a shareholder agreement). This information is compiled as part of the schedules to the SPA and may be referred to post transaction to ensure existence and accuracy. The warranties are usually organised across fundamental, commercial, and other warranties such as tax. The SPA usually contain an indemnification clause which protects the other party from an omitted or missed representation which may lead to a post-transaction financial loss. It is a crucial part of the DD process that both parties provide all information up front in their representations and warranties to avoid costly legal disputes trying to enforce indemnification clauses after the transaction closes.

Commercial due diligence (CDD)

Commercial due diligence (CDD) is the undertaking by a buyer and/or investor to evaluate the commercial attractiveness of target. It provides a full overview and in-depth assessment of the target's internal and external environment, the strategic direction of the business, the market opportunities, and commercial positioning while highlighting any potential risks of the acquisition and/or the investment. CDD focuses on the overall value of the business by investigating holistically the areas of market environment, competitive landscape, the institution's capabilities, and the likelihood of achieving projections. It includes competition benchmarking through assessing competitor information through multiple sources, including agency interviews and desktop research. The most effective methods for the CDD include conducting interviews with industry experts, independent primary and secondary market research, analysis of competitors using a wide range of techniques, along with detailed industry knowledge and expertise, as well as internal and external research.

A CDD is structured across the following areas with their key components:

1. Business overview
   - Outline commercial positioning and value proposition
   - Describe business model
   - Describe organisational overview and operating model
   - Outline capability system
2. Market structure, size, and future growth
   - Describe core characteristics from market environment while sizing it
   - Describe growth and value driver for respective market and industry
   - Illustrate current trends and disruptions
3. Competitive landscape and position
   - Describe key competitors
   - Illustrate competitive dynamics
   - Apply benchmark data for peer comparison
4. Strengths, weaknesses, opportunities, threats (SWOT) analysis
   - Describe internal strengths and weaknesses
   - Describe external opportunities and threats
   - Conclude on respective positioning and addressable elements

Operational and technology due diligence (OTDD)

Operational and technology due diligence (OTDD) is a comprehensive review of the target's operational aspects in accordance with delivery requirements and available capability system. The OTDD examines the TOM, the operational functions, the organisational structure, structural processes, technology platform, and system architecture and aims to identify operational risks which the potential buyer and/or investor should consider before acquiring or investing in the business. It also covers the potential for performance improvement and synergies from a value-creation perspective as well the full assessment of the technology platform. Given the importance of financial technology, the technology assessment has become by itself a due diligence component often with its own dedicated title, that is, operational and technology due diligence. The OTDD is a crucial input factor in developing an achievable standalone business plan and prepare the postdeal integration plan including the realisation of synergies.

A OTDD is structured across the following areas with their key components:

1. Operating model and cost base
   - Outline the standalone operating model and cost base
   - Define services and describe shared-service structure with group (if applicable)
   - Describe third-party service relationships with areas of spend

2. Organisation and people
- Outline organisation charts by functions and locations with respective number of employees and employment costs
- Detail employees who may transfer as part of the deal
- Outline gaps in key personnel such as senior management and experts
- Detail employment benefits such as pension and insurance arrangements
- Outline disaster recovery and business continuity plan

3. Technology
- Describe system architecture
- Provide details of software applications
- Provide details of IT infrastructure
- Provide details of IT outsourcing
- Outline the product and technology development roadmap
- Provide relationships between group and business, and how the standalone is getting impacted
- Provide overview of current and historical IT operating expenses (OPEX) and capital expenditures (CAPEX) including recharges to the group
- Provide estimates of the one-off costs required to implement the standalone IT operating model including estimates for costs to novate or replace software licences and outsourcing arrangements

4. Intellectual property (IP)
- Detail all shared IP, and IP will be transferred
- Outline plans for brands and logos
- Outline potential standalone rebranding plans

5. Properties and facilities
- Detail property portfolio
- Outline facilities and respective arrangements

6. Separation and integration considerations
- Outline available separation plans including key roles and responsibilities
- Outline specific carve-out plans including assets, people, processes, and systems
- Forecast one-off separation costs
- Outline service-level and transition service agreements with key areas where long-term arrangements will be required
- Details of contracts for novation and change of control clauses

Financial and technical due diligence (FDD)

The financial due diligence (FDD) establishes an understanding of historic and actual financial performance, as well as forecasting the financial position and solvency of an institution on behalf of the buyer or an investor. The result allows for an informed valuation of the company as it was covered in Chapter 3 with regard to the different methods available. It also has the advantage of providing investors with an understanding of the target company's assets, liabilities, and operations management structure in the respective umbrella of financial reporting. Usually, a minimum period of three years is required for all documents, ranging from published accounts to internal statements, management information, and similar documents.

An FDD is structured across the following areas with their key components:

1. View on consolidated and individual balance sheets
2. View on consolidated and individual income/profit and loss statements
3. View on consolidated and individual cash-flow statements
4. Assessment of capital and liquidity considerations
5. Asset-quality review
6. Regulatory considerations such as legal entity structure and capital requirements
7. Legal requirements
8. Tax implications

The findings of the FDD also provides the base for the completion accounts after the closing of the transaction, which defines the normalised working capital and any price adjustments to the previously agreed purchase price. It is advisable to outline the principles of the completion accounts in the term sheet as its preempts difficult negotiations as the financial situation becomes more transparent.

The legal and tax assessment can include a variety of complex documentation from certificates of incorporation, operating agreements, by-laws, licencing, permits intellectual property rights, supplier and customer contracts, and so on. It is ultimately about the legitimacy of the business to do business and need to be carefully reviewed.

Integrated DD view across all dimensions

Combining the commercial, operational, and financial dimensions lead to an integrated assessment and decision base. It covers a series of core outcomes such as commercial and competitor positioning, business and strategic plan review, operational and financial planning, working capital assessment, TOM and operational risk considerations, technology capabilities, risk and process capacity planning, sales and marketing effectiveness assessment, procurement and supply review, people, and resources assessment as well as value creation plan including integration plans and synergy benefit assessments. In its assessment, it needs to be granular with focus on the details of a situation while in its judgement it needs to be comprehensive and conclusive. The integrated view allows establishment of a more elaborated view on valuation and the purchase price that will be further shape the negotiations.

The DD will establish early on in the process a series of red flags on weaknesses and challenges of the target. These red flags should be articulated as initial hypotheses and validated as the DD moves on. They can be commercial with regard to the market positioning and the overall financial potential of a product given the competitor situation. Common strategic red flags are the lack of a clear articulation of the value proposition or a very fragmented competitor situation. It may also be operational with inefficiencies and hidden or much higher costs than are reported in the financials or the management information systems. The technology platform may use legacy systems and outdated programme language, runs its hardware out of support software with multiple vendors, or has gaps in its security policy. There are organisational issues with regard to reporting lines, key-person dependencies, and the use of contractors. Financially, important elements are not captured on the balance sheet or intangibles and goodwill are overstated which leads to unreasonable expectations with regard to valuation. The red flags must be transparently communicated to the deal principal and the deal team.

Deal execution

The execution of a transaction follows the conclusion of the DD process. In practice, negotiations and other activities are being performed simultaneously after agreeing on the terms through a LOI. The execution phase leads to the signing of the SPA and the closing of the deal. The determination of the final accounts is a crucial step in the closing process and may together with other materials cause adverse changes the transaction price. It is the time where the stakes are the highest and where typically things can go sideways. An internal and external communication strategy and plan needs to be defined and followed in a disciplined manner as part of the transaction management office (TMO).

6.1.3 Value creation plan

The value creation plan captures and measures opportunities across a defined methodology. A value creation plan is a blueprint of quantifiable and measurable value creation initiatives across the engagement life cycle. It can be in the form of a business plan for a greenfield build-up and scale-up venture. It can be an M&A transaction such as divestments/disposals, joint ventures, and acquisition that follows the outlined phases of the transaction life cycle. In a first step, the value creation plan defines the sources and drivers of value creation within an institution, business, industry, and marketplace. The second step is driven by the value metrics that quantify the performance impact of the value creation initiative. It is defined by the valuation methodology and the applied KPIs. It should start as early as possible in the process with a first scratch during the DD.

Value drivers

Value drivers are activities that create value measured financially through a metric in a high-impact situation across the engagement life cycle. They may improve the commercial positioning, reduce costs through operational improvement, reduce risk, and promote growth in accordance with an overarching objective of the institution and business. This objective may include increasing shareholder value or establishing a differentiating competitive edge. There are different categories of value drivers such as commercial drivers, operational drivers, or technical (usually financial) drivers that can be applied generically across an organisation or specifically a business. Depending on an institution's understanding of value, different metrics or KPI are applied to measure the value impact. Value drivers must be defined at an explicit and measurable level where specific action can be taken towards its realization. Exhibit 6.2 outlines the different value drivers across their commercial, operational, and financial dimensions.

Value metrics

Chapter 2 discussed a group of financial metrics and KPI to measure value contribution. As we outlined, the most fundamental driver across all methodologies is cash generation. Cash generation is measured by cash flow or a cash-flow proxy such as earnings before interest, taxes, depreciation, and amortization (EBITDA). Operating income measured as earnings before interest and taxes (EBIT), which measures as a preinterest earning metric the profitability of a business's operations, is the base of return on investment (ROI) assessment. In financial services with its different risk-taking

242

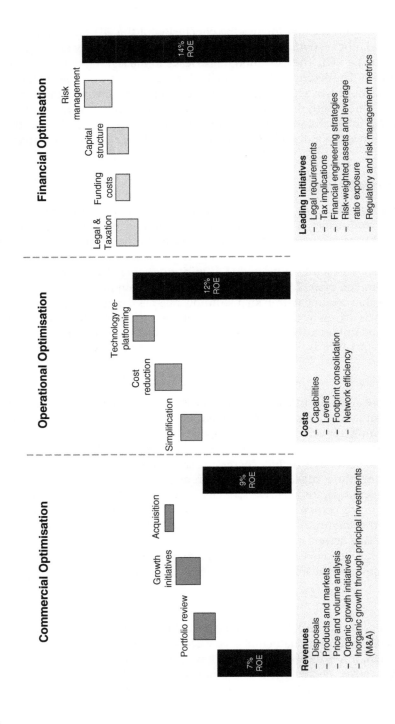

Exhibit 6.2 The value creation with drivers across categories

businesses though, the excess of return on equity (ROE), measured through profit above allocated equity capital to cost of equity, is the closest proxy of a profitability and cash measure. We therefore suggest a focus on ROE as the value metric for financial services businesses. However, the use of the respective KPI should always be clarified in the context of a specific engagement and its value creation plan.

Although individual KPI can be applied on a specific value driver, the proposed ROE measure is used across the value creation plan, organised across the three dimensions of commercial, operational, and financial optimisation. The value drivers and metrics are combined in a value creation plan that describes and outlines each individual step across categories. It is an important part of the transaction roadmap towards value realisation across all stages of a high-impact situation. At the same time, the value creation plan provides the base for value optimisation across commercial, operational, and financial initiatives. It outlines each opportunity and hence initiatives on how to increase value across categories and hence becomes an important input factor in negotiations in particular with regard to valuation. Each initiative drives value creation through strategic repositioning and performance improvement that may extract unrealised value of a business.

Plan establishment and execution strategy

If the value drivers have been identified, described, and quantified, a comprehensive operational value creation plan can be established.

It usually is organised across the following sections:

1. Executive summary with scope and objectives
2. Situational and financial assessment
   - Describes the current situation of the institution with its businesses
   - Outlines the financial situation with past performance
   - Defines the liquidity plan and working capital needs (ultimately evaluates the runway if the institution's is loss making; see the section on crisis management in Chapter 5)
3. Strategic identity with its pillars
   - Defines the winning aspiration for the institution that typically starts with its vision, mission statements, and set purpose and further outlines the value proposition and growth initiatives
   - Describes the playing field with its market and competitive dynamics (opportunities and threats)
   - Outlines the target customer segments with their requirements (marketing positioning)
   - Describes the institution's products and pricing assumptions
   - Outlines the institution's strengths and weaknesses relative to its competitors and where they intersect by establishing its core capability set
   - Concludes in a coherent execution roadmap with winning initiatives that are realistic and measurable through agreed KPIs, and provides a long-lasting competitive advantage in the marketplace

4. Operating model
   - Describes the current as-is operating model with its functional organisation and cost and full-time equivalency distribution
   - Defines the TOM with its go-forward functional organisation to deliver the strategic pillars
5. Financial forecast
   - Outlines the go-forward financial and liquidity forecast
   - Identifies the institution's financing needs and requests
6. Operational blueprint in accordance with the execution roadmap
   - Sets the execution strategy with its milestones
   - Identifies key performance improvement initiatives towards operational excellence
   - Outlines status quo of already initiated actions
   - Details initiatives for commercial value optimisation (markets, customers, and products) across the defined KPIs
   - Details initiatives for operational value optimisation (TOM and operational excellence) across the defined KPIs
   - Describes initiatives for financial value optimisation (legal structure, tax considerations, and financial requirements) across the defined KPIs
   - Concludes in a comprehensive action plan with timeline
7. Communication protocol and timeline
8. Tactical plan

The value creation plan usually has a number of appendices that compile detailed analyses and critical company documents for further discussions with key shareholders and stakeholders. To be successful and impactful this plan must be action oriented and milestone based. It must be aligned across key shareholders and stakeholders, and built consensus and trust among them. The actions and milestones are focused on the optimisation across the commercial, operational, and financial dimensions of the business as outlined in the following section on value optimisation. It concludes in the post-deal operational blueprint for value realisation that outlines the execution strategy with its pillars.

6.2   VALUE OPTIMISATION

Value optimisation can be pursued across three categories: commercial operational, which includes technology; and financial initiatives. The objective is to maximise and protect value in a specific situation. The following section covers these initiatives in detail and is organised accordingly.

6.2.1   Commercial optimisation

The commercial optimisation focuses on optimising market and client parameters, as well as product portfolios in coherence with the institution's market positioning and overall strategic objectives. It may start with a portfolio review and focus on specific organic growth initiatives and M&A such as divestments and bolt-on strategies.

This section is a direct application of the frameworks that were covered in Chapter 2 under strategic decision making.

Sales and marketing effectiveness

At the core of commercial optimisation are the right product and customer mix and pricing considerations while establishing an effective sales and marketing model. The product and customer mix may be refined while growth strategies to new markets are established. Segmentation and differentiation analyses are applied to get a better client understanding and target market analysis identified. Entire product lines may be cut, added, or extended, depending on the outcome of this analysis. This may require investments to build new capabilities and skill sets. The institution may adapt its pricing strategy in accordance with its costs, competition, and perceived client value to become more competitive in the marketplace. Detailed contribution and break-even analyses may further improve profit per customer. Unprofitable customer relationships may be terminated unless they have a broader franchise value for the company.

Partnership and alliances

A business may be repositioned on a standalone basis, absorbed and integrated in a larger and more established organisation, and/or combined with another business to reach the respective scale and combine capabilities. The transaction acts as trigger event to accelerate the commercialisation and monetisation of a business, technology, and/or specific corporate situations. Businesses may have built strong capabilities, technology, and products but are missing the scale to be commercially successful. Such a situation may require a strategic repositioning and reorganisation combined with well-articulated growth initiatives which may include the acquisition of other capabilities. In the financial industry, a certain size is required that often can only be reached on a global scale. The global financial centres such as New York, London, and Hong Kong have a fundamental role from a distribution and skill perspective. Several European FinTech players in Berlin, Paris, and Zurich developed innovative, high-quality technology but struggled to market their solutions outside of their home market. Many companies built satellite offices in London and started working out of shared workspaces and accelerator facilities. They had become under former Chancellor of the Exchequer George Osborn a harbour of bringing financial and technology talent together. The City of London with its global financial industry became a scalable distribution platform for the start-up community across the European markets. At the completion of this book, the future outlook of London as Europe's financial centre remains unchallenged but uncertain after the United Kingdom's decision to leave the EU and its single market.

To allow emerging technologies to have an impact on financial institutions' technology replatforming requirements scale remains of essence. At the same time, many of these emerging technology solutions will eventually be integrated in the ecosystem of incumbent financial from a commercial and operational perspective. Many FinTech businesses offered specific components in analytics and decision making through machine learning (ML) as well as workflow and infrastructure management through software. Those components have to be integrated in a scalable operational platform that provides the respective business services. A ML technology for credit underwriting must be combined with a core software to support a lending business. A natural language processing (NLP) technology that filters unstructured data from proprietary and public sources must be integrated in software solutions that combines it with traditional financial data and provides comprehensive analytics across the investment process. Buy-to-build strategies can provide the platform to make this happen and scale the business. Often partnerships and strategic alliances further facilitate scalability across businesses and segments.

6.2.2 Operational optimisation

Operational and technology optimisation links back to adapting the as-is operating model and designing a new TOM while driving business performance improvement initiatives. The transformational impact of technology has a crucial role in streamlining the operating models and automating processes. The core objective remains on increasing operational efficiency.

Business transformation

Business transformation includes business process, product and client simplification, cost reduction, and targeted technology replatforming that were discussed extensively in Chapters 1, 4, and 5. Business development over time often results in high organisational complexity with unfocused layers. Simplifying an organisational structure and shedding capabilities, businesses, and product as well as services provide the base for a broader cost reduction programme. Given the fragmented technology platforms in financial services, a broader replatforming is part of these solutions in which technology innovation allows new approaches in resolving the cost situation.

Technology replatforming

Emerging technologies and technology innovation have fundamentally shaped the operating platforms of financial institutions and become the core component of value creation. They allow for increased automation and standardisation and hence are an important factor for operational efficiency and performance improvement. Chapter 4, introduced open platforms model through application programming interface (API), cloud computing for crucial data management application, and other innovations to improve infrastructure elements. As we discussed, API allows new forms of operating models to integrate best-in-class services with an efficient software solution at its core. Data are the lifeblood of any modern organisation, and trust is the currency of our engagements with clients while harnessing data through analytics gives organisations a clear path to improve performance. All these dimensions should be embedded into the operating model of an organisation. From the perspective of value optimisation, the core focus is on replacing ineffective technology solutions while integrating new emerging technologies. During the growth years, financial institutions had neglected their technology stacks and had to catch up with innovation that became the norm in other industries.

6.2.3   Financial optimisation

Financial optimisation links back to specific technical initiatives such as legal, regulation, taxation, capital, financing, and risk management that were extensively covered in previous chapters.

Legal structure across corporate, regulatory, and taxation requirements

A transaction may offer the opportunity to optimise the legal structure of a corporation. Often there are historical legal complexities that can be resolved with a NewCo. NewCo is a term used for a proposed legal entity, that is, a subsidiary, during a fresh start or spin-off before getting assigned an operating name. In a distressed scenario and in preparation of a fire sale, a hive-off structure may be applied that follows specific requirements under bankruptcy and insolvency proceedings. This may apply a reorganisation under court protection which may allow some flexibility in executing the new legal entity strategy. Ring-fencing and recovery and resolution requirements may apply additional restrictions and opportunities from a regulatory perspective. Most financial institutions implemented new legal entity strategies after the Global Financial Crisis (GFC) with the incoming regulatory requirements such as those of the European Bank for Reconstruction and Development.

Tax optimisation allow substantial savings or mitigates negative financial implications in a reorganisation and transactional structure. Tax considerations can have a strong impact on a legal reorganisation because of specific financial implications in case of a profit realisation, partial liquidation, or deferred losses that can no longer be monetised in a new legal structure. Net operating loss (NOL) is a crucial topic in case certain tax-deductible expenses exceed taxable revenues for a taxable year. The most common application is the use of losses in one year to offset the profits of other years. Many financial institutions used their steep losses during the GFC to offset their profits that follows during the postcrisis recovery. Taxation remains a very technical field that requires expert advice.

Financing, capital structuring, and risk management

Financial engineering aims to optimise the capital structure and to cheapen the funding requirements through targeted strategies. The core driver and starting point for such strategies are capital requirements and the available financing streams. It can be implemented through leverage either through debt or the application of specific financial instruments across the capital structure. Both topics were extensively covered in Chapter 2 and are usually applied in a very specific framework.

Debt allows the gearing of the capital structure for performance improvement. The applications of financial instruments may add another element to optimise financing and manage risk. Often in funding new businesses and/or the acquisition of distressed businesses, mezzanine capital such as convertible loans are used for investors. They can be structured with optional and mandatory features. Other instruments are conventional bank loans unsecured or secured. Financial institutions such as banks may have access to central bank funding and the interbank lending market. Financial instruments and insurance contracts may further allow to manage risk given by the uncertainty of a situation and or an event. However, the more complex a financial optimisation strategy, the higher the risk and the less transparent they are. Morgan Stanley, for instance, reported at the end of 2007, a loss of almost US$10 billion because of a hedging strategy related to subprime exposure. There are different perspectives of what happened from an actual error in selecting the tranches to the application of a wrong hedge ratio. The ratio of being long the AAA senior tranche and funding the position through shorting BBB junior tranche may have been miscalculated.

6.3   VALUE REALISATION

Once the value creation has been planned and the different initiatives optimised, the last step is fully focused on execution and harvesting value across the engagement and transaction life cycle. In a transactional situation, value realisation is a postcompletion phase that starts with detailed planning after signing the SPA. It is common that after the closing of a transaction, the deal team transitions the leadership responsibilities to an implementation team. Similar for growth initiatives, when a dedicated implementation team is getting appointed by the executive management team. Those teams focus on implementing the value creation plan. The implementation team is organised through a central programme management structure and the individual steps outlined in the operational blueprint with a 100-day plan at its core. The following section focuses on the post-deal environment but the same principles apply for a growth initiatives. Exhibit 6.3 outlines the different components of a transactional situation.

6.3.1   Governance and central programme management

After signing, the deal team needs to mobilise the implementation team and organise it around the governance of a central programme management entity. A central programme management allows an efficient execution to realise the anticipated benefits from the previously defined value creation initiatives. It is organised around a group of execution specialists, defining and maintaining the standards and processes related to project management within an organisation. The central function is often known as programme management office (PMO)[1] or in the context of a transaction as transaction management office (TMO). The term smart is often added to emphasise the available execution capabilities, the skill sets, and expertise of its team members to drive specific engagement situations.

Each goal of the central programme management should target a specific area of focus across clearly defined objectives and milestones. The objectives themselves should be relevant, attainable, quantifiable, and time bound, based on available resources and existing constraints. They should further align to overarching objectives with a conclusive timeline that defines the implementation phase. Dependencies and constraints

---

[1]The word project is more common than programme under the term PMO. However, we use programme as standard definition.

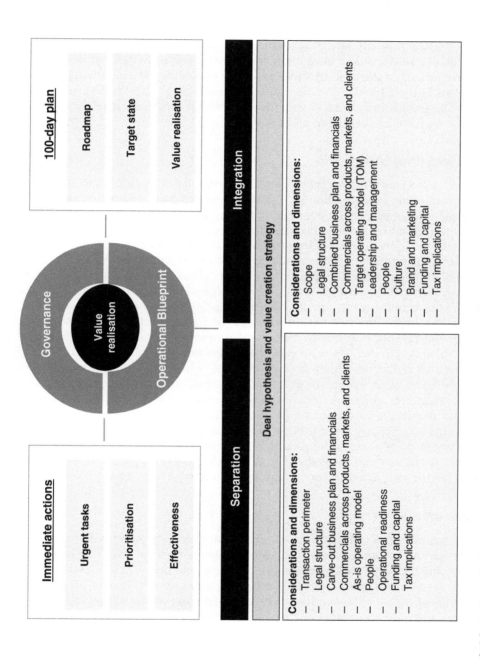

Exhibit 6.3 Value realisation across separation and integration considerations

249

should be understood and prioritised accordingly. Smart programme management has become a discipline on its own with specialist groups available in-house and externally through dedicated advisory firms. Most of these groups follow a standardised template in executing the roadmap of the defined blueprint. Given the transactional circumstances, the TMO usually further takes the shape of a separation management office (SMO) for a carve-out and an integration management office (IMO) for an acquisition. It directly reports to the deal principal and implements the execution framework in accordance with the 100-day and the respective succession plans as derivatives of it. To reach the milestones in accordance with the value creation plan is a crucial core element in the successful value realisation phase.

6.3.2 Operational blueprint

A value-creation plan is further specified by the operational blueprint. It operationalises the roadmap of the value creation plan. The blueprint moves value realisation from a conceptual to an operational level, outlines the key activities, and prioritises the value levers with regard to their execution schedule. It is to be seen as a plan of plan rather than details the individual execution steps across different dimensions of the postdeal implementation phase such as the central role of the programme management and the responsibilities across business functions. It consolidates all defined initiatives in an executable format for rapid and more long-term targeted value realisation. It details the TOM and the technology platform and sets up the processes on how to establish, build, and scale the services, moving toward an envisaged end-target state.

The value creation plan targets performance improvement as core of the value realisation which is reflected in the blueprint. This includes the rightsizing of functional areas and cost reduction initiatives (e.g. synergies) while initiating growth activities across the board to accelerate the commercial development in case of an integrated and combined unit. Once the top priorities of the blueprint are identified, making it successful requires a laser focus on monitoring key performance benchmarks. This prepares the base for day one readiness with its immediate action list and a 100-day plan. The blueprint ensures the successful implementation while specific considerations for separation and integration apply. A well-defined separation or integration strategy is to be articulated and communicated in a consistent manner.

Immediate action list

In every transaction, a series of issues come up that need to be addressed immediately after completion. Communication and alignment while working across the cultures of the seller and the buyer are key elements for day one readiness. There are several tools available for prioritising an immediate action list based on the level of urgency and importance of each implementation task. A prioritisation matrix allows rapid identification of the activities that should be focussed on, along with the ones that should be filtered out. It challenges the role of habitual activities and focusses on regaining control of the environment with its external demands that the implementation team is operating under. By excluding work-intensive activities that provide minimal value to long-term objectives under the deal hypothesis, time can be freed or things that matter from a value-creation perspective. Each task is then positioned on the prioritisation matrix, thus providing a visual representation of which critical activities should be focused on, and resources and effort be allocated respectively.

100-day plan

The 100-day plan can take a variety of formats with different meanings. In the definition applied here, it details the first 100 days of the postcompletion execution and describes the most important tasks and quick wins for value realisation beyond the immediate action list. It is at the core of the operational blueprint. By visualizing forward and detailing individual steps, the plan provides the implementation team clear goals and benchmarks and allows them to be agile and responsive when inevitable obstacles arise during the first 100 days after a transaction. It challenges the process and manages the issues, costs, and risks around the implementation and value realisation. The implementation should stay focused on maximising the value levers across functions from the front office, operations, and technology to shared functions. Rules of engagement should be clearly defined and clearly communicated, with specific and definitive accountabilities. The governance and central programme management allow the implementation team to keep control over this process.

Separation considerations

Disposing a business can be substantially more complex than acquiring one as it needs to be separated from its existing operational structure. The focus of the programme management during a separation is on efficiently disposing the business while minimising business disruptions and avoiding any negative implications or perception from a stakeholder perspective (e.g. clients). The separation considerations start with the standalone cost base and respective cost reduction initiatives, and the operational considerations around the technology separation. Usually, transition service agreements (TSAs) and service-level agreements (SLAs) are applied under a master service agreement (MSA) in ensuring these objectives and mitigating any issues during the transition period. This often includes regulatory approval and includes a comprehensive understanding across shared functions, group structure, and business services.

The seller needs to work with the buyer to define a separation plan. It describes the governance for the transition, outlining the services with their timeline. The TSA and SLA are usually defined by a standardised legal template and aggregated through specific process and service description. The TSA is transitionary and therefore timed for a specific period during the separation and/or until certain milestones are reached. TSAs are often required to maintain business continuity from completion until a standalone service provision can be established. This allows a faster deal close and smoother transition but also mitigate the risks associated with the transition. The SLA reflects a more long-term solution to replace the services internally in case they are required on an ongoing basis. The services provided, the associated costs, and responsibilities of each party are documented by function as well as the associated service levels. To limit dependency, these services are provided for a limited period of time but may contain an extension and/or conversion in a long-term agreement. The separation programme requires robust project management to oversee the cutover to business processes that are independent from the vendor group. This should be accompanied by a transactional risk memorandum that can be transparently discussed and communicated to stakeholders in each organisation. A well-defined governance and reporting structure are key in a successful separation that can also manage the wider organisational implications.

In April 2015, General Electric announced under the project name "Hubble" a massive divestment programme for its finance arm, GE Capital. The refocus of the conglomerate on its industrial operations was the biggest strategic shift in its over 100-year corporate history. GE Capital started in 1905 with financing for utilities and consumer appliances. It was substantially trimmed after the GFC but was still ranked as the seventh-largest US bank and designated as systemically important financial institution (SIFI) by its regulators. Hubble targeted several businesses units and included the selling of US$165 billion in loans. The company eventually kept only a small number of its financial businesses with main focus on aircraft leasing and energy finance. The programme was a massive undertaking with huge complexities and costs given the variety and scale of the individual businesses. It succeeded by following a disciplined approach with a clear governance and reporting lines. The article in the *Harvard Business Review* with the title "GE Capital after the Crisis" provides an interesting case study on the 2 successful execution of Hubble.[2]

Another example but sold as one entity is the divestment of Barclays Group's African business unit Barclays Africa Group, also known under its brand name Absa Group. Absa Group had been one of the largest financial institutions in Africa and was separately listed at the Johannesburg stock exchange. The divestment was announced in 2016 and structured as a three-year programme. Barclays Group continuously reduced its shareholding to a minority stake in 2017 by several block transactions of its shares. The separation programme itself comprised the gradual replacement of operational, technology, and regulatory compliance services that were provided to Absa by Barclays Group. This included the migration of core banking platforms and digital channels to Absa's different African regional operations. The programme also completed a brand transitioning from Barclays to Absa and ended in an almost century-long presence of Barclays in several African countries.

As we previously discussed, several other global European banks established large-scale disposal programmes to streamline and refocus their wholesale businesses across their corporate, institutional, and global market units. Those programmes were part of a multiyear restructuring and transformation journey of those institutions while their international operations were reorganised. The execution strategy included the establishment of dedicated noncore and legacy units for these nonstrategic, subscale, and distressed businesses. Many transactions were in particular focused on streamlining infrastructure and related cost challenges. After years of restructuring, UBS initiated Project Mercury with the objective to make its investment banking businesses self-sufficient from a capital and regulatory perspective which also included the set-up of a separate legal entity. Several of its investment banking businesses were critically dependent on UBS' shared services and corporate infrastructure and needed

---

[2]See Coates John D., John Dionne and David S. Scharfstein (2017). *GE Capital after the Crisis*; Harvard Business Review.

to be organised separately. Similar to RBS in Britain, Deutsche Bank established a large-scale divestment programme as part of its reorganisation to refocus on its German home market. Its Global Transaction Banking division, for instance, sold its subscale Corporate Services business to Vistra. Vistra is a global corporate service provider that has been consolidating through its technology platforms different businesses from financial institutions. This included the management and administration of specialised purpose vehicles and asset-holding companies to banks, nonbank financial institutions, and corporations at a large scale. Through SLAs, these services were still available for the clients of the disposing institutions, in this case Deutsche Bank, while the associated costs and capital requirements were reduced accordingly.

Integration considerations

Similar to a separation, the integration covers dimensions from strategy, branding and marketing, people, and functional considerations. The core focus is on realising synergies that have been identified during the transaction process. The programme management is naturally focused on harvesting and managing these synergies while executing the 100-day plan. Information on synergies has been more or less available pre-signing and closing depending on the nature of transaction (e.g. public versus private transactions). After the closing, the TMO can establish a design authority that details the initial hypotheses and establishes a more granular view on how the synergies can be realised. All synergy initiatives should focus on maximising value creation strategically, commercially, and operationally. Given the huge importance of technology in financial institutions, a lot of synergies can be realised by system integration. At the same time, technology challenges may be a deal breaker for such transactions.

The execution requires clear focus and prioritisation of synergies. Revenue synergies are usually a fraction of cost synergies and are often driven by increased effectiveness in existing markets than new market opportunities. Cost synergies can add up to 30% of the total operating cost base. They range from portfolio rationalisation and strategic operating model shifts to business simplification and process improvement as well as headcount and activity reduction and consolidating technology platforms, applications, and data centres. A successful integration will leverage the relative capabilities of both organisations whilst emphasising important differences in positioning and cultural elements. At the same time, a new entity will be designed or integrated in an existing set-up and established culture. This requires a balanced approached in keeping accepted elements while introducing new features.

As we outlined previously, neo and challenger banks started to emerge in the United States, United Kingdom, and continental Europe during the last 10 years after the GFC. Some of them have been built as greenfield build-ups applying new technology solutions as outlined in Chapter 4. Others are built through carve-outs and scale-up situations from existing banking structures such as the large high street banks such as Lloyds or RBS. In many cases, buy-to-build strategies were applied in scaling and growing existing challenger banking platforms. In the United Kingdom, the market for challenger banks started to consolidate on an accelerated basis over the last few years. FirstRand, the South African financial services provider, acquired Aldermore Group for GB£1.1 billion in late 2017 to merge it its regional Motor Finance

Corporation MotoNovo. Shortly after in 2018, Virgin Money, Britain's first challenger bank, was sold to Clydesdale and Yorkshire Banking Group for GB£1.7 billion, and OneSavings Bank merged with Chartered Court Financial Services in 2019 for GB£1.6 billion deal. According to more recent press reports in late 2020, JP Morgan Chase and Lloyds Banking Group had shown interests in acquiring one of the challenger banks such as Starling Bank as it had grown to a 2 million customer base. As a foreign bank, JP Morgan Chase targets its UK customer base whilst Lloyds as a local high street bank aims to integrate its technology platform. Starling successfully extended its Series D funding round from March 2021 with an additional investment over GB£50 million by Goldman Sachs Growth Equity. JP Morgan Chase announced the launch of its digital consumer bank in the United Kingdom in the first quarter of 2021 which was followed by the acquisition of UK robo-adviser Nutmeg in June 2021. Chapter 7 further elaborates on the role of challenger banks with its specialty finance offering in rebuilding the banking industry in Europe. The successful execution of these transactions is crucially dependent on the logic and smooth management of the integration considerations.

6.3.3   Targeted implementation

The postcompletion implementation phase of an M&A transaction targets the outcome originally envisaged by the investment hypothesis of a deal. It harvests the deal by solving a specific issue or is part of a financial institution's broader transformation journey. This journey is driven by specific objectives and based on a set of initial hypotheses. Both in a case of a disposal and acquisition, the transaction may implement a targeted strategic option, right-size the business, augment the customer proposition, improve performance, realise synergies, scale and grow the business, optimise the capital structure, and/or establish an augmented TOM. At its core, the transaction needs to be aligned with the core capabilities on which the business is based and further plans to grow with.

In financial services, M&A will drive the consolidation and remains an important strategic option to resolve the ongoing performance issues in financial institutions. However, it goes beyond this operational assessment and provides through commercial focus and scale a response to the ongoing challenges of the viability of business model in financial services. Technology solutions remains the core of any principal investment considerations of a financial institution. The outlined value-creation approach defines a KPI-driven framework to execute those objective with a transaction-driven and growth mindset. At the same time, regulatory requirements and organisational complexity need to be managed and incorporated in all activities. Large deals are challenging to facilitate and execute, given the organisational complexity and regulatory challenges. A consistent execution model remains key for a successful implementation.

RESOURCES AND FURTHER READING

Carlisle, Tobias E (2014). *Deep Value*; Wiley.
Collins, Jim (2009). *How the Mighty Fall*; Harper Collins.
Deibel, Walker (2018). *Buy Then Build*; Lioncrest.

Depamphilis, Donald M. (2015). *Mergers, Acquisitions and Other Restructuring Activities*; Elsevier.

Graham, Benjamin (2003). *The Intelligent Investor*; Revised Edition, Harper & Brothers.

Graham, Benjamin (2009). *Security Analysis*; 6th Edition, McGraw-Hill Book Companies.

Harnish, Verne (2014). *Scaling Up*; Gazelles.

Johnson, Luke (2012). *Start It Up*; Penguin.

Koller, Tim et al. (2020). *Valuation*; Wiley.

Shapiro, Alan C. and Sheldon D. Balbier (2000). *Modern Corporate Finance: A Multidisciplinary Approach to Value Creation*; Prentice Hall.

Thakor, Anjan V. (2000). *Becoming a Better Value Creator: How to Improve the Company's Bottom Line—and Your Own*; Jossey Bass.

Thiel, Peter and Blake Masters (2014), *Zero to One*; Penguin Random House.

Zeisberger, Claudia, Michael Prahl and Bowen White (2017). *Mastering Private Equity: Transformation via Venture Capital, Minority Investments and Buyouts*; Wiley.

Three

Conclusion

The third and last part of this book synthesises the previous chapters and applies the management framework to rebuilding the global banking industry. The final chapter conclusively discusses several ideas that were introduced previously with the objective to provide a comprehensive answer to the hypotheses that were articulated in the Introduction.

CHAPTER 7

Rebuilding the Global Banking Industry

T his final chapter summarises the major findings of this book while applying it specifically to the current situation of the global banking industry. It aims to answer conclusively the six core hypotheses that were introduced at the beginning of the book and drove its narrative across the different chapters. It synthesises the major findings across the six core chapters and establishes an overarching view on how the banking industry can be reorganised and repositioned as an ongoing process. The focus of the analysis remains on commercial and institutional banking business with emphasis on European financial institutions.

7.1   THE INDUSTRY'S CHANGE AND GROWTH AGENDA

Chapter 1 introduced hypothesis-driven problem solving and the core principles of strategic decision making such as coherence and best-practice comparison. It proposed a multi- and interdisciplinary approach to solve commercial and operational challenges from an institutional perspective. The first core hypothesis of this book states that global and large domestic financial institutions have become unmanageable due to their size, complexity, and incoherent capabilities which has challenged the overall value creation in the sector since the outbreak of the Global Financial Crisis (GFC) in 2007. The banking sector has struggled genuinely with value creation by not being able to cover the cost of its businesses. Analytically, value creation is measured by the excess of the return on equity (ROE) over an institution's costs of capital. The ROE of most of the large global banks remain below their costs of capital with no clear path out of this current paradigm. As a result, most of these banks trade at the time of writing at a price-to-book ratio way below one. At the same time, technology innovation such as artificial intelligence (AI), machine learning (ML), cloud computing (CC), application programming interface (API), and distributed ledger technology (DLT) are changing the operating models and organisational structures of the industry. Specialisation and platform applications have become key which requires the rethinking of traditional commercial and operational models. Those technology solutions are valued at a much higher multiple than their established counterparts and usually operate at a much lower cost base.

Business performance improvement, measured across tangible KPIs such as the reduction of cost-income ratios back to profitable and competitive levels, can be achieved only through a clearly defined commercial focus, coherent alignment of operational capabilities, and the respective product and services fit. Chapter 1 on strategic decision making further covered portfolio optimisation and divestments as core tools to focus businesses and specialise financial institutions and service providers. It is followed by technology replatforming and disciplined cost-reduction initiatives. Vertical M&A across business units will remain an instrument of an outstanding sector consolidation wave that applies to global financial institutions in particular. In the second half of 2020, the Spanish banking sector was now going through another consolidation wave with a series of simultaneous merger processes. CaixaBank and Bankia announced a tie-up deal over €4.3 billion in September, followed by the smaller regional banks Unicaja and Liberbank that were in process of agreeing on a proposed merger to create the country's fifth-biggest lender in December. BBVA bank and Sabadell had just previously abandoned a potential merger in late November that would create a lender with over €850 billion assets while BBVA was also selling its US division. As we previously elaborated, the Spanish banking sector had already shrunk from 55 lenders to 12 since the GFC, and this new consolidation wave is expected to reduce this to half a dozen. The process started with the creation of Bankia back in 2010 that was formed by the merger of several regional savings banks before it had to be bailed out in 2012 by the government. La Caixa assimilated in a similar fashion seven regional savings banks, and Santander acquired Banco Popular in 2017. Spain has been Europe's largest bank restructuring with a reduction of almost 40% of the banking industry's workforce and around 50% of its branch network. Through these recent M&A activities, the process entered a next chapter and may further provide the direction of what is to come in many other European countries.

Within this analysis, we need to keep in mind that a successful commercial model in banking and financial services is based on risk transfer and respective services that support those capabilities across the value chain, for example, analytics, management systems, and efficient operating platforms. It remains crucially important that an institution has a strong balance sheet and markets it frequently (preferred daily) to market prices or its fair value. This is a core principle to successfully manage the boom and bust cycle of the financial system as discussed in Chapter 2. As we outlined in Chapter 3, there are several financial instruments available to manage this volatility but the management team needs to have a transparent decision base to protect its balance sheet. As we emphasised numerous times in this book, the success of Goldman Sachs and J.P. Morgan has been based fundamentally in their disciplined approach to their balance sheet management and technology platforms.

The financial industry needs to reshape itself accordingly across the ongoing transformation life cycle through combining operational restructuring with the emerging technology agenda. This combination drives the strategic roadmap and going-forward target-operating-model (TOM) design. New technology-enabled players are emerging that will facilitate this transformation. There is inherent value in specialised finance businesses with their risk-transfer capabilities such as dedicated lending, trading, and related risk-transfer services across specific client segments and product portfolios. Specialty finance operates at a much lower cost-income ratio and higher ROE targets than large-scale, aggregated financial businesses. However, it remains open how they can become commercially effective at a larger aggregated scale in this highly regulated environment that has protected the incumbent structure of the industry.

The disciplined integration of emerging technologies in the incumbent structures as well as the focus and the specialisation of businesses may be the answers to these challenges.

7.2 THE TRANSFORMATIONAL IMPACT OF TECHNOLOGY

The going-forward TOM of financial institutions is based on the four technology components that were introduced in Chapter 4. It ensures the effective delivery of the commercial model across decision making and operational efficiency. Open architecture and straight-through processing are the core principles of the going-forward TOM design. The emerging technology agenda that was introduced facilitates the implementation of new TOM across the principle of open architecture, delivered through API, cloud computing, and automation, which will help to bring down and control costs. Platform solutions with core software applications connect through API integration layers specialised best-in-class provider. The regulatory requirements, however, are managed centrally by the platform provider. An incumbent bank may take on this role while offering a broad spectrum of services to its targeted client base. Non-value-added services in the back office have kept the cost base elevated and unmanageable for many financial institutions. A dedicated technology infrastructure utility through the cooperation among several financial institutions and technology players may bring a solution for those cost layers as a broader industry solution. At the same time, DLT will bring new applications in the areas of payments and post-trade service services which remain in an early stage of its development. Decentralised units with DLT as core technology and principle may further stabilise the overall financial system and make it less dependent on a few large institutions, and the respective government and regulatory interventions in case of financial stress.

Financial decision making has become heavily supported by ML, further evolving the long-term applications of algorithms in banking and financial services across research and analytics, lending and credit underwriting, securities trading and marketing, investment advisory, and risk and capital management. The current algorithms are evolving from the assumptions of the perfect-market paradigm and incorporate learning mechanisms of the distressed cycle such as feedback loops, dislocations, and full-blown banking crises. This applies in particular to microanalysis on credit and equity that is core to the lending and investment businesses. Neural networks and deep learning may move the application of ML and potentially more broadly AI outside of standardised decision-making frameworks. Natural language processing (NLP) supports the processing of large amount of internal and external data. However, there have been several events over the last years when algorithmic trading seems to have destabilised markets and accelerated sharp price corrections of over 5%. Numerai, an AI-run hedge fund in San Francisco, uses open source technologies and crowd sourcing to predict market through engaging a network of thousands of anonymous data scientists. The fund frequently hosts crowd events in which data scientists submit their predictions in exchange for the potential to earn some amount of US dollars and cryptocurrency called Numeraire. It is at the edge of combining emerging technologies with quantitative financial decision making. The combination and aggregation of innovative technology to efficient commercial and operational solutions are at the core of this development. These technologies must be integrated across the operational requirements of the incumbent financial institutions.

7.3   SPECIALISATION AND INCLUSIVE RISK TRANSFER

The management of size and complexity with their diverse capability requirements as become a core value driver as well as target of the numerous business transformation initiatives for the financial industry since the GFC. Financial institutions need to become smaller and more focused while establishing an open-architecture platform to become profitable and competitive again. Client-centricity and specialisation remain key. As smaller and technology-enabled players and business solutions are emerging, specialised neo-banking and asset management platforms to transfer and manage risk effectively are built. Financial inclusion remains a core topic for these platforms as several client segments in European banking remain underserved. The funding of small to midsize enterprises (SME), for instance, has moved up on the political agendas as governments fight the economic distortions of the coronavirus crisis. The following section discusses the hypothesis that specialty finance platforms provide the answer to close the gaps in the successful repositioning of the European banking industry. It also reintroduces the notion of the traditional merchant banking model as a specific solution for the SME market and answers to the perpetual state of crisis in the European banking industry.

Specialty finance has become a widely used term in today's banking environment. It has historically been defined as any financing activity that takes place outside the traditional banking system. Specialty finance businesses have been established as alternative lending and investing platforms that make loans to client segments that often find it difficult to obtain financing in the traditional credit application process: a variety of consumer solutions such as retail point-of-sale (POS) instalment lending, car financing, and payroll deduction loans. Commercial solutions such as supply chain finance, trade finance, accounts receivable factoring, small ticket equipment lending and leasing, merchant cash advances, and peer-to-peer lending usually fall under this definition. Since the GFC, a variety of offerings has emerged from specialised purpose vehicles (SPV), fund structures, peer-to-peer platforms, and fully licensed banking organisations. We use the term broadly for specialised lending and investment businesses that target consumer and commercial borrowers that are not adequately covered by the traditional banking channels. Their approach is in particular focused on the performance of the underlying asset, and the financing is often provided through highly structured asset-backed facilities and forms of securitisation. The structuring is a key provision and capability in specialty finance to mitigate and manage the underlying risk exposure. Many deals isolate the assets' performance in targeted structure (e.g. bankruptcy-remote SPV) with the objective to separate the performance of the collateral from the performance of the operating company.

Specialty lenders assess each loan request in a more tailored and effective manner, looking at available data such as intention to pay, ability to pay, and the asset value of pledged collateral as opposed to the more ratio-driven, formulaic approach that traditional banks have been following in their credit assessment. Their credit process is typically much more flexible with willingness to perform a deep dive approach to assess the loan request and accessible investment committees that can approve it. Specialty finance firms are able to invest in specific client segments because of the time they invest in understanding each situation and, in many instances, their ability to determine the liquidation value of the collateral pledged to secure the loan. This level of underwriting allows specialty finance companies to provide financing to borrowers, or in situations declined by traditional lenders while obtaining a premium price to cover the work and the risk. This dedicated approach applies in a similar fashion to equity investments where big data and ML-based algorithms are used to screen and assess the investment universe. Technology and a nimble operating models have an important role to play in the commercial approach of such providers.

Digital banking models with their technology-enabled services, applying the going-forward TOM design that we outlined across this book, will, for instance, facilitate a deeper coverage of the SME segment. SMEs are the backbone of European economies but the funding opportunities remain constraints as a result of fragmentation, scale, and the punitive treatment of unrated exposure under the Basel capital framework. Specialised lending capabilities in the SME space, supported and enabled by technology for credit underwriting and loan facilitation, allow a neo-banking model to merge finance and technology in one coherent service package. We need to keep in mind that technology applications are dependent on the available sources of information, which leads to a fundamental requirement of accumulating huge amounts of market and client data. A universal service offering starting with merchant acquiring, account management, lending, and advisory services delivers these datasets, which brings us back to the inherent value of banking platform with an open-source architecture. Consequently, there is a role for specialised lenders but also one of an incumbent player that has the platform in place and fulfils the respective regulatory requirements. The going-forward commercial and operational model in banking and finance is therefore based on specialisation but also cooperation. Many of the current neo banks, in particular in the United Kingdom but also across Europe, the Middle East, and Asia in the retail and consumer space, have built their capabilities from scratch, acquiring massive amounts of data while struggling in successfully commercialising their business model. A different mindset has to be found that combines the new and the old in a successful going-forward TOM for the banking industry.

The revival of the traditional and the establishment of a new merchant banking model are a natural next step in this journey in particular for the repositioning of corporate and institutional businesses, that is, the SME market. Historically, the term merchant bank was a British term used to describe investment banks. Today, however, their business models differ. Merchant banks do not deal with the public but serve smaller and midsize corporations and entrepreneurial clients with their primary functions of risk underwriting, financing, and advisory. Several of today's merchant banks such as the dedicated divisions of Goldman Sachs or Rothschild & Co. serve these clients, usually smaller businesses, under the umbrella of coinvesting and culture of partnership. Risk sharing and coinvesting are core principles and ideals in accordance with which the going-forward banking industry and the incumbent financial institutions have to transform. The historian Niall Ferguson praises in his biography of Siegmund Warburg, written during and shortly published after the GFC, the aspirations of the high financiers during Warburg's period to the ideals of high moral and aesthetic standards and what can be learnt in a time of crisis. Client-centricity and customer closeness are core attributes and takeaways that can be applied to modern banking. Successful finance is about specialised risk-taking and respective distribution. The more decentralised the system, the less sensitive are its institutions towards price dislocations and financial stress. In a backward-looking and historical analysis, it feels that both attributes got somehow lost in the sheer complexity of modern banking organisation and were the core of the public criticisms that hit financial institutions post GFC.

The global financial industry, particularly in Europe, seems to have been in a continuous and almost perpetual state of crisis since the collapse of the US subprime mortgage market in August 2007. From a value creation perspective, this simply means that returns and profits need to be in excess of cost of capital for shareholders, and clients trust their financial institutions with their service needs. Both these engines seem to have been broken for years now. Risk transfer has a crucially important economic function and contributes massively to economic growth. This fact is often forgotten in the recent public debate about the purpose of banking in modern societies. The combination of innovative technology solutions and specialised value propositions on an integrated platform under the principles of risk sharing and coinvesting is the core driver in these reorganisation and repositioning efforts. With this book we hope to contribute to an elevated discussion—pointing out the needs of the banking industry to reposition and transform itself through a new approach and mindset and to a more inclusive and effective contributor to growth and wealth building over the generations to come.

RESOURCES AND FURTHER READING

Cohan, William D. (2008). *The Last Tycoons: The Secret History of Lazard Frères & Co.*; Penguin.
Ellis, Charles D. (2009). *The Partnership: The Making of Goldman Sachs*; Penguin.
Ferguson, Niall (1999). *The House of Rothschild Volume 2: The World's Banker: 1849–1999*; Penguin.
Ferguson, Niall (2008). *High Financier: The Lives and Time of Siegmund Warburg*; Penguin.

Afterword and Acknowledgment

It feels just around the corner but it has been 14 years since the Global Financial Crisis (GFC) erupted and an eternity to see how slow global financial institutions have been adjusting to the new realities of the postcrisis environment. Much of this experience has been part of my own professional journey. After all these years, I truly believe that technology innovation and less complexity through more specialised financial services shape the future of the financial industry. It is a challenge and opportunity at the same time for the industry. The different chapters referenced the literature that has influenced my thinking and has been a crucial part of the journey. I have always been a passionate reader and remain fascinated by the technical challenges of financial problems. However, the problem-solving process has changed fundamentally and is today driven now by technological and no longer by financial innovation. The intellectual curiosity remains the same, and the biographical references at the end of each chapter are a reference to that. What remains is to thank teachers, mentors, colleagues, and organisations alike who profoundly impacted the methodology of this book. This acknowledgment is organised across the different chapters.

Chapter 1 on strategic decision making has been heavily influenced by my time at Booz & Company (now Strategy& as part of the PwC network). I thank my former colleagues for all the valuable discussions and insights in the various engagements and, most important, Alan Gemes who had fundamental impact on my understanding of capability-driven strategy. The results of our combined work were published in *strategy + business* in the article "Banking's Biggest Hurdle: Its Own Strategy—Why Coherent Institutions Were the First to Rebound After the Financial Crisis". The application of system theory and macro-history has been fundamentally driven by my studies at the University of St. Gallen–HSG, and the inspiration of my late father's work in the area of cybernetics as well as many discussions with mentors and business associates over the years. I further would like to mention the fruitful collaboration with Gagan Bhatnagar, Tim Powers, James Nodder, Mike Magee, Miles Kennedy, Shazia Azim, and Sohail Shaikh on bank restructuring and the broader transformation agenda of financial institutions. I am grateful for their insights, knowledge, and experience during the numerous performance improvement engagements over the years. Much of the content on strategy were augmented by the training curricula at the Goldman Sachs University and the experienced hire programme at Booz & Company.

Chapter 2 is a reflection of a lifelong fascination for financial decision making from more straightforward corporate finance challenges to complex financial transactions as well as core interests in financial stress and systematic crises. I had to cut the chapter substantially given the extensive materials available with several unpublished chapters and research from my time as a PhD student at the University of Zurich. The chapter leverages in many ways the curricula of the Chartered Financial Analyst (CFA) designations by the CFA Institute, the programme of International Financial Reporting of the Association of Chartered Certified Accountants, and the rigorous finance courses of the Goldman Sachs University. There are so many people on this journey to be grateful for from Professors Heinz Zimmermann, Rudolf Volkart, Hans Geiger, and Markus Leippold as academic advisors to early mentors at Invesco and Stepstone Global such as Roger Yates, Hans-Joerg Baumann, Meinrad Wyser, and many others who were part of this journey and fascination.

Chapter 3 on risk and asset-liability management is heavily influenced by my experience at Goldman Sachs. I have been blessed to have had the opportunity during one of the most challenging periods for the financial systems to work with many talented risk managers such as Michael de Lathauwer, Carl Faker, Stefan Bollinger, Stuart Cash, Chris Milner, Etienne Common, Thomas Hansen, Arun Assumall, Christoph Hansmeyer, Urban Angehrn, Peter Gassmann, Sebastian Fritz-Morgenthal, and many others. I further recommend the curriculum of the Financial Risk Manager (FRM) designation of the Global Association of Risk Professionals (GARP) for interested readers who look for a structured programme on the topic of risk and asset-liability management.

Chapter 4 on technology management and innovation is at the core of the introduced methodology and represents the future of the industry. To work with technology-driven solutions has become my core focus in particular around the integration of emerging technologies in the ecosystem of financial institutions. Applying advanced machine learning algorithms for risk analysis and predictive analytics, combining it with innovative software and blockchain solutions and building efficient technology platforms has become a true fascination and passion. I thank Steve Davies, Robert Churcher, Daniel Diemers, Marcus Brauchlin, Beat Wittmann, Michael Appenzeller, Thomas Oeschger, Andreas Pusch, Yannick Hausmann, Adrian Peyer, Wojciech Gryc, Greg Borel, Kelvin Malayapillay, Dan Schleifer, Terry Thorsen, Arif Babayev, Herman Klein Wassink and many others for their insight and experience and the continuous cooperation in this field.

Chapter 5 on turnaround and transformation as well as Chapter 6 on value creation combine the previous chapters into a comprehensive methodology that can be applied to financial institutions within a commercial and operational environment. It is shaped by specific legal and regulatory requirements such as Basel III/IV or the European Bank Recovery and Resolution Directive (BRRD). The section on legal frameworks of Chapter 6 leverages several aspects of the Certified Turnaround Professional (CTP) curriculum of the Turnaround Management Association (TMA), applying it specifically to the financial industry. I can strongly recommend the programme of the TMA with its international chapters across the globe. At the same time, I thank Colin Brereton and Jose de Ochoa, with whom I worked closely after the merger of Booz & Company and PwC as part of EMEA Financial Market Solutions, for sharing their long-term experience and insights in this field. I further express my appreciation and gratitude to Caio Gilberti, Tim Allen, Hein Marais, Andrew Turner, and many of the other Deal Value Architects with whom I had the opportunity to work with on PwC's Deals platform across operational restructuring and merger and acquisition advisory.

This book aims to establish an experienced-based methodology for decision makers in the financial industry. The methodology applies and leverages existing ideas and research in a comprehensive decision framework that is based on my own professional experience. I am grateful for feedback and further discussions on the different topics and can always be reached through EES at www.eesadvisory.com.

Joerg Ruetschi, August 2021

Bibliography

A

Ahamed, Liaquat (2020). *Lords of Finance: The Bankers Who Broke the World*; 2nd Edition, The Penguin Press.

Alber, Robert Z. and Charles P. Kindleberger (2015). *Manias, Panics and Crashes: A History of Financial Crises*; 7th Edition, Palgrave Macmillan.

Ansoff, Igor H. (1988), *Corporate Strategy*; Business Library.

Arslanian, Henri and Fabrice Fischer (2019). *The Future of Finance: The Impact of FinTech, AI, and Crypto on Financial Services*; Palgrave Macmillan.

B

Bernanke, Ben (2015). *The Courage to Act*; W.W. Norton & Company.

Bernanke, Ben, Timothy T. Geithner and Henry M. Paulson (2019). *Firefighting—The Financial Crisis and Its Lessons*; Penguin Books.

Besanko, David et al. (2000). *Economics of Strategy*; Wiley.

Bessis, Joel (2015). *Risk Management in Banking*; Wiley.

Biehl, Mattias (2015). *API Architecture*; API University Series – Volume 2.

Biehl, Mattias (2016). *API Design*; API University Series – Volume 3.

Black, F. and M. Scholes (1973). "The Pricing of Options and Corporate Liabilities"; *Journal of Political Economy*, 81.

Bookstaber, R. (2000). "Understanding and Monitoring the Liquidity Crisis Cycle"; *Financial Analysts Journal*, September/October 2000.

Bookstaber R. (2017). *The End of Theory—Financial Crises, the Failure of Economics, and the Sweep of Human Interaction*; Princeton University Press.

Bocij, Paul, Andrew Greasley and Simon Hickie (2018). *Business Information Systems: Technology, Development and Management for the Modern Business*; Pearson.

Brookshear, Glenn J. and Dennis Brylow (2015). *Computer Science*; Pearson.

C

Carlisle, Tobias E (2014). *Deep Value*; Wiley.

Chancellor, Edward (1998). *Devil Take the Hindmost. A History of Financial Speculation*; Farrar, Strauss and Giroux, New York

Coates John D., John Dionne and David S. Scharfstein (2017). "GE Capital after the Crisis"; *Harvard Business Review*.

Cochrane, John N. (2009). *Asset Pricing*; Princeton University Press.

Cohan, William D. (2008). *The Last Tycoons: The Secret History of Lazard Frères & Co.*; Penguin.

Coleman, Thomas (2011). *A Practical Guide to Risk Management*; The Research Foundation of CFA Institute.

Collins, Jim (2009). *How the Mighty Fall*; Harper Collins.

Copeland, Thomas, J. Fred Weston and Kuldeep Shastri (2014). *Financial Theory and Corporate Policy*; Limited Edition, Pearson.

Cox, J. C., S. A. Ross and M. Rubinstein (1979). "Option Pricing: A Simplified Approach"; Journal of Financial Economics, 7

Couto, Vinay, John Plansky and Deniz Caglar (2016). *Fit for Growth: A Guide to Strategic Cost Cutting, Restructuring and Renewal*; Wiley.

Crouhy, Michel, Dan Galai et al (2013). *The Essentials of Risk Management*; 2nd Edition, McGraw Hill.

D

Dalio, Ray (2018). *Big Debt Crises*; Bridgewater.

Damodaran, Aswath (2012). *Investment Valuation*; University Edition, Wiley.

Deibel, Walker (2018). *Buy Then Build*; Lioncrest.

Depamphilis, Donald M. (2014). *Mergers, Acquisitions and Other Restructuring Activities*; Elsevier.

E

Ellis Charles D. (2009). *The Partnership: The Making of Goldman Sachs*; Penguin.

Epstein David G. and Steve H. Nickles (2007). *Principles of Bankruptcy Law*; Thomson/West.

Evans, Vaughan (2013). *Key Strategy Tools*; FT Publishing.

F

Ferguson, Niall (1999). *The House of Rothschild Volume 2: The World's Banker: 1849–1999*; Penguin.

Ferguson, Niall (2007). *The Ascent of Money: A Financial History of the World*; Penguin.

Ferguson, Niall (2008). *High Financier: The Lives and Times of Siegmund Warburg*; Penguin.

Freedman, Lawrence (2013). *Strategy—A History*; Oxford University Press.

G

Geithner, Timothy F. (2014). *Stress Test*; Broadway Books.

Gemes, Alan and Joerg Ruetschi (2016). "Banking's Biggest Hurdle: Its Own Strategy—Why Coherent Institutions Were the First to Rebound After the Financial Crisis"; *strategy + business*

Goetzmann, William N. (2017). *Money Changes Everything: How Finance Made Civilization Possible*; Princeton University Press.

Graham, Benjamin (2003). *The Intelligent Investor*; Revised Edition, Harper & Brothers.

Graham, Benjamin and David Dodd (2008). *Security Analysis*; 6th Edition, McGraw-Hill.

Grossmann, S. J. (1988a). "An Analysis of the Implication for Stock and Future Price Volatility of Program Trading and Dynamic Hedging Strategies"; *Journal of Business*, 61.

Grossmann, S. J. (1988b). "Insurance Seen and Unseen: The Impact on Markets"; *Journal of Portfolio Management*, Summer 1988.

Grossmann, S. J. and M. H. Miller (1988). "Liquidity and Market Structure"; *Journal of Finance*, 43.

Guttag, John (2021). *Introduction to Computation and Programming Using Python*; 3rd Edition, The MIT Press.

H

Harnish, Verne (2014). *Scaling Up*; Gazelles.

Harrison, J. M. and D. Kreps (1979). Martingales and Arbitrage in Multiperiod Securities Markets; *Journal of Economic Theory*, 20.

Harrison, J. M. and S. Pliska (1981). Martingales and Stochastic Integrals in the Theory of Continuous Trading; Stochastic Processes and Their Applications, Volume 11.

Harrison, J. M. and S. Pliska (1983). A Stochastic Calculus Model of Continuous Trading: Complete Markets; Stochastic Processes and Their Applications, Volume 15.

Hull, John C. (2017). *Options, Futures and Other Derivatives*; Global Edition, Pearson Prentice Hall.

Hull, John C. (2018). *Risk Management and Financial Institutions*; 5th Edition, Wiley Finance.

I

Ingersoll, Jonathan E (1987). *Theory of Financial Decision Making*; Rowman & Littlefield.

Isaacson, Walter (2014). *The Innovators*; Simon & Schuster.

J

Jarrow, Robert A. (2019). Introduction to Derivative Securities, Financial Markets, and Risk Management; 2nd Edition, World Scientific.

Johnson, Luke (2012). *Start It Up*; Penguin.

Jorion, Philippe (2006). *Value at Risk: The New Benchmark for Managing Financial Risk*; 3rd Edition, McGraw-Hill.

Jorion, Philippe (2013). *Financial Risk Manager Handbook*; Wiley Finance.

K

Kaplan Robert S. and David P. Norton (1996). *The Balanced Scorecard: Translating Strategy into Action*; President and Fellows of Harvard College.

Karatzas Ioannis and Steven Shreve (2001). *Methods of Mathematical Finance*; Springer Applications of Mathematics.

Kay John and Mervyn King (2020). *Radical Uncertainty; Decision-making for an Unknowable Future*; The Bridge Street Press.

Kiechel, Walter III (2010). *The Lords of Strategy*; Harvard Business Press.

Kindleberger, Charles P. (1992) *Manias, Panics, and Crashes. A History of Financial Crisis*; John Wiley & Sons, New York

King, Mervyn (2016). *The End of Alchemy—Money, Banking and the Future of the Global Economy*; Little Brown.

Koller Tim, Marc Goedhart and David Wessels (2020). *Valuation*; 7th Edition, Wiley.

L

Leinwand, Paul and Cesare Mainardi (2010). *The Essential Advantage: How to Win with a Capabilities-Driven Strategy*; Harvard Business Review Press.

Leinwand, Paul and Cesare Mainardi (2016). *Strategy That Works*; Harvard Business Review Press.

Lekatis, George (2016). *Understanding Basel III, What Is Different*; Smashwords Edition.

Lewis, Antony (2021). *The Basics of Bitcoins and Blockchains*; Mango Publishing.

Lewis, Michael (2014). *Flash Boys: A Wall Street Revolt*; W. W. Norton & Company.

Lowenstein, Roger (2014). *When Genius Failed: The Rise and Fall of Long-Term Capital Management*; Random House, New York.

M

Malkiel, Burton G. (2019). *A Random Walk Down Wall Street*; W.W. Norton & Company.

Mckeown, M. (2019). *The Strategy Book*; Pearson

Meadows, Donella (2008). *Thinking in Systems: A Primer*; Chelsea Green Publishing.

Merton R. C. (1973). "The Theory of Rational Option Pricing"; *Bell Journal of Economics and Management Science*, 4.

Mintzberg, Henry (1993). *Rise and Fall of Strategic Planning*; Pearson Education Limited.

Mougayar, William (2016) *The Business of Blockchain*; John Wiley & Sons.

N

Neftci, S.H. (2002). *An Introduction to the Mathematics of Financial Derivatives*; 2nd Edition, Academic Press.

Neisen, Martin and Stefan Röth (2017). *Basel IV: The Next Generation of Risk Weighted Assets*; Wiley Finance.

O

O'callaghan, Shaun (2010), *Turnaround Leadership*; KoganPage.

P

Paulson, Henry, Jr (2010). *On the Brink*; Business Plus.

Pignataro, Paul (2013). *Financial Modeling & Valuation: A Practical Guide to Investment Banking and Private Equity*; Wiley.

Porter, Michael E. (1980). *Competitive Strategy: Techniques for Analyzing Industries and Competitors*; Free Press.

Pusch, Andreas (2020). "Navigating a Sea of Information, News and Opinions with Augmented Human Intelligence," Chapter 4 of *The AI Book* by Susanne Chishti et al; John Wiley & Sons.

R

Rasiel, Ethan M. and Paul N. Friga (2010) *The McKinsey Mind*; McGraw Hill, New York.

Reinhart, Carmen M. and Kenneth S. Rogoff (2009). *This Time Is Different*; Princeton University Press.

Ridley, Matt (2020). *How Innovation Works*; Harper Collins Publisher.

Rosenbaum Joshua and Joshua Pearl (2013). *Investment Banking*; Wiley.

Ruetschi, Joerg (2005). *Liquidity in Financial Markets: Theory and Application in the Swiss Securities Market Structure*; Haupt.

Rumelt, Richard (2011). *Good Strategy, Bad Strategy*; Profile Books.

Rutherford, Albert (2018). *The Systems Thinker*; Kindle Direct Publishing

Ruttiens, Alain (2013). *Mathematics of the Financial Markets*; Wiley Finance.

Ruparelia, Nayan (2013). *Cloud Computing*; The MIT Press.

S

Scardovi, Claudio (2015). *Holistic Active Management of Non-Performing Loans*; Springer.

Scardovi, Claudio (2016). *Restructuring and Innovation in Banking*; Springer.

Scardovia, Claudio (2017). *Digital Transformation in Financial Services*; Springer.

Shapiro, Alan C. and Sheldon D. Balbier (2000). *Modern Corporate Finance: A Multidisciplinary Approach to Value Creation*; Prentice Hall.

Sironi, Paolo. F (2016). *FinTech Innovation: From Robo-Advisor to Goal Based Investing and Gamification*; Wiley.

SLATTER, STUART and DAVID LOVETT (1999). *Corporate Turnaround*; Penguin Books.

Stewart, G. B. (1999). *The Quest for Value*; HarperCollins.

T

Taleb, Nassim N. (1998). *Fooled by Randomness: The Hidden Role of Chance in Life and in the Markets*; Penguin.

Taleb, Nassim N. (2008). *The Black Swan: The Impact of the Highly Improbable*; Penguin.

Tapscott, Don and Alex Tapscott (2016). *Blockchain Revolution*; Penguin.

Tegmark Max (2017). *LIFE 3.0: Being Human in the Age of Artificial Intelligence*; Penguin.

Thakor, Anjan V. (2000). *Becoming a Better Value Creator: How to Improve the Company's Bottom Line—and Your Own*; Jossey Bass.

Thiel, Peter and Blake Masters (2014); *Zero to One*; Penguin Random House.

W

Warwick, Kevin (2013). *Artificial Intelligence*; Routledge.

William, Jacob (2016). *Blockchain*; Simple Guides.

Wooldridge, Michael (2020). *The Road to Conscious Machines*; Pelican Book.

V

Van Zwieten, Kristin (2019). *Principles of Corporate Insolvency Law*; Sweet & Maxwell.

Z

Zeisberger, Claudia, Michael Prahl and Bowen White (2017). *Mastering Private Equity: Transformation via Venture Capital, Minority Investments and Buyouts*; Wiley.

Index

100 day plans 251

A

ABN Amro Bank N.V. 33
ABS *see* asset-backed securities
absolute priority rule 211
acquisitions, decision making 32–33
action plans 11–12, 21–23
adequacy, of capital 145
adequate protection 210–211
advanced measurement approach (AMA) 161
AI *see* artificial intelligence
algorithms 173–176
alliances 245–246
allocation mechanisms, capital management 148–149
ALM *see* asset-liability management
AMA *see* advanced measurement approach
American options 132–133
AMM *see* automated market maker
analysis
  action plans 11–12
  balance sheets 38–41
  baselines 10–11
  capabilities 14–16, 20–21
  cash flow statements 41–44
  coherence 13–17
  competitive advantage 14
  elimination 11
  financial 35–47
  financial ratios 44–45
  financial statements 35–44
  framework formation 10–11
  framing 10–11
  identity setting 16–17
  liquidity risk 88–90, 161–163
  market dislocations 91–92
  market positioning 14–16, 20–21
  modelling 60–85
  problem solving 8–12
  product fit 16, 20–21
  refinement 11
  service fit 16, 20–21
  strategic 7–17
  stress 86–99
  systems theory 12–13
  valuation 47–60
analytics, machine learning 189–190
ANNs *see* artificial neural networks
APIs *see* application programming interfaces
application programming interfaces (APIs) 169–171
APT *see* arbitrage pricing theory
arbitrage pricing theory (APT) 52, 73–74, 116
arbitrage-free models 69–71
artificial intelligence (AI) 173–177
artificial neural networks (ANNs) 174–176
as-is operating models 23–24
Asian options 134–135
asset swap (ASW) spread 130
asset swaps 124–125
asset-backed securities (ABS) 139
asset-based loans 118
asset-liability management (ALM) 101–164
  Basel framework 149–164
  capital allocation 148–149
  capital management 145–163
  cash instruments 117–120
  commodity risk 112–113
  credit risk 113–116, 154–157
  enterprise-wide risk management 142–143
  equity risk 116
  financial engineering 116–141
  foreign exchange risk 112
  forwards 120–124
  funding mix 147–148
  futures 120–124
  interest-rate risk 103–111
  liquidity requirements 161–163
  market risk 157–160
  net stable funding ratio 163
  operational risk 160–161
  regulatory capital 151–153
  risk management 141–164
  risk transfer 101–116
  risk-weighted assets 154–161
  securitisation 138–141
  swaps 124–131
  swaptions 137–138
  value-at-risk 143–145

asset-liquidity-price ratio 88
assets
   balance sheet 38–40
   disposals 226
   liquidity 88–89
   management 102
   non-performing 224–226
   see also capital . . .
ASW spread *see* asset swap spread
ASX *see* Australian Securities Exchange
augmented decision making 189–193
Australian Securities Exchange (ASX) 188
automated market maker (AMM) model 198
automation
   capital management 192–193
   credit underwriting 190
   investment advisory 192
   risk management 192–193
   robotics 176–177
   trading 191
average continuously compounded return 62
average simple returns of n subperiods 61

B

bail-ins 214, 215
bailouts 212–215
Bakkt project 197
balance sheets 38–41
balance-sheet restructuring 224
balanced scorecard (BSC) 24–26
bank panic of 1907 97
Bank Recovery and Resolution Directive (BRRD)
   213–215
banking crises 87
bankruptcy
   absolute priority rule 211
   automatic stay 210–211
   court protection 209–210
   Europe 207–209
   fulcrum security 211–212
   United States 206–207
Basel framework 149–164
   advanced measurement approach 161
   context and development 149–150
   counterparty credit risk 157, 159
   credit risk 154–157
   GFC effects 150
   interest rate risk 159–160
   leverage ratio exposure 152
   liquidity coverage ratio 162–163
   liquidity requirements 161–163
   market risk 157–160
   methodological framework 150–151
   Minimum Requirements for own Funds and
      Eligible Liabilities 151–152, 153

net stable funding ratio 163
   operational risk 160–161
   output floor 161
   regulatory capital 151–153
   risk-weighted assets 154–161
   securitisation framework 156–157
   standardised approach 155–156, 160
   Total Loss Absorbing Capacity 151–152, 153
baselines, problem solving 10–11
basic indicator approach (BIA) 160
basis point value (BPV) 110–111
basket options 135–136
BCG *see* Boston Consulting Group
benchmarking 26
   credit indices 115–116
   interest rates 103–105
Bermuda options 133–134
best practice 26
BIA *see* basic indicator approach
binomial trees 83–85
Bitcoin 178, 179, 180, 182, 194–195
Black Thursday 97
Black-Scholes-Merton formula 75–76
blockchains
   technology 178–182
   see also cryptocurrencies; distributed ledger
      technologies
bonds 119, 121–123, 124–125
book value per share (BVPS) 60
bootstrapping 107
Boston Consulting Group (BCG) 26
Brownian motion 75–76
BSC *see* balanced scorecard
bubble phase, financial stress cycle 87
business performance improvement 26–32
business portfolios, optimisation 27
business transformation 246
BVPS *see* book value per share

C

callable instruments, convexity 109
capabilities 14–16
capability-driven strategy (CDS) 14–17
CAPEX *see* capital expenditure
capital adequacy 145, 151–163
   liquidity requirements 161–163
   risk-weighting 154–161
capital asset pricing model (CAPM) 52, 72–73
capital expenditure (CAPEX) 38, 44
capital management 145–149
   adequacy 145, 151–153
   allocation mechanisms 148–149
   automation 192–193
   Basel framework 151–163
   credit risk 154–157

funding mix 147–148
leverage ratio exposure 152
liquidity requirements 161–163
market risk 157–160
net stable funding ratio 163
operational risk 160–161
output floors 161
recapitalisation 226–228
restructuring 227–228
risk-weighted assets 154–161
structure 145–147
systemically important financial institutions 152
capital market line (CML) 71–72
capital structure 145–147, 227–228
capital-protected payoff strategies 132
CAPM *see* capital asset pricing model
caps, interest-rate options 136–137
CART *see* classification and regression trees
cash flow statements 41–44
cash flows
  discounted 54–55, 57
  free 50–52
  investing 43
  operating 41–43
  restructuring 223–224
  swaps 124–125
cash instruments 117–120
CC *see* cloud computing
CCE *see* cryptocurrency exchanges
CDD *see* commercial due diligence
CDOs *see* collateralised debt obligations
CDS *see* capability-driven strategy; credit default
    swaps
central bank rates 104–105
challenger banks, post GFC 21
change agenda 259–261
Citigroup, formation 33
classification and regression trees (CART) 174
client fit, optimisation 27–28
cliquet options 134
cloud computing (CC) 31, 171–173
CMBX 116
CML *see* capital market line
COBOL 185
CoCo *see* contingent convertible capital
COGS *see* cost of goods sold
coherence 13–17
collars 137
collateral, loans 117–118
collateralised debt obligations (CDOs) 139–140
commercial due diligence (CDD) 237–238
commercial optimisation 244–246
commodities finance 102
commodities futures 123–124
commodity risk 112–113

communication, turnaround plans 222–223
competitive advantage 14–16
complementary assets 14–16, 245–246
complete market paradigm 70–71
concave pay-off strategies 133–134
conditional value-at-risk (CVaR) 144
constant maturity swaps (CMS) 127
consulting firms, benchmarks 26
contingent claims 74–85, 132–138
  Asian options 134–135
  barrier options 135
  basket options 135–136
  Bermuda options 133–134
  Black-Scholes-Merton formula 75–76
  cliquet options 134
  CRR method 84–85
  equal probability approach 85
  exotic options 133–136
  forward-start options 134
  framework 74–75
  fundamental partial differential equation 75–82
  Greeks 79–82
  implied volatility 82–83
  interest-rate options 136–138
  knock in/out features 135
  martingale transformation 77–79
  multi-asset options 135–136
  numerical methods 83–85
  path-dependent options 134–135
  replicating portfolio 81–82
  swaptions 137–138
  time-dependent options 133–134
  vanilla options 132–133
contingent convertible capital (CoCo) 146
continuous return calculations 62
continuously compounded return 61
contribution margin 47
convex pay-off strategies 133
convexity 109, 111, 122–123
Cook ratio 149
core tier-one capital 145–146, 152
corporate renewal 229
correlation products 140–141
cost of goods sold (COGS) 29–31
cost reduction 29–31
counterparty credit risk, Basel framework 157, 159
Counterparty Risk Management Policy Group
    (CRMPG) 90
court protection 209–210
Cox, Ross, and Rubenstein (CRR) method 84–85
CPython 185
credit benchmarks 115–116
credit default swaps (CDS) 128–130
credit default swaptions 138
credit options 138

credit risk 113–116, 154–157
credit spread options 138
credit spreads 115
credit underwriting 190
credit value adjustment (CVA) 159
crisis management 217–220
CRM *see* credit risk, mitigation
CRMPG *see* Counterparty Risk Management Policy
    Group
cross-currency swaps 128
crowdfunding 199
CRR method *see* Cox, Ross, and Rubenstein
crypto assets 181–182
cryptocurrencies 177–182, 187–188, 193–199
    Bitcoin 178, 179, 180, 182, 194–195
    crowdfunding 199
    cryptography 179–180
    decentralised finance 197–199
    Ether 178, 179, 180, 182, 188, 195
    mining 180–181
    regulation 196, 197
    smart contracts 182, 188
    stablecoins 197–198
    synthetic trading 198–199
    technology 178–181
    Tether 198
    tokens 181
    USD Coin 198
    XRP 187, 195–196
cryptocurrency exchanges (CCE) 196–197
cryptography 179–180
cubic spline interpolation 107
currency risk 112
current assets 38
CVA *see* credit value adjustment
CVaR *see* conditional value-at-risk
cycle of financial stress 86–87
Cyprus
    post-GFC 215
    see also Europe

D

DAH *see* Digital Asset Holdings
DCF *see* discounted cash flows
DD *see* due diligence
DDM *see* dividend discount model
DDR *see* digital depository receipts
DE *see* effective duration
deal execution, mergers and acquisitions 241
deal strategy, mergers and acquisitions 235–236
debt 147–148
debt restructuring 224
decentralised finance (DeFi) 197–199
decision making
    augmented 189–193

financial 35–100
    analysis 35–47
    arbitrage free models 69–71
    arbitrage pricing theory 52, 73–74
    asset pricing 68–74
    Black-Scholes-Merton formula 75–76
    CAPM 72–73
    contingent claims 74–85
    CRR method 84–85
    equal-probability approach 85
    fundamental partial differential equation
        75–82
    Greeks 79–82
    implied volatility 82–83
    liquidity risk 88–90
    macro-historical conclusions 99
    market dislocations 87, 90–96
    market efficiency 53–55
    martingale transformation 77–78
    modelling 60–85
    negative capital effect 94–96
    risk management 92–96
    stress evaluation 86–99
    systemic crises 96–99
    valuation 47–60
strategic 7–34
    action plans 11–12, 21–23
    analysis 7–17
    balanced scorecard 24–26
    baselines 10–11
    benchmarking 26
    capability-driven strategy 14–17
    coherence 13–17
    framing 10–11
    identity 16–17
    impact assessments 17–20
    mergers and acquisitions 32–33
    operating model 23–24
    operational excellence 23–26
    optionalities 20–21
    performance improvement 26–32
    planning 17–23
    portfolio choices 20–21
    response plans 21–23
    roadmaps 17
    systems theory 12–13
    target operating models 23–25
default
    CDS premium calculation 129–130
    collateralised debt obligations 140–141
    correlation products 140–141
    risk assessment 114–115
    secured loans 118
deferred taxes 38–39
DeFi *see* decentralised finance

degree of financial leverage (DFL) 46
degree of leverage (DL) 47
degree of operating leverage (DOL) 47
delta (Δ) 79–80
delta-neutral asset position 94
deployment models, cloud computing 172
deposit accounts 147
derivatives 27, 28–29
   smart contracts 188
   see also options pricing
DFL *see* degree of financial leverage
Digital Asset Holdings (DAH) 188
digital assets 181–182
digital depository receipts (DDR) 181
direct lending 190–191
discounted cash flows (DCF) 54–55, 57
dislocation phase, financial stress cycle 87
disposals 28, 226, 249, 251–253
distressed assets 224–226
distressed companies
   valuation 60
   see also turnaround
distributed ledger technologies (DLT) 177–182,
   187–188, 193–199
   assets 181–182, 193–197
   concept 177–178
   cryptography 179–180
   decentralised finance 187–189
   mining 180–181
   networks 178–179
   smart contracts 182, 188
   technology 178–181
   tokens 181
   see also cryptocurrencies
diversification 14
divestments 28, 251–253
dividend discount model (DDM) 45–46, 49–50,
   53–54
dividend swaps 130–131
DJ-AIGCI *see* Dow Jones-AIG Commodity Index
DL *see* degree of leverage
DLT *see* distributed ledger technologies
DMod *see* Modified duration
DOL *see* degree of operating leverage
dollar value change (DV01) 110
Dow Jones-AIG Commodity Index
   (DJ-AIGCI) 113
due diligence (DD) 236–240
   commercial 237–238
   financial 239–240
   operational and technology 238–239
   representations and warranties 237
DuPont equation 45
duration measures 109–111
DV01 *see* dollar value change

dynamic feedback loops 93–94
dynamic price investors 91, 93–94
dynamic system theory 12–13

E

EAD *see* exposure at default
earnings before interest, taxes, depreciation, and
   amortisation (EBITDA) 38, 44, 52
earnings before interest and taxes (EBIT) 44, 50–52
earnings before taxes (EBT) 37
earnings per share (EPS) 45
EBIT *see* earnings before interest and taxes
EBITDA *see* earnings before interest, taxes,
   depreciation, and amortisation
EBT *see* earnings before taxes
ECN *see* enhanced capital notes
economic profit (EP) 58, 148
economic value added (EVA) 27, 51–52, 57–58
ecosystems, strategic analysis 12–13
effective duration (DE) 111
elimination, strategic analysis 11
emerging technologies *see* innovation
EMIR *see* European Market Infrastructure
   Regulation
endogenous liquidity risk 90
enhanced capital notes (ECN) 146
enterprise value (EV) 54–60
enterprise-wide risk management 142–143
EP *see* economic profit
EPS *see* earnings per share
equal probability approach 85
equity, balance sheet 39, 40–41
equity capital 120
equity futures 124
equity risk 116
equity swaps 130–131
equity tranches 140
equity value
   discounted cash flows 54–55, 57
   dividend discount model 53–54
   economic profit 58
   economic value added 51–52, 57–58
   leveraged buyout analysis 55–57
ES *see* expected shortfall
Ether 178, 179, 180, 182, 188, 195
Eurodollar futures 121–123
Europe
   bankruptcy and insolvency legislation 207–209
   post-Global Financial Crisis 212–227
European Market Infrastructure Regulation (EMIR)
   216
European options 132–133
European Stability Mechanism (ESM) 213–215
EV *see* enterprise value
EVA *see* economic value added

EVAN *see* extreme value analysis
excellence
  balanced scorecard 24–26
  benchmarking 26
  best practice 26
  operational 23–26
  TOM 23–25
exchanges, cryptocurrencies 196–197
exogenous liquidity risk 90–96
exotic derivatives 27–28
expected shortfall (ES) 144
exposure at default (EAD) 114
extreme value analysis (EVAN) 144–145

F

factoring loans 118
fair value through profit and loss (FVTPL) 41
Fannie Mae 99
Federal Home Loan Mortgage Corp (FHLMC) 99
Federal National Mortgage Association (FNMA) 99
Federal Savings and Loan Insurance Corporation (FSLIC) 98
feedback, market dislocations 93–94
FHLMC *see* Federal Home Loan Mortgage Corp
financial analysis 35–47
  balance sheets 38–41
  cash flow statements 41–44
  financial statements 35–44
  income statements 36–38
  leverage 46–47
  ratios 44–45
financial decision making *see* decision making, financial
financial due diligence (FDD) 239–240
financial engineering 116–141
  cash instruments 117–120
  forwards 120
  futures 120–124
  options 132–138
  securitisation 138–141
  swaps 124–131
  swaptions 137–138
financial infrastructure 186–188
financial institutions, reorganisation/wind-down, overview 205
financial leverage (FL) 46
financial modelling *see* modelling
financial optimisation 247–248
financial ratios 44–45
financial restructuring 223–228
  cash flows 223–224
  disposals 226
  non-performing assets 224–226
  recapitalisation 226–228

Financial Services (Banking Reform) Act of 2013 215
financial statements 35–44
financial stress *see* stress
financial valuation *see* valuation
financing cash flows 44
first-to-default (FTD) baskets 141
fixed costs 46–47
FL *see* financial leverage
floors, interest-rate options 136–137
FNMA *see* Federal National Mortgage Association
forced liquidations, negative capital effect 94–96
foreign exchange (FX) futures 123
foreign exchange (FX) risk 112
foreign exchange (FX) swaps 128
forward rate agreements (FRA) 105, 120, 122–123
forward rates 107–108
forward-start options 134
forwards 120–124
FRA *see* forward rate agreements
framing, strategic analysis 10–11
Freddie Mac 99
free cash flows 50–52
front-to-back optimisation 28–29
FSLIC *see* Federal Savings and Loan Insurance Corporation
FTD *see* first-to-default
FTE *see* full time equivalent
fulcrum security 211–212
full time equivalent (FTE) requirements 28–29
fundamental partial differential equation (FPDE) 75–82
  Black-Scholes-Merton Derivation 75–76
  Greeks 79–82
  martingale transformation 77–79
funding liquidity 89–90
futures 120–124
  commodities 123–124
  equities 124
  foreign exchange 123
  interest-rate 121–123
FVTPL *see* fair value through profit and loss
FX *see* foreign exchange

G

G20 reform 212–217
game theory 20
gamma (Γ) 80
Germany
  Global Financial Crisis 214
  see also Europe
GFC *see* Global Financial Crisis
Girsanov theorem 77

Global Financial Crisis (GFC)
  anatomy 98–99
  bail-ins 215
  bailouts 212–215
  Basel framework effects 150
  Europe 212–217
  G20 reform 212–217
  liquidity facilities 223–224
  M&A activities 32–33
  market infrastructure reforms 216–217
  non-performing loans 224–226
  RBS 21
  recovery and resolution 213–215
  repositioning effects 21, 203–204
  ring-fencing 215–216
  risk weighting adjustments 27
  structural reforms 213–216
  UBS 16, 21
  United States 212
Goldman Sachs 14, 16, 31
governance 248–250
government bond futures 121
government interest rates 104
government-sponsored enterprises (GSE) 99
Gramm-Leach-Bliley Act 32
great crash 1929 97
Great Depression 97–98
Greece, Global Financial Crisis 214
growth
  industry agenda 259–261
  initiatives 232–233
  mergers and acquisitions 233–241
  value creation plans 241–244
GSE *see* government-sponsored enterprises

H

heat map analysis 17–19
hedging
  Black-Scholes-Martin formula 75–76
  feedback loops 93–94
  fundamental partial differential equation
    75–82
  Greeks 79–82
  replicating portfolio 81–82
high-frequency trading 191
high-impact situations 233
HSH Nordbank 214
hybrid tier-one capital 146
hypothesis-driven problem solving
    8–12

I

ICO *see* initial coin offering
idea generation, M&A 233–235
IIN *see* Interbank Information Network

illiquidity
  market dislocations 87, 90–96
  risk analysis 88–90
IM *see* investment memorandum
immediate action lists 250–251
impact assessments 17–20
impacts of innovation 182–199
implied volatility 82–83
improvement, business performance 26–32
inclusive risk transfer 262–264
industry agenda 259–261
initial coin offering (ICO) 199
innovation 165–200, 168–199
  APIs 169–171
  artificial intelligence 173–177
  blockchains 178–181
  capital management 192–193
  change and growth agenda 259–261
  cloud computing 171–173
  crowdfunding 199
  cryptocurrencies 178–182, 187–188, 193–199
  decentralised finance 197–199
  decision making 189–193
  distributed ledger technologies 177–182,
    187–188, 193–199
  emerging technologies 168–182
  financial stress cycle 87
  future impacts 261–262
  infrastructure 169–173, 186–188
  investment advisory 192
  machine learning 173–176
  natural language processing 176, 189–190
  open architectures 182–185
  operational efficiency 182–188
  payment services 186–187, 188
  peer-to-peer lending 190–191
  post-trade capital markets 187–188
  replatforming 31–32, 167–168
  risk management 192–193
  robotic process automation 176–177
  securities trading and marketing 191
  smart contracts 182, 188
  speciality finance 262–264
  synthetic trading 198–199
  transformational impacts 182–199
  underwriting 190
insolvency 220
  absolute priority rule 211
  automatic stay 210–211
  court protection 209–210
  Europe 207–209
  fulcrum security 211–212
  United States 206–207
insurance 92
intangible assets 38

Interbank Information Network (IIN) 187
interest rate options 136–138
interest rate risk 103–111
    Basel framework 159–160
    benchmarking 103–105
    convexity 109, 111
    duration measures 109–111
interest rate swaps (IRS) 104–105, 125–127
    plain-vanilla 125–127
    swaptions 137–138
interest rates
    central banks 104–105
    forward rates 107–108
    LIBOR 104–105
    OIS swap rate 104
    term structures 108
    yield curve 106–107
interest-rate futures 121–123
internal rate of return (IRR) 56
internal-rating based (IRB) approach 156
International Swaps and Derivatives Association
        (ISDA) 106
intrinsic value 231–244
    growth initiatives 232–233
    mergers and acquisitions 233–241
    value creation plans 241–244
inventories 38
investing cash flows 43
investment advisory automation 192
investment memorandum (IM) 232–233
IRB approach *see* internal-rating based approach
IRR *see* internal rate of return
IRS *see* interest rate swaps
ISDA *see* International Swaps and Derivatives
        Association
issue trees 10
Italy
    post-GFC 215
    see also Europe
Itô's lemma 76

J
JPM coin 188
JPMorgan Chase 32, 188

K
key performance indicators (KPIs) 23, 26–27
key rate duration (KRD) 111
knock-in/-out features 135
know your customer (KYC) 188
KPIs *see* key performance indicators
KRD *see* key rate duration
KYC *see* know your customer

L
LBO *see* leveraged buyout
LCR *see* liquidity coverage ratio
legal principles
    securitisation 139
    turnaround/restructuring 205–212
Lehman Brothers 212
lending
    innovations 190–191
    loans 117–119, 124–125
letters of intent (LOI) 235–236
leverage analysis 46–47
leverage ratio exposure (LRE), Basel III 152
leveraged beta 72–73
leveraged buyout (LBO) analysis 55–57
leveraged loans 118
LGD *see* loss given default
liabilities, balance sheet 39, 40
LIBID *see* London Interbank Bid Rate
LIBOR *see* London Interbank Offered Rate
LIBOR–OIS spread 104–105
liquidity
    cash flow restructuring 223–224
    decentralised pools 198–199
    global financial crisis 223–224
liquidity coverage ratio (LCR) 162–163, 224
liquidity risk 88–90, 161–163, 197–198
loans 117–119, 124–125
    non-performing 224–226
LOI *see* letters of intent
London Interbank Bid Rate (LIBID) 105
London Interbank Offered Rate (LIBOR)
        104–105
loss given default (LGD) 114
LRE *see* leverage ratio exposure

M
M&A *see* mergers and acquisitions
Macaulay duration 110
machine learning (ML) 173–176, 189–193
McKinsey 26
macro risks 102–113
    commodities 112–113
    currency/exchange 112
    interest rates 103–111
management
    of risk *see* risk management
    technology 166–168
management information systems (MIS) 26
market dislocations 87, 90–99
    analysis 91–92
    dynamic asset allocation 92–93
    feedback loops 93–94
    negative capital effect 94–96
    path dependency 94

systemic crises 96–99
value-at-risk 92–93
market efficiency 63–65
market equilibrium 71–73
market liquidity 88–89
market positioning 14–16
market price of risk 78
market reforms, post-GFC 216–217
market risk 157–160
  parameter estimation 157–158
  in trading book 158–159
market value added (MVA) 58
marketing, machine learning 191
marketing optimisation 245
Markov property 64–65
martingale property 63–64
martingale transformation 77–79
MECE *see* mutually exclusive collectively
    exhaustive
mergers and acquisitions (M&A) 233–241
  deal execution 241
  deal strategy 235–236
  decision making 32–33
  due diligence 236–240
  generation, origination and preparation 233–235
  high-impact situations 233
  offer process 235–236
  representations and warranties 237
  sales and purchase agreement 236
  term sheet 236
  transaction life cycle 234
  value realisation 249, 253–254
mezzanine capital 119
mezzanine tranches 140
micro risks 103, 113–116
  credit risk 113–116
  equity risk 116
Minimum Requirements for own
    Funds and Eligible Liabilities
    (MREL) 151–152, 153
minimum variance portfolio (MVP) 71–73
mining 180–181
MIS *see* management information systems
mission statements 16–17
mitigation, credit risk 156
ML *see* machine learning
modelling 60–85
  APT 73–74
  arbitrage free 69–71
  asset pricing 68–74
  binomial trees 83–85
  Black-Scholes-Merton formula 75–76
  CAPM 72–73
  contingent claims 74–85
  CRR method 84–85

equal probability approach 85
  financial 60–85
  fundamental partial differential equation 75–82
  Greeks 79–82
  implied volatility 82–83
  market efficiency 53–55, 63–65
  market equilibrium 71–73
  Markov property 64–65
  martingale property 63–64
  martingale transformation 77–79
  normal distribution 65–67
  numerical methods 83–85
  replicating portfolio 81–82
  return properties 61–62
  risk premiums 68–69
  risk properties 62–63
  stochastic processes 65–67
Modified duration (DMod) 110
mortgage loans 117–118
MREL *see* Minimum Requirements for own Funds
    and Eligible Liabilities
Mt. Gox 197
multi-asset options 135–136
mutually exclusive collectively exhaustive (MECE)
    10
MVP *see* minimum variance portfolio

N
Nakamoto, Satoshi 178, 194
natural language processing (NLP) 176, 189–190
negative capital effect 94–96
negative feedback traders 93
net interest margin (NIM) 103, 223
net operating assets (NOA) 57–58
net operating profit less adjusted taxes (NOPLAT)
    51–52
net operating profits after taxes (NOPAT) 51–52,
    57–58
net stable funding ratio (NSFR) 163, 224
NIM *see* net interest margin
NLP *see* natural language processing
NOA *see* net operating assets
noise traders 91, 94
non-callable instruments, convexity 109
non-performing loans (NPLs) 224–226
noncurrent assets 38
nonperforming assets (NPAs) 224–226
NOPAT *see* net operating profits after taxes
NOPLAT *see* net operating profit less adjusted taxes
normal distribution 62, 65–67
NPAs *see* nonperforming assets
NPLs *see* non-performing loans
NSFR *see* net stable funding ratio
numerical methods, options pricing 83–85

O

object finance 102
offer process, mergers and acquisitions 235–236
OIS *see* Overnight Indexed Swap
OL *see* operating leverage
onboarding 188
open architecture 31–32, 182–185
open-loop payment systems 187
operating cash flows 41–43
operating leverage (OL) 46–47
operating models 23–24
operational excellence 23–26
operational optimisation 246
operational restructuring 228–229
operational risk 160–161
operational and technology due diligence (OTDD) 238–239
optimisation
    commercial 244–246
    financial 247–248
    operational 246
    portfolios 27–28
    value creation 244–248
options 132–138
    American 132–133
    Asian 134–135
    barrier 135
    basket 135–136
    Bermuda 133–134
    cliquet 134
    credit 138
    European 132–133
    exotic 133–136
    forward-start 134
    interest-rate 136–138
    knock out/in features 135
    multi-asset 135–136
    path-dependent 134–135
    put-call parity 133
    quantity adjusting 136
    swaptions 137–138
    time-dependent 133–134
    vanilla 132–133
options pricing 74–85
    Black-Scholes-Merton formula 75–76
    CRR method 84–85
    equal probability approach 85
    framework 74–75
    fundamental partial differential equation 75–82
    Greeks 79–82
    implied volatility 82–83
    martingale transformation 77–79
    numerical methods 83–85
    replicating portfolio 81–82
origination, mergers and acquisitions 233–235
output floor, Basel framework 161
Overnight Indexed Swap (OIS) rates 104

P

P/B *see* price-to-book ratio
P/E *see* price-earnings ratio
par asset swaps 125
partnerships 245–246
path dependency, market dislocations 94
payer swaptions 138
payment services 186–187, 188
    see also cryptocurrencies
PD *see* probability of default
peer-to-peer lending 190–191
peer-to-peer payment services 187
perfect market paradigm 69–70
performance improvement 26–32
    cost reductions 29–31
    divestments/disposals 28
    front-to-back optimisation 28–29
    portfolio optimisation 27–28
    restructurings 228–229
    technology replatforming 31–32
performance tracking 21–23
permissioned blockchains 179
permissionless blockchains 179
pillars of the Basel framework 151–152
plain-vanilla interest-rate swaps 125–127
planning, strategic *see* strategic planning
portfolio choices 20–21
portfolio insurance 92
portfolio modelling
    asset prices 73–74
    asset pricing 68–74
    capital market line 71–72
    contingent claims 74–85
    CRR method 84–85
    Greeks 79–82
    implied volatility 82–83
    market equilibrium 71–73
    minimum variance 71–73
    replicating portfolio 81–82
    risk and return 61–67
    security market line 72
portfolio optimisation 27–28, 244–248
Portugal
    post-GFC 215
    see also Europe
PoS *see* proof-of-stake
positive feedback traders 93
post-trade capital markets 187–188
PoW *see* proof-of-work

price to tangible book value (PTBV) 60
price-to-book ratio (P/B) 60
price–earnings ratio (P/E) 45, 60
private blockchains 179
private keys 179–180
private wealth management 102
probability of default (PD) 114
problem solving
    action plans 11–12
    baselines 10–11
    elimination 11
    framing 10–11
    hypothesis-driven 8–12
    refinement 11
    systems theory 12–13
process automation, robotic 176–177
product fit 16, 20–21, 27–28
programming languages 185
proof-of-stake (PoS) mining 181
proof-of-work (PoW) mining 180–181, 194
PTBV *see* price to tangible book value
public blockchains 179
public keys 179–180
put-call parity 133
Python 185

Q

quantity adjusting options (quanto) 136

R

R *see* recovery rate
ratched options 134
RBS *see* Royal Bank of Scotland
real-time gross settlement (RTGS) systems 188
recapitalisation 226–228
receiver swaptions 138
recovery rate (R) 114
reference data consortia 188
refinement, strategic analysis 11
regulation of cryptocurrencies 196, 197
regulatory capital 151–153
reorganisation 204–217
    financial institutions 212–217
    legal principles 205–212
    market infrastructure 216–217
    structural reform 213–216
replatforming 31–32, 167–168, 246
replicating portfolio 81–82
REPO *see* retro purchase agreements
representations, due diligence 237
research, machine learning 189–190
reset options 134
residual income (RI) method 51–52
Resolution Trust Corporation (RTC) 98
response plans 21–23

restructuring 223–229
    automatic stay 210–211
    balance sheet 224
    cash flows 223–224
    court protection 209–210
    financial 223–228
    legal concepts 209–212
    legislative frameworks 206–209
    market infrastructure 216–217
    operational 228–229
    overview 205
    ring-fencing 215–216
    strategic analysis 10–11
retention rate 54–55
retro purchase agreements (REPO) 126–127
return on assets (ROA) 44–45
return on attributed equity (ROAE) 58, 148
return on debt (ROD) 46
return on equity (ROE) 21, 44–45
return on invested capital (ROIC) 44–45
return on tangible equity (ROTE) 37
revolving loans 118
RI method *see* residual income method
ring-fencing 215–216
Ripple Labs 187, 195–196
risk
    collateralised debt obligations 140
    correlation products 140–141
    dynamic asset allocation 92–93
    feedback loops 93–94
    liquidity 88–90, 161–163, 197–198
    management 92–96
    pricing taxonomy 102–116
    taking, principles of 101–102
risk management 141–164
    automation 192–193
    Basel framework 149–164
    capital management 145–149, 151–163
    credit risk 154–157
    enterprise-wide 142–143
    expected shortfall 144
    extreme value analysis 144–145
    liquidity coverage ratio 162–163
    liquidity requirements 161–163
    market risk 157–160
    net stable funding ratio 163
    operational risk 160–161
    regulatory capital 151–153
    risk-weighted assets 154–161
    value-at-risk 143–145
risk premiums 68–69, 71–73
risk transfer 101–116
    commodities 112–113
    credit risk 113–116
    equity risk 116

risk transfer (*Continued*)
  foreign exchange 112
  inclusive 262–264
  interest rates 103–111
risk weighting, post-GFC 27
risk-weighted assets (RWA) 154–161
  credit risk 154–157
  principles 154
ROA *see* return on assets
roadmaps, planning 17
ROAE *see* return on attributed equity
robo-advisor technology 192
robotic process automation (RPA) 176–177
ROD *see* return on debt
ROE *see* return on equity
ROIC *see* return on invested capital
ROTE *see* return on tangible equity
Royal Bank of Scotland (RBS) 21
RPA *see* robotic process automation
RTC *see* Resolution Trust Corporation
RWA *see* risk-weighted assets

S

S&L *see* savings and loans
St Galler Management Model 12–13
sales optimisation 245
sales and purchase agreement (SPA) 236
Santander Group, formation 33
savings accounts 147
savings and loans (S&L) crisis 98
scenario analysis 19–20
SDE *see* stochastic differential equations
SecDB *see* Securities DataBase
secured loans 117–119
Securities DataBase (SecDB) 31
securities dealers 91
securities trading and marketing 102, 191
securitisation 138–141
  collateralised debt obligations 139–140
  correlation products 140–141
  credit risk 156–157
  legal process 139
security interest 118
security market line (SML) 72
senior tranches 140
separation plans 249, 251–253
service fit 16, 20–21, 27–28
SFI *see* systemically important financial institutions
SGR *see* sustainable growth rate
short-term interest-rate (STIR) futures 121–123
short-term survival financing 227
simple one-period returns 61
smart contracts 182, 188
SML *see* security market line
SPA *see* sales and purchase agreement

Spain
  post-GFC 214–215
  see also Europe
special purpose vehicles (SPV) 138–141
specialisation 262–264
speciality finance 102
stablecoins 197–198
staffing requirements 28–29
standardised approach (SA)
  credit risk 155–156
  operational risk 160
statement of changes in equity 40–41
statements of cash flows 41–44
STIR futures *see* short-term interest-rate futures
stochastic differential equations (SDE) 76
stop-loss strategies 92
strategic analysis 7–17
  action plans 11–12
  baselines 10–11
  capabilities 14–16, 20–21
  coherence 13–17
  competitive advantage 14
  elimination 11
  framing 10–11
  identity setting 16–17
  market positioning 14–16, 20–21
  problem solving 8–12
  product fit 16, 20–21
  refinement 11
  service fit 16, 20–21
  systems theory 12–13
strategic decision making 7–34
  action plans 11–12, 21–23
  analysis 7–17
  balanced scorecard 24–26
  baselines 10–11
  benchmarking 26
  capability-driven strategy 14–17
  coherence 13–17
  framing 10–11
  identity 16–17
  impact assessments 17–20
  mergers and acquisitions 32–33
  operating model 23–24
  operational excellence 23–26
  optionalities 20–21
  performance improvement 26–32
  planning 17–23
  portfolio choices 20–21
  response plans 21–23
  roadmaps 17
  systems theory 12–13
  target operating models 23–25
strategic identity 16–17
strategic options 20–21

strategic planning 17–23
  action plans 21–23
  impact assessments 17–20
  options/portfolio choices 20–21
  response plans 21–23
  roadmaps 17
  target operating models 23–25
stress 86–99
  asset liquidity 88–89
  cycle 86–87
  dynamic asset allocation 92–93
  funding liquidity 89–90
  liquidity risk 88–90
  macro-historical issues 99
  market dislocations 87, 90–96
  negative capital effect 94–96
  path dependency 94
  systemic crises 96–99
  tests under Basel framework 151
  value-at-risk 92–93
STRIPs 106–107
structural reform, post GFC 213–216
structure
  of capital 145–147
  turnaround plans 221–222
structured derivatives 28–29
submartingales 77
survival financing 227
sustainable growth rate (SGR) 53
swaps 124–131
  assets 124–125
  constant maturity 127
  credit default 128–130
  cross-currency 128
  equity 130–131
  foreign exchange 128
  interest-rate 104–105, 125–127
swaptions 137–138
SWOT analysis 19
synthetic trading 198–199
systemic crises 96–99
  bank panic of 1907 97
  Global Financial 98–99
  Great Depression 97–98
  savings and loans, US 98
systemically important financial institutions (SFI)
  152

T

T1 capital 145–146, 152
T2 capital 146–147
tails, clients/products 27–28
target operating models (TOM) 23–25
TDAG *see* transaction-based directed acyclic graphs

technical liquidity constraints, negative capital
  effect 94–96
technology 165–200
  analytics 189–190
  APIs 169–171
  artificial intelligence 173–177
  augmented decision making 189–193
  blockchains 178–181
  capital management 192–193
  cloud computing 171–173
  credit underwriting 190
  crowdfunding 199
  cryptocurrencies 178–182, 187–188, 193–199
  decision making 189–193
  distributed ledgers 177–182, 187–188, 193–199
  future impacts 261–262
  infrastructure transformation 169–173, 186–188
  machine learning 173–176
  management 166–168
  natural language processing 176, 189–190
  open architectures 182–185
  open-loop payment systems 187
  operational efficiency 182–188
  payment services 186–187, 188
  post-trade capital markets 187–188
  replatforming 31–32, 167–168, 246
  research 189–190
  risk management 192–193
  robo-advisors 192
  robotic process automation 176–177
  smart contracts 182, 188
  specialisation 262–264
  synthetic trading 198–199
  trading and marketing 191
term loans 118
term sheets (TS) 236
term structures
  interest rates 108
  volatility 83
Tether 198
theta (Θ) 80–81
tier-one (T1) capital 145–146, 152
tier-two (T2) capital 146–147
TLAC *see* Total Loss Absorbing Capacity
tokens 181
TOM *see* target operating models
"Too Big to Fail" 213–215
Total Loss Absorbing Capacity (TLAC) 151–152,
  153
total return swaps (TRS) 125
traders 91, 93–94
trading, synthetic 198–199
trading book, market risk 158–159
tranches, collateralised debt obligations 139–140

transaction-based directed acyclic graphs (TDAG) 178
Treasury-bond futures 121
Troubled Asset Relief programme 212
TRS *see* total return swaps
TS *see* term sheets
turnaround 203–230
   automatic stay 210–211
   bail-ins 214
   bailouts 212–215
   cash flow restructuring 223–224
   corporate renewal 229
   court protection 209–210
   crisis management 217–220
   definition 203
   disposals 226
   distressed assets 224–226
   financial restructuring 223–228
   G20 reform 212–217
   Global Financial Crisis 203–204
   insolvency 220
   legal concepts 209–212
   legislative frameworks 206–209
   market infrastructure reforms 216–217
   nonperforming assets 224–226
   operational restructuring 228–229
   overview 205
   plans 220–223
   process 217–229
   recapitalisation 226–228
   reorganisation 204–217
   ring-fencing 215–216
   structural reforms 213–216
   wind-down 204–217

U

UBS 16, 21
UK Vickert reforms 215
underwriting 102, 190
Uniswap 198
United Kingdom (UK)
   post-GFC 213–215
   see also Europe
United States (US)
   bankruptcy and insolvency 206–207
   post-GFC 212, 216
unsecured loans 117–119
US savings and loans crisis 98
USC *see* utility settlement coin
USD Coin (USDC) 198
utility settlement coin (USC) 188

V

valuation 47–60
   Asian options 134–135

asset swaps 125
barrier options 135
basket options 135–136
Bermuda options 133–134
cliquet options 134
collars 137
commodities futures 123–124
contingent claims 74–85
credit default swap premia 129–130
discounted cash flows 50–52, 54–55, 57
distressed companies 60
dividend discount model 45–46, 53–54
dividend swaps 131
dynamic methods 49–50
economic profit 58
economic value added 51–52, 57–58
equity swaps 130–132
expected shortfall 144
foreign exchange futures 123
forwards prices 120
free cash flows 50–52
interest-rate instruments 105–106, 121–122, 126–127
leveraged buyout analysis 55–57
market value added 58
modelling 61–85
price-earnings ratio 45, 60
price-to-book ratio 60
price-to-book values 60
price–earnings ratio 45, 45, 60
quantity adjusting options 136
static methods 49
vanilla options 132–133
weighted average cost of capital 51–53
value, definition 48–49
value creation 231–244
   growth initiatives 232–233
   mergers and acquisitions 233–241
   plans 241–244
value drivers 241
value investors 91–92
value metrics 241–243
value optimisation 224–228
value realisation 228–254
   100 day plans 251
   disposals 249, 251–253
   governance 248–250
   immediate action lists 250–251
   integrations 249, 253–254
   operational blueprints 250–254
   targeted implementation 254
value-at-risk (VaR) 92–93, 143–145
vanilla equity swaps 130
vanilla options 132–133
VaR *see* value-at-risk

variable costs 46–47
variance swaps 131–132
Vega (ν) 82–83
vision 16–17
volatility
    implied 82–83
    term structure 83
volatility swaps 131–132
Volcker, P. 98

W

WACC *see* weighted average cost of capital
warranties, due diligence 237
weighted average cost of capital (WACC) 51–53
wholesale funding 147
winding-down 204–217
    financial institutions 212–217
    legal concepts 209–212

legislative frameworks 206–209
overview 205
workout 224

X

XRP 187, 195–196

Y

yield curve 106–107
yield-to-maturity (YTM) 105–106
yield-to-yield asset swaps 125
YTM *see* yield-to-maturity

Z

Z-scores 114–115
z-spread 129–130
zone of insolvency 220